Prague

THE ROUGH GUIDE

There are more than one hundred Rough Guide titles
covering destinations from Amsterdam to Zimbabwe

Forthcoming titles include
Bangkok • Barbados • Japan • Jordan • Syria

Rough Guide Reference Series
Classical Music • European Football • The Internet • Jazz • Opera
Reggae • Rock Music • World Music

Rough Guide Phrasebooks
Czech • French • German • Greek • Hindi & Urdu
Hungarian • Indonesian • Italian • Japanese • Mandarin Chinese
Mexican Spanish • Polish • Portuguese • Russian • Spanish
Thai • Turkish • Vietnamese

Rough Guides on the Internet
http://www.roughguides.com

Rough Guide Credits

Text Editor:	Sarah Dallas
Series Editor:	Mark Ellingham
Editorial:	Martin Dunford, Jonathan Buckley, Samantha Cook, Jo Mead, Kate Berens, Amanda Tomlin, Ann-Marie Shaw, Paul Gray, Chris Schüler, Helena Smith, Caroline Osborne, Kieran Falconer, Judith Bamber, Olivia Eccleshall, Orla Duane (UK); Andrew Rosenberg
Online Editors:	Alan Spicer, Kate Hands (UK); Geronimo Madrid (US)
Production:	Susanne Hillen, Andy Hilliard, Judy Pang, Link Hall, Nicola Williamson, Helen Ostick, James Morris
Picture Research:	Eleanor Hill
Cartography:	Maxine Burke, Melissa Flack, Nichola Goodliffe
Finance:	John Fisher, Celia Crowley, Neeta Mistry
Marketing & Publicity:	Richard Trillo, Simon Carloss, Niki Smith (UK); Jean-Marie Kelly, SoRelle Braun (US)
Administration:	Tania Hummel, Alexander Mark Rogers

Acknowledgements

Special thanks to David, Mira and in particular Laďa for the loan of his flat. Thanks also to Petr, Tim and Anděla, Kate, Josh and Stan. The editor would like to thank Stratigraphics for cartography; Gareth Nash for proofreading; and Judy Pang for typesetting and production.

Thanks also to the following people who contributed to the production of the book with their letters and comments: Ilana Barnett, J Bartlett, Mark Baverstock, Neil Bennett, Rebecca Bishop, Sylvia Blakely, Alexandra Cameron, Colin Chamberlain, Tracy Cheung, Victoria Coddington, Mark Corner, Ian Davey, Lisa Dierbeck, Dafyd Downes, Sylvia Forrest, Debbie Goode, Paul Guscin, Richard Hardy, PG Huggins, Philip Horton, JR Hunter, Paul Kabrna, David Key, Thao Lee, Rose & Ted Longman, Lisa Malyon, Dave Manton, Maria McHale, Metter Kia Krabbe Meyer, Ian Nancollas, Peter Noorlander, Barry Redhead, Jim Redshaw, Nancy Sands, Jane Scotti, Jamie Segust, Chris Smith, Dominic Snowdon, Geoff Stansfield, Alan Sutcliffe, Emma Symonds, Liza Taylor, Katharine Turner, Francoise Vidal, Sophia Walton and Herreman Yvan.

This edition published May 1998 by Rough Guides Ltd, 1 Mercer Street, London WC2H 9QJ. Previous editions published 1992, 1995.

Distributed by the Penguin Group:

Penguin Books Ltd, 27 Wrights Lane, London W8 5TZ.

Penguin Books USA Inc, 375 Hudson Street, New York 10014, USA.

Penguin Books Australia Ltd, 487 Maroondah Highway, PO Box 257, Ringwood, Victoria 3134, Australia.

Penguin Books Canada Ltd, 10 Alcorn Avenue, Toronto, Ontario, Canada M4V 1E4.

Penguin Books (NZ) Ltd, 182–190 Wairau Road, Auckland 10, New Zealand.

Printed in England by Clays Ltd, St Ives PLC

Typography and **original design** by Jonathan Dear and The Crowd Roars.

Illustrations throughout by Edward Briant.

Prague

THE ROUGH GUIDE

Written and researched by
Rob Humphreys

With additional research by
David Charap

THE ROUGH GUIDES

Help us update

We've gone to a lot of trouble to ensure that this new edition of the *Rough Guide to Prague* is up-to-date and accurate. However, things are still changing at an extraordinary speed in Prague and if you find we've missed something good or covered something which has now gone, then please write; suggestions, comments or corrections are much appreciated. We'll credit all contributions, and send a copy of the next edition (or any other *Rough Guide* if you prefer) for the best letters.

Please mark all letters "Rough Guide to Prague update" and send to:
Rough Guides, 1 Mercer St, London WC2H 9QJ or
Rough Guides, 375 Hudson St, 9th floor, New York, NY 10014.

Email should be sent to:
mail@roughguides.co.uk

Online updates about Rough Guide titles can be found on our Web site at http://www.roughguides.com

The Author

Rob Humphreys joined Rough Guides in 1989, having worked as a failed actor, taxi driver and male model. He has travelled extensively in central and eastern Europe, writing guides to Prague, the Czech and Slovak Republics, and St Petersburg, as well as London. He has lived in London since 1988.

Rough Guides

Travel Guides • Phrasebooks • Music and Reference Guides

We set out to do something different when the first Rough Guide was published in 1982. Mark Ellingham, just out of University, was travelling in Greece. He brought along the popular guides of the day, but found they were all lacking in some way. They were either strong on ruins and museums but went on for pages without mentioning a beach or taverna. Or they were so conscious of the need to save money that they lost sight of Greece's cultural and historical significance. Also, none of the books told him anything about Greece's contemporary life – its politics, its culture, its people, and how they lived.

So with no job in prospect, Mark decided to write his own guidebook, one which aimed to provide practical information that was second to none, detailing the best beaches and the hottest clubs and restaurants, while also giving hard hitting accounts of every sight, both famous and obscure, and providing up-to-the-minute information on contemporary culture. It was a guide that encouraged independent travellers to find the best of Greece, and was a great success, getting shortlisted for the Thomas Cook travel guide award, and encouraging Mark, along with three friends, to expand the series.

The Rough Guide list grew rapidly and the letters flooded in, indicating a much broader readership than had been anticipated, but one which uniformly appreciated the Rough Guides' mix of practical detail and humour, irreverence and enthusiasm. Things haven't changed. The same four friends who began the series are still the caretakers of the Rough Guide mission today: to provide the most reliable, up-to-date and entertaining information to independent-minded travellers of all ages, on all budgets.

We now publish more than 100 titles and have offices in London and New York. The travel guides are written and researched by a dedicated team of more than 100 authors, based in Britain, Europe, the USA and Australia. We have also created a unique series of phrasebooks to accompany the travel series, along with the acclaimed series of music guides, and a best-selling pocket guide to the Internet and World Wide Web. We also publish comprehensive travel information on our Web site: http://www.roughguides.com

Contents

Part Four: Contexts 247

Index 285

List of Maps

MAP SYMBOLS

━━━ Railway		ⓘ	Tourist office
═══ Road		⊠	Post office
- - - - Path		Ⓜ	Metro station
– – – Ferry route		✡	Synagogue
──── Waterway		✚	Church
━ ━ ━ Chapter division boundary		✝ Christian Cemetery	
▲ Peak		Jewish Cemetery	
◉ Hotel		Park	
		Building	

Introduction

P rague (Praha to the Czechs) is one of the least "Eastern" European cities you could imagine. Architecturally, and in terms of city sights, it is a revelation: few other cities, anywhere in Europe, look so good – and no other European capital can present six hundred years of architecture so completely untouched by natural disaster or war. Culturally, it has always looked towards Paris rather than Moscow, and after four decades of Soviet-imposed isolation the city is now keen to re-establish its position as the political and cultural centre of *Mitteleuropa*.

One of Prague's most appealing characteristics is that its artistic wealth is not hidden away inside grand museums and galleries, but displayed in the streets and squares. Its town-planning took place in medieval times, its palaces and churches were decorated with a rich mantle of Baroque, and the whole lot has escaped the vanities and excesses of postwar redevelopment. Prague's unique compactness allows you to walk from the grandeur of the city's castle district, via a series of intimate Baroque lanes, across a medieval stone bridge, through one of the most alluring central squares on the continent, and end up sipping coffee on Wenceslas Square, the modern hub of the city, in under half an hour.

As well as having a rich history, Czechs have been at the forefront of European **culture** for much of the modern era. Before World War I, Prague boasted a Cubist movement second only to Paris, and, between the wars, a modernist architectural flowering to rival Bauhaus. Today, its writers, artists and film directors continue to exert a profound influence on European culture, out of all proportion to their numbers.

The city's recent history has attracted the attention of the west like no other capital in the former eastern bloc. The 1968 **Prague Spring** captured the imagination of a generation, with an explosion of cultural energy which, for a moment, made the "third way" between communism and capitalism seem a real possibility. Then, in

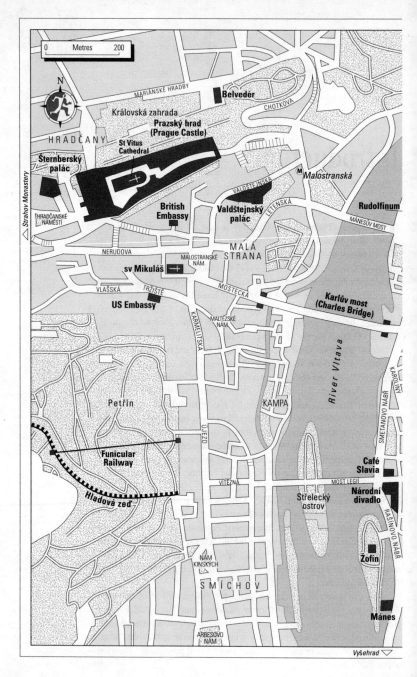

Metres 200

N

Strahov Monastery

MARIÁNSKÉ HRADBY

Belvedér

CHOTKOVA

Královská zahrada

Prazský hrad
(Prague Castle)

HRADČANY

St Vitus
Cathedral

M Malostranská

Šternberský
palác

VALDŠTEJNSKÁ

LETENSKÁ

Rudolfinum

HRADČANSKÉ
NÁMĚSTÍ

British
Embassy

Valdštejnský
palác

MÁNESŮV MOST

NERUDOVA

MALÁ
STRANA

MALOSTRANSKÉ
NÁM.

sv Mikuláš

VLAŠSKÁ

TRŽIŠTĚ

MOSTECKÁ

Karlův most
(Charles Bridge)

US Embassy

MALTÉZSKÉ
NÁM.

KARMELITSKÁ

River Vltava

KAROLINY

Petřín

KAMPA

SMETANOVO NÁBŘ

ÚJEZD

Funicular
Railway

VÍTĚZNÁ

Café
Slavia

MOST LEGII

Hladová zeď

Střelecký
ostrov

Národní
divadlo

RAŠÍNOVO NÁBŘ

NÁM.
KINSKÝCH

Žofín

SMÍCHOV

Mánes

ARBESOVO
NÁM.

Vyšehrad

PRAGUE

Letná

NÁBŘ. EDVARDA BENEŠE

ŠVERMŮV MOST

River Vltava

NÁBŘ. LUDVIKA SVOBODY

NA FRANTIŠKU

NÁBŘ. EDVARDA BENEŠE

ČECHŮV MOST

Anežský klášter

KOZÍ

KLIMENTSKÁ

DUŠNÍ

REVOLUČNÍ

SOUKENICKÁ

Staronová synagóga

PAŘÍŽSKÁ

ŠIROKÁ

RYBNÁ

DLOUHÁ

NOVÉ MĚSTO

17 LISTOPADU

MAISELOVA

DLOUHÁ

MASNÁ

NA POŘÍČÍ

UPM

Starý židovský hřbitov

DLOUHÁ

RYBNÁ

Masarykovo nádraží

NÁM. JANA PALACHA

Staroměstská

JOSEFOV

NÁM. REPUBLIKY

KAPROVA

sv Mikuláš

Hus Monument

Týn Church

Obecní dům

Náměstí Republiky

KŘIŽOVNICKÁ

STAROMĚSTSKÉ NÁM.

CELETNÁ

HYBERNSKÁ

Klementinum

i Staroměstská radnice

OVOCNÝ TRH

Prašná brána

KARLOVA

MELANTRICHOVA

i PIS

SENOVÁŽNÉ NÁM.

STARÉ MĚSTO

Stavovské divadlo

NEKÁZANKA

Betlémská kaple

RYTÍŘSKÁ

NA PŘÍKOPĚ

PANSKÁ

Praha hlavní nádraží i

BETLÉMSKÉ NÁM.

JIHELNÝ TRH

M Můstek

HINDŘIŠSKÁ

SVĚTLÉ

BARTOLOMĚJSKÁ

JUNGMANNOVO NÁM.

Můstek M

NÁRODNÍ

NÁRODNÍ

Grand Hotel Evropa

OPLETALOVA

Státní opera

Národní třída M

VÁCLAVSKÉ NÁMĚSTÍ (WENCESLAS SQUARE)

VODIČKOVA

WILSONOVA

OSTROVNÍ

NOVÉ MĚSTO

SPÁLENÁ

JUNGMANNOVA

Muzeum M

ŠTĚPÁNSKÁ

KRAKOVSKÁ

Národní muzeum

Novoměstská radnice

VE SMEČKÁCH

LEGEROVÁ

MYSLÍKOVA

ŽITNÁ

ŽITNÁ

KARLOVO NÁMĚSTÍ

the messy, sometimes bloody, upheavals of 1989, Czechoslovakia, and in particular Prague, outshone the rest with its unequivocably positive "**Velvet Revolution**". True to its pacifist past, the country shrugged off forty years of communism without so much as a shot being fired.

The exhilarating popular unity of that period, and the feeling of participating in history itself have now gone. Few Czechs continue to talk about the events of 1989 as a "revolution". Disorientation at the speed of change, the break with Slovakia, and the first real taste of western vices in the capital have taken their toll. **Economically**, too, the country is going through some difficult times. Ninety percent of state-owned property has been "restituted", that is given back to its pre-1948 owners in various states of disrepair. Foreign companies have bought up huge slices of Czech industry for a song and the traditional heavy industrial base has shrunk considerably.

Walking the streets of the city centre, you'd be forgiven for thinking otherwise. But then Prague is in a privileged position vis-à-vis the rest of the country – as the place where the majority of the country's new businesses and corporations have made their head offices, and, of course, thanks to its potential for attracting western tourists. The feeling in much of the rest of the country is that Prague has prospered at the expense of other cities and regions. Which is not surprising, given that it is something like seven times the size of any other city in Bohemia, all the government ministries are based here, and it's where all the big decisions are made.

That's not to say that Prague doesn't have more than its fair share of problems. Its recent mini-boom may have brought crowds of tourists and hordes of, mostly American, expats, but it has done little to improve life for much of the city's population. The westernized shops and restaurants in the centre, with their glitzy window-dressing, are out of reach for most Praguers. Racial tensions, suppressed under the police state, have surfaced once more, with a spate of skinhead attacks on the city's considerable Romany and Vietnamese communities, which the police seem either powerless or unwilling to prevent. The lifestyle gulf between Party and non-Party members has been replaced by the western malaise of rich and poor. There's nothing new in this, but it does serve as a sobering footnote to the city's glowing image in the west.

Prague is also trying to come to terms with its more distant past. Both the forced, and frequently violent, removal of the German minority and the virtual extinction of the Jewish population had a marked effect on the city, but were never discussed openly under the previous regime. Much of the current retrospection is positive, a cultural rediscovery of the cosmopolitan interwar period, when the city was ethnically far more diverse. There is also the extremely sensitive matter of the events of the last war: the degree of collaboration with the Nazis and of acquiescence in the fate of the Jews. These are issues that need to be addressed if the city is to break free from the monocultural straitjacket which makes it stand out amongst the multicultural capitals of the west.

When to go

Lying at the heart of central Europe, Prague has a continental climate: winters can be bitterly cold, summers correspondingly scorching. The best times to visit, in terms of weather, are late spring and early autumn. Summer in the city can be pretty stifling, but the real reason for avoiding the peak season is that it can get uncomfortably crowded in the centre – finding a place to eat in the evening, let alone securing a room, can become fraught with difficulties. If you're looking for good weather, April is the earliest you can expect at least some sunny days, and October is the last warm month. If you don't mind the cold, the city looks beautiful in the snowy winter months.

Average temperatures (°F) and Rainfall											
	Jan	Feb	Mar	April	May	June	July	Aug	Sept	Oct	Nov	Dec
Min °C	-5	-4	-1	3	8	11	13	13	9	5	1	-3
Max °C	0	1	7	12	18	21	23	22	18	12	5	1
mm	18	18	18	27	48	54	68	55	31	33	20	21

Prague: Basics

Getting there from Britain and Ireland

By far the most convenient way to get to Prague is **by plane**. The flight from London takes just under two hours (compared with more than 24 hours by train), and there are at least four daily direct flights from London throughout the year.

By plane

Both Czech Airlines (ČSA) and British Airways (BA) run two daily **scheduled flights** from London to Prague. ČSA fly out of Heathrow (Terminal 2), and less frequently from Stansted, while British Airways fly from Heathrow (Terminal 1) only. British Midland also fly daily out of Heathrow (Terminal 1), but only ČSA fly five times a week direct from Manchester.

The cheapest tickets with the above airlines go by various names at various times of the year, but are usually valid for one or two months, require you to stay at least one Saturday night, and don't allow for change or cancellation. Booking tickets through the airlines themselves is rarely the cheapest option, though prices are usually fairly competitive: from as little as £165-195 return from London (£195-225 from Manchester), plus tax (currently £20-25 per person). Fares vary according to season – they tend to be highest from April to October and in the two weeks around Christmas – though some kind of economy fare is usually available all year round.

Discounted flights to Prague now feature in most of the "bucket shop" adverts of the various London freebie magazines, *Time Out*, *The Evening Standard* and the travel sections of the quality Sunday papers, where return fares can be bought for as little as £130. You might also try specialist agents, such as Campus Travel or STA (see box on p.4 for details). Note, however, that in peak season discount flights are often booked up weeks in advance. It might also be worth considering flying to a neighbouring European city like Berlin, Leipzig or Vienna, for which return fares can be as little as £100 – again, you'll find the cheapest fares in the sources quoted above.

Package deals and city breaks

Several tour operators offer simple flight and accommodation **package deals** to Prague, which for a short trip can often be much better value than travelling independently. ČEDOK offers a city break with a return flight from London and two nights' accommodation in a three-star hotel for around £300 high season and £250 in low season; the same deal with private accommodation costs around £200 all year round. Travelscene also offers a two-night city break including flights and accommodation for around £300. With these packages, there's no compulsion to go on any organized tours once you're there. A list of the main agents can be found in the box on p.4.

Flights from Ireland

There are no direct flights from anywhere in Ireland to Prague. The cheapest way of making the journey is to fly to London and pick up a

Airlines	
British Airways	☎ 0345/222111
British Midland	☎ 0345/554554
Czech Airlines (ČSA)	
London	☎ 0171/255 1898
Manchester	☎ 0161/489 5840

Agents and operators in Britain

Bohemian Promotions
61 Mere Rd, Erdington,
Birmingham B23 7LL ☎0121/373 9107
Offers a full range of accommodation in Prague.

Bridgewater Travel
217 Mouton Rd, Mouton Village,
Manchester M30 9PA ☎0161/707 8547
Accommodation and package deals.

Campus Travel (Eurotrain)
52 Grosvenor Gdns,
London SW1 ☎0171/730 3402

541 Bristol Rd,
Selly Oak, Birmingham ☎0121/414 1848

61 Ditchling Rd, Brighton ☎01273/570226

37–39 Queen's Rd,
Clifton, Bristol ☎0117/929 2494

5 Emmanuel St, Cambridge ☎01223/324283

53 Forest Rd, Edinburgh ☎0131/668 3303

122 George St,Glasgow ☎0141/553 1818

166 Deansgate, Manchester ☎0161/273 1721

105–106 St Aldates, Oxford ☎01865/242067
Student/youth travel specialists; branches also in YHA shops and universities around Britain.

ČEDOK
4th Floor, 53–54 Haymarket,
London SW1 ☎0171/836 4414
Former state-owned tourist board offering flights, accommodation and package deals.

Czech Tourist Centre
16 Frognal Parade, Finchley Rd,
London NW3 ☎0171/794 3263
Accommodation, bus tickets, flights and lots more.

Czech Travel Ltd
Trinity House, 1 Trinity Square,
South Woodham Ferrers,
Essex CM3 5JX ☎01245/328647
Rooms and flats for rent in Prague.

Czechbook Agency
Jopes Mill, Trebrownbridge,
Near Liskeard,
Cornwall PL14 3PX ☎01503/240629
Cheap private and self-catering accommodation in Prague.

Czechdays
89 Valence Road,
Lewes BN7 1SJ ☎01273/474738
Cheap rooms in Prague suburbs.

Czechscene
1 Thon Lea, Evesham,
Worcestershire WR11 6TN ☎01386/442782
B&B and self-catering flats available in Prague.

Holiday Services
1 Charnwood Drive, Ripley,
Derby DE5 3TB ☎01773/747426
Cheap flights and accommodation.

Martin Randal Travel
10 Barley Mow Passage,
London W4 4PH ☎0181/742 3355
Specialist cultural guided tours of Prague.

STA Travel
86 Old Brompton Rd, London SW7;
117 Euston Rd, London NW1;
38 Store St, London WC1 ☎0171/361 6161

25 Queen's Rd, Bristol ☎0117/929 3399

38 Sidney St, Cambridge ☎01223/366966

88 Vicar Lane, Leeds ☎0113/244 9212

75 Deansgate, Manchester ☎0161/834 0668

36 George St, Oxford ☎01865/792800
Independent travel and discount flight specialists; offices also at universities of Aberdeen, Birmingham, Canterbury, Cardiff, Coventry, Durham, Glasgow, Loughborough, Nottingham, Warwick and Sheffield.

TK Travel
14 Buckstone Close,
London SE23 ☎0181/699 8065
B&B and self-catering apartments for rent in Prague.

Travellers' Czech Ltd
203 Main Road,Biggin Hill,
Kent TN16 3JU ☎01959/540700
Private accommodation in, and packages to, Prague.

Travelscene
11–15 St Ann's Rd,
Harrow, Middlesex HA1 ☎0181/427 4445
Two-night breaks and upwards in Prague.

Airlines in Ireland

Aer Lingus

Belfast	☎ 0645/737747
Dublin	☎ 01/844 4777
Cork	☎ 021/327155
Limerick	☎ 061/474239

British Airways

Belfast	☎ 0345/222111
Dublin contact *Aer Lingus*	

British Midland

Belfast	☎ 0345/554554
Dublin	☎ 01/283 8833

Jersey European

Belfast	☎ 0990/676676

Ryanair

Dublin	☎ 01/609 7800

Agents and operators in Ireland

USIT

Fountain Centre, College St, Belfast BT1	☎ 01849/324073
10–11 Market Parade, Patrick Street, Cork	☎ 021/270900
33 Ferryquay St, Derry	☎ 01504/371888
Aston Quay, Dublin 2	☎ 01/602 1600
Victoria Place, Eyre Square, Galway	☎ 091/565177
Central Buildings, O'Connell St, Waterford	☎ 051/872601

Student/youth specialists for flights and trains.

Budget Travel

134 Lower Baggot St, Dublin 2	☎ 01/661 1866

Discounted airfares.

Joe Walsh Tours

34 Grafton St, Dublin 2	☎ 01/671 8751
69 Upper O'Connell St, Dublin 2	☎ 01/676 3053
8–11 Baggot St, Dublin 2	☎ 01/676 8915
117 St Patrick St, Cork	☎ 021/277959

General budget fares agent.

Student & Group Travel

1st Floor, 71 Dame St, Dublin 2	☎ 01/677 7834

Student and group specialists.

Thomas Cook

11 Donegal Place, Belfast	☎ 01232/242341
118 Grafton St, Dublin	☎ 01/677 1721

Package holiday and flight agent with occasional discount offers.

---

connecting flight or package (see p.3). Discount travel agents, such as USIT, may be able to organize both flights. As usual, the cheapest tickets are only available if you make sure you stay away over a Saturday night, and fly mid-week (Mon–Thurs).

There are numerous daily flights **from Dublin to London**, operated by Ryanair, Aer Lingus and British Midland; the cheapest is Ryanair, which costs from around IR£70 return to Stansted, though the price of the bus and underground journeys across London may make the total cost greater than Aer Lingus or British Midland IR£80 fares to Heathrow. **From Belfast**, there are British Airways and British Midland flights from Belfast International to Heathrow for around £75, subject to various restrictions. The less flexible the ticket the cheaper the price, though it's always

worth enquiring with Jersey European, who fly from Belfast City airport to Gatwick for £75 return or less.

From Dublin you can slightly undercut the plane's price by getting a Eurotrain ticket to London, but from Belfast you'll save nothing by taking the train and ferry instead of a plane.

Another way of getting to Prague from Ireland is to opt for a **package tour** with an operator such as Thomas Cook, who offer a seven-day trip to Prague for around IR£500; see box for more details.

By train

From London to Prague takes just under 24 hours by **train**, though if you go via the Channel Tunnel, you can cut the journey time by around six hours.

The routes

Trains leave Victoria station daily at around 8am, arriving in Prague the following morning. The main route is **by catamaran** from Ramsgate to Ostend, then by train via Brussels, Cologne, Frankfurt and Nuremberg, entering the Czech Republic by the Schirnding/Cheb border crossing. You'll have to change at Cologne (Köln) in the early evening, and during the winter timetable (Oct–May), you also have to change at Brussels.

Travelling **via Eurostar**, you can leave from London Waterloo International some four hours later, and connect with the aforementioned route at Brussels. Although you can travel **via Paris**, there is no longer a direct overnight service, which means you'll have to change in Frankfurt towards midnight, or get to Paris the night before and take the direct daytime train.

Although you can simply crash out on the seats, you won't get much sleep as the train passes across the Czech border during the early hours of the morning. To reserve a **couchette** for the final, overnight leg of the journey from Cologne to Prague (around £12 one-way), go to any British train station with an international desk; if you book over the phone with British Rail International, you'll be charged a £5 fee.

Tickets and passes

A **standard rail ticket** from London (bookable through some high-street travel agents or at London's mainline stations) will currently set you back around £200 return (via Ramsgate–Ostend): tickets are valid for two months and allow you to stop off en route. Travelling via Eurostar is a lot less hassle, and, depending on when you travel and how flexible you want to be, costs virtually the same: there's a discount fare of £69 return to Brussels, plus a £140 return from Brussels to Prague. However, to qualify for discount fare to Brussels, you can only travel mid-week and have to say exactly which train you're taking for your outward and return journeys.

Those under 26 can purchase a discounted **BIJ** ticket, available from British Rail, Eurotrain or Wasteels, thus saving around £30 on the return fare via catamaran. Eurotrain also offer a range of **Explorer** tickets, which allow you to go and come back a different route: for example, the "Eastern Explorer", currently £256, covers London–Amsterdam–Hannover–Berlin–Prague–Budapest–Vienna–Salzburg–Basel–Luxembourg–Brussels–

Train information

International Rail Centre
Victoria Station,
London SW1   ☎ 0990/848848

Eurostar
EPS House,
Waterloo Station, London SE1 ☎ 0345/303030

Eurotrain
52 Grosvenor Gdns,
London SW1   ☎ 0171/730 3402

Wasteels
Victoria Station (by platform 2),
London SW1   ☎ 0171/834 7066

Bus information

Bohemia Euroexpress International
Czech Tourist Centre
16 Frognal Parade,
London NW3   ☎ 0171/794 3264

Capital Express
57 Princedale Rd,
London W11   ☎ 0171/243 0488

Eurolines
52 Grosvenor Gdns,
London SW1   ☎ 0990/143219

Kingscourt Express
15 Balham High Rd,
London SW12   ☎ 0181/673 7500

Cross-Channel information

Holyman Sally Ferries   ☎ 0990/595522
Hoverspeed   ☎ 0990/240241
Le Shuttle   ☎ 0990/353535

P&O European Ferries   ☎ 0990/980980
Stena Line   ☎ 0990/707070

London. Travellers over 60 can get a 30 percent discount on the standard London to Prague ticket price by purchasing a **Rail Europe Senior Card** at a cost of £5. However, before you can buy this card, you must already possess a British Senior Card (£18); both are valid for a year.

If you're planning to visit Prague as part of a more extensive trip around Europe, it may be worth purchasing an **InterRail pass**, available from British Rail or travel agents; the only restriction is that you must have been resident in Europe for at least six months. Under the current system travellers will need a three-zone pass to get to Prague and back: this costs £249 for one month for those under 26, and £275 a month for those aged 26 and over. In addition to free travel on the European rail networks specified on your ticket, you're also entitled to discounts in Britain and on Eurostar and cross-Channel ferries. Either way, though, you're only really going to get your money back if you do a lot of travelling. For the latest information, visit British Rail's home page at *www.britrail.com*.

By bus

The cheapest way to get to Prague is by **bus**. There are direct services from London's Victoria Station more or less daily throughout the year, all of which take around 24 hours to reach Prague's main bus terminal, Florenc. Prices between companies vary very slightly so it's worth ringing round to find the best deal; a return ticket currently costs around £80 for those under 26, or around £90 for those over 26. Addresses and telephone numbers for all current operators are in the box opposite. The journey is long but just about bearable – make sure you bring along enough to eat, drink and read, and a small amount of Belgian and German currency for coffee and any spending en route. There are stops for around half an hour every four hours or so, and the routine is broken by the ferry (included in the cost of the ticket).

By car

Driving to Prague is not the most relaxing option – even if you're into driving virtually non-stop, it'll take the best part of two days – but with two or more passengers it can work out relatively inexpensive. The quickest way of taking your car over to the continent is to drive to the **Channel Tunnel**, where Le Shuttle operates 24 hours a day, carrying cars, motorcycles, buses and their passengers between Folkestone and Calais and takes 35 minutes. At peak times, services run every fifteen minutes; during the night, they run hourly. You must turn up at least 25 minutes before departure; Standard return fares cost £149 per vehicle (passengers included), with discounts in the low season.

Cheaper cross-Channel options are the conventional **ferry**, **catamaran** or **hovercraft** links between Dover and Calais, and Ramsgate and Dunkirk or Ostend. **Fares** vary enormously with the time of year, month and even day that you travel, and the size of your car. The Dover–Calais run, operated by Stena Sealink and P&O, starts at about £150 return for a small car and two adults in the high season. Sally Lines charge slightly less for the Ramsgate–Dunkirk crossing; from £120 return high season. The cheapest Hoverspeed route is Folkestone–Boulogne, which costs around £140 return in high season.

The most direct route from northern France to Prague is via Brussels, Liège (Luik), Cologne (Köln), Frankfurt, Würzburg and Nuremberg (Nürnberg), entering the country at the **Waidhaus–Rozvadov** border crossing: a distance of over 1000km or roughly twelve hours' solid driving. Motorways in Belgium and Germany are free, but to travel on any motorways within the Czech Republic, you need authorization in the form of a *dálniční známka*, which can be purchased from all border crossings and most garages and post offices.

Travel insurance

Though not compulsory for a trip to Prague, **travel insurance** including medical cover is a good idea. **In Britain**, travel insurance schemes are sold by all travel agents. ISIS policies, originally designed for students but now available to all comers, are available from any of the youth/student travel companies listed on pp.4–5, and offer comprehensive insurance covering medical expenses, theft and baggage loss for £20 for two weeks. Alternatively, try specialist, low-priced firms like Endsleigh Insurance (☎0171/436 4451) or Columbus Travel Insurance (☎0171/375 0011), who both offer similarly priced policies.

If you do have to pay for any medical treatment or drugs when in Prague, keep the receipts for claiming on your insurance once you're home. If you have anything stolen (including money) register the loss immediately with the local police – without their report you won't be able to claim. For the address of the main police stations in Prague, see p.29.

Getting there from the USA and Canada

The quickest and easiest way to reach Prague from the US or Canada is **to fly**. One of the most convenient options is Czech Airlines (ČSA), who operate non-stop flights from New York and Chicago daily in the summer and several times a week during the rest of the year. From Toronto and Montreal, ČSA operate non-stop flights every day except Sunday in the summer, and twice a week during the rest of the year. Flying time from New York to Prague is around 8 hours and 30 minutes; the flight from Toronto to Prague takes about 10 hours.

In addition, the major carriers offer dozens of one- and two-stop flights from any number of North American gateways via major European cities. However, if money rather than convenience is your top priority, you might want to think about buying a cheap transatlantic flight to London or Frankfurt and making your way to Prague overland by train, bus or car (see pp.5–6 for details).

To save any hassle, and sometimes even money, you may also want to consider some form of package tour – names and addresses of agents specializing in travel to Prague and details of some of the various options are given below.

If you're flying from North America, bear in mind that high season lasts from June to the end of August; shoulder season runs from mid- to end of December and low season from the start of November to mid-December, and then after Christmas to the end of March. Ticket prices quoted in this section are for midweek travel; weekend flights cost around $50 extra. All prices we've quoted are round-trip, exclusive of taxes and subject to availability and change.

Airlines serving Prague

Air New Zealand
USA	☎ 1-800/262-1234
Canada	☎ 1-800/663-5494

British Airways
USA	☎ 1-800/247-9297
Canada	☎ 1-800/668-1059

Delta ☎ 1-800/241-4141

Continental ☎ 1-800/231-0856

Czech Airlines (CSA)
USA	☎ 1-800/223-2365; 212/765 6022
Montreal	☎ 1-800/561 5171
Toronto	☎ 1-800/641 0641

Finnair ☎ 1-800/950-5000

KLM
USA	☎ 1-800/374-7747
Canada	☎ 1-800/361-5073

SAS ☎ 1-800/221-2350

Lufthansa
USA	☎ 1-800/645-3880
Canada	☎ 1-800/563-5954

Flights from the US

Discounted tickets and special offers aside, the cheapest way to get from the US to Prague is with an **Apex** (Advance Purchase Excursion) ticket. This carries certain restrictions: you'll most likely have to book – and pay – 21 days before departure; you'll be restricted as to the time you spend abroad (such as a minimum seven days, maximum stay three months, must include a Saturday night etc) and will face penalties if you change your schedule. There are also winter **Super Apex** tickets, sometimes known as "Eurosavers" – slightly cheaper than an ordinary Apex, but limiting your stay to between 7 and 21 days. Some airlines issue **Special Apex** tickets to those under 24, often extending the maximum stay to a year. The lowest scheduled Apex fares from New York (Newark) to Prague are $738 (low season); $898 (shoulder) and $1058 (high); from Chicago add on $100 and from Los Angeles $250.

Discount agents, advertised in Sunday newspaper travel sections such as that in the *New York Times*, can usually do better than any Apex fare. Agents come in several guises. **Consolidators** buy up large blocks of tickets that airlines don't think they'll be able to sell at their published fares, and sell them at a discount. Besides being cheap, consolidators normally don't impose advance purchase requirements (although in busy times you'll want to book ahead to be sure of getting a ticket), but they do often charge very stiff fees for date changes. Also, these companies' margins are tiny, so they make their money by dealing in volume – don't expect them to entertain lots of questions. **Discount agents** also wheel and deal in blocks of tickets offloaded by the airlines, but they also offer a range of travel-related services such as travel insurance, rail passes, youth and student ID cards, car rental, tours, and the like. These agencies tend to be most worthwhile to students and the under-26s, who can often benefit from special fares and deals. **Travel clubs** are another option for those who travel a lot – most charge an annual membership fee, which may be worth it for discounts on air tickets and car rental.

As with all fares, but particularly in the case of flights to the Czech Republic, you'd be well advised to shop around. Airlines often run special limited offers with considerable reductions on prices, and sometimes with less restrictions than on regular Apex fares. If you're travelling from the East Coast for example, Finnair is definitely worth looking into, while Air New Zealand often operate good-value flights from the West Coast; their flight from Los Angeles to London (from where you can pick up dirt cheap flights to Prague) is one of the best kept secrets in the business.

Flights from Canada

Getting **flights from Canada to Prague** is no problem. ČSA flies non-stop twice a week from Toronto for CDN$1342 (high season), CDN$922 (low season). It's less straightforward arranging an inexpensive connection from elsewhere in the country. Your best bet is Lufthansa, who fly more or less daily from several major Canadian cities to Prague via Frankfurt, usually in partnership with local carriers. Fares from Montreal are the same as from Toronto. From Vancouver or from Calgary expect to pay from CDN$1709 in high season, CDN$1226 during low season. A good source for discount flights, especially if you're a **student** or **under 26**, is Travel Cuts (see box on p.10 for address and phone number).

Flights via Europe

Since direct flights to Prague are usually more expensive than flights to other European cities, it may be worth your while to fly to another country and make your way overland from there. Munich, Berlin, Frankfurt and Vienna are the closest major European cities to Prague. Airlines offering flights to Prague **via Europe** include Lufthansa (via Frankfurt), SAS (via Copenhagen), KLM (via Amsterdam) and Delta, but check the routing of their flights – many involve lengthy stopovers and multiple changes of

---

Rail contacts in North America

CIT Tours
9501 W. Devon Ave, Suite 502,
Rosemont, IL 60018 ☎ 1-800/223-7987

DER Tours/GermanRail
9501 W Divon Ave, Suite 400
Rosemont, IL 60018 ☎ 1-800/421-2929

Rail Europe
226 Westchester Ave
White Plains, NY 10604 ☎ 1-800/438 7245

ScanTours
1535 6th St, Suite 205
Santa Monica, CA 90401 ☎ 1-800/223-7226

Discount agents, consolidators and travel clubs in North America

Council Travel
205 E 42nd St,
New York, NY 10017 ☎ 1-800/226-8624
*Nationwide US student travel organization
with branches (among others) in San
Francisco, Los Angeles, Washington DC,
Austin, Seattle, Chicago and Minneapolis.*

Encore Travel Club
4501 Forbes Blvd,
Lanham, MD 20706 ☎ 1-800/444-9800
East-coast discount travel club.

Interworld Travel
800 Douglass Rd,
Miami, FL 33134 ☎ 305/443-4929
Southeastern consolidator.

New Frontiers/Nouvelles Frontières
12 E 33rd St,
New York, NY 10016 ☎ 1-800/366-6387

Sherbrooke East, Suite 720,
Montreal, H2L 1L3 ☎ 514/526-8444
*Discount travel firm with branches in
Los Angeles, San Francisco, Montreal and
Quebec City.*

STA Travel
10 Downing St
New York, NY 100014 ☎ 1-800/777-0112
*Worldwide specialist in independent travel
with branches in the Los Angeles, San
Francisco and Boston areas.*

Travac
Head office: 989 6th Ave,
New York, NY 10018 ☎ 1-800/872-8800
*Consolidator and charter broker, with
another branch in Orlando.*

Travel Avenue
10 S Riverside, Suite 1404,
Chicago, IL 60606 ☎ -800/333-3335
Discount travel agent.

Travel Cuts
187 College St,
Toronto, ON M5T 1P7 ☎ 416/979-2406
*Canadian student travel organization with
branches all over the country.*

Travelers Advantage
3033 S Parker Rd, Suite 900,
Aurora, CO 80014 ☎ 1-800/548-1116
Discount travel club.

UniTravel
1177 N Warson Rd,
St Louis, MO 63132 ☎ 1-800/325-2222
Consolidator.

plane. Lufthansa currently offers a limited round-trip special fare to Berlin from New York for $358 (low season); from Berlin you can reach Prague by train in well under twelve hours.

"**Open-jaw**" fares provide more flexibility, enabling you to fly into one city and out of another. If you're lucky enough to catch one of their limited special offers, you can fly with Lufthansa from New York into Berlin, then out of Prague two weeks later, for as little as $490 (low season). See "Getting There from Britain", on p.3, for a more complete rundown of trans-European options.

Eurail Passes are not valid in the Czech Republic, but if you're visiting Prague as part of a more extensive tour of Europe, they may be worth considering. The all-country pass, which you must purchase before you leave for Europe, allows unlimited free travel on the railways of seventeen European countries. The **Eurail**

Youthpass (for under-26s) costs US$365 for fifteen days, $587 for one month or $832 for two months; if you're 26 or over you'll have to buy a first-class pass, available in fifteen-day ($522), 21-day ($678), one-month ($838), two-month ($1188) and three-month ($1468) increments.

You stand a better chance of getting your money's worth out of a **Eurail Flexipass**, which is good for a certain number of travel days in a two-month period. This, too, comes in under-26/first-class versions: ten days, $431/$616; fifteen days, $568/$812. If you're travelling in a group of two or more, you might also want to consider the **Eurail Saverpass**. This costs $444 for fifteen consecutive days, $576 for 21; $712 for a month; $1010 for two months or $1248 for three. There's also a **Flexi Saverpass** at $524 for ten days or $690 for fifteen.

Another possibility is the **European East pass**, valid for travel in Hungary, Austria, Poland,

Slovakia and the Czech Republic. Any five days in one month costs $195; and you can add on a maximum of five extra days for $21 per day. Finally, there's a **Czech Flexipass** which is valid for travel within the Czech Republic for five days out of fifteen and costs around $69.

Package tours

Travel agents specializing in Eastern Europe, are your best sources of up-to-date advice on travel to Prague, as well as being a good way of finding out about any other cheap flight deals that might be available. Among commercial tour operators offering good packages to Prague, Tradesco's range of products include the "Prague Classic", an eight-day package from $962, while Fugazy offer a seven-night package from around $600 to $1000 (low season) and from $1300 to $1800 (high season), depending on the standard of hotel. A list of specialist travel agents is given in the box below.

Specialist agents in North America

American-International Homestays
P.O. Box 1754, Nederland,
CO 80466   ☎1-800/876-2048; 303/642-3088
Arranges accommodation with English-speaking families. Bed and Breakfast at $59 (single) or $89 (double) per night; also packages with dinner and city guide.

Backroads
801 Cedar St,
Berkeley, CA 94710   ☎1-800/462-2848
Six-day hiking/canoeing/rafting tour with hotel accomodation starting and finishing in Prague for $1798 (land only).

La Bohème
875 N Michigan Ave, Suite 3530, Chicago, IL 60611   ☎1-888/LA BOHEME; 312/440-0866
Customized tour operators specializing in the Czech Republic and Central Europe.

Carpati International
Gypsy Trail Rd,
Carmel, NY 10512   ☎1-800/447-8742
Fully independent and group tours.

Czech & Slovak Travel Service
7033 Sunset Boulevard, Suite 210,
Los Angeles, CA 90028   ☎213/389-2157
All-inclusive packages to Central and Eastern European destinations.

Delta Vacations
53 Summer St, Keene,
NH 03431   ☎1-800/872-7786
Five-day/three-night city breaks from $899.

Different Strokes Tours
1841 Broadway
New York, NY 10023   ☎1-800/668 3301
Customised tour service for gay and lesbian travellers.

Eastern Europe Tours
600 Stewart St, Suite 524
Seattle, WA 98101   ☎206/448 8400
"Chateaus, Museums and Spas" is a seven-night tour based mostly in Prague for around $1460 (not including flights).

Elderhostel
75 Federal St,
Boston, MA 02110   ☎1-617/426-8056
Specialists in educational and activity programs, cruises and homestays for senior travellers (companions may be younger). Offers two all-inclusive three-week packages: 'Exploring Prague' ($3365) and 'Prague and the New World Order' (from $3049).

Europe Train Tours
198 E Boston Post Rd,
Mararoneck, NY 10543   ☎1-800/551-2085
Customized tours by rail, with special rates on Swiss Air.

Fugazy International
770 US-1,
North Brunswick, NJ 08902   ☎1-800/828-4488
Customized tours to Prague.

Tradesco
6033 Century Blvd, Suite 670,
Los Angeles,
CA 90045-6415   ☎1-800/833-3402
Wide variety of European packages, including city breaks to Prague and a three-night Prague Music Tour.

Unique World Travel
39 Beechwood Ave,
Manhasset, NY 11030   ☎1-516/627 2636
Unique operate cruises which include Prague in their itineraries.

Travel insurance companies in North America

Most travel agents will arrange travel insurance at no extra charge. The following insurance companies can be called directly.

Access America	☎1-800/284-8300	**International Student Insurance Service**	
Carefree Travel		**(ISIS)** – sold by STA Travel ☎1-800/777-0112	
Insurance	☎1-800/323-3149	**Travel Guard**	☎1-800/826-1300
Desjardins Travel Insurance		**Travel Insurance Services**	☎1-800/937-1387
– Canada only	☎1-800/463-7830		

Travel insurance

Before buying travel insurance, check any existing insurance policies to make sure that you're not already covered. Canadian provincial health plans, for example, typically provide some overseas medical coverage, although they are unlikely to pick up the full tab in the event of a mishap. Holders of official **student/teacher/youth cards** are entitled to accident coverage and hospital in-patient benefits – the annual membership is far less than the cost of comparable insurance. **Students** may also find that their student health coverage extends during the vacations and for one term beyond the date of last enrollment. Bank and credit cards (particularly American Express) often provide certain levels of medical or other insurance, and travel insurance may also be included if you use a major credit or charge card to pay for your trip. **Homeowners' or renters'** insurance often covers theft or loss of documents, money and valuables while overseas.

After exhausting the possibilities above, you might want to contact a specialist **travel insurance** company; your travel agent can usually recommend one, or see the box above.

Travel insurance **policies** vary: some are comprehensive while others cover only certain risks (accidents, illnesses, delayed or lost luggage, cancelled flights, etc.). In particular, ask whether the policy pays medical costs up front or reimburses you later, and whether it provides for medical evacuation to your home country. For policies that include lost or stolen luggage, check exactly what is and isn't covered, and make sure the per-article limit will cover your most valuable possession.

Most North American travel policies apply only to items lost, stolen or damaged while in the custody of an identifiable, responsible third party – hotel porter, airline, luggage consignment, etc. Even in these cases you will have to contact the local police within a certain time limit to have a complete report made out so that your insurer can process the claim.

The best **premiums** are usually to be had through student/youth travel agencies – ISIS policies, for example, cost between $48 and $69 for fifteen days (depending on level of coverage), betwenn $80 and $105 for a month, and from $149 to $207 for two months.

Getting there from Australia and New Zealand

There are no direct flights to Prague from Australia or New Zealand – whichever route you fly will involve stopping off on the way. A number of mid-priced combinations with Qantas or Air New Zealand – such as Czechoslovak Airlines (ČSA), Alitalia, Olympic Airways, Lufthansa, KLM and Aeroflot – can get you to Prague for around A\$1999/NZ\$2350 in low season and around A\$2499/NZ\$2799 in high season via either a transfer or stopover in their Asian and European cities. Another option is to get a cheap flight to Frankfurt with Garuda, Malaysia Airlines or Philippine Airlines (from around A\$1550/NZ\$2099) and then continue on to Prague by road or rail. As most fares to Europe are common rated (ie you pay the same no matter what your destination), this option rarely works out cheaper than buying a discounted airfare all the way, but can be a good idea if you intend to take in Prague as part of a wider European experience.

"**Round-the-world**" (RTW) flights, valid for up to a year, are another good option – especially from New Zealand, where airlines offer fewer bonuses to fly with them. Qantas/British Airway's "Global

Explorer" fare, starting at A\$2599/NZ\$3089, is probably the most versatile, allowing four sectors within Europe (including Prague), additional sectors for A\$/NZ\$120 each and routing via the US, Asia and Africa.

Tickets purchased direct from the airlines tend to be expensive – you'll get much better deals on fares from your local travel agent, as well as the latest information on limited specials, fly-drive, accommodation packages, stopovers en route and round-the-world fares. Some of the best discounts are through Flight Centres and STA (see box for telephone numbers), who can also advise on visa regulations. Seat availability on most international flights out of Australia and New Zealand is often limited so it's best to book at least three weeks ahead.

Fares vary according to the season and you can expect to pay from A\$/NZ\$400 to \$600 more for high-season fares (from mid-May to the end of August and from December to mid-January); shoulder season is from March to mid-May and September; low season is the rest of the year.

From Australia

The nearest to a direct flight to Prague **from Australia** is with Czechoslovak Airlines (ČSA) in conjunction with Qantas via Bangkok/Singapore for around A\$1850 (low season), A\$2100 (shoulder season) and A\$2200 (high season). However, the lowest fares, for around A\$1750–\$2499, are with Olympic Airways via Athens, Lufthansa via Frankfurt and Alitalia via Rome, while Aeroflot fares to Budapest via Moscow start from A\$1850. Slightly pricier is the Ansett/Swiss Air flight via Zurich (A\$1950–2300) and KLM's fares start from A\$2100. Other major carriers, such as Qantas and British Airways, offer return trips to Prague with stopovers en route from A\$2499.

From New Zealand

There are very few options **from New Zealand** to Prague, and all involve combinations of air-

Airlines in Australia and New Zealand

☎008 and ☎003 numbers are toll-free, but only apply if dialled outside the city in the address.
☎13 0000 are charged at the local rate nationwide.

Aeroflot
Sydney 2000   ☎ 02/9262 2233
No NZ office.

Air France
Sydney   ☎ 02/9321 1000
Auckland   ☎ 09/303 3521

Alitalia
Sydney   ☎ 02/9247 1308
Auckland   ☎ 09/379 4457

Ansett Australia
Australia   ☎ 13 1767
New Zealand   ☎ 09/796 409

British Airways
Sydney   ☎ 02/9258 3300
Auckland   ☎ 09/356 8690

Cathay Pacific
Australia   ☎ 13 1747
New Zealand   ☎ 09/379 0861

Czech Airlines
Australia   ☎ 02/9247 6196

Garuda
Sydney   ☎ 02/9334 9944 & 1800/800 873
Auckland   ☎ 09/366 1855

Japan Airlines
Sydney   ☎ 02/9272 1111
Auckland   ☎ 09/379 9906

Lufthansa
Sydney   ☎ 02/9367 3888
Auckland   ☎ 09/303 1529

Malaysia Airlines
Sydney   ☎ 13 2627
Auckland   ☎ 09/373 2741

Olympic Airlines
Sydney   ☎ 02/9251 2044
No NZ office

Philippine Airlines
Australia   ☎ 02/9262 3333

Qantas
Sydney   ☎ 13 1211
Auckland   ☎ 09/357 8900 & 0800/808 767

Thai Airways
Sydney   ☎ 13 1960
Auckland   ☎ 09/377 3886

lines to take you via Asia or the US to a European hub city, and then on to Prague. The best deal is with Qantas to either Los Angeles, Singapore or Bangkok, where you connect with Alitalia via Rome; fares start at NZ$2350 in low season and rise to NZ$2799 in high season. There is also an Air New Zealand/Lufthansa combination via Singapore or Los Angeles starting at NZ$2399. You'll get good-value flights to a range of other European destinations with Japanese Airlines (overnighting in Tokyo), Garuda, via either Bali or Jakarta and Malaysia Airlines via Kuala Lumper – all from around NZ$2099. As with Australia, major carriers such as Qantas and British Airways include returns to Prague with their London service and stopovers en route from NZ$2800 to $3500. Qantas/BA's Round-the-World fare costs only a little more at NZ$3089 to $3599.

Most flights are out of Auckland, so you'll need to add on around NZ$100 to $300 for Christchurch and Wellington connections.

Travel insurance

In Australia and New Zealand **travel insurance** is available from most travel agents or direct from

Travel insurance companies in Australia and New Zealand

Cover More
9/32 Walker St, North Sydney
☎ 02/9202 8000 & 1800/251 881

Ready Plan
141 Walker St, Dandenong, Melbourne
☎ 03/9791 5077 & 1800/337 462

10/ 63 Albert St, Auckland ☎ 09/379 3208

Discount and specialist agents in Australia and New Zealand

Anywhere Travel
345 Anzac Parade, Kingsford, Sydney
☎02/9663 0411

Brisbane Discount Travel
260 Queen St, Brisbane ☎07/3229 9211

Budget Travel
16 Fort St, Auckland ☎09/366 0061 & 0-
800/808 040

Destinations Unlimited
3 Milford Rd, Auckland ☎09/373 4033

Flight Centres
82 Elizabeth St, Sydney ☎13 1600
205 Queen St, Auckland ☎09/309 6171

Northern Gateway
22 Cavenagh St, Darwin ☎08/8941 1394

STA Travel
702 Harris St, Ultimo, Sydney; 256 Flinders St,
Melbourne; other offices in state capitals and
major universities, nearest branch ☎13 1776;
fastfare telesales ☎1-300/360 960; 10 High St,
Auckland ☎09/309 0458; fastfare telesales
☎09/366 6673. Plus branches in Wellington,
Christchurch, Dunedin, Palmerston North,
Hamilton and at major universities.
www.statravelaus.com.au; email:
traveller@statravelaus.com.au

Thomas Cook
175 Pitt St, Sydney; 257 Collins St, Melbourne;
plus branches in other state capitals; local
branch ☎13 1771; direct telesales ☎1-800/063
913; 96 Anzac Ave, Auckland ☎09/379 3920

Tymtro Travel
Level 8, 130 Pitt St, Sydney ☎02/9223 2211 or
1300/652 969

Specialist operators

Australians Studying Abroad
1/970 High St, Armadale, Melbourne
☎03/9509 1955 & 1800/645 755
Art and culture tours drawing on the signifi-
cance of the Hapsburg cities of Budapest,
Prague and Vienna.

Contal Travel
446 George St, Brisbane ☎07/3236 2929
http://www.contaltours.com
Prague accommodation, car rental and day
tours.

Eastern Europe Travel Bureau
75 King St, Sydney ☎02/9262 1144;
fax 9262 4479

343 Little Collins St, Melbourne ☎03/9600
0299; fax 9670 1793

131 Elizabeth St, Brisbane ☎07/3229 9716
Prague accommodation, three- to four-day
city-stays, homestays, tours and concerts. Also
branches in Adelaide and Perth.

Eastern Eurotours
Seabank Centre, level 9, 17 Marine Parade,
Southport QLD 4215 ☎07/5591 0326 & 1-800
242 353
Prague accommodation and city tours.

Eurolynx
3/20 Fort St, Auckland ☎09/379 9716
Prague accommodation and city sightseeing
tours.

Gateway Travel
48 The Boulevarde, Strathfield, Sydney
☎02/9745 3333
Can arrange accomodation in Prague and
city tours.

---

insurance companies (see box opposite), for
periods ranging from a few days to a year or
even longer. Although most policies are similar
in premium and coverage, if you plan to indulge
in high-risk activities such as mountaineering,
bungy jumping or scuba diving without a certificate, check the policy carefully to make sure
you'll be covered.

A typical policy for the Czech Republic will cost
around A$100/NZ$110 for two weeks, A$170/
NZ$190 for one month and A$250/NZ$275 for
two months.

Red Tape and visas

British, Irish, US, Canadian and all EU nationals need only a **full passport** to enter the Czech Republic, though the passport itself must be valid for at least six months beyond your return date. However, Canada has recently introduced visa requirements for Czech citizens. So far, no retaliatory measures have been taken but you'd be wise to double-check with the embassy or consulate in case there's a change in policy.

At the time of writing Australian and New Zealand citizens still need a **visa** (valid for up to thirty days), available from a Czech embassy or consulate – the process should take no more than two days and is free. Along with your application form you'll need a valid

---

Czech embassies and consulates

Australia
169 Military Rd,
Dover Heights,
Sydney,
NSW 2030 ☎ 02/9371 8877 & 02/9371 7307

Austria
Penzingerstrasse 11–13,
1140 Vienna ☎ 0222/894 1200

Belgium
555 rue Engeland,
1180 Bruxelles-Uccle ☎ 02/374 1203

Canada
541 Sussex Drive,
Ottawa,
Ontario K1N 6Z6 ☎ 613/562 3875;

1305 Avenue des Pins West,
Montreal,
Quebec H3G 1B2 ☎ 514/849-4495

France
15 avenue Charles Floquet,
75343 Paris ☎ 40 65 13 00

Germany
Wilhelmstrasse 44,
10117 Berlin ☎ 030/220 0481

Ireland
57 Northumberland Rd,
Ballsbridge,
Dublin 4 ☎ 01/668 1135

New Zealand
48 Hair St,
Wainuiomata
Wellington ☎ 44/564 6001

UK
28 Kensington Palace Gdns,
London W8 4QY ☎ 0171/243 1115
Visa hotline ☎ 0891/171267

USA
3900 Spring of Freedom St, NW,
Washington DC 20008 ☎ 202/274 9100;

1109 Madison Ave,
New York, NY 10028 ☎ 212/717-5643; 10990

Wilshire Blvd,
Suite 1100,
Los Angeles, CA ☎ 310/473-0889)

Foreign consulates and embassies in Prague are listed on p.244.

---

passport and two passport photgraphs (four for a multiple entry visa) and a SAE if applying by post.

Officially visitors are supposed to notify the local police within thirty days of their arrival, though if you're staying at a hotel this will all be done for you. EU nationals are allowed to stay for up to three months; US citizens get six months; other nationals should check with their Czech consulate. To stay longer, you either need a really good excuse, or a residence permit (*občanský průkaz*), which is difficult to obtain unless you're studying here or have a job (and, therefore, a work permit). Many people avoid this bureaucratic nightmare – which can take up to six months – by simply leaving the country for a few days when their time runs out, making sure they get their passport stamped upon re-entry, but the legality of this is somewhat doubtful, and the Prague police are clamping down on foreigners working or staying here illegally.

If you already have a work permit and need a residence permit, you'll have to fill in the application form known as *povolení k pobytu*, which you can only get by going in person to the second floor of the Úřad práce (Department of Employment), Zborovská 11, Smíchov. Then go to the head passport office at Olšanská 2, Žižkov, Prague. You should bring with you your passport, your work permit, a 1000kč stamp (*kolková známka*) and a letter from the owner of the property you're staying in. You also need to bring with you a certificate saying that you have a clean criminal record, obtainable in person from the Rejstřík trestu, náměstí Hrdinů, Nusle, as long as you go armed with a 50kč *kolková známka*.

Customs allowances into the Czech Republic are 250 cigarettes or 50 cigars, 1 litre of spirits and 2 litres of wine. Allowances when taking goods from the Czech Republic into EU countries are the same. These allowances may change in the future, though, so if in doubt, check with customs before you leave for Prague.

Health matters

No inoculations are required for the Czech Republic, and on a short visit you're unlikely to fall victim to anything worse than an upset stomach. However, if you suffer from a respiratory problem, avoid coming to Prague during the winter months, when sulphur dioxide levels in the city centre regularly reach three or four times World Health Organisation safety levels (see box on p.18).

Pharmacies, Doctors and Hospitals

Reciprocal arrangements between the Czech Republic and the EU mean that EU citizens are entitled to free emergency medical care, with a charge only for imported drugs and certain specialized treatments. Citizens from all other countries should have their own health insurance, and even EU residents would be well-advised to take out their own health policies, as the reciprocal agreement only covers emergency treatment and not a visit to a doctor.

24-hr pharmacies

Belgická 37, Vinohrady; metro náměstí Míru; ☎24 23 72 07

Koněvova 210, Žižkov; tram #5, #9, #26; ☎644 18 95

Štefánikova 6, Břevnov; metro Anděl; ☎53 70 39

Emergency dentist

Vladislavova 22, Nové Město ☎24 22 76 63; Mon–Thurs 7pm–7am; Fri–Sun 24hr.

If you should become ill, the easiest course of action is to go to a **pharmacy** (*lékárna*). Pharmacists are willing to give advice (though language may be a problem), and are able to dispense many drugs available only on prescription in other countries. They usually keep normal shop hours, but several outlying ones are open round the clock (there's a list below). The next step up is to go to a **medical centre** (*poliklinika*); the most central one is at Palackého 5, Nové Město; metro Národní třída.

If language proves an insurmountable barrier, and you wish to see an **English-speaking doctor**, you should go to the Nemocnice na Homolce, Roentgenova 2, Motol; bus #167 from metro Anděl. This is a privately run **hospital** specifically geared towards foreigners – take your passport and at least 1000kč to put down as a deposit. If it's an **emergency**, dial ☎155 for an ambulance and you'll be taken to the nearest hospital.

Pollution in Prague

Don't be fooled by the outward beauty of Prague's buildings. The city is sick, suffering some of the highest levels of sulphur dioxide of any European capital. And the worst place to be is the old town itself: every winter the **pollution** in the Staré Město exceeds the WHO safety limits. On at least ten days during each winter, pollution levels rise to nearly three times the WHO safety levels, forcing the municipal authorities to introduce a total ban on non-essential traffic, domestic and foreign, within the city.

Between October and March, Prague is plagued by a lethal cocktail of winter weather, the city's basin-like topography, and the brown coal which provides energy for industry and most of the city's heating. The heavy, cold air sits in the basin, trapped in by the warmer air above, and thus preventing the sulphur dioxide and carbon monoxide from dispersing. Car ownership looks set to rise dramatically over the next decade, and a year-round ban on cars in the city centre is a serious possibility.

Information and maps

The Czech tourist board – known as the Czech Centre – remains in its infancy and is of limited use, though it has a handful of good maps and pamphlets to give away. The staff are

---

Czech centres abroad

Austria
Herrengasse 17,
1010 Vienna   ☎ 535 2361

Canada
P.O. Box 198,
Exchange Tower, 2 First Canadian Place,
14th Floor, Toronto
Ontario M5X 1A6   ☎ 416/367 3432

Germany
Leipzigerstrasse 60,
Berlin   ☎ 030/204 4770

UK
95 Great Portland St,
London W1 5RA   ☎ 0171/291 9924

USA
1109–1111 Madison Ave,
New York, NY 10028   ☎ 212/288 0830

---

generally helpful and should be able to answer any queries you have about the country (see below for addresses of Czech Centres abroad).

Maps

For wandering round the centre of Prague, the **maps** produced in this book should be sufficient, but if you crave greater detail, or are staying out in the suburbs, you may need to buy something more comprehensive. The best maps of Prague are produced by *Kartografie Praha*, whose 1:20,000 booklet (*plán města*) covers the whole city and includes the tram and bus routes, too. This, or something similar, should be available from the map suppliers listed below, though you'll get it more easily and cheaply in Prague itself at PIS offices (Prague Information Service), most bookstores (*knihkupectví*) and some hotels. For more details on maps available in Prague, see box below.

Surfing Prague

Welcome to the Czech Republic
The Foreign Ministry's very own home page, with basic information on the country.
http://www.czech.cz/

Do města/Downtown
Prague's useful fortnightly listings leaflet on-line.
http://www.cz/downtown/

Ticketpro
Prague's largest ticket agency is, of course, on-line so you can book concert tickets ahead.
http://www.ticketpro.cz/

Radio Prague
An informative site well worth visiting, with updated news and weather as audio or text.
http://www.radio.cz/

Map and guide outlets

Australia and New Zealand

Bowyangs, 372 Little Bourke St, Melbourne; ☎ 03/9670 4383

The Map Shop, 16a Peel St, Adelaide; ☎ 08/8231 2033

Perth Map Centre, 891 Hay St, Perth; ☎ 09/9322 5733

Speciality Maps, 58 Albert St, Auckland; ☎ 09/307 2217

Travel Bookshop, 175 Liverpool St, Sydney; ☎ 02/9241 3554

Worldwide Maps and Guides, 187 George St, Brisbane; ☎ 07/3221 4330

Canada

Open Air Books and Maps, 25 Toronto St, Toronto M5R 2C1; ☎ 416/363 0719

Ulysses Travel Bookshop, 4176 St-Denis, Montreal; ☎ 514/843 9447

World Wide Books and Maps, 736 Granville St, Vancouver; ☎ 604/687 3320

UK

Blackwell's, 53 Broad St, Oxford OX1 3BQ; ☎ 01865/792792

Daunt Books, 83 Marylebone High St, London W1 ☎ 0171/224 2295; 193 Haverstock Hill, London NW3; ☎ 0171/794 4006

Heffers, 3rd Floor, Heffers Stationery, 19 Sidney St, Cambridge CB2 3HL; ☎ 01223/568467

John Smith and Sons, 57–61 St Vincent St, Glasgow; ☎ 0141/221 7472

National Map Centre, 22–24 Caxton St, London SW1; ☎ 0171/222 2466

Newcastle Map Shop, 55 Grey St, Newcastle-upon-Tyne, NE1 6EF; ☎ 0191/261 5622

Stanfords, 12–14 Long Acre, London WC2E 9LP; ☎ 0171/836 1321

US

Adventurous Traveler Bookstore, PO Box 1468, Williston, VT 05495; ☎ 1-800/282-3963; http://www.adventuroustraveler.com/

Book Passage, 51 Tama; Vista Blvd, Corte madera, CA 94925; ☎ 415/927-0960

The Complete Traveler Bookstore, 199 Madison Ave, New York, NY 10016; ☎ 212/685-9007

Map Link, 30 S La Petera Lane, Unit #5, Santa Barbara, CA 93117; ☎ 805/692-6777

The Map Store Inc., 1636 1st St, Washington DC 20006; ☎ 202/628 2608

Rand McNally has 24 stores across the US; phone ☎ 1-800/333-0136 (ext 2111) for the address of your nearest store, or for direct mail maps.

Travel Book & Language Center, 4931 Cordell Ave, Betheada, MD 20814; ☎ 1-800/220 2665

Traveler's Bookstore, 22 W 52nd St, New York, NY 10019; ☎ 212/664-0995

Costs, money and banks

In general terms, Prague is still incredibly cheap for westerners. The one exception is accommodation, which is comparable with many EU countries. At the time of writing, inflation was pretty much under control, though before you get to thinking everything is rosy in the Czech Republic, it's worth bearing in mind that the average monthly wage for Czechs is currently around 6000kč (£120/$190).

You'll find more precise costs for accommodation, food and drink in the relevant sections of the book: see "Accommodation" (p.195) and "Eating and Drinking" (p.204). At the bottom end of the scale, if you stay in a hostel and stick to pubs and takeaways, you could get by on as little as £10/$16 a day. If you stay in private accommodation or cheapish hotels, and eat in slightly fancier restaurants, then you could easily spend £25/$40 a day. The good thing about Prague, however, is that once you've accounted for your room, most restaurants, pubs, museums and galleries, beer and even taxis and nightclubs are far from expensive.

Tipping is normal practice in cafés, bars, restaurants and taxis, though this is usually done by simply rounding up the total. For example, if the waiter tots up the bill and asks you for 74kč, you should hand him a 100kč note and say "take 80kč".

Czech currency

The currency in the Czech Republic is the Czech crown or *koruna česká* (abbreviated to kč), which is divided into one hundred relatively worthless hellers or *halíře* (abbreviated to h). At the time of going to press there were around 60kč to the pound sterling and around 35kč to the US dollar. The crown's value is likely to fall further in the future as the political and economic stability of the country is looking uncertain.

Notes come in 20kč, 50kč, 100kč, 200kč, 500kč, 1000kč (less frequently 2000kč and 5000kč) denominations; coins as 1kč, 2kč, 5kč, 10kč, 20kč and 50kč, plus 10h, 20h and 50h.

Travellers' cheques and credit cards

Probably the safest and easiest way to carry your funds is in **travellers' cheques** – sterling, US dollars or Deutschmarks are all equally acceptable. American Express and Thomas Cook are the most widely used – you can get them, for a small commission (usually one percent of the amount ordered), from any bank and some building societies, whether or not you have an account, and from branches of American Express and Thomas Cook. The cheques can be exchanged commission-free at the companies' respective Prague branches (for addresses, see below).

Credit cards like Visa, Master Card (Access) and Amex are becoming more widely accepted: most upmarket hotels, restaurants and shops should take plastic. You can also withdraw cash from the automatic teller/cashpoint machines which are now a feature of downtown Prague, though you shouldn't rely solely on this method. It's a good idea to keep at least some hard currency in **cash** for emergencies, as it will be accepted almost anywhere. If you lose your credit card, ring the Prague credit card hotline on ☎ 236 66 88.

Changing money

The 24-hour exchange desk at the **airport** run by the Československá obchodní banka is, somewhat surprisingly, an excellent place to change money, regularly charging a mere one or two percent commission. Most Czech **banks** will be

Central moneychanging outlets

American Express, Václavské náměstí 56, Nové Město; ☎24 22 98 83

Česká spořitelna, Na příkopě 20, Nové Město; ☎26 36 96

Komerční banka, Na příkopě 33, Nové Město; ☎24 02 11 11

Thomas Cook, Václavské náměstí 47, Nové Město; ☎26 31 06

Živnostenká banka, Na příkopě 20, Nové Město; ☎24 12 11 11

prepared to change travellers' cheques, accept Eurocheques, and give cash advances on credit cards – look for the window marked *směnárna*. Commissions at banks are fairly reasonable (generally three percent or under) but the queues and the bureaucracy can mean a long wait. Quicker, but more of a ripoff in terms of commission are the exchange outlets (around five percent commission is the norm) which can be found on just about every street corner in the centre of Prague.

Banking hours are usually Monday to Friday 8am to 5pm, often with a break at lunchtime. Outside of these times, you may find the odd bank open, but otherwise you'll have to rely on the exchange outlets and the international hotels.

Cash emergencies

When you buy your travellers' cheques, make a note of the emergency phone number given. On your trip keep a record of all cheques and note which ones you spend – and report any loss or theft immediately. All being well, you should get the missing cheques reissued within a couple of days. Things can get trickier if you lose your credit card: your bank should be able to give you details of the number to call if this happens, but you won't be provided with a replacement card until you get home.

Assuming you know someone who is prepared to send you the money, the quickest and easiest way to have funds sent out to you in an emergency is to do it through **Western Union**, who will wire the money to you in a couple of hours (some banks will also do this via Western Union); get your sponsor to phone ☎0800/833833 in the UK or ☎1-800/325-6000 in North America. The Prague office of Western Union is at Sport Turist Special, Národní třída 33 (Mon–Fri 9am–6pm, Sat & Sun 10am–2pm; ☎24 22 95 24).

If you have a few days' leeway, you can simply get your bank to wire your money to a Czech bank, a process that shouldn't take more than a couple of working days. If you can last out the week, then an **international money order**, exchangeable at any post office, is by far the cheapest way of sending money.

If you're in really dire straits, get in touch with your **consulate** in Prague, who will usually let you make one phone call home free of charge, and will – in worst cases only – repatriate you, but will never, under any circumstances, lend you money.

Disabled travellers

In the past, very little attention has been paid to the needs of the disabled anywhere in the Czech Republic. Attitudes are slowly changing, but there is still a long way to go, and the chronic shortage of funds for almost anything is not helping matters.

Transport is a major problem, since buses and trams are virtually impossible for wheelchairs, though some metro stations now have facilities for the disabled, and the two railway stations (Hlavní nádraží and Nádraží Holešovice) actually have self-operating lifts.

Contacts for disabled travellers

Australia and New Zealand
ACROD (Australian Council for Rehabilitation of the Disabled), PO Box 60, Curtain, ACT 2605; ☎06/682 4333

Barrier Free Travel, 36 Wheatley St, North Bellingen, NSW 2454; ☎066/551733

Disabled Persons Assembly, PO Box 10-138, The Terrace, Wellington; ☎04/472 2626

Canada
Jewish Rehabilitation Hospital, 3205 Place Alton Goldbloom, Chomedy Laval, Quebec H7V 1RT; ☎514/688-9550, ext 226
Guidebooks and travel information.

Twin Peaks Press, Box 129, Vancouver, WA 98666; ☎360/694-2462 or 1-800/637-2256
Publisher of the Directory of Travel Agencies for the Disabled ($19.95), listing more than 370 agencies worldwide; Travel for the Disabled ($19.95); the Directory of Accessible Van Rentals ($9.95) and Wheelchair Vagabond ($14.95), which is full of personal tips.

Czech Republic
Prague Wheelchair Association, Pražská organizace vozíčkářů, Benediktská 6, Nové Mesto, Prague; ☎232 58 31, fax 24 81 62 31
Disabled-run organization that can provide assistance when you're in Prague, and which also produces the Accessible Prague guidebook.

UK and Ireland
Disability Action Group, 2 Annadale Ave, Belfast BT7 3JH ☎01232 491011
Information about access for disabled travellers abroad.

Holiday Care Service, 2nd Floor, Imperial Building, Victoria Rd, Horley, Surrey RH6 7PZ; ☎01293/774535
Information on all aspects of travel.

Tripscope, The Courtyard, Evelyn Rd, London W4 5JL; ☎0181/994 9294
Information, access guides, tours and exchange programmes.

RADAR (The Royal Association for Disability and Rehabilitation), 12 City Forum, 250 City Rd, London EC1V 8AF; ☎0171/250 3222
Information on all aspects of travel.

USA
Directions Unlimited, 720 N Bedford Rd, Bedford Hills, NY 10507; ☎91-800/533-5343
Tour operator specializing in custom tours for people with disabilities.

Mobility International USA, PO Box 10767, Eugene, OR 97440; ☎ 541/343-1284
Information and referral services, access guides, tours and exchange programs. Annual membership $25 (includes quarterly newsletter).

Society for the Advancement of Travel for the Handicapped (SATH), 347 5th Ave, Suite 610, New York, NY 10016 ☎212/447-7284; http://www.sittravel.com/
Non-profit-making travel industry referral service that passes queries on to its members as appropriate; allow plenty of time for a response.

Travel Information Service ☎215/456 9600
Telephone information and referral service; phone enquiries only.

At the time of writing, none of the **car rental** companies could offer vehicles with hand controls in Prague. If you're driving to Prague, most cross-Channel ferries now have adequate facilities, as does British Airways for those who are flying.

For a list of wheelchair-friendly **hotels**, restaurants, metro stations and so forth, order the guide book *Accessible Prague/Přístupná Praha* from the Prague Wheelchair Association, listed on previous page.

Post and phones

Post

The **main post office** (*pošta*) in Prague is at Jindřišská 14 (☎24 22 88 56), just off Wenceslas Square. It is open 24 hours a day, although it operates a reduced service during the night. Make sure you queue at the right counter, as there are a large number to choose from. The whole building is currently undergoing a major overhaul, but at the time of writing *známky* (stamps) were sold from windows 12 to 16; phone cards (*telefonní karty*) from window 19; and *balíky* (parcels) weighing under 2kg are dealt with at windows 6 and 7. Each postal district in Prague has several post offices, though these have far less comprehensive hours and services.

Poste restante (pronounced as five syllables in Czech) letters to Prague will arrive at the main post office mentioned above (the postcode is 110 00 PRAHA 1); go to window 17 (Mon–Fri 7am–8pm, Sat 7am–1pm). Alternatively, American Express, at Václavské náměstí 56

(Mon–Fri 9am–6pm, Sat 9am–noon), will hold mail for a month for credit card and/or cheque holders.

Outbound post is reasonably reliable, with letters or cards taking around five working days to Britain and Ireland, and one week to ten days to North America or Australasia. You can buy **stamps** from newsagents, tobacconists and some kiosks, as well as at the post offices. If you want to send an **email** or go on-line, head for one of Prague's internet cafés (see p.214).

To send a **parcel over 2kg** (but below 15kg) you must go to the Pošta-Celnice parcel office at the junction of Plzeňská and Vrchlického in Prague 5 (tram #4, #6, #7 or #9 from metro Anděl). After filling in two separate forms for shipping and customs, you then have a choice of sending your parcel by ship, air or express. Alternatively, you can save a lot of hassle, and get the parcel there in no time at all, by paying considerably more at a courier company like DHL, Běžecká 1, Strahov (☎310 4111).

Some foreign countries in Czech

Australia – Austrálie

Austria – Rakousko

Canada – Kanada

Eire – Irsko

Germany – Německo

Great Britain – Velká Británie

Hungary – Maďarsko

Netherlands – Nizozemí

New Zealand – Nový Zéland

USA – Spojené státy americké

Phones

Prague's **telephone system** is gradually being digitalized, but phone numbers can still vary in length from six to eight digits. The majority of public phones in the centre of Prague take only **phone cards** (*telefonní karty*), currently available in 50, 100 and 150 units from post offices, tobacconists and some shops (prices vary). You can make international calls from all card phones (calls cost over 30kč a minute to Britain and Ireland, over 60kč to the US, Canada and Australia, and a whopping 90kč to New Zealand). There are instructions in English, and if you press the appropriate button the language on the digital read-out will change to English. If you have any problems, ring ☎0149 to get through to international information.

In **coin-operated phones**, you need to insert a minimum of 3kč to make a local call, 5kč for long-distance – if you stock up with enough coins, it is perfectly possible to make an international phone call. The **dialling tone** is a short followed by a long pulse; the **ringing tone** is long and regular; **engaged** is short and rapid (not to be confused with the connecting tone which is very short and rapid). The standard Czech response is *prosím*; the word for extension is *linka*.

You can also make phone calls from the **telephone exchange** situated in the main post office

Dialling codes	
To Prague	
From Britain & Ireland	☎00 420 2
From USA & Canada	☎011 420 2
From Australia & New Zealand	☎0011 420 2
Phoning from elsewhere in the Czech Republic, the Prague city code is ☎02	
From Prague	
UK	☎0044
Eire	☎00353
Australia	☎0061
New Zealand	☎0064
USA and Canada	☎001

(see above for address). Write down the town and number you want, leave a deposit of around 200kč and wait for your name to be called out. Avoid making any calls from hotels, where the surcharge is usually outrageous. To make a **collect call**, which will probably cost the recipient less than it costs you, you need to get through to the international operator in the country you're phoning: ring ☎00 420 00 44 01 for the UK; ☎00 420 001 01 for the US; ☎00 420 001 51 for Canada; these calls are not free.

Opening hours, holidays and festivals

Shops in Prague are generally open Monday to Friday from 9am to 5pm, though most supermarkets and tourist shops stay open later. Smaller shops may close for lunch for an hour some time between noon and 2pm. Some shops close by noon or 1pm on Saturday, and only a few open on Sunday. Most pubs and restaurants tend to close between 10 and 11pm, with food often difficult to obtain (especially in pubs) after 9pm.

Opening hours for **museums and galleries** are generally 9 or 10am to 5 or 6pm every day except Monday (when they are closed) all year

round. Full opening hours are detailed in the text. Ticket prices to museums and galleries are so negligible (rarely more than 50kč) that we haven't included them in the text – notable exceptions, such as Prague Castle and the Jewish Museum, where entrance charges are high, are given in full.

Getting into **churches** can present more of a problem. Most of the more central ones operate in much the same way as museums and occasionally even have an entry charge, particularly for their crypts or cloisters. Most other churches are kept locked, opening only for worship in the early morning (around 7 or 8am) and/or the evening (around 6 or 7pm). Synagogues in Josefov follow museum hours, except that they close on Saturdays rather than Mondays.

Outside Prague, in the high season, **castles and chateaux** open from 9am to noon, and again from 1 to 4pm. On Mondays and from the end of October to the beginning of April, apart from a few notable exceptions, most places are closed. In April and October, opening hours are often restricted to weekends and public holidays only. Whatever the time of year, if you want to see the interior of a castle or chateau, you're more than likely to have to go on a **guided tour** (nearly always in Czech) that can last for an hour or more. Ask for an *anglický text*, an often unintentionally hilarious English resumé of the castle's history. Guided tours invariably set off on the hour, and the last one leaves an hour before the actual closing time: in practice, this means the last morning tour will usually set off at 11am, and the last afternoon tour will often be at 3pm. Again, ticket prices are relatively low, rarely exceeding 100kč.

Closed for technical reasons

Don't be too surprised if one or two of Prague's museums and galleries are "closed for technical reasons", "closed due to illness", or, more permanently, "closed for reconstruction". Notices are rarely more specific than that, but the widespread shortage of staff and funds is often behind the closure. It's impossible to predict what will be closed when, but it's a good idea to make alternative plans when visiting galleries and museums, just in case.

National holidays

National holidays were always a potential source of contention with the old regime, and they remain controversial even today. **May Day**, once a nationwide compulsory march under dull Commie slogans, remains a public holiday, though only the skinheads and anarchists bother to slug it out on the streets nowadays. Of the other *slavné májové dny* (Glorious May Days), as they used to be known, **May 5**, the beginning of the 1945 Prague Uprising, has been binned, and VE Day is now celebrated along

---

National holidays

January 1

Easter Monday

May 1

May 8 (VE Day)

July 5 (Introduction of Christianity)

July 6 (Death of Jan Hus)

October 28 (Foundation of the Republic)

December 24

December 25

December 26

---

with the western Allies on **May 8**, and not on May 9, as it was under the Communists, and still is in Russia. To scupper any celebration of the founding of the First Republic on **October 28**, the Communists hijacked the date for their very own Nationalization Day. Some Czechs argue that whichever way you look at it, this Czechoslovak/Communist holiday – which the extreme right-wing Republican Party regularly disrupt – should be ditched in favour of September 28, the feast day of the country's patron saint, St Wenceslas.

Festivals

Prague's **annual festive calendar** is light compared to most European capitals, with just a couple of cultural events in addition to the usual religious festivities. To find out what's going on, check out one of the listings magazines mentioned on p.27.

The city's most famous festival is the **Pražské jaro** (Prague Spring), not to be confused with the political events of 1968. It begins every year on May 12, the anniversary of Smetana's death, with a procession from Smetana's grave in Vyšehrad to the Obecní dům, where the composer's *Má vlast* (My Country) is performed in the presence of the president. It ends three weeks later, on June 2, with Beethoven's Ninth Symphony, and generally attracts several top-class performers. Tickets can be extremely hard to come by, so book well in advance (see p.230).

A new highlight in the city's cultural calendar is **Tanec Praha** (Dance Prague), an international festival of modern dance which takes place throughout the city in June. Prague's **International Film**

Festival, in the second half of July, appears to have failed in its attempt to usurp Karlovy Vary's more established festival (in mid-July) as the country's foremost filmic forum, though it still showcases some interesting work. In October, Prague also puts on a modest **International Jazz Festival**, which attracts all the best names in Czech jazz as well as at least one big foreign artist.

The rest of Prague's stirrings are mostly of a religious nature. At **Easter** (*Velikonoce*), the age-old sexist ritual of whipping girls' calves with braided birch twigs tied together with ribbons (*pomlázky*) is still practised. To prevent such a fate, the girls are supposed to offer the boys a coloured easter egg and pour a bucket of cold water over them. What may once have been an innocent bucolic frolic has now become another excuse for Czech men to harass any woman who dares to venture onto the street during this period.

Halloween comes early to the Czech Republic, on April 30, when the "**Burning of the Witches**" (*pálení čarodějnic*) takes place. Bonfires are lit across the country, old brooms thrown out and burned, as everyone celebrates the end of the long winter. On December 4, the feast day of Saint Barbara, cherry tree branches are bought as decorations, the aim being to get them to blossom before Christmas.

On the evening of **December 5**, numerous trios, dressed up as *svatý Mikuláš* (Saint Nicholas), an angel and a devil, tour round the neighbourhoods, the angel handing out sweets and fruit to children who've been good, while the devil dishes out coal and potatoes to those who've been naughty. The Czech Saint Nicholas has white hair and a beard, and dresses not in red but in a white priest's outfit, with a bishop's mitre.

With a week or so to go, large barrels are set up in the streets from which huge quantities of live carp (*kapr*), the traditional Christmas dish, are sold. **Christmas Eve** (*štědrý večer*) is traditionally a day of fasting, broken only when the evening star appears, signalling the beginning of the Christmas feast of carp, potato salad, schnitzel and sweet breads. Only after the meal are the children allowed to open their presents, which miraculously appear beneath the tree, thanks not to Santa Claus, but to *Ježíšek* (Baby Jesus).

Birthdays are much less important for the Czechs than **saints' name days**, which fall on the same day each year. Thus popular names like Jan or Anna are practically national celebrations, and an excuse for everyone to get drunk since you're bound to know at least one person with those names.

The media

It's a sign of the times that the most famous **Czech newspaper**, *Lidové noviny* (the best-known *samizdat* or underground publication under the Communists) is now owned by a Swiss company, Ringier. In fact over half the Czech press is now foreign-owned, including the country's most popular daily, *Blesk*, a sensationalist tabloid with lurid colour pictures, naked women and reactionary politics.

The next most popular paper is *Mlada fronta dnes*, former mouthpiece of the Communist youth movement, now a centre-right daily with solid coverage of local and international news. Third in the popularity stakes is *Právo* (formerly the official mouthpiece of the Communist Party *Rudé právo* or "Red Justice"), a surprisingly suc-

cessful "left-wing daily". The other positive independent political voice is the weekly *Respekt*, which prides itself on its investigative journalism. If all you want is yesterday's international and domestic football results, pick up a copy of the daily *Sport*.

The **English-language** weekly to look out for is *The Prague Post*, a quality paper with strong business coverage and a useful pull-out **listings** section. More comprehensive listings are to be found in the monthly listings magazine *Přehled*, which is in Czech, but should be easily decipherable.

The entire range of **foreign newspapers** is now available from the kiosks on Wenceslas Square and elsewhere. They're generally a day old, though one that you can buy on the day of issue is the European edition of *The Guardian*, printed in Frankfurt (it arrives on the streets of Prague around mid-morning).

In the **magazine** market, you'll find the best coverage of contemporary Czech politics in English in *The New Presence/Nová přítomnost*, a bi-lingual current affairs magazine, directly inspired by the Masaryk-funded *Přítomnost*, which was one of the leading periodicals of the First Republic. Various arty magazines run by ex-pats have come and gone over the years – the literary *Trafika* is probably the best known of the genre – but it's still worth calling in at **The Globe** bookstore (see p.241) for the latest titles.

TV and radio

Česká televize's two state-owned channels, *ČT1* and *ČT2* have both been eclipsed as far as ratings go by the runaway success of the commercial channel, *Nova*. The latter features lots of Amercian sitcoms dubbed into Czech, plenty of game shows and the most comprehensive coverage of Czech football. *Prima*, the other commercial channel, has yet to make any significant inroads into *Nova*'s audience monopoly. *ČT2* is your best bet for foreign films with subtitles; it also shows news in English from the BBC on Monday to Friday at 8am, and on Saturday and Sunday at 7am.

On the **radio**, the BBC World Service now broadcasts loud and clear on 101.1FM, mostly in English, with occasional Czech news summaries. As far as domestic **radio** goes, the most popular station is still, as in Communist days, the state-run *Česká rozhlas* news-orientated *Radio Praha* (92.6/102.7FM), on which Havel broadcasts his presidential Sunday evening chat; an English-language news summary goes out Monday to Friday at 5.30pm. The three top FM music channels are *Evropa 2* (88.2FM) and *Kiss FM* (98FM) which dish out bland Euro-pop, and *Country Radio* (89.5FM) which panders to the Czechs' strange obsession with American country and western music. More interesting are *Radio 1* (91.9FM), which plays a wide range of indie rock from east and west, and broadcasts a brief news summary at 7am Monday to Friday. Classical music lovers are now catered for by the excellent *Classic FM* (97.7/98.7FM).

Trouble and the police

Despite their change of name from *Veřejná bezpečnost* or *VB*, as the former Communist police were known, to **Policie**, the national police force are still extremely unpopular, certainly among the younger generation, and they know it. Their participation in the November 17 demo destroyed what little credibility they had left after forty years of Communist control.

Public confidence in their competence has also suffered a severe blow due to the dramatic rise in the level of **crime** since 1989. The murder rate has quadrupled, prostitution is widespread and corruption is rife in Prague. However, you shouldn't be unduly paranoid: the crime rate is still very low compared with most European or North American cities. Pickpockets are the biggest hassle, especially in summer around the most popular tourist sights and on the trams and metro.

There are two main types of police nowadays: the aforementioned *Policie* and the municipal police (see below). The **Policie**, in khaki-green uniforms (hence their nickname – *žáby* or "frogs") with red lapels and a red band on their caps are the national force, with the power of arrest, and are under the control of the Ministry of Interior. If you do need the police, though – and above all if you're reporting a serious crime – you should always go to the **Městská policie** (municipal police), run by the Prague city authorities, distinguishable by their all-black uniforms.

In addition, there are various private security guards, who also dress in black – hence their nickname, *Cerné šerií* (Black Sheriffs) – employed mostly by hotels and banks. They are often very officious, incompetent and trigger-happy. They are allowed to carry guns, but have no powers of arrest, and you are not legally obliged to show them your ID.

Avoiding trouble

Almost all the problems encountered by tourists in Prague are to do with **petty crime** – mostly theft from cars and hotel rooms – rather than more serious physical confrontations. Sensible precautions include making photocopies of your passport, leaving passport and tickets in the hotel safe and noting down travellers' cheque and credit card numbers. If you have a car, don't leave anything in view when you park it; take the cassette/radio with you if you can. Vehicles are rarely stolen, but luggage and valuables left in cars do make a tempting target and rental cars are easy to spot.

In theory, you're supposed to carry some form of **identification** at all times, and the police can stop you in the street and demand it. In practice, they're rarely bothered if you're clearly a foreigner (unless you're driving). In any case, the police are now so deferential that they tend to confine themselves to socially acceptable activities like traffic control and harassing Romanies.

What to do if you're robbed

If you are unlucky enough to have something stolen, you will need to **go to the police** to report it, not least because your insurance company will require a police report. It's unlikely that there'll be anyone there who speaks English, and even less likely that your belongings will be retrieved but, at the very least, you should get a statement detailing what you've lost for your insurance claim. Try the phrase *byl jsem oloupen* or (if you're a woman) *byla jsem oloupena* – "I have been robbed".

The following is a list of the main police stations for each of Prague's ten postal districts.

Prague 1 – Bartolomějská 6

Prague 2 – Legerova 2

Prague 3 – Lupáčova 11

Prague 4 – U plynárny 2

Prague 5 – Nádražní 16a

Prague 6 – V. P. Čkalova 18

Prague 7 – Fr. Křížka 24

Prague 8 – Rosenbergových 1

Prague 9 – Jandova 1

Prague 10 – Přípotoční 300

Emergencies	
Ambulance	☎ 155
Police	☎ 158
Fire	☎ 150

Sexual harassment

As far as **sexual harassment** is concerned, things are, if anything, marginally less intimidating than in western Europe, although without the familiar linguistic and cultural signs, it's easier to misinterpret situations. Specific places to avoid going after dark include Wenceslas Square, Uhelný trh, the main train stations, Hlavní nádraží and nádraží Holešovice.

Finding work

Unless you're fluent in Czech, have some particular skill and have applied for a job advertised in your home country, the only real chance of long-term work in Prague is teaching English, either privately or in one of the many language schools. With English having replaced Russian on most school syllabuses, there's a constant shortage of English teachers, though you're more likely to strike lucky anywhere else in the country other than Prague.

Obviously it's best to have a TEFL (Teaching English as a Foreign Language) or ESL (English as a Second Language) certificate, but you may find that even without that qualification many language schools will still take you on. Finding a teaching job is mainly a question of perusing the English-language weekly *Prague Post*, the thrice-weekly Czech advertiser *Annonce*, and scouring the notice boards in the American and British cultural centres (see "Directory" on p.243). Other options are to try advertising private lessons (better paid, but harder to make a living at) on the university notice boards, or in *Annonce*. With unemployment creeping steadily upwards, finding temporary work of any kind is extremely unlikely.

If you have a legitimate job, getting a **work permit** should be easy, but getting a **residence permit** is a lengthy and bureaucratic process which, unless your employers are prepared to do it on your behalf, is not worth the hassle. If you want to be legitimate, however, you'll find details of how to obtain a residence permit on p.17.

The City

Introducing the city

With a population of just one and a quarter million, **Prague** is one of the smallest capital cities in Europe. It originally developed as four separate, self-governing towns and a Jewish ghetto, whose individual identities and medieval street plans have been preserved, more or less intact, to this day. Almost everything of any historical interest lies within these central districts, the majority of which are easy to master quickly on foot. Only in the last hundred years has Prague spread beyond its ancient perimeter, and its suburbs now stretch across the hills for miles on every side. There's a cheap and efficient transport system on which to explore them – a decent map is all you need to find your way around.

The castle district or **Hradčany** (Chapter One) spreads across the hill on the left bank of the River Vltava where the first Slavs settled in the seventh or eighth century. At its eastern end is the Pražský hrad or Prague Castle (known simply as the *Hrad* in Czech), which contains a whole series of important historical buildings, including the city's cathedral, the seat of the president, and the royal palace and gardens, as well as a host of museums and galleries. The rest of Hradčany lies to the west of the castle: a sleepy district ranging in scale from the miniature cottages of Nový Svět to the gargantuan facade of the Černínský palác.

Squeezed between the castle hill and the river are the Baroque palaces and houses of the "Little Quarter" or **Malá Strana** (Chapter Two) – around 150 acres of twisting cobbled streets and secret walled gardens – home to most of the city's embassies and dominated by one of the landmarks of the left bank, the green dome and tower of the church of sv Mikuláš. At the southern end of Malá Strana, a funicular railway carries you out of the cramped streets to the top of Petřín hill, the city's most central leafy escape, with a wonderful view across the river.

The twisting matrix of streets is at its most confusing in the original medieval hub of the city, **Staré Město** (Chapter Three) – literally, the "Old Town" – on the right bank of the Vltava. The Karlův most,

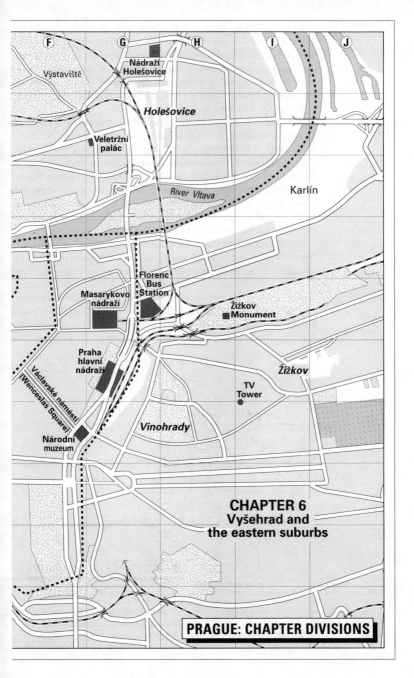

Výstaviště

Nádraží
Holešovice

Holešovice

Veletržní
palác

River Vltava

Karlín

Florenc
Bus
Station

Masarykovo
nádraží

Žižkov
Monument

Praha
hlavní
nádraží

Žižkov

Václavské náměstí
(Wenceslas Square)

TV
Tower

Vinohrady

Národní
muzeum

CHAPTER 6
Vyšehrad and
the eastern suburbs

PRAGUE: CHAPTER DIVISIONS

or **Charles Bridge**, its main link with the opposite bank, is easily the city's most popular historical monument, bristling with Baroque statuary and one of the most beautiful places from which to view the castle. Staré Město's other great showpiece is its main square, **Staroměstské náměstí**, where it's easy to sit for hours, soaking up the sights – the astronomical clock, the Hus monument and the spiky towers of the Týn church.

Nothing else in Staré Město can quite match these two spots, but it's worth spending at least an afternoon exploring the quarter's backstreets and alleyways, and in the process losing the crowds. Enclosed within the boundaries of Staré Město, to the northwest of the main square, is the Jewish quarter or **Josefov** (Chapter Four). The ghetto walls have long since gone, and the whole area was remodelled at the turn of the century, but six synagogues, a medieval cemetery and a town hall survive as powerful reminders of a community which has existed here for over a millennium.

South and east of the old town is the large sprawling district of **Nové Město** (Chapter Five), whose main arteries make up the city's commercial and business centre. Despite its name – literally, "New Town" – Nové Město was founded back in the fourteenth century, and even its outer reaches are worth taking the trouble to explore. The nexus of Nové Město is Václavské náměstí or **Wenceslas Square**, focus of the political upheavals of the modern-day republic and a showcase of twentieth-century architecture. The district also

PRAGUE'S POSTAL DISTRICTS

1. Hradčany, Malá Strana, Staré Město, Josefov and Nové Město.
2. Nové Město, Vinohrady, Vyšehrad and Nusle.
3. Vinohrady and Žižkov.
4. Nusle, Podolí, Braník, Krč and the southeastern suburbs.
5. Smíchov and the southwestern suburbs

6. Dejvice, Střešvice, Břevnov and the northwestern suburbs
7. Holešovice, Bubeneč and Troja
8. Karlín, Libeň and the northern suburbs
9. Vysočany and the northeastern suburbs
10. Vršovice, Strašnice and the eastern suburbs

contains numerous potent symbols of the Czech struggle for nationhood, such as the Národní muzeum (National Museum), Národní divadlo (National Theatre) and the Art Nouveau extravaganza of the Obecní dům.

Further afield lie various **suburbs**, most of which developed only in the last hundred years or so. The single exception is **Vyšehrad**, one of the original fortress settlements of the newly arrived Slavs in the last millennium. Nowadays, it's a peaceful escape from the city, and its cemetery is the final resting place for leading Czech artists of the modern age, including Smetana and Dvořák. To the east is the once wealthy residential suburb of **Vinohrady**, peppered with parks and squares; and **Žižkov**, traditionally a working-class district, whose two landmarks – the Žižkov monument and the futuristic TV tower – are visible for miles around. All of these areas are covered in Chapter Six.

Nineteenth-century suburbs also sprang up to the north of the city centre in **Holešovice**, which boasts two huge swathes of greenery: the Letná plain, overlooking the city; and the Stromovka park, beyond which lie the city chateau of **Troja** and the zoo. Further west, leafy interwar suburbs like **Dejvice** and **Střešovice**, dotted with modernist family villas, give an entirely different angle on Prague. All these places are covered in Chapter Seven.

If you're keen to head **out of the city** entirely, there's a wide choice of destinations within an hour or so's journey from Prague. The medieval mining town of **Kutná Hora**, east of Prague, boasts one of central Europe's most stunning pieces of ecclesiastical architecture, plus a host of other attractions. The royal hideaway of **Karlštejn**, 30km or so southwest of Prague, is an obvious day-trip, though the castle of **Konopiště**, some 40km southeast of the city, is perhaps more rewarding for those in search of period interiors. Last of all, the legacy of the war hangs over two places to the northwest: **Lidice**, which was razed to the ground by the Nazis; and the ghetto town of **Terezín** (Theresienstadt), through which most of the country's Jews passed, en route to the extermination camps. The above destinations are all covered in Chapter Eight.

Arrival in Prague

If you fly into Prague, you'll find yourself more than 10km northwest of the city centre, with only a bus link to get you into town. By contrast, both the international train stations and the main bus terminal are linked to the centre by the fast and efficient metro system. Driving into Prague is easy enough, though the city authorities, quite rightly, make it very awkward for drivers to enter the old town, and finding a parking space is also extremely difficult.

By Air

Prague's airport, **Ruzyně** (☎334 11 11), though still overstretched, now has most of the facilities you'd expect of a European capital city airport, with shops, cafés, 24-hour exchange facilities and a variety of accommodation agencies (see p.195) and car rental outlets (see p.44).

The airport is linked to the city by a cheap, regular **express bus service** (daily 8.30am–7pm), which stops first at Dejvická metro station, at the end of metro line A (journey time 20min) and ends up at the ČSA offices on V celnici, near náměstí Republiky (journey time 30min); to obtain a ticket simply pay the driver. There's an even cheaper **local bus** connection, too: bus #119 (daily: 5am–8pm every 10–15min, 8pm–5am every 30min; journey time 20–25min) stops frequently and ends its journey outside Dejvická metro station; you must buy your ticket from the orange machine just inside the airport exit, or from the newsagents at the other end of the airport. If you arrive after midnight, you can catch a night bus #510 to Divoká Šárka, the terminus for night tram #51, which will take you to Národní in the centre of town; you'll need to buy a ticket for both the bus and the tram from the range machine at the airport.

Alternatively, **taxis** from the airport into the centre cost over 500kč; make sure the driver turns on the meter, or, if in doubt, agree on a price before getting in.

By train and bus

International trains arrive either at the old Art-Nouveau **Praha hlavní nádraží**, on the edge of Nové Město and Vinohrady, or at **Praha-Holešovice**, which lies in an industrial suburb north of the city centre. At both stations you'll find exchange outlets (there's even a branch of the PIS tourist office at Hlavní nádraží), as well as a 24-hour left-luggage office (see p.245) and accommodation agencies (see p.195). Both stations are on metro lines, and Hlavní nádraží is only a five-minute walk from Václavské náměstí (Wenceslas Square). Some **domestic train** services wind up at the central **Masarykovo nádraží** on Hybernská (metro náměstí Republiky) or in the suburban station of **Smíchovské nádraží** (metro Smíchovské nádraží).

If you're catching a **train out of Prague**, don't leave buying your ticket until the last minute, as the queues can be long and slow. You can buy international train tickets at either Praha hlavní nádraží (currently at windows 16–24) or Praha-Holešovice.

Prague's **main bus terminal** is **Praha-Florenc** (metro Florenc), on the eastern edge of Nové Město, where virtually all long-distance international and domestic services terminate. It's a confusing (and ugly) place to end up, but its facilities include a 24-hour left luggage office and you can make a quick exit to the adjacent metro station.

Information and maps

Once in Prague, the main tourist office is the **Prague Information Service** or **PIS** (Pražská informační služba), whose main branch is at Na příkopě 20, Nové Město (Mon–Fri 8.30am–7pm, Sat & Sun 9am–5pm; ☎26 40 22). The staff speak at least four languages between them, including English, and will be able to answer most enquiries; they can organize private accommodation for you, sell maps and guides and they act as a general ticket agency, too. PIS also distributes some useful free publications, including *Prague Cultural Events*, a monthly English-language booklet listing the major events, concerts and exhibitions, and a fortnightly leaflet *Do města/Downtown*, which concentrates on cinema, art exhibitions and club listings. There are additional PIS offices in the main train station, Praha hlavní nádraží, within the Staroměstská radnice on Staroměstské náměstí, plus a summer-only office in the Malá Strana bridge tower on the Charles Bridge.

The PIS should be able to furnish you with a quick reference **map** of central Prague, but to locate a specific street, or find your way round the suburbs, you'll need a detailed city map (*plán města*). *Kartografie Praha* produces the cheapest and most comprehensive ones: the 1:20,000 map covers the city centre as well as many of the suburbs and has a full street index, and the metro, tram and bus routes marked on – available in both booklet form (handier to carry about and leaf through) and the fold-out variety (better for the overall picture). You can get hold of either, and any other maps you may

---

Prague card

If you're in Prague for a long weekend, it's worth considering buying a **Prague Card**, which gives you free travel on the public transport system and free entry into Prague Castle, plus virtually all the city's public art galleries and museums (with the notable exception of the sights of the Jewish Musem). The ticket currently costs 430kč, lasts for three days and is available from the ČSA desk at the airport, the Amex office on Wencelas Square, ČEDOK and various other travel agencies in town.

want, from *PIS* offices, street kiosks, most bookshops (*knihku-pectví*) and some hotels.

Another good source of information is the weekly **English-language paper**, *Prague Post*, which carries listings on the latest exhibitions, shows, gigs and events around the capital.

City transport

The centre of Prague, where most of the city's sights are concentrated, is reasonably small and best explored on foot. At some point, however, in order to cross the city quickly or reach some of the more widely dispersed attractions, you'll need to use the city's cheap and efficient public transport system (*dopravní podnik* or *DP*), which comprises the metro and a network of trams and buses. To get a clearer picture, it's essential to invest in a **city map** (see above), which marks all the tram, bus and metro lines.

Tickets and passes

A single **ticket** (*lístek* or *jízdenka*) for the two central zones (*2 pásma*) comes in two basic versions. The 8kč version (*zlevněná*) allows you to travel for up to fifteen minutes on the trams or buses, or up to four stops on the metro; it's known as a *nepřestupní jíz-denka*, or "no change ticket", although you can in fact change metro lines (but not buses or trams). The 12kč version (*plnocenná*) is valid for one hour at peak times (an hour and a half off-peak), during which you may change trams, buses or metro lines as many times as you like, hence its name, *přestupní jízdenka*, or "changing ticket". Half-price tickets are available for those aged 6 to 15, bikes and other large objects; under-6s travel free.

Tickets must be bought beforehand either from a tobacconist (*tabák*), street kiosk, newsagents, PIS office or any place that displays the yellow *DP* sticker. You can also buy tickets from the new ticket machines found at some bus and tram stops and inside all metro stations; after you've pressed the right button (see above), you must press *výdej/enter* before putting your money in. The machines give change, but if you don't have enough coins, the person on duty in the metro office by the barriers will usually be able to give you change or sell you a ticket.

When you enter the metro, or board a tram or bus, you must validate your ticket by placing it in one of the electronic machines to hand. Buy as many tickets in advance as you think you'll need, to avoid the problem of trying to hoard change for the machines, or finding a machine that actually works. To save hassle, and money, think about investing in a Prague Card (see box on p.39). Alternatively, you can buy a one-day **tourist pass** (*turistická síťová jízdenka*) for 70kč; no photos or ID are needed, and you can get the pass either from the ticket machines or *DP* outlets. There are also three-day (160kč), seven-day (220kč) and fifteen-day (300kč) passes available, though these can usually be bought only from *DP* windows at metro stations.

Most Praguers buy a monthly or quarterly **travel pass** (*průkaz*), which is why you see so few of them punching tickets. To do this, present ID and a passport-sized photo to the windows marked *DP* at major metro stations and ask for a *měsíční jízdenka*. Monthly passes currently cost around 360kč. There's nothing to stop people from freeloading on the system, of course, since there are no barriers. However, plain-clothes **inspectors** make spot checks and will issue an on-the-spot fine of 200kč to anyone caught without a valid ticket or pass; controllers should show you their ID (a small metal disc), and give you a receipt (*paragon*).

The metro

Prague's futuristic Soviet-built **metro** is fast, smooth and ultra-clean, running daily from 5am to midnight with trains every two minutes during peak hours, slowing down to every five to ten minutes by late in the evening. Its three lines (with a fourth planned) intersect at various points in the city centre and the route plans are easy to follow (see map at the back of the book).

The stations are fairly discreetly marked above ground with the metro logo, in green (line A), yellow (line B) or red (line C). The constant bleeping at metro entrances is to enable blind people to locate the escalators, which are a free-for-all, with no fast lane. Once inside the metro, it's worth knowing that *výstup* means exit and *přestup*

An extension eastwards on line B to Černy Most is due to open at the end of 1998.

PRAGUE'S METRO

will lead you to one of the connecting lines at an interchange. The digital clock at the end of the platform tells you what time it is and how long it was since the last train.

Trams and buses

The electric **tram** (*tramvaj*) **system**, in operation since 1891, negogiates Prague's hills and cobbles with remarkable dexterity. Modern Škoda rolling stock is gradually being introduced, but many of Prague's red trams (now plastered over with advertising) still date back to the 1950s. After the metro, trams are the fastest and most efficient way of getting around, running every six to eight minutes at peak times, and every five to fifteen minutes at other times – check the timetables posted at every stop (*zastávka*), which list the departures times from that specific stop, and bear in mind that Czech trams rival Swiss trains in their punctuality.

Tram #22, which runs from Vinohrady to Hradčany via the centre of town and Malá Strana, is a good way to get to grips with the lie of the land, and a cheap way of sightseeing. From Easter to October, an interwar tram (#91) runs from Výstaviště to náměstí Republiky via Malá Strana (Sat & Sun hourly 1–7pm). Some lines

---

Night trams

#51
Nádraží Strašnice, metro Želivského, metro Flora, nám. Míru, nám. I. P. Pavlova, Lazarská, Národní, metro Staroměstská, nábř. kpt. Jaroše, metro Hradčanská, metro Dejvická, Evropská, **Divoká Šárka**.

#52
Hlubočepy, metro Anděl, Lazarská, Masarykovo nádraží, metro Florenc, metro Křižíkova, metro Palmovka, **Lehovec**.

#53
Metro Pankrác, Lazarská, Masarykovo nádraží, nábř. kpt Jaroše, nádraží Holešovice, Trojská, **Vozovna Kobylisy**.

#54
Nádraží Braník, Lazarská, Národní, metro Staroměstská, nábř. kpt Jaroše, nádraží Holešovice, metro Palmovka, **sídliště Jáblice**.

#55
Ústřední dílny DP, metro Strašnická, Vršovická, Karlovo nám., Lazarská, Václavské nám., Masarykovo nádraží, metro Florenc, metro Křižíkova, metro Palmovka, **Lehovec**.

#56
Spořilov, Nuselská, Bělehradská, Lazarská, Masarykovo nádraží, metro Florenc, metro Hradčanská, **Petříny**.

#57
Nádraží Hostivař, Radošovická, nám. Míru, Lazarská, Národní, metro Malostranská, metro Hradčanská, **Bílá hora**.

#58
Spojovací, metro Želivského, metro Flora, Olšanské nám., Lazarská, Národní, metro Anděl, **sídliště Řepy**.

operate only during rush hour (Mon–Fri 6.30–8.30am & 3–6pm), others run seven days a week (5am–midnight) and the whole system slows down during July and August for the holidays. **Night trams** (*noční tramvaje*) run roughly every forty minutes from around midnight to 5am, and all pass by Lazarská and Spálená in Nové Město (see box above).

You'll rarely need to get on a Prague **bus** (*autobus*), which for the most part keep well out of the centre of town. If you're intent upon visiting the zoo or staying in some of the city's more obscure suburbs, though, you may need to use them: their hours of operation are similar to those of the trams (though generally less frequent), and route numbers are given in the text where appropriate. **Night buses** (*noční autobusy*) run just once an hour between midnight and 5am.

Taxis

Taxis come in all shapes and sizes, and, theoretically at least, are extremely cheap. After experiments with de-regulation, the local authorities have set a ceiling on fares: 25kč initial fare, plus 17kč per kilometre and 4kč per minute of waiting time. Tourists, however, are seen as easy prey by many Prague taxi drivers, and stories of overcharging are too numerous to mention. A few tips to avoid such a situation are: hail a cab, rather than pick one up at the taxi ranks, many of which are controlled by the local mafia; if the meter isn't switched on, ask the driver to do so – *zapněte taxametr, prosím*; and, if you suspect you've been overcharged, asking for a receipt – *prosím, dejte mi potrzení* – should have the desired effect. The following cab companies have fairly good reputations: *Profitaxi* ☎61 04 55 55 or 61 04 55 50; *AAA taxi* ☎312 21 12 or 33 99.

Car rental

You really don't need a **car** in Prague, since much of the city centre is pedestrianized and the public transport system is so cheap and efficient. Should you want to drive out of Prague, however, **car rental** is easy to arrange but pricey; if you book with a big company you're looking at a whopping £80/$128 per day for a small car (£450/$720 for a week, with special rates at the weekend). All the major car rental firms have offices in Prague. You'll get a much cheaper deal if you go to a local agent, though with very little of the back-up you'd get from an international firm should something go wrong. In order to rent a car, you'll need to be at least 21 and have been driving for at least a year.

Driving in Prague

Rules and regulations on Czech roads are pretty stringent – a legacy of the police state – though less strictly adhered to by Czechs

Car rental firms in Prague

Avis
Klimentská 46,
Nové Město
☎21 85 12 25; fax 21 85 12 29

Budget
Hotel Intercontinental,
nám. Curieových,
Staré Město
☎24 88 99 95; fax 231 95 95

Europcar
Pařížská 28,
Staré Město
☎24 81 05 15; fax 24 81 19 20

Hertz
Karlovo nám. 28,
Nové Město
☎29 18 51; fax 29 78 36

Josef Rejzek
U Gabrielky 535
Nebušice
☎38 11 88/

nowadays. On-the-spot fines are still regularly handed out, up to a maximum of 500kč. The basic rules are driving on the right (introduced by the Nazis in 1939); compulsory wearing of seatbelts; and no alcohol at all in your blood when you're driving. Watch out for restricted streets, most notably Wenceslas Square, and don't overtake a tram when passengers are getting on and off if there's no safety island for them. Speed limits are 110kph on motorways, 90kph on other roads and 60kph in all cities. In addition, there's a special limit of 30kph for level crossings (you'll soon realize why if you try ignoring it). As in other continental countries, a yellow diamond means you have right of way; a black line through it means you don't. If you have **car trouble**, dial ☎154 at the nearest phone and wait for assistance.

Petrol (*benzín*) comes in two types: *super* (96 octane) and *special* (90 octane); diesel (*nafta*) is also available but two-stroke fuel (*mix*), which powers the old East German Trabants and Wartburgs, is being phased out. **Lead-free** petrol (*natural* or *bezolovnatý*) is available from most petrol stations in and around Prague. Remember, though, that 24-hour petrol stations aren't as widespread as in western European capitals.

Vehicle crime is on the increase and western cars are a favourite target – never leave anything visible or valuable in the car. The other big nightmare is **parking**. Spaces in the centre are expensive and few and far between, and illegally parked cars are quickly towed away. If this happens, you'll find the **car pound** on Černokostelecká, way out in Prague 10 (tram #11). If you're staying in a private room outside the centre, you'll have no problems; if you're at a hotel in the centre, they'll probably have a few parking spaces reserved for guests in the neighbouring streets, though whether you'll find one vacant is another matter. Otherwise, your best option is to park near a metro station out of the centre.

Cycling

Cycling as a leisure activity is beginning to catch on in the Czech Republic, but only the brave (or foolish) use it as a form of transport in Prague. The combination of cobbled streets, tram lines and sulphurous air is enough to put most people off. Facilities for **bike rental** are still not that widespread, but if you're determined to give cycling a go, head for *Landa* (Šumavská 33, Vinohrady; Mon–Fri only; ☎253 99 82; metro náměstí Míru) – both rent out mountain bikes all year round. A bike (*kolo*) needs a half-price ticket to travel on the metro or the train (they're not allowed on trams and buses); they travel in the guard van on trains, and in the last carriage of the metro.

Chapter 1

Hradčany

HRADČANY's *raison d'être* is its castle, or **Hrad**, built on the site of one of the original hill settlements of the Slav tribes who migrated here in the seventh or eighth century AD. The Přemyslid prince, Bořivoj I, erected the first castle here sometime in the late ninth century, and, since then, whoever has occupied the Hrad has exercised authority over the Czech Lands. Consequently, unlike the city's other districts, Hradčany has never had a real identity of its own – it became a royal town only in 1598 – existing instead as a mere appendage, its inhabitants serving and working for their masters in the Hrad. The same is still true now. For although the odd café or *pivnice* (pub) survives in amongst the palaces (and even in the Hrad itself), there's very little real life here beyond the stream of tourists who trek through the castle and the civil servants who work either for the president or in the multifarious ministries whose departmental tentacles spread right across Hradčany and down into Malá Strana.

Stretched out along a high spur above the River Vltava, Hradčany shows a suitable disdain for the public transport system. There's a choice of **approaches** from Malá Strana, all of which involve at least some walking. From Malostranská metro station, most people take the steep short cut up the Staré zámecké schody, which brings you into the castle from its rear end. A better approach is up the stately Zámecké schody, where you can stop and admire the view, before entering the castle via the main gates. The alternative to all this climbing is to take tram #22 from Malostranská metro, which tackles the hairpin bends of Chotkova with ease, and deposits you either outside the Královská zahrada (Royal Gardens) to the north of the Hrad, or, if you prefer, outside the gates of the Strahovský klášter (monastery), at the far western edge of Hradčany.

Pražský hrad (Prague Castle)

Viewed from the Charles Bridge, **Pražský hrad** (popularly known as the Hrad) stands aloof from the rest of the city, protected, not by bastions and castellated towers, but by its palatial Neoclassical facade – an "immense unbroken sheer blank wall", as Hilaire Belloc described it – breached only by the great mass of St Vitus Cathedral. It's *the* picture-postcard image of Prague, though for the Czechs the castle has been an object of disdain as much as admiration, its alternating fortunes mirroring the shifts in the nation's history. The golden age and the dark ages, Masaryk's liberalism and Gottwald's terror – all emanated from the Hrad. When the first posters appeared in December 1989 demanding "*HAVEL NA HRAD*" (Havel to the Castle), they weren't asking for his reincarceration. Havel's occupancy of the Hrad was the sign that the reins of government had finally been wrested from the Communist regime.

The site has been successively built on since the first castle was erected here in the ninth century, but two **architects** in particular bear responsibility for the present outward appearance of the Hrad. The first is **Nicolo Pacassi**, court architect to Empress Maria Theresa, whose austere restorations went hand in hand with the deliberate run-down of the Hrad until it was little more than an administrative barracks. For the Czechs, his grey-green eighteenth-century cover-up, which hides a variety of much older buildings, is unforgivable. Less apparent, though no less controversial, is the hand of **Josip Plečnik**, the Slovene architect who was commissioned by T. G. Masaryk, president of the newly founded Czechoslovak Republic, to restore and modernize the castle in the 1920s (for more on Plečnik, see box on p.50). For a map of Prague Castle, see the colour maps at the back of the book.

Visiting the castle

You can wander freely through the streets, courtyards and gardens of the castle and watch the changing of the guard without a ticket. A single ticket, costing 100kč and valid for three days, will give you entry to four sights within the castle: the choir, crypt and tower of the cathedral; the Old Royal Palace; the Basilica of sv Jiří and the Mihulka tower. Tickets are available from the main information centre or from any one of the aforementioned sights. To see the art collections of the Jiřský klášter, the toys at the Muzeum hraček, the

The grounds of Prague Castle are open daily: April–Oct 5am–midnight; Nov–March 6am–11pm; sights within the castle (unless otherwise stated) are open daily: April–Oct 9am–5pm; Nov–March 9am–4pm.

museum in the Lobkovický palác, or any of the special art exhibitions held in the Obrazárna Pražského hradu, Císařská konírna or Jízdárna, you must buy separate tickets on entry.

Within the castle precincts there are several cafés and restaurants, which are by no means as extortionate as you might expect from their location. If you simply want a quick cup of coffee and a place to write some postcards, head for the *Café Poet*, which has tables outside in the shade and is hidden away in the peaceful and little-visited Zahrada na baště.

The first and second courtyards

The **first courtyard** (první nádvoří), which opens on to Hradčanské náměstí, is guarded by Ignaz Platzer's *Battling Titans* – two gargantuan figures, one on each of the gate piers, wielding club and dagger and about to inflict fatal blows on their respective victims. Below them stand a couple of impassive presidential sentries, sporting blue uniforms that deliberately recall those of the First Republic. They were designed by the Oscar-winning costume designer for Miloš Forman's film *Amadeus*, and chosen by Havel himself. The hourly **changing of the guard** is a fairly subdued affair, but every day at noon there's a much more elaborate parade, accompanied by a brass ensemble which appears at the first-floor windows to play local rock star Michal Kocáb's gentle, slightly comical, modern fanfare.

To reach the **second courtyard** (druhé nádvoří), you must pass through the early Baroque Matyášova brána (Matthias Gate) originally a freestanding triumphal arch in the middle of the long-since defunct moat, now set into one of Pacassi's blank walls. Grand stairways on either side lead to the presidential apartments in the south wing, and to the **Španělský sál** (Spanish Hall) and **Rudofova galerie** (Rudolf Gallery) in the north wing – two of the most stunning rooms in the entire complex. Sadly, both are generally out of bounds, though concerts are occasionally held in the Španělský sál. The latter was decked out with gilded chandeliers and lined with mirrors for Emperor Franz-Josef I's coronation, though in the end he never turned up; under the Communists it was used for Politburo meetings; and more recently still it was discovered that behind the mirrors some eighteenth-century trompe l'oeil murals have been preserved.

Once you've entered the rectangular courtyard, there's little escape from the monotonous onslaught of Pacassi's plastering and the smooth granite paving added in the 1960s. It's an unwelcoming and impersonal space, relieved only by an early Baroque stone fountain and wrought-iron well grille, and Anselmo Lurago's **chapel of sv Kříž**, which cowers in one corner. Its richly painted interior, dating mostly from the mid-nineteenth century, used to house the castle treasury, a macabre selection of medieval reliquaries.

In the north wing of the courtyard are the former **Císařská konírna** (Imperial Stables), which still boast their original, magnificent

*Plečnik also
built one of
Prague's most
unusual
churches, in
Vinohrady
(see p.155).*

Josip Plečnik: postmodernist in the making

Born in Ljubljana, **Josip Plečnik** (1872–1957) studied under the great Viennese architect Otto Wagner at the turn of the century, and was appointed the chief architect to Prague Castle shortly after the foundation of the First Republic. Despite having the backing of the leading Czech architect Jan Kotěra, and President Masaryk himself, controversy surrounded him as soon as the appointment was announced; his non-Czech background and, moreover, his quirky, eclectic style placed him at odds with the architectural establishment of the day. He remained so until his rediscovery in the 1980s by the newly ascendant postmodernist movement. Several leading postmodern architects, among them Richard Rogers, James Stirling, Robert Venturi and Denise Scott-Brown, have made special trips to Prague to see Plečnik's work, which, like their own, borrows elements from any number of genres from classical to Assyrian architecture.

Plečnik's most conspicuous contributions to the castle are the fir-tree flag poles in the first courtyard and the granite obelisk in the third courtyard, but his light-hearted touch is to be seen throughout the castle grounds: check out the jokey palm tree with roped-on copper leaves outside the Jízdárna; the Bull Staircase, which leads down to the Zahrada na valech; or the impressive Sloupová síň (Hall of Columns), which contains the stairs going up to the Španělský sál, and can be peeked at through the glass doors between the first and second courtyards. However, much of Plečnik's work – in particular the president's private apartments – remains hidden from public view, though thanks partly to Havel (a keen Plečnik fan), there are plans to increase public access wherever possible.

Renaissance vaulting dating from the reign of Rudolf II. Along with the neighbouring **Obrazárna Pražského hradu** (Prague Castle Picture Gallery), the stables are now used to house temporary exhibitions, mostly drawn from remnants of the imperial collection begun by the Habsburgs' most avid art collector, Emperor Rudolf II (see p.61). The collection contains works by the likes of Rubens, Veronese and Titian, but the best of what Rudolf amassed was either taken as booty by the marauding Saxons and Swedes, or sold off by his successors. Most sorely missed are the works of Giuseppe Arcimboldo, whose portraits of Rudolf – a surrealist collage of fruit, with his eyes as cherries, cheeks as apples and hair as grapes – now reside in Vienna and Madrid.

St Vitus Cathedral

St Vitus Cathedral (katedrála sv Víta) takes up so much of the third courtyard that it's difficult to get an overall impression of this chaotic Gothic edifice. Its asymmetrical appearance is the product of a long and chequered history, for although the foundation stone was laid in 1344, the cathedral was not completed until 1929 – exactly 1000 years after the foundation of the first church within the Hrad.

The site of the present cathedral was originally a sacrificial altar to the heathen fertility god **Svantovit**, which partly explains why the

first church, founded in 929 by Prince Václav, was dedicated to Saint
Vitus (*svatý Vít* in Czech), who allegedly exorcized the Emperor
Diocletian's son and was thereafter known as the patron saint of
epilepsy and of the convulsive disorder, Sydenham's chorea (hence
its popular name, St Vitus' Dance). The inspiration for the medieval
cathedral came from Emperor Charles IV, who, while still only heir
to the throne, not only wangled an independent archbishopric for
Prague, but also managed to gather together the relics of Saint Vitus.

Inspired by the cathedral at Narbonne, Charles commissioned the
Frenchman **Matthias of Arras** to start work on a similar structure.
Matthias died eight years into the job in 1352, with the cathedral
barely started, and Charles summoned **Peter Parler**, a precocious
23-year-old from a family of great German masons, to continue the
work. For the next 46 years, Parler imprinted his slightly flashier,
more inventive *SonderGotik* ("Unusual Gothic") style on the city,
but the cathedral got no further than the construction of the choir
and the south transept before his death in 1399.

Little significant work was carried out during the next four centuries and the half-built cathedral became a symbol of the Czechs'
frustrated aspirations to nationhood. Not until the Czech national
revival or *národní obrození* of the nineteenth century did building
begin again in earnest, with the foundation, in 1859, of the **Union for
the Completion of the Cathedral**. A succession of architects,
including Josef Mocker and Kamil Hilbert, oversaw the completion of
the entire west end, and, with the help of countless other Czech
artists and sculptors, the building was transformed into a treasure-
house of Czech art. The cathedral was finally given an official opening ceremony in 1929, though work, in fact, continued right up to
and beyond World War II.

The exterior

The sooty Prague air has made it hard now to differentiate between the
two building periods. Close inspection, however, reveals that the **western facade**, including the twin spires, sports the rigorous if unimaginative work of the neo-Gothic restorers (their besuited portraits can be
found below the rose window), while the **eastern section** – best viewed
from the Belvedere – shows the building's authentic Gothic roots. The
south door (see Zlatá brána, below) is also pure Parler. Oddly then, it's
above the south door that the cathedral's tallest steeple reveals the
most conspicuous stylistic join: Pacassi's Baroque topping resting
absurdly on a Renaissance parapet of light stone, which is itself glued
onto the blackened body of the original Gothic tower.

The nave

The cathedral is the country's largest, and once inside, it's difficult
not to be impressed by the sheer height of the **nave**. This is the
newest part of the building, and, consequently, is decorated mostly

with twentieth-century furnishings. Of the later additions to the church, the most striking is František Bílek's **wooden crucifix**, in the north aisle, which breaks free of the neo-Gothic strictures that hamper other contemporary works inside.

Also worth some attention are the cathedral's modern **stained-glass** windows, which on sunny days send shafts of rainbow light into the nave. Beautiful though the effect is, it's entirely out of keeping with Parler's original concept, which was to have almost exclusively clear-glass windows. The most unusual windows are those by František Kysela, which look as though they have been shattered into hundreds of tiny pieces, a technique used to greatest effect in the rose window over the west door with its kaleidoscopic *Creation of the World* (1921).

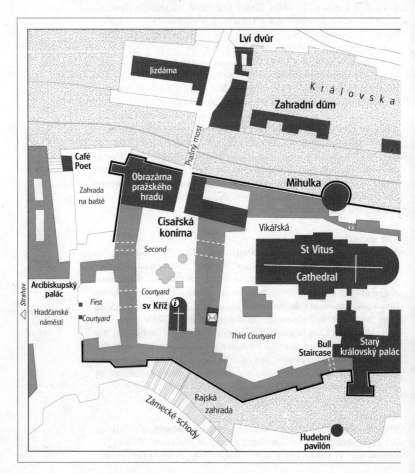

In keeping with its secular nature, two of the works from the time of the First Republic were paid for by financial institutions: the *Cyril and Methodius* window, in the third chapel in the north wall, was commissioned from Alfons Mucha by the *Banka Slavie*; while on the opposite side of the nave, the window on the theme *Those Who Sow in Tears Shall Reap in Joy* was sponsored by a Prague insurance company.

Chapel of sv Václav

Of the cathedral's 22 side chapels, the grand **Chapel of sv Václav**, by the south door, is easily the main attraction. Although officially dedicated to Saint Vitus, spiritually the cathedral belongs as much to the Přemyslid prince, Václav (Wenceslas, of "Good King" fame; see box

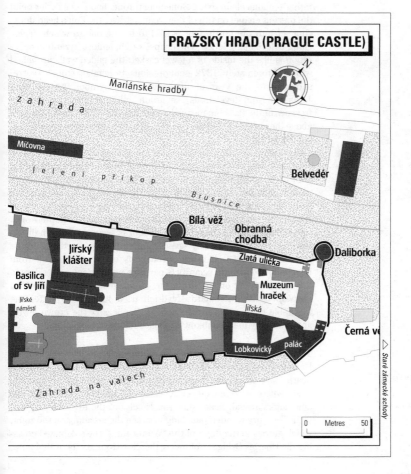

PRAŽSKÝ HRAD (PRAGUE CASTLE)

Mariánské hradby

zahrada

Mičovna

Jelení příkop

Brusnice

Belvedér

Bílá věž

Obranná chodba

Zlatá ulička

Daliborka

Jiřský klášter

Muzeum hraček

Basilica of sv Jiří

Jiřské náměstí

Jiřská

Lobkovický palác

Černá v

Zahrada na valech

0   Metres   50

▷ Staré zámecké schody

Pražský hrad

Entry to the main nave, the Chapel of sv Václav and to all services is free; the cathedral is open for services only on Sunday until noon. To enter the ambulatory, crypt or chancel where the most interesting monuments are located, you must have a castle ticket, available from the box office in the south transept. The entrance to the South Tower, which you can climb (April–Oct Mon–Sat 9am–4.30pm, Sun noon–4.30pm) is inside the cathedral.

opposite), the country's patron saint, who was killed by his pagan brother, Boleslav the Cruel. Ten years later, in 939, Boleslav repented, converted, and apparently transferred his brother's remains to this very spot. Charles, who was keen to promote the cult of Wenceslas in order to cement his own Luxembourgeois dynasty's rather tenuous claim to the Bohemian throne, had Peter Parler build the present chapel on top of the original grave; the lion's head **door-ring** set into the north door is said to be the one to which Václav clung before being killed. The chapel's rich, almost Byzantine decoration is like the inside of a jewel casket: the gilded walls are inlaid with approximately 1372 semiprecious Bohemian stones (corresponding to the year of its creation and symbolizing the New Jerusalem from Revelations), set around ethereal fourteenth-century frescoes of the Passion; meanwhile the tragedy of Wenceslas unfolds above the cornice in the later paintings of the Litoměřice school, dating from 1509.

Though a dazzling testament to the golden age of Charles IV's reign, it's not just the chapel's artistic merit which draws visitors. A door in the south wall gives access to a staircase leading to the coronation chamber (rarely open to the public) which houses the **Bohemian crown jewels**, including the gold crown of Saint Wenceslas, studded with some of the largest sapphires in the world. Closed to the public since 1867, the door is secured by seven different locks, the keys kept by seven different people, starting with the president himself – like the seven seals of the holy scroll from Revelations. The tight security is partly to prevent any pretenders to the throne trying on the headgear, an allegedly fatal act: the Nazi *Reichsprotektor* Reinhard Heydrich tried it, only to suffer the inevitable consequences (see p.140). Replicas of the crown jewels are on display in the Lobkowicz Palace (see p.62).

The chancel

Having sated yourself on Wenceslas Chapel, buy a ticket from the nearby box office, and head off to the north choir aisle – the only place where you can currently enter the **chancel**. Following the ambulatory round, make sure you check out the high-relief seventeenth-century wooden panelling between the arcading on the right, which glories in the flight of the "Winter King" (he's depicted crossing the Charles Bridge), following the disastrous Battle of Bílá hora.

Good King Wenceslas

As it turns out, there's very little substance to the story related in the nine-teenth-century English Christmas carol, *Good King Wenceslas*, by J.M. Neale, itself a reworking of the medieval carol *Tempus adest floridum*. For a start, **Václav** was only a duke and never a king (though he did become a saint); he wasn't even that "good", except in comparison with the rest of his family; the St Agnes fountain, by which "yonder peasant dwelt", wasn't built until the thirteenth century; and he was killed a good three months before the Feast of Stephen.

Born in 907, Václav inherited his title at the tender age of thirteen. His Christian grandmother, Ludmila, was appointed regent in preference to Drahomíra, his pagan mother, who had Ludmila murdered in a fit of jeal-ousy the following year. On coming of age in 925, Václav became duke in his own right and took a vow of celibacy, intent on promoting Christianity throughout the dukedom. Even so, the local Christians didn't take to him, and when he began making conciliatory overtures to the neighbouring Germans, they persuaded his pagan younger brother, Boleslav the Cruel, to do away with him. On September 20, 929, Václav was stabbed to death by Boleslav at the entrance to a church just outside Prague.

The remains of various early Czech rulers are scattered throughout the side chapels, most notably those of Přemysl Otakar I and II, in the Saxon Chapel (the fifth one along), whose limestone tombs are the work of Peter Parler and his workshop; you can also pay your respects to Rudolf II's internal organs buried in the chapel vault.

Slap bang in the middle of the ambulatory, close to the Saxon Chapel, is the perfect Baroque answer to the medieval chapel of sv Václav, the **Tomb of St John of Nepomuk**, plonked here in 1736. It's a work of grotesque excess, designed by Johann Bernhard Fischer von Erlach's son, Johann Michael, and sculpted in solid sil-ver with free-flying angels holding up the heavy drapery of the bal-dachin. Where Charles sought to promote Wenceslas as the nation's preferred saint, the Jesuits, with Habsburg backing, replaced him with another Czech martyr, John of Nepomuk (Jan Nepomucký), who had been arrested, tortured, and then thrown – bound and gagged – off the Charles Bridge in 1393 on the orders of Václav IV, allegedly for refusing to divulge the secrets of the queen's confession. A cluster of stars was said to have appeared over the spot where he drowned, hence the halo of stars on every subsequent portrayal of the saint.

The Jesuits, in their efforts to get him canonized, exhumed his corpse and produced what they claimed to be his tongue – alive and licking, so to speak (it was in fact his very dead brain). In 1729, he duly became a saint, and, on the lid of the tomb, back-to-back with the martyr himself, a cherub points to his severed tongue, sadly no longer the "real" thing. The more prosaic reason for John of Nepomuk's death was simply that he was caught up in a dispute between the archbishop and the king over the appointment of the abbot of Kladruby, and backed the wrong side. John was tortured on the rack along with two other priests, who were then made to sign a document denying that they had been maltreated; John, however, died before he could sign, and his dead body was secretly dumped in the river. The Vatican finally admitted this in 1961, some 232 years after his canonization.

Between the tomb of St John of Nepomuk and the chapel of sv Václav, Bohemia's one and only Polish ruler, Vladislav Jagiello, built a **Royal Oratory**, connected to his bedroom in the Royal Palace by a covered bridge. The balustrade sports heraldic shields from Bohemia's (at the time) quite considerable lands, while the hanging vault is smothered in an unusual branch-like decoration, courtesy of Benedikt Ried. To the left, the statue of a miner is a reminder of just how important Kutná Hora's silver mines were in funding such artistic ventures.

The Imperial Mausoleum and the Royal Crypt

At the centre of the choir, within a fine Renaissance grill, cherubs irreverently lark about on the sixteenth-century marble **Imperial Mausoleum**, commissioned by Rudolf II and containing his grandfather Ferdinand I, his Polish grandmother, and his father Maximilian II, the first Habsburgs to wear the Bohemian crown. Rudolf himself rests beneath them, in one of the two pewter coffins in the somewhat cramped **Royal Crypt** (the entrance is beside the Royal Oratory); his coffin features yet more cherubs, brandishing quills, while the other one contains the remains of Maria Amelia, daughter of the Empress Maria Theresa. A good number of other Czech kings and queens are buried here, too, reinterred this century in incongruously modern 1930s sarcophagi, among them the Hussite King George of Poděbrady, Charles IV and, sharing a single sarcophagus, all four of his wives.

The third courtyard and the Starý královský palác

There's a post office in the west wing of the third courtyard, open Mon–Fri 8am–7pm, Sat & Sun 10am–7pm.

The rest of the **third courtyard** (třetí nádvoří) reveals yet more Pacassi plasterwork, the monotony broken by just a couple of distractions. A fourteenth-century **bronze statue**, executed by a couple of Transylvanian Saxon sculptors, depicts a rather diminutive Saint George astride a disturbingly large horse (actually two hundred years younger than the rest of the ensemble), slaying an extremely puny dragon; the original is in the Convent of sv Jiří (see below). Apart from Plečnik's polished granite **monolith**, an unfinished work celebrating the tenth anniversary of the foundation of Czechoslovakia, the only other reason for hanging about in the third courtyard is to clock Parler's **Zlatá brána** (Golden Gate), decorated with a multicoloured fourteenth-century mosaic of the *Last Judgement*, scheduled to receive sorely needed restoration during the course of 1998, courtesy of the Getty Foundation.

Starý královský palác (Old Royal Palace)

Across the courtyard from the Zlatá brána, the **Starý královský palác** (Old Royal Palace) was home to the princes and kings of Bohemia from the eleventh to the sixteenth centuries. It's a sandwich of royal apartments, built one on top of the other by successive generations, but left largely unfurnished and unused for the last three hundred years. The original Romanesque palace of Soběslav I now forms the cellars of the present building, above which Charles IV built his own Gothic chambers; these days you enter at the third and top floor, built at the end of the fifteenth century.

Immediately past the antechamber (which now serves as a ticket office) is the bare expanse of the massive **Vladislavský sál** (Vladislav Hall), the work of Benedikt Ried, the German mason appointed by Vladislav Jagiello as his court architect. It displays some remarkable, sweeping rib-vaulting which forms floral patterns on the ceiling, the petals reaching almost to the floor. It was here that the early Bohemian kings were elected, and since 1918 every president from Masaryk to Havel has been sworn into office in the hall. In medieval times, the hall was also used for banquets and jousting tournaments, which explains the ramp-like **Riders' Staircase** in the north wing (now the exit).

From a staircase in the southwest corner of the hall, you can gain access to the Ludvík Wing. The rooms themselves are pretty uninspiring but the furthest one, the **Bohemian Chancellery**, was the scene of Prague's **second defenestration**. After almost two centuries of uneasy coexistence between Catholics and Protestants, matters came to a head over the succession to the throne of the Habsburg archduke Ferdinand, a notoriously intolerant Catholic. On May 23, 1618, a posse of more than one hundred Protestant nobles, led by Count Thurn, marched to the chancellery for a showdown with Jaroslav Bořita z Martinic and Vilém Slavata, the two Catholic governors appointed by Ferdinand I. After a "stormy discussion", the two councillors (and their personal secretary, Filip Fabricius) were thrown out of the window. As a contemporary historian recounted: "No mercy was granted them and they were both thrown dressed in their cloaks with their rapiers and decoration head-first out of the western window into a moat beneath the palace. They loudly screamed *ach, ach, oweh!* and attempted to hold on to the narrow window-ledge, but Thurn beat their knuckles with the hilt of his sword until they were both obliged to let go." There's some controversy about the exact window from which they were ejected, although it's agreed that they survived to tell the tale, landing in a medieval dung heap below, and – so the story goes – precipitating the Thirty Years' War.

At the far end of the hall, to the right, there's an outdoor **viewing platform**, from which you can contemplate the councillors' trajectory, and enjoy a magnificent view of Prague (at its best in the late afternoon). At the far end of the hall, you can look down onto **the** chapel of

Pražský hrad

Details of the first defenestration are on p.141.

Všech svatých, which Parler added to Charles IV's palace, but which had to be rebuilt after the 1541 fire, and has since been Baroquified. Its only point of interest is the remains of the Czech saint, Procopius, which are contained within an eighteenth-century wooden tomb along the north wall. To the right of the Riders' Staircase, a door leads into the vaulted room of the Diet, whose (purely decorative) ribs imitate those of the Vladislav Hall. The room is laid out as if for a seventeenth-century session of the Diet: the king on his throne, the archbishop to his right, the judiciary to his left, the nobility facing him, and representatives from towns across Bohemia (with just one collective vote) confined to the gallery by the window.

A staircase to the left of the Riders' Staircase will take you up to the sparsely furnished rooms of the New Land Rolls, whose walls are tattooed with coats-of-arms. More rewarding, though, is the quick canter down the Riders' Staircase to the **Gothic and Romanesque chambers** of the palace, equally bare, but containing a couple of interesting models showing the castle at various stages in its development. Also on display are copies of busts by Peter Parler's workshop, which are virtually hidden from view in the triforium of the cathedral. As well as the architect's remarkable self-portrait, there are portraits of Charles IV and his four wives, including the formidable fourth spouse, Elizabeth of Pomerania, who used to bend horseshoes and tear chained mail to shreds with her bare hands.

The Basilica and Convent of sv Jiří

The only exit from the Royal Palace is via the Riders' Staircase, which deposits you in Jiřské náměstí. Don't be fooled by the uninspiring red Baroque facade of the **Basilica of sv Jiří** (St George) which dominates the square; inside is Prague's most beautiful Romanesque building, meticulously scrubbed clean and restored to re-create something like the honey-coloured stone basilica that replaced the original tenth-century church in 1173. The double staircase to the chancel is a remarkably harmonious late Baroque addition and now provides a perfect stage for chamber music concerts. The choir vault contains a rare early thirteenth-century painting of the New Jerusalem from Revelations – not to be confused with the very patchy sixteenth-century painting on the apse – while to the right of the chancel, only partially visible, are sixteenth-century frescoes of the **burial chapel of sv Ludmila**, grandmother of Saint Wenceslas, who was strangled by her own daughter-in-law in 921 (see box on p.55), thus becoming Bohemia's first Christian martyr and saint. There's a replica of the recumbent Ludmila, which you can inspect at close quarters, in the south aisle.

There are several other equally atmospheric concert venues in Prague; see p.230 for a more comprehensive list.

Jiřský klášter (the old Bohemian art collection)

Next door is Bohemia's first monastery, the **Jiřský klášter** (St George's Convent) founded in 973 by Mlada, sister of the

Přemyslid prince Boleslav the Pious, who became its first abbess. Like most of the country's religious institutions, it was closed down and turned into a barracks by Joseph II in 1782, and now houses the Národní galerie's **old Bohemian art collection** (Staré české umění), which spans the Gothic and Baroque period. The exhibition is arranged chronologically, starting in the crypt with a remarkable collection of Gothic art, which first flourished here under the patronage of Charles IV.

The **earliest works** are almost exclusively symbolical depictions of the Madonna and Child, the artists known only by their works and locations, not by name. Here you'll find – among other things – the monumental tympanum from the church of Panna Maria Sněžná in Prague and nine panels from the altarpiece of the Cistercian monastery at Vyšší Brod. The first named artist is **Master Theodoric**, who painted over one hundred panels for Charles IV's castle at Karlštejn (see p.190); just six are on display here, their larger-than-life portraits overflowing onto the edges of the panels.

On the next floor, are paintings by the **Master of Třeboň**, whose work shows even greater variety of balance and depth, moving ever closer to realistic portraiture. The following room contains the stone-carved tympanum from the Týn church (see p.100) – originally coloured and gilded – with high-relief figures by Peter Parler's workshop, whose mastery of composition and depth heralded a new stage in the development of Bohemian art. The last room on this floor is devoted to a series of superb sixteenth-century woodcuts by **Master I. P.**, including an incredibly detailed scene *Christ the Redeemer before Death*, a skeleton whose entrails are in the process of being devoured by a frog.

The transition from this to the next floor, where you are immediately thrown into the overtly sensual and erotic **Mannerist paintings** of Rudolf II's reign, is something of a shock. Few works survive from Rudolf's superlative collection, but make sure you check out Paulus Roy's clever optical illusion, *The Portrait of Three Emperors*, and Josef Heintz's riotous orgy in his *Last Judgement*. The rest of the gallery is given over to Czech **Baroque art**, as pursued by the likes of Bohemia's Karel Škréta and Petr Brandl, whose paintings and sculptures fill chapels and churches across the Czech Lands. Michael Leopold Willmann's portrait of St Bartholomew being skinned alive is disturbingly gruesome, but aside from the works of Jan Kupecký and the statues of Matthias Bernhard Braun and Ferdinand Maximilian Brokof, this section is unlikely to hold your attention for long.

Zlatá ulička and the castle towers

Around the corner from the convent is the **Zlatá ulička** (Golden Lane), a seemingly blind alley of miniature cottages in dolly-mixture colours. The contrast in scale with the rest of the Hrad makes this

Pražský hrad

The Jiřský klášter is open Tues–Sun 10am–6pm. Entry is not covered by the general castle admission; tickets are available from the ticket office inside the cloisters.

by far the most popular sight in the entire complex, and during the day, at least, the whole street is mobbed, so if you want to try and re-capture some of the original atmosphere, you really need to come back in the evening. Originally built in the sixteenth century for the 24 members of Rudolf II's castle guard, the lane allegedly takes its name from the goldsmiths who followed (and modified the build-ings) a century later, though the only house which survives from the sixteenth century is no. 13, the least cute of the lot. By the nine-teenth century, the whole street had become a kind of palace slum, attracting artists and craftsmen, its two most famous inhabitants being Jaroslav Seifert, the Czech Nobel prize-winning poet, and Franz Kafka. Kafka's youngest sister, Ottla, rented no. 22, and dur-ing a creative period in the winter of 1916 he came here in the evenings to write short stories. Finally, in 1951, the Communists kicked out the last residents and turned most of the houses into sou-venir shops for tourists.

At no. 12, at the eastern end of Zlatá ulička, is a throughway to the **Černá věž** (Black Tower), standing at the top of the Staré zamecké schody, which leads down to Malostranská metro. There's no access to the Černá věž but at the other end of the lane, at no. 24, you can climb a flight of stairs to the **Obranná chodba** (defence corridor), which is lined with wooden shields, suits of armour and period cos-tumes. The **Bílá věž** (white tower) at the western end of the corridor, was the city's main prison from Rudolf's reign onwards. Edward Kelley, the English alchemist, was locked up here by Rudolf for fail-ing to turn base metal into gold, while the emperor's treasurer hanged himself by his gold cord on the treasury keys, after being accused of embezzlement. There's a reconstructed torture chamber on the first floor, and in the shop on the floor above you can kit your-self out as a medieval knight with replica swords and maces, not to mention chastity belts and various torture instruments.

In the opposite direction, the corridor leads to a shooting range, where for small fee, you can have a few shots with a cross-bow. The tower, which lies beyond is the **Daliborka**, dedicated to its first pris-oner, the young Czech noble, Dalibor, accused of supporting a peas-ants' revolt at the beginning of the fifteenth century. According to Prague legend, he learnt to play the violin while imprisoned here, and his playing could be heard all over the castle – a tale that provided material for Smetana's opera *Dalibor* – until his execution in 1498.

To get inside the castle's other tower, the Prašná věž (Powder Tower) or **Mihulka**, which once served as the workshop of gun-smith and bell-founder Tomáš Jaroš, you'll have to backtrack to Vikářská, the street which runs along the north side of the cathe-dral. The powder tower's name comes from the lamprey (*mihule*), an eel-like fish supposedly bred here for royal consumption, though it's actually more noteworthy as the place where Rudolf's team of alchemists (including Kelley) were put to work trying to

Rudolf II (1576–1612)

In 1583 Emperor **Rudolf II** switched the imperial court from Vienna to Prague. This was to be the first and last occasion in which Prague would hold centre-stage in the Habsburg Empire, and as such is seen as something of a second golden age for the city (the first being under Holy Roman Emperor Charles IV, for more on whom, see p.92). Bad-tempered, paranoid and probably insane, Rudolf had little interest in the affairs of state – instead, he holed up in the Hrad and indulged his own personal passions of alchemy, astrology and art. Thus, Rudolfine Prague played host to an impressive array of international artists including the idiosyncratic Giuseppe Arcimboldo, whose surrealist portraits were composed entirely of fruit and vegetables. The astrologers, Johannes Kepler and Tycho Brahe, were summoned to Rudolf's court to chart the planetary movements and assuage Rudolf's superstitions. And the English alchemists, Edward Kelley and John Dee, were employed in order to discover the secret of the philosopher's stone, the mythical substance that would transmute base metal into gold.

Accompanied by his pet African lion, Otakar, Rudolf spent less and less time in public, hiding out in the Hrad, where he "loved to paint, weave and dabble in inlaying and watchmaking", according to modern novelist Angelo Maria Ripellino. With the Turks rapidly approaching the gates of Vienna, Rudolf spent his days amassing exotic curios for his strange and vast *Kunst- und Wunderkammer*, which contained such items as "two nails from Noah's Ark...a lump of clay out of which God formed Adam...and large mandrake roots in the shape of little men reclining on soft velvet cushions in small cases resembling doll beds". He refused to marry, though he sired numerous bastards, since he had been warned in a horoscope that a legitimate heir would rob him of the throne. He was also especially wary of the numerous religious orders who inhabited Prague at the time, having been warned in another horoscope that he would be killed by a monk. In the end, he was relieved of his throne by his younger brother, Matthias, in 1611, and died the following year the day after the death of his beloved pet lion.

discover the secret of the philosopher's stone (see box). Despite its colourful history, the exhibition currently on display within the tower is dull, with just a pair of furry slippers and hat belonging to Ferdinand I to get excited about.

Muzeum hraček (Toy Museum) and the Lobkovický palác

If you continue east down Jiřská, which runs parallel with Zlatá ulička, you'll come to the courtyard of the former Purkrabství (Burgrave's House) on the left, which hides a café, exhibition space and **Muzeum hraček** (Toy Museum). With brief, Czech-only captions and unimaginative displays, the museum is a disappointing venture, which fails to live up to its potential. The succession of glass cabinets contains everything from toy cars and motorbikes to robots and even Barbie dolls, but there are only a few buttons for younger kids to

The Muzeum hraček is open daily 9.30am–5.30pm; admission requires a separate ticket, available from the ticket office on the ground floor.

press, and unless you're really lost for something to do, you could happily skip the whole enterprise.

Lobkovický palác

The Lobkovický palác is open Tues–Sun 9am–5pm; admission requires a separate ticket available from the ticket office on the ground floor.

The hotchpotch historical collection in the **Lobkovický palác** (Lobkowicz Palace), on the opposite side of Jiřská, is marginally more rewarding, despite the ropey English text provided. The exhibition actually begins on the top floor, though by no means all the objects on display deserve attention; the following is a quick run-down of some of the more memorable exhibits. The first cabinet worth more than a passing nod is in the second room, and contains copies of the Bohemian crown jewels (the originals are hidden away above the Chapel of sv Václav in the cathedral and are very rarely on view). Next door, in the Hussite room, there's an interesting six-teenth-century carving of *The Last Supper*, originally an altarpiece from the Bethlehem Chapel, while, further on, Petr Vok's splendid funereal shield, constructed out of wood covered with cloth shot through with gold, hangs on the wall.

All things post-1620 and pre-1848 are displayed in the six rooms downstairs, starting with the sword of the famous Prague execution-er, Jan Mydlář, who could lop a man's head off with just one chop, a skill he demonstrated on 24 of the 27 Protestant leaders who were executed on Staroměstské náměstí in 1621; Mydlář's invoice cover-ing labour and expenses is displayed beside the sword. Several rooms on are some more unusual exhibits – three contemporary scaled-down models of eighteenth-century altars, and further on still, three carved marionettes from later that century, among the oldest surviving in Bohemia.

The Castle Gardens

The Hrad boasts some of the city's loveliest gardens, particularly in terms of views. The Jižní zahrady (South Gardens) enjoy wonderful vistas over the city and link up the terraced gardens of Malá Strana, while Královska zahrada (Royal Gardens) allow a better view of the cathedral and the Vltava's many bridges.

Jižní zahrady

For recuperation and a superlative view over the rest of Prague – not to mention a chance to inspect some of Plečnik's quirky additions to the castle – head for the **Jižní zahrady** (South Gardens), accessible via Plečnik's copper-canopied Bull Staircase on the south side of the third courtyard. Originally laid out in the sixteenth century, but thor-oughly remodelled in the 1920s by Josip Plečnik, the first garden you come to, the **Zahrada na valech** (Garden on the Ramparts), features an observation terrace and colonnaded pavilion, below which is an earlier eighteenth-century music pavilion (hudební pavilón). Two sandstone obelisks further east record the arrival of Slavata and

The gardens are open May–Oct daily 10am–6pm.

Martinic after their defenestration from the royal palace above (see p.57); beyond them lies yet another of Plečnik's observation pavilions. In the opposite direction, beyond the Baroque fountain lies the smaller **Rajská zahrada** (Paradise Garden), on whose lawn Plečnik plonked a forty-ton granite basin suspended on two small blocks. From here, a quick slog up the monumental staircase will bring you out onto Hradčanské náměstí.

The Královská zahrada and Belvedér

Before exploring the rest of Hradčany, it's worth taking a stroll in the most verdant of all the castle's gardens, the **Královská zahrada** (Royal Gardens), situated beyond the castle walls to the north. To get there, pass through the north gate of the second courtyard and cross the **Prašný most** (Powder Bridge), erected in the sixteenth century to connect the newly established royal gardens with the Hrad (the original wooden structure has long since been replaced). Below lies the wooded **Jelení příkop** (Stag Ditch), once used by the Habsburgs for growing figs and lemons, and storing game for the royal hunts, but now populated only by bored castle guards.

Beyond the bridge, opposite the former riding school or **Jízdárna** (now used for temporary art exhibitions) is the entrance to the Královská zahrada themselves, founded by Emperor Ferdinand I in the 1530s on the site of a former vineyard. Burned down by the Saxons and Swedes during the Thirty Years' War, and blown up by the Prussians, the gardens were only saved from French attack in 1741 by the payment of thirty pineapples. Today, this is one of the best-kept gardens in the capital, with fully functioning fountains and immaculately cropped lawns. Consequently, it's a very popular spot, though more a place for admiring the azaleas and almond trees than lounging around on the grass. It was here that tulips brought from Turkey were first acclimatized to Europe, before being exported to the Netherlands, and every spring there's an impressive, disciplined crop.

The Jízdárna is open Tues–Sun 10am–6pm.

At the entrance to the gardens is the **Lví dvůr** (Lion's Court), now a restaurant but originally built by Rudolf II to house his private zoo, which included leopards, lynxes, bears, wolves and lions, all of whom lived in heated cages to protect them from the Prague winter. Rudolf was also responsible for the Renaissance ball-game court, known as the **Míčovna** (occasionally open to the public for concerts and exhibitions), built into the south terrace and tattooed with sgraffito by his court architect Bonifaz Wolmut. If you look carefully at the top row of allegorical figures on either side of the sandstone half-columns, you can see that the figure of Industry, between Justice and Peace, is holding a hammer and sickle and a copy of the Five-Year Plan, thoughtfully added by restorers in the 1950s. Incidentally the guarded ochre building to the right of the Míčovna, the **Zahradní dům**, is one of Havel's presidential pads, built as a summer house by Dientzenhofer only to be destroyed during the Prussian bombard-

The gardens are open May–Oct Tues–Sun 10am–5.45pm.

ment of 1757. It was later restored by Pavel Janák who added the building's two modern wings on a postwar whim of the ill-fated President Beneš.

At the end of the gardens is Prague's most celebrated Renaissance legacy, Letohrádek královny Anny (Queen Anne's Summer Palace), popularly known as the **Belvedér**, a delicately arcaded summerhouse topped by an inverted copper ship's hull, built by Ferdinand I for his wife, Anne (though she didn't live long enough to see it completed). It was designed by the Genoese architect Paolo della Stella, one of a number of Italian masons who settled in Prague in the sixteenth century, and is decorated by a series of lovely figural reliefs depicting scenes from mythology. Unlike the gardens, the Belvedér is open for most of the year and is mostly used for exhibitions by contemporary artists; if the gardens are closed you'll have to leave the Královská zahrada and head down Mariánské hradby. At the centre of the palace's miniature formal garden is the **Zpívající fontána** (Singing Fountain), built shortly after the palace and named for the musical sound of the drops of water falling in the metal bowls below – you have to stick your ears up close to get the full effect. From the garden terrace, you also have an unrivalled view of the castle's finest treasure – the cathedral.

The Belvedér is open Tues–Sun 10am–6pm.

The Chotkovy sady and the Bílkova vila are both within easy walking distance of the Belvedér; see p.160 for details.

From Hradčanské náměstí to the Strahovský klášter

The monumental scale and appearance of the rest of Hradčany, outside the castle, is a direct result of the **great fire of 1541**, which swept up from Malá Strana and wiped out most of the old dwelling places belonging to the serfs, tradesmen, clergy and masons who had settled here in the Middle Ages. With the Turks at the gates of Vienna, the Habsburg nobility were more inclined to pursue their major building projects in Prague instead, and, following the Battle of Bílá hora in 1620, the palaces of the exiled (or executed) Protestant nobility were up for grabs too. The newly ensconced Catholic aristocrats were keen to spend some of their expropriated wealth, and over the next two centuries, they turned Hradčany into a grand architectural showpiece. As the Turkish threat subsided, the political focus of the empire gradually shifted back to Vienna and the building spree stopped. For the last two hundred years, Hradčany has been frozen in time, and, two world wars on, its buildings have survived better than those of any other central European capital.

Hradčanské náměstí

Hradčanské náměstí fans out from the castle gates, surrounded by the oversized palaces of the old Catholic nobility. For the most part, it's a tranquil space that's overlooked by the tour groups marching through, intent on the Hrad. The one spot everyone heads for is the ramparts in the southeastern corner, by the top of the Zámecké schody, which allow an unrivalled view over the reddish-brown rooftops of Malá Strana, past the famous dome and tower of the church of sv Mikuláš and beyond, to the spires of Staré Město. Only the occasional bookish Praguer or tired traveller makes use of the square's central green patch, which is marked by a giant green wrought-iron lamppost decked with eight separate lamps – one of the few that have survived from the 1860s.

From Hradčanské náměstí to the Strahovský klášter

Until the great fire of 1541, the square was the hub of Hradčany, lined with medieval shops and stalls but with no real market as such. After the fire, the developers moved in; the **Martinický palác** at no. 8 was one of the more modest newcomers, built in 1620 by one of the councillors who survived the second defenestration. Its rich sgraffito decoration, which continues in the inner courtyard, was only discovered during restoration work in the 1970s, and was part of the reason it was featured as Mozart's house in the film *Amadeus*. Mathey's rather cold, formal **Toskánský palác** (now in the hands of the Foreign Ministry) was built on a more ambitious scale, replacing the row of butchers' shops that once filled the west end of the square.

The powerful Lobkowicz family replaced seven houses on the south side of the square with the over-the-top sgraffitoed pile at no. 2, known as the **Schwarzenberský palác** after its last aristocratic owners (the present-day Count Schwarzenberg, Karl, is one of the republic's leading capitalists). For a brief period, it belonged to the Rožmberk family, whose last in line, Petr Vok, held the infamous banquet which proved fatal to the Danish astronomer Tycho Brahe. So as not to offend his host, Tycho refrained from leaving the table before Vok, only to burst his bladder, after which he staggered off to his house in Nový Svět, where he died five days later.

All of which makes the **Vojenské historické muzeum** (Museum of Military History), which now occupies the palace, seem considerably less gruesome. Predictably enough, it was the Nazis who founded the museum, though the Czechs themselves have a long history of manufacturing top-class weaponry to world powers (Semtex is probably their best-known export) – it's no coincidence that of the two Czech words to have made it into the English language, one is pistol (from *pišťale*, a Hussite weapon); the other is robot (from Karel Čapek's play *R.U.R.*). The museum is currently desperately underfunded, and, somewhat surprisingly, many of the captions are in English. Among the ostentatious Habsburg uniforms and finely crafted instruments of death, all of which are pre-1914, you'll find the first Colt 45 produced outside the USA, maunfactured in 1849 for the Austrian Navy, a field altar donated by Prince Eugène of Savoy, and a mannekin of General Windischgrätz surveying Prague, as he did before bombing it into submission in 1848. Prague's post-1914 military collections are housed at the Army Museum on Žižkov Hill (see p.158).

The museum is open May–Oct Tues–Sun 10am–5.30pm.

From Hradčanské náměstí to the Strahovský klášter

The Archbishop's Palace is open to the public only on Maundy Thursday – the Thursday before Easter.

The Šternberský palác is open Tues–Sun 10am–6pm; tickets for the gallery allow free entry into the Jiřský klášter, Anežský klášter and Jízdárna.

The adjacent **Salmovský palác**, at no. 1, was another Schwarzenberg pile, which served as the Swedish Embassy until the 1970s when the dissident writer Pavel Kohout took refuge there. Frustrated in their attempts to force him out, the Communists closed the embassy down and left it to rot, though it looks likely, eventually, to be turned into a hotel. On the opposite side of the square, just outside the castle gates, stands the sumptuous **Arcibiskupský palác** (Archbishop's Palace), seat of the archbishop of Prague since the beginning of the Roman Catholic church's suzerainty over the Czechs, following the Battle of Bílá hora. The Rococo exterior only hints at the even more extravagant furnishings inside.

Šternberský palác – the old European art collection

A passage down the side of the archbishop's palace leads to the early eighteenth-century **Šternberský palác**, which houses the Národní's galerie's **old European art collection** (Staré evropské umění), mostly ranging from the fourteenth to the eighteenth century, but excluding works by Czech artists of the period (you'll find them in the Jiřský klášter in the Hrad). It would be fair to say that the collection is relatively modest in comparison with those of other major European capitals, though the handful of masterpieces makes a visit here worthwhile. To see the late nineteenth- and twentieth-century European art which used to be housed here, you need to pay a visit to the Národní Galerie's modern and contemporary art collection in the Veletržní palác (see p.164).

The **first floor** kicks off with Florentine religious art, most notably a series of exquisite miniature triptychs by Bernardo Daddi, plus several gilded polyptychs by the Venetian artist Antonio Vivarini. Moving swiftly into the gallery's large Flemish contingent, it's worth checking out Dieric Bouts' *Lamentation*, a complex composition crowded with figures in medieval garb, and the bizarre *Well of Life*, painted around 1500 by an unknown artist. The latter features a squatting Christ depicted as a Gothic fountain issuing forth blood which angels in turn serve in goblets to passing punters. One of the most eye-catching works is Jan Gossaert's *St Luke Drawing the Virgin*, an excercise in architectural geometry and perspective which used to hang in the cathedral. The section ends with a series of canvases by the Brueghel family; before you head upstairs, though, don't miss the side rooms containing Orthodox icons from Venice and the Balkans to northern Russia.

The **second floor** contains one of the most prized paintings in the whole collection, the *Feast of the Rosary* by Albrecht Dürer, depicting, among others, the Virgin Mary, the Pope, the Holy Roman Emperor, and even a self-portrait of Dürer himself (top right). This was one of Rudolf's most prized aquisitions (he was an avid Dürer fan), which was transported on foot across the Alps to Prague (he didn't trust wheeled transport with such a precious object). There are other outstanding works here, too: two richly coloured Bronzino portraits, a Rembrandt, a Canaletto of the Thames, a whole series by the Saxon master, Lucas Cranach – including the striking, almost minimalist *Portrait of an Old Man* – and a mesmerizing *Praying Christ* by El Greco. Rubens' colossal *Murder of St Thomas* is difficult to miss, with its pink-buttocked cherubs hovering over the bloody scene. Nearby, in the hugely expanded (and uneven) Dutch section, there's a wonderful portrait of an arrogant "young gun" named Jasper by Frans Hals. A few of the rooms in the gallery have preserved their original decor, the best of which is the Chinoiserie of the Činský kabinet.

From Hradčanské náměstí to the Strahovský klášter

Nový Svět to Loreta

At the other end of Hradčanské náměstí, Kanovnická heads off towards the northwest corner of Hradčany. Nestling in this shallow dip, **Nový Svět** (meaning "New World", though not Dvořák's) provides a glimpse of life on a totally different scale from Hradčanské náměstí. Similar in many ways to the Zlatá ulička in the Hrad, this cluster of brightly coloured cottages, which curls around the corner into Černínská, is all that's left of Hradčany's medieval slums, painted up and sanitized in the eighteenth and nineteenth centuries. Despite having all the same ingredients for mass tourist appeal as Zlatá ulička, it remains remarkably undisturbed, save for a few swish wine bars, and Gambra, a surrealist art gallery at Černínská 5 (Wed–Sun noon–6pm), which sells works by, among others, the renowned Czech animator, Jan Švankmajer, and his wife Eva, who live nearby.

Up the hill from Nový Svět, Loretánské náměstí is dominated by the phenomenal 135-metre-long facade of the **Černínský palác**, decorated with thirty Palladian half-columns and supported by a swathe of diamond-pointed rustication. For all its grandeur – it's the largest palace in Prague, for the sake of which two whole streets were demolished – it's a pretty brutal building, commissioned in the 1660s by Count Humprecht Jan Černín, one-time imperial ambassador to Venice and a man of monumental self-importance. After quarrelling with the master of Italian Baroque, Giovanni Bernini, and disagreeing with Prague's own Carlo Lurago, Count Černín settled on Francesco Caratti as his architect, only to have the finished building panned by critics as a tasteless mass of stone. The grandiose plans, which were nowhere near completion when the count died, nearly bankrupted future generations of Černíns, who were eventually forced to sell the palace in 1851 to the Austrian state, which converted it into military barracks.

Since the First Republic, the palace has housed the Ministry of Foreign Affairs, and during the war it was, for a while, the Nazi *Reichsprotektor*'s residence. On March 10, 1948, it was the scene of

The Černínský palác is not open to the public.

From
Hradčanské
náměstí to
the
Strahovský
klášter

Prague's third – and most widely mourned – defenestration. Only days after the Communist coup, **Jan Masaryk**, the only son of the founder of the Republic, and the last non-Communist in Gottwald's cabinet, plunged 45 feet to his death from the top-floor bathroom window of the palace. Whether it was suicide (he had been suffering from bouts of depression, partly induced by the country's political path) or murder will probably never be satisfactorily resolved, but for most people Masaryk's death cast a dark shadow over the newly established regime.

Loreta

*The Loreta is
open
Tues–Sun
9am–12.15pm
& 1–4.30pm.*

The facade of the **Loreta**, immediately opposite the Černínský palác, was built by the Dientzenhofers, a Bavarian family of architects, in the early part of the eighteenth century, and is the perfect antidote to Caratti's humourless monster. It's all hot flourishes and twirls, topped by a tower which lights up like a Chinese lantern at night – and by day clanks out the hymn *We Greet Thee a Thousand Times* on its 27 Dutch bells.

The facade and the cloisters, which were provided a century earlier to shelter pilgrims from the elements, are, in fact, just the outer casing for the focus of the complex, the **Santa Casa**, founded by Kateřina Lobkowicz in 1626 and smothered in a mantle of stucco depicting the building's miraculous transportation from the Holy Land. Legend has it that the Santa Casa (Mary's home in Nazareth), under threat from the heathen Turks, was transported by a host of angels to a small village in Dalmatia and from there, via a number of brief stopoffs, to a small laurel grove (*lauretum* in Latin, hence Loreta) in northern Italy. News of the miracle spread across the Catholic lands, prompting a spate of copy-cat shrines, and during the Counter-Reformation, the cult was actively encouraged in an attempt to broaden the popular appeal of Catholicism. The Prague Loreta is one of fifty to be built in the Czech Lands, each of the shrines following an identical design, with pride of place given to a lime-wood statue of the *Black Madonna and Child*, encased in silver.

*The Lobkowicz
family gave
Prague its
other famous
pilgrimage
shrine, the
pražské
Jezulátko (see
p.82).*

Behind the Santa Casa, the Dientzenhofers built the much larger **Church of Narození Páně** (Church of the Nativity), packed with some fairly gruesome Baroque kitsch. On either side of the main altar are glass cabinets containing the (fully clothed) skeletons of Saint Felicissimus and Saint Marcia, and next to them, paintings of Saint Apolena – who had her teeth smashed in during her martyrdom and is now invoked for toothache – and Saint Agatha, carrying her severed breasts on a dish. Last but not least of the weird and wonderful saints in Loreto is Saint Wilgefortis, a painting of whom is in the final chapel of the cloisters. Daughter of the King of Portugal, she was due to marry the King of Sicily, despite having taken a vow of virginity. God intervened and she grew a beard, whereupon the King of Sicily broke off the marriage and her father had her crucified.

Wilgefortis thus became the patron saint of unhappily married women, and is traditionally depicted bearded on the cross.

You can get some idea of the Santa Casa's serious financial backing in the **treasury** (situated on the first floor of the west wing), much ransacked over the years but still stuffed full of gold. The padded ceilings and low lighting create a kind of giant jewellery box for the master exhibit, a tasteless Viennese silver monstrance studded with 6222 diamonds, standing over three feet high and weighing nearly two stone. It was constructed in 1699 to a design by Fischer von Erlach, on the posthumous orders of one of the Kolovrat family who had made the Loreto sole heir to her fortune.

From Hradčanské náměstí to the Strahovský klášter

Strahovský klášter

Continuing westwards from Loretánské náměstí, Pohořelec, an arcaded street-cum-square, leads to the chunky remnants of the zigzag eighteenth-century fortifications that mark the edge of the old city, as defined by Charles IV back in the fourteenth century. Close by, to the left, is the **Strahovský klášter** (Strahov Monastery), founded in 1140 by the Premonstratensian order. Strahov was one of the lucky few to escape Joseph II's 1783 dissolution of the monasteries, a feat it managed by declaring itself a scholarly institution – the monks had, in fact, amassed one of the finest libraries in Bohemia. It continued to function until shortly after the Communists took power, when, along with all other religious establishments, it was closed down and most of its inmates thrown into prison; following the happy events of 1989, the monks have returned.

The Baroque entrance to the monastery is topped by a statue of Saint Norbert, founder of the Premonstratensian order, whose relics were brought here in 1627. Just inside the cobbled outer courtyard is a tiny deconsecrated church built by Rudolf II and dedicated to **sv Roch**, protector against plagues, one of which had very nearly rampaged through Prague in 1599; it's now an art gallery. The other church in this peaceful little courtyard is the still functioning monastery church, first built back in the twelfth century, and given its last remodelling in Baroque times by Jean-Baptiste Mathey; it's recently been restored to its former glory, with lots of colourful frescoes relating Saint Norbert's life, and is definitely worth a quick peek.

It's the monastery's two **libraries**, though, that are the real reason for visiting Strahov, however; the entrance for both is to the right as you enter the outer courtyard. The first library you come to is the later of the two, the **Filosofický sál** (Philosophical Hall), built in some haste in the 1780s, in order to accommodate the books and bookcases from Louka, a Premonstratensian monastery in Moravia that failed to escape Joseph's decree. The walnut bookcases are so tall they touch the library's lofty ceiling, which is busily decorated with frescoes by the Viennese painter Franz Maulpertsch on *The*

The libraries are open daily 9am–noon & 1–5pm.

From
Hradčanské
náměstí to
the
Strahovský
klášter

Struggle of Mankind to Know Real Wisdom. Don't, whatever you do, miss the collection of curios exhibited in the glass cabinets outside the library, which features shells, turtles, crabs, lobsters, dried-up sea monsters, plastic fruit, moths and even a whale's penis. The other main room is the low-ceilinged **Teologický sál** (Theological Hall), studded with ancient globes, its wedding-cake stucco framing frescoes on a similar theme, executed by one of the monks seventy years earlier.

An archway on the far side of the church contains the ticket office for the **Strahovská obrazárna** (Strahov Gallery), situated above the cloisters, and accessible from the door on the right, beyond the ticket office. The gallery's collection of religious art, church plate and reliquaries – a mere fraction of the monastery's total – may not be to everyone's taste, but it does contain the odd gem from Rudolf II's collection, including a portrait of the emperor himself by his court painter, Hans von Aachen, plus a superb portrait of Rembrandt's elderly mother by Gerrit Dou.

*The
Strahovská
obrazárna is
open
Tues–Sun
9am–noon &
12.30–5pm.*

If you leave the monastery through the narrow doorway in the eastern wall, you enter the gardens and orchards of the **Strahovská zahrada**, from where you can see the whole city in perspective. The gardens form part of wooded hill known as Petřín, and the path to the right contours round to the Stations of the Cross that lead up to the miniature Eiffel Tower known as the Rozhledna (see p.84). Alternatively, you can catch tram #22 from outside Strahov's main entrance to Malostranská metro or the centre of town.

Chapter 2

Malá Strana

More than anywhere else, **MALÁ STRANA**, the "Little Quarter", conforms to the image of Prague as the ultimate Baroque city. It was here that film director Miloš Forman chose to shoot many of the street scenes in *Amadeus*, judging that its picturesque alleyways resembled Mozart's Vienna more than Vienna itself. And it's true; the streets have changed very little since Mozart walked them, as he often did on his frequent visits to Prague between 1787 and 1791. Unlike Hradčany, its main square is filled with city life during the day; while around practically every corner, narrow cobbled streets lead to some quiet walled garden, the perfect inner-city escape.

Foolishly, many visitors never stray from the well-trodden paths that link the Charles Bridge with Hradčany, thus bypassing most of Malá Strana. This is easy to do given that the whole town takes up a mere 600 square metres of land squeezed in between the river and the Hrad, but it means missing out on one of the greatest pleasures of Malá Strana – casually exploring its hilly eighteenth-century backstreets.

Long before the Přemyslid king, Otakar II, decided to establish a German community here in 1257, a mixture of Jews, merchants and monks had settled on the slopes below the castle. But, as with Hradčany, it was the fire of 1541 – which devastated the entire left bank of the Vltava – and the expulsion of the Protestants after 1620, that together had the greatest impact on the visual and social make-up of the quarter. In place of the old Gothic town, the newly ascendant Catholic nobility built numerous palaces here, though generally without quite the same destructive glee as up in Hradčany.

In 1918, the majority of these buildings became home to the foreign embassies of the newly established First Republic, and after 1948 the rest of the real estate was turned into flats to alleviate the postwar housing shortage. The cycle has come full circle again since 1989, and property in Malá Strana – much of it in need of repair – is now among the most sought after in Prague. The restitution law has brought back many former owners, while many of the old tenants have been forced out by rent increases – the face of Malá Strana is beginning to change once more.

Some of the city's best restaurants and jazz clubs are located within Malá Strana; see Chapters 10 and 11 for details.

MALÁ STRANA

Malostranské náměstí and around

The main focus of Malá Strana has always been the sloping, cobbled **Malostranské náměstí**, which is dominated and divided into two by the church of sv Mikuláš (see below). Trams and cars hurtle across it, regularly dodged by a procession of people – some heading up the hill to the Hrad, others pausing for coffee and cakes at the numerous bars and restaurants hidden in the square's arcades and Gothic vaults. The most famous (and the most central) of the cafés is the **Malostranská kavárna**, established in 1874, and an occasional haunt of Kafka, Brod, Werfel and friends in the 1920s.

On every side, Neoclassical facades line the square, their facades imitating the colour and grandeur of those of Hradčanské and Staroměstské náměstí. The largest Baroque re-development, the **Lichtenštejnský palác**, takes up the square's entire west side and is home to the university music faculty, as well as a concert venue, art gallery and café. Its pleasing frontage hides a history linked to repression: first as the home of Karl von Liechtenstein, the man who pronounced the death sentence on the 27 Protestant leaders in 1621; then as headquarters for the Swedes during the 1648 siege; and later as base to the Austrian General Windischgrätz, scourge of the 1848 revolution.

On the north side, distinguished by its two little turrets and rather shocking pistachio and vanilla colour scheme, is the **dům Smiřických** (no. 18), where the Protestant posse met up in 1618 to decide how to get rid of Emperor Ferdinand's Catholic governors:

Mozart in Prague

Mozart made the first of several visits to Prague with his wife Constanze in 1787, staying with his friend and patron Count Thun in what is now the British Embassy (Thunovská 14). A year earlier, his opera *The Marriage of Figaro*, which had failed to please the opera snobs in Vienna, had been given a rapturous reception at Prague's Nostitz Theater (now the Stavovské divadlo; see p.104); and on his arrival in 1787, Mozart was already flavour of the month, as he wrote in his diary: "Here they talk about nothing but Figaro. Nothing is played, sung or whistled but Figaro. Nothing, nothing but Figaro. Certainly a great honour for me!" Encouraged by this, he chose to premiere his next opera, *Don Giovanni*, later that year, in Prague rather than Vienna. He arrived with an incomplete score in hand, and wrote the overture at the Dušeks' Bertramka villa in Smíchov (see p.174), dedicating it to the "good people of Prague". Apart from a brief sojourn whilst on a concert tour, Mozart's fourth and final visit to Prague took place in 1791, the year of his death. The climax of the stay was the première of Mozart's final opera, *La Clemenza di Tito*, commissioned for the coronation of Leopold II as King of Bohemia (and according to tradition written on the coach from Vienna to Prague). Mozart's funeral in Vienna was a low-key affair according to most sources, but in Prague four thousand people turned out for his memorial service, held in Malá Strana's church of sv Mikuláš to the strains of his *Requiem Mass*.

whether to attack them with daggers, or, as they eventually attempted to do, kill them by chucking them out of the window (see p.57). Sněmovní, the side street which runs alongside the palace's western facade, takes its name from the **Sněmovna**, the Neocloassical palace at no. 4, which served as the provincial Diet in the nineteenth century, the National Assembly of the First Republic in 1918, the Czech National Council after 1968, and finally, since 1993, home to the lower house of the Czech parliament, the Chamber of Deputies.

Malostranské náměstí and around

The church of sv Mikuláš

Towering above the square, and the whole of Malá Strana, is the church of **sv Mikuláš** (St Nicholas), easily the most magnificent Baroque building in the city, and one of the last great structures to be built on the left bank, begun in 1702. For Christoph Dientzenhofer, a German immigrant from a dynasty of Bavarian architects, this was his most prestigious commission and is, without doubt, his finest work. For the Jesuits, who were already ensconced in the adjoining college, it was their most ambitious project yet in Bohemia, and the ultimate symbol of their stranglehold on the country. When Christoph died in 1722, it was left to his son Kilian Ignaz Dientzenhofer, along with Kilian's son-in-law, Anselmo Lurago, to finish the project, which they did with a masterful flourish, adding the giant green dome and tower – now among the most characteristic landmarks on Prague's left bank. Sadly for the Jesuits, they were able to enjoy the finished product for just twenty years, before they were banished from the Habsburg Empire in 1773.

The church is open daily 9am–4pm; there is a small admission charge.

Nothing about the relatively plain west facade prepares you for the overwhelming High Baroque **interior**. The fresco in the nave, by Johann Lukas Kracker, is one of the largest paintings in Europe, covering an area of more than 1500 square metres and portraying some of the more fanciful miraculous feats of Saint Nicholas. Apart from his role as Santa Claus, he is depicted here rescuing sailors in distress, saving women from prostitution by throwing them bags of gold, and reprieving from death three unjustly condemned men. Even given the overwhelming proportions of the nave, the dome at the far end of the church, built by the younger Dientzenhofer, remains impressive, thanks, more than anything, to its sheer height. Leering over you as you gaze up at the dome are Ignaz Platzer's four terrifyingly oversized and stern Church Fathers, leaving no doubt as to the gravity of the Jesuit message.

Nerudova

The most important of the various streets leading up to the Hrad from Malostranské náměstí is **Nerudova**, named after the Czech journalist and writer Jan Neruda (1834–91), who was born at *U dvou slunců* (The Two Suns), at no. 47, a former inn at the top of

Nerudova was once famous for its pubs; sadly, only a few of the originals remain, see p.215 for details.

The pharmacy
is open
Tues–Fri
noon–6pm, Sat
& Sun
10am–6pm.

The Galerie
Josefa Sudka
is open
Tues–Sun
10am–noon &
1–6pm.

the street. His tales of Malá Strana immortalized bohemian life on Prague's left bank, though he's perhaps best known in the West via the Chilean Nobel prize-winner, Pablo Neruda, who took his pen name from the lesser-known Czech. Historically, this is Prague's **artists' quarter**, and although few of the present inhabitants are names to conjure with, the various private galleries and craft shops that have sprouted up over the last few years continue the tradition.

The houses that line the steep climb up to the Hrad are typically restrained, many retaining their medieval barn doors, and most adorned with their own peculiar house signs (see box below). A short way up the hill, you'll pass two of the street's fancier buildings: at no. 5 is the **Morzinský palác**, now the Romanian Embassy, its doorway designed by Giovanni Santini and supported by two Moors (a pun on the owner's name) sculpted by Brokof; diagonally opposite, at no. 20, two giant eagles by Braun hold up the portal of the **Thun-Hohenštejnský palác**, now the Italian Embassy (also by Santini). Further up the street, according to Prague legend, Casanova and Mozart are thought to have met up at a ball given by the aristocrat owners of no. 33, the Bretfeldský palác, in 1791, while the latter was in town for the première of *La Clemenza di Tito* (see box on p.74). On the opposite side of the street, at no. 32, the former Dittrich pharmacy, dating from 1821, has been restored

---

House Signs

As well as preserving their Gothic or Romanesque foundations, many houses throughout Prague retain their ancient **house signs**, which you'll see carved into the gables, on hanging wooden signs, or inscribed on the facade. The system originated in medieval times, and still survives today, though it's now used predominantly by *pivnice* (pubs), restaurants and *vinárny* (wine bars).

Some signs were deliberately chosen to draw custom to the business of the house, like *U zeleného hroznu* (The Green Bunch of Grapes), a wine shop in the Malá Strana; others, like *U železných dveří* (The Iron Door), simply referred to some distinguishing feature of the house, often long since disappeared. The pervasive use of *zlatý* (gold) in the house names derives from the city's popular epithet, *Zlatá Praha* (Golden Prague), referring either to the halcyon days of Charles IV, when the new Gothic copper roofing shone like gold, or the period of alchemy under Rudolf II, depending on your viewpoint. Religious names, like *U černé Matky boží* (The Black Madonna), were popular, too, especially during the Counter-Reformation.

In the 1770s, the Habsburgs, in their rationalizing fashion, introduced a numerical system, with each house in the city entered onto a register according to a strict chronology; later, the conventional system of progressive street numbering was introduced. So don't be surprised if seventeenth-century pubs like *U medvídků* (The Little Bears) have, in addition to a house sign, two numbers: in this case 7 and 345; the former, Habsburg number, written on a red background, the latter, modern number, on blue.

---

to its former glory and now houses a small and mildly diverting Expozice historických lékáren, whose prize exhibits are its leech bottles and a large dried fruit fish.

Halfway up the hill, Nerudova halts at a crossroads where it meets the cobbled hairpin of Ke Hradu, which the royal coronation procession used to ascend; continuing west along Úvoz (The Cutting) takes you to the Strahovský klášter (see p.69). On the south side of Úvoz, the houses come to an end, and a view opens up over the picturesque jumble of Malá Strana's red-tiled roofs, while to the north, narrow stairways squeeze between the towering buildings of Hradčany, emerging on the path to the Loreta.

Tržiště and Vlašská

Running (very) roughly parallel to Nerudova – and linked to it by several side streets and steps – is Tržiště, which sets off from the south side of Malostranské náměstí. Halfway up on the left is the Schönbornský palác, now the US Embassy. The entrance, and the renowned gardens, are nowadays watched over by closed-circuit TV and machine-gun-toting GIs – a far cry from the dilapidated palace in which Kafka rented an apartment in March 1917, and where he suffered his first bout of tuberculosis.

As Tržiště swings to the right, bear left up Vlašská, home to yet another Lobkovický palác, now the German Embassy. In the summer of 1989, several thousand East Germans climbed over the garden wall and entered the embassy compound to demand West German citizenship, which had been every German's right since partition. The neighbouring streets were soon jam-packed with abandoned Trabants, as the beautiful palace gardens became a muddy home to the refugees. Finally, the Czechoslovak government gave in and organized special trains to take the East Germans over the federal border, cheered on their way by thousands of Praguers, and thus prompted the exodus that eventually brought about *Die Wende*.

The palace itself is a particularly refined building, best viewed from the rear – you'll have to approach it from Petřín (see p.83). The gardens, laid out in the early nineteenth century by Václav Skalník (who went on to landscape the spa at Mariánské Lázně), are no longer open to the public but you should be able to see David Černý's sculpture, *Quo Vadis?*, a gold Trabant on legs, erected in memory of the fleeing East Germans.

Valdštejnské náměstí and around

To the north of Malostranské náměstí, up Tomášská, lies the Valdštejnský palác, which takes up the whole of the eastern side of Valdštejnské náměstí and Valdštejnská. As early as 1621, Albrecht von Waldstein started to build a palace which would reflect his status

Valdštejnské náměstí and around

Waldstein

Albrecht von Waldstein (known to the Czechs as Albrecht z Valdštejna, and to the English as Wallenstein – the name given to him by the German playwright Schiller in his tragic trilogy) was the most notorious warlord of the Thirty Years' War. If the imperial astrologer Johannes Kepler is to be believed, this is all because he was born at four in the afternoon on September 14, 1583. According to Kepler's horoscope Waldstein was destined to be greedy, deceitful, unloved and unloving. Sure enough at an early age he tried to kill a servant, for which he was expelled from his Lutheran school. Recuperating in Italy, he converted to Catholicism (an astute career move) and married a wealthy widow who conveniently died shortly after the marriage. Waldstein used his new fortune to cultivate a friendship with Prince Ferdinand, heir to the Habsburg Empire, who in turn thought that a tame Bohemian noble could come in handy.

Within five years of the Battle of Bílá hora in 1620 (see p.173), Waldstein owned a quarter of Bohemia, either by compulsory purchase or in return for money or troops loaned to Ferdinand. It was a good time to go into property: Ferdinand's imperial armies, who were busy restoring Catholicism throughout Europe, provided a ready-made market for agricultural produce. And as a rising general, Waldstein could get away with a certain amount of insider trading, marching armies with as many as 125,000 men over enemy territory or land owned by rivals, laying fields waste and then selling his troops supplies from his own pristine Bohemian estates.

As Waldstein ranged further afield in Germany, conquering Jutland, Pomerania, Alsace and most of Brandenburg on Ferdinand's behalf, his demands for reward grew ever more outrageous. Already Duke of Friedland and Governor of Prague, Waldstein was appointed Duke of Mecklenburg in 1628. This upset not only the existing duke, who had backed Ferdinand's opponents, but even the Emperor's loyalist supporters. If Ferdinand thought fit to hand one of the greatest German titles to this Czech upstart, what family's inheritance could be secure? By 1630, Waldstein had earned himself the right to keep his hat on in the imperial presence as well as the dubious honour of handing the Emperor a napkin after he had used his fingerbowl. However, at this point Waldstein's services became too expensive for Ferdinand, so the duke was relieved of his command.

The following year, the Saxons occupied Prague, and the Emperor was forced to reinstate Waldstein. Ferdinand couldn't afford to do without the supplies from Waldstein's estates, but knew he was mortgaging large chunks of the Empire to pay for his services. More alarmingly, there were persistent rumours that Waldstein was about to declare himself King of Bohemia and defect to the French enemy. In 1634, Waldstein openly rebelled against Ferdinand, who immediately hatched a plot to murder Waldstein, sending a motley posse including English, Irish and Scottish mercenaries to the border town of Cheb (Eger), where they cut the general down in his nightshirt as he tried to rise from his sickbed. Some see him as the first man to unify Germany since Charlemagne, others see him as a wily Czech hero. In reality he was probably just another ambitious, violent man, as his stars had predicted.

as commander of the Imperial Catholic armies of the Thirty Years' War. By buying, confiscating, and then destroying 26 houses, three gardens and a brick factory, he succeeded in ripping apart a densely populated area of Malá Strana to make way for one of the first, largest and, quite frankly, most unappealing Baroque palaces in the city – at least from the outside.

The Czech upper house, or Senát, now uses the palace and only the former stables, housing the **Pedagogické muzeum**, are accessible to the public. This is a small and none too exciting exhibition on Czech education and, in particular, the influential teachings of Jan Amos Komenský (1592–1670) – often anglicized to John Comenius – who was forced to leave his homeland after the victory of Waldstein's Catholic armies, eventually settling in Protestant England. To get to the exhibition, go through the main gateway and continue straight across the first courtyard; the museum is on your right. The only way to get to see the palace's magnificent main hall – used in the filming of *Amadeus* – is to go to one of the concerts occasionally held there.

If you've no interest in pedagogical matters, the palace's formal gardens, the **Valdštejnská zahrada** – accessible only from a doorway in the palace walls along Letenská – are a good place to take a breather from the city streets. The focus of the gardens is the gigantic Italianate *sala terrena*, a monumental loggia decorated with frescoes of the Trojan Wars, which stands at the end of an avenue of sculptures by Adriaen de Vries. The originals, which were intended to form a fountain, were taken off as booty by the Swedes in 1648 and now adorn the royal gardens in Drottningholm. In addition, there's a café, a pseudo grotto along the south wall, with quasi-stalactites and a door which once led to Waldstein's observatory, and a small aviary, home to the gardens' peacock population.

On the opposite side of the gardens, the palace's former riding school, **Valdštejnská jízdárna**, has been converted into a gallery, which puts on temporary exhibitions of fine art and photography organized by the National Gallery. The riding school is accessible only from the courtyard of the nearby Malostranská metro station.

Letenská and sv Tomáš

Walking southwest along **Letenská** from the gardens back towards Malostranské náměstí, takes you past **U svatého Tomáše**, the oldest *pivnice* in Prague, established in 1352 by Augustinian monks who brewed their own lethal dark beer on the premises. Unfortunately, the Communists succeeded in kicking out the monks and closing down the brewery – the surviving pub is now shamelessly touristy and overpriced. Better preserved are the neighbouring cloisters and priory church of **sv Tomáš** (St Thomas), which bear few traces of their Gothic origins since Kilian Ignaz Dientzenhofer's rebuilding in the 1720s. The rich burghers of Malá Strana spared no expense, buy-

Valdštejnské náměstí and around

The Pedagogické muzeum is open Tues–Sun 10am–12.30pm & 1–5pm.

The Valdštejnská zahrada is open May–Sept daily 9am–7pm.

The Valdštejnská jízdárna is open Tues–Sun 10am–6pm.

ing a couple of Rubens for the altarpiece and two dead saints (St Just and St Boniface) to give the church extra kudos. The Rubens now hang in the National Gallery, but the saints' fully dressed skeletons survive, as do Václav Vavřinec Reiner's frescoes and Dientzenhofer's glorious dome.

Malá Strana's terraced gardens

One of the chief joys of Malá Strana is its **terraced gardens**, hidden away behind the Baroque palaces on Valdštejnská, on the slopes below the castle, where the royal vineyards used to be, and commanding superb views over Prague. After lengthy restoration, all the gardens, except the Polish Embassy's Fürstenberská zahrada, are once more open to the public. In fact, now you can climb all the way up through the gardens to the Zahrada na valech beneath the Hrad itself.

The best loved of the three adjoining gardens is the **Kolovratská** or **Černínská zahrada**, which makes the most of its cramped site with a jumble of balustrades and terraces which culminate in a small *sala terrena* by Giovanni Alliprandi, as does the **Ledeburská zahrada** to the west. The largest of the gardens is the central **Pálffyovská zahrada**, made up of two older plots, joined together and renovated in Rococo style in 1751.

Another option is to seek out the **Vojanovy sady**, securely concealed behind a ring of high walls off U lužického semináře. Originally a monastic garden belonging to the Carmelites, it's now an informal public park, with sleeping babies, weeping willows, and lots of grass on which to lounge about; outdoor art exhibitions and occasional concerts also take place here. One final Malá Strana Baroque garden worth exploring is the Vrtbovská zahrada, off Karmelitská (see below).

Southern Malá Strana

Karmelitská is the busy cobbled street that runs south from Malostranské náměstí along the base of Petřín towards the industrial suburb of Smíchov, becoming Újezd at roughly its halfway point. Between here and the River Vltava are some of Malá Strana's most picturesque and secluded streets. Although there are no major sights around here, the island of **Kampa**, in particular, makes up one of the most peaceful stretches of riverfront in Prague.

Maltézské náměstí and around

From the trams and traffic fumes of Karmelitská, it's a relief to cut across to the calm restraint of **Maltézské náměstí**, one of a number of delightful little squares between here and the river. It takes its name from the Order of the Knights of St John of Jerusalem (better known by their later title, the Maltese Knights), who in 1160 founded the nearby church of **Panna Maria pod řetězem** (Saint Mary below-the-chain), so called because it was the Knights' job to guard the Judith Bridge. The original Romanesque church was pulled down by the Knights themselves in the fourteenth century, but only the chancel and towers were successfully rebuilt by the time of the Hussite Wars. The two severe Gothic towers are still standing and the apse is now thoroughly Baroque, but the nave remains unfinished, an open, grassy, ivy-strewn space inhabited only by a fig tree and its companion.

The Knights have recently returned to reclaim (and restore) the church and the adjacent Grand Priory, which backs onto **Velkopřevorské náměstí**, another pretty little square to the south, which echoes to the sound of music from the nearby Prague conservatoire. Following the violent death of John Lennon in 1980, Prague's youth established an ad hoc shrine smothered in graffiti tributes to the ex-Beatle along the Grand Priory's garden wall. The running battle between police and graffiti artists continued well into the Nineties, with the Maltese Knights taking an equally dim view of the mural. On the opposite side of the square from the wall, sitting pretty in pink behind a row of chestnut trees, is the Rococo **Buquoyský palác**, built for a French family and appropriately enough now the French Embassy.

Kampa

The two or three streets that make up **Kampa**, the largest of the Vltava's islands, contain no notable palaces or museums; just a couple of old mills, an exquisite main square, and a serene riverside park – in other words, plenty enough diversion for a lazy summer afternoon. The island is separated from the left bank by Prague's "Little Venice", a thin strip of water called **Čertovka** (Devil's Stream), which used to power several mill-wheels until the last one ceased to function in 1936. In contrast to the rest of the left bank, the fire of 1541 had a positive effect on Kampa, since the flotsam from the blaze effectively stabilized the island's shifting shoreline. Nevertheless, Kampa was still subject to frequent flooding right up until the Vltava was dammed in the 1950s.

For much of its history, the island was the city's main wash house, a fact commemorated by the church of sv Jan Křtitel Na Prádle (St John-the-Baptist at the Cleaners) on Říční, near the southernmost tip of the island. It wasn't until the sixteenth and seventeenth centuries that the Nostitz family, who owned Kampa, began to develop the northern half of the island; the southern half was left untouched, and today is laid out as a public park, with riverside views across to Staré Město. To the north, the oval main square, **Na Kampě**, once a pottery market, is studded with slender acacia trees and cut through by the Charles Bridge, to which it is connected by a double flight of steps.

Karmelitská and Újezd

On the corner of Karmelitská and Tržiště, at no. 25, is the entrance to one of the most elusive of Malá Strana's many Baroque gardens, the **Vrtbovská zahrada**, founded on the site of the former vineyards of the **Vrtbovský palác**. Laid out on Tuscan-style terraces, dotted with ornamental urns and statues of the gods by Matthias Bernhard Braun, the gardens twist their way up the lower slopes of Petřín Hill to an observation terrace, from where there's a spectacular rooftop perspective on the city. After being closed for fifteen years, these gardens, like those off Valdštejnská, finally re-opened to the public in 1997.

Further down, on the same side of the street, is the rather plain church of **Panna Maria Vítězná**, which was begun in early Baroque style by German Lutherans in 1611, and later handed over to the Carmelites after the Battle of Bílá hora. The main reason for coming here is to see the *pražské Jezulátko* or *Bambino di Praga*, a high-kitsch wax effigy of the infant Jesus as a precocious three-year old, enthroned in a glass case illuminated with strip-lights, donated by one of the Lobkowicz family's Spanish brides in 1628. Attributed with miraculous powers, the *pražské Jezulátko* became an object of international pilgrimage equal in stature to the Santa Casa in Loreta, similarly inspiring a whole series of replicas. It continues to attract visitors (as the multilingual prayer cards attest) and boasts a vast personal wardrobe of expensive swaddling clothes – 72 separate outfits at the last count – regularly changed by the Carmelite nuns.

A block or so further south, Karmelitská becomes Újezd, on the east side of which is the Michnův palác, at no. 40, built on the site of another former nunnery, this time Dominican. The facade and gateway still incorporates elements of the Renaissance summer palace built by the Kinský family around 1580. From 1787 the building was used as an armoury and fell into disrepair until the Czech nationalist sports movement *Sokol* bought it in 1921. Nowadays, it is home to the university's sports faculty and the **Tyršovo muzeum**, which focuses on the history of Czech sport. **Sport** played an important part in the Czech national revival (*národní obrození*) through *Sokol*, the extremely popular nationalist organization set up in 1862, in direct response to the German *Turnverband* physical education movement. The Communists outlawed *Sokol* (as the Nazis had also done) and, in its place, established a tradition of *Spartakiáda*, extravaganzas of synchronized gymnastics held every five years in the Strahov stadium, behind Petřín. Even the *Spartakiáda* were popular, but, indelibly tainted by their political past, the last one, due to have been held in 1990, was cancelled. The museum, named after one of *Sokol*'s founders, Miroslav Tyrš, fails to mention the *Spartakiáda*, and instead traces the history of *Sokol*, which has since re-formed, and focuses on the postwar Olympic successes of the likes of the Czech long-distance runner (and Party stooge), Emil Zátopek.

The Tyršovo muzeum is open Tues–Sat 9am–5pm, Sun 10am–5pm.

Petřín

The scaled-down version of the Eiffel Tower is the most obvious landmark on the wooded hill of **Petřín**, the largest green space in the city centre. The tower is just one of the exhibits built for the 1891 Prague Exhibition, whose modest legacy includes the **funicular railway** (lanová dráha) which climbs up from a station just off Újezd. The original funicular was powered by a simple but ingenious system whereby two carriages, one at either end of the steep track, were fitted with large watertanks that were alternately filled at the top and emptied at the bottom; it was replaced in the 1960s by the current electric system. As the carriages pass each other at the halfway station of Nebozízek, you can get out and soak in the view from the restaurant of the same name.

The funicular runs every 10–15 minutes, 9.15am–8.45pm – tickets are the same as for the rest of the public transport system and travel passes are valid.

Along the Hunger Wall

At the top of the hill, it's possible to trace the southernmost perimeter wall of the old city – popularly known as the **Hladová zeď** (Hunger Wall) – as it creeps eastwards back down to Újezd, and northwestwards to the Strahovský klášter. Instigated in the 1460s by Charles IV, it was much lauded at the time (and later by the Communists) as a great public work which provided employment for the burgeoning ranks of the city's destitute (hence its name); in fact, much of the wall's construction was paid for by the expropriation of Jewish property.

Follow the wall southeast and you come to the aromatic **Růžový sad** (Rose Garden), whose colour-co-ordinated rose beds are laid out in front of Petřín's observatory, the **Štefánikova hvězdárna**, which offers a range of telescopes for use by the city's amateur astronomers. A little further down the hill, on the other side of the wall from the observatory, stands a bust of the leading Czech Romantic poet **Karel Hynek Mácha**, who penned the poem *Máj* (May), on the subject of unrequited love. In spring, and in particular on the first of May, the statue remains a popular place of pilgrimage for courting couples.

The observatory is open Tues–Fri 2–6pm & 8–10pm, Sat & Sun 10am–noon, 2–6pm & 8–10pm; shorter hours in winter.

Another curiosity, hidden in the trees on the southern side of the Hladová zeď, is a **wooden church** that was brought here, log by log, from an Orthodox village in Carpatho-Ruthenia (now part of Ukraine) in 1929. Churches like this are still common in eastern Slovakia, and this is a particularly ornate example from the eighteenth century, with multiple domes like piles of giant acorns.

Back at the Růžový sad, follow the wall northwest and you'll come to Palliardi's twin-towered church of **sv Vavřinec** (St Lawrence), from which derives the German name for Petřín – Laurenziberg. Dotted along the path that leads to Strahov are the Stations of the Cross, culminating in the sgraffitoed Calvary Chapel, just beyond the church. Opposite the church are a series of buildings from the 1891

Petřín

The Rozhledna is open April–Oct daily 9.30am–7pm; Nov–March Sat & Sun 9.30am–7pm.

The Mirror Maze is open daily: April–Oct 10am–7pm; Nov–March 10am–4pm.

Exhibition, starting with the diminutive **Rozhledna**, an octagonal interpretation – though a mere fifth of the size – of the Eiffel Tower which shocked Paris in 1889, and a tribute to the city's strong cultural and political links with Paris at the time; naturally, the view from the public gallery is terrific in fine weather.

The next building along is the **Bludiště**, a mini neo-Gothic castle complete with mock drawbridge. The first section of the interior features a **mirror maze**, a stroke of infantile genius by the exhibition organizers. This is followed by an action-packed, life-sized diorama of the Prague students' and Jews' victory over the Swedes on the Charles Bridge in 1648. The humour of the convex and concave mirrors that lie beyond the diorama is so simple, it has both adults and kids giggling away. From the tower and maze, the path with the Stations of the Cross will eventually lead you to the perimeter wall of the Strahovský klášter (see p.69), giving great views over Petřín's palatial orchards and the sea of red tiles below.

Chapter 3

Staré Město

S TARÉ MĚSTO, literally the "Old Town", is Prague's most central, vital ingredient. Most of the capital's busiest markets, shops, restaurants and pubs are in this area, and during the day a gaggle of shoppers and tourists fills its complex web of narrow streets. Yet despite all the commercial activity, there are still plenty of residential streets, giving the area a lived-in feel that is rarely found in European city centres. The district is bounded on one side by the river, on the other by the arc of Národní, Na příkopě and Revoluční, and at its heart is **Staroměstské náměstí**, Prague's showpiece main square, easily the most magnificent in central Europe.

Merchants and craftsmen began settling in what is now Staré Město as early as the tenth century, and in the mid-thirteenth century it was granted town status, with jurisdiction over its own affairs. The fire of 1541, which ripped through the quarters on the other side of the river, never reached Staré Město, though the 1689 conflagration made up for it. Nevertheless, the victorious Catholic nobles built fewer large palaces here than on the left bank, leaving the medieval street plan intact with the exception of the Klementinum (the Jesuits' powerhouse) and the Jewish Quarter, Josefov, which was largely reconstructed in the late nineteenth century (see p.110). Like so much of Prague, however, Staré Město is still, on the surface, overwhelmingly Baroque, built literally on top of its Gothic predecessor to guard against the floods which plagued the town.

From the Karlův most to Malé náměstí

In their explorations of Staré Město, most people unknowingly retrace the **králová cesta**, the traditional route of the coronation procession from the medieval gateway, the Prašná brána (see p.135), to the Hrad. Established by the Přemyslids, the route was followed, with a few minor variations, by every king until the Emperor Ferdinand IV in 1836, the last of the Habsburgs to both-

86

STARÉ MĚSTO

er having himself crowned in Prague. It's also the most direct route from the Charles Bridge to Prague's main square, Staroměstské náměstí, and therefore a natural choice. However, many of the real treasures of Staré Město lie away from the *králová cesta*, so if you want to escape the crowds, it's worth heading off into the quarter's silent, twisted matrix of streets, then simply following your nose – for details of specific sights to the south of Karlova, see p.94.

The Karlův most (Charles Bridge)

The **Karlův most**, or Charles Bridge – which for over four hundred years was the only link between the two halves of Prague – is by far the city's most familiar monument. It's an impressive piece of medieval engineering, aligned slightly askew between two mighty Gothic gateways, but its fame is due almost entirely to the magnificent Baroque statues, additions to the original structure, that punctuate its length. Individually, only a few of the works are outstanding, but taken collectively, set against the backdrop of the Hrad, the effect is breathtaking.

The bridge was begun in 1357 to replace an earlier structure which had been swept away by one of the Vltava's frequent floods in 1342. Charles IV commissioned his young German court architect, Peter Parler, to carry out the work, which was finally completed in the early fifteenth century. Given its strategic significance, it comes as no surprise that the bridge has played an important part in Prague's history: in 1648, it was the site of the last battle of the Thirty Years' War, fought between the besieging Swedes and an ad hoc army of Prague's students and Jews; in 1744, the invading Prussians were defeated at the same spot; and in 1848, it formed the front line between the revolutionaries on the Staré Město side, and the reactionary forces on the left bank. For the first four hundred years it was known simply as the Prague or Stone Bridge – only in 1870 was it officially named after its patron. Since 1950, the bridge has been closed to vehicles, and is now one of the most popular places to hang out, day and night; apart from the steady stream of sightseers, the niches created by the bridge-piers are keenly fought over by souvenir hawkers and buskers.

Building the bridge

There are countless legends regarding the bridge's initial construction: the most persistent is that the builders mixed eggs (and, in some versions, wine) with the mortar to strengthen it. Having quickly depleted the city's egg supply, orders were sent out for contributions from the surrounding villages: the villagers of Velvary, who were worried that raw eggs wouldn't have quite the right consistency, hard-boiled theirs, and from Unhošt curd, cheese and whey were sent to bond the bricks even harder.

A bronze crucifix has stood on the bridge since its construction, but the first sculpture wasn't added until 1683, when St John of Nepomuk appeared. His statue was such a propaganda success with the Catholic church authorities that another 21 were added between 1706 and 1714. These included works by Prague's leading Baroque sculptors, led by Matthias Bernhard Braun and Ferdinand Maximilian Brokof; the Max brothers unimaginatively filled in the remaining piers in the mid-nineteenth century. The original sculptures, mostly crafted in sandstone, have weathered badly over the years and are gradually being replaced by copies.

From the
Karlův most
to Malé
náměstí

The Malá Strana bridge towers
The following account of the statuary starts from the Malá Strana side, where two unequal **bridge towers**, connected by a castellated arch, form the entrance to the bridge. The smaller, stumpy tower was once part of the original Judith Bridge (named after the wife of Vladislav I, who built the twelfth-century original); the taller of the two, crowned by one of the pinnacled wedge-spires more commonly associated with Prague's right bank, contains an exhibition relaying the history of the towers, the bridge itself, and the story of St John of Nepomuk (see p.55). You can also walk out onto the balcony that connects the two towers for a bird's-eye view of the seething masses pouring across the bridge.

The bridge
tower is open
daily
April–Oct
9am–5.30pm.

The statues
In the first statue group on the north side, paid for by the university medical faculty, Jesus is flanked by **Saint Cosmas and Saint Damian** (**1**), both dressed in medieval doctors' garb – they were renowned for offering their medical services free of charge to the poor. Opposite stands **Saint Wenceslas** (**2**), added by Czech nationalists in the nineteenth century. On the next pier, Brokof's **Saint Vitus** (**3**) is depicted as a Roman legionary, his foot being gently nibbled by one of the lions that went on to devour him in a Roman amphitheatre. Facing him is one of the most striking sculptural groups, the founders of the **Trinitarian Order** (**4**), again by Brokof: Saints John of Matha, Felix of Valois and his pet stag (plus, for some unknown reason, Saint Ivan), whose good works included ransoming persecuted Christians – three petrified souls can be seen through the prison bars below – from the infidels, represented by a bored Turkish jailor and his rabid dog.

Amid all the blackened sandstone, the lightly coloured figure of the (at the time) only recently canonized Servite friar, **Saint Philip Benizi** (**5**), stands out as the only marble statue on the bridge. At his feet sits the papal crown, which he refused to accept when it was offered to him in 1268. Opposite stands Prague's second bishop, the youthful **Saint Adalbert** (**6**), who was hounded out of the city on more than one occasion by the blissfully pagan citizens of Prague. Another (at the time) recently canonized saint is **Cajetan** (**7**), founder of the Theatine Order (and of a whole chain of non-profit-making pawnshops in Naples), who stands in front of a column of cherubs sporting a sacred heart.

One of the most successful statues is that of the blind Cistercian nun, **Saint Lutgard (8)**, sculpted by Braun when he was just 26 years old. She is depicted here in the middle of her celebrated vision, in which Christ appeared so that she could kiss his wounds. The Augustinians sponsored the next duo, on the other side of the steps leading down to Kampa Island: **Saint Augustine (9)**, and one of his later followers, **Saint Nicholas of Tolentino (10)**, who is depicted dishing out bread to the poor. On the top-floor balcony of the house immediately behind Saint Nicholas of Tolentino is a strange collection of objects – a Madonna, a mangle and a lantern. The story goes that the Madonna was retrieved from the river during a particularly bad flood, and saved the house from further inundation. She then went on to save a washerwoman whose sleeves got caught in the mangle; as for the lantern, if it goes out while you're passing by, it means you'll die within the year.

Next pier along, the apostle **Saint Jude Thaddaeus (11)**, patron saint of those in dire straits, holds the club with which the pagans beat him to death. On the opposite side, the Dominican friar **Saint Vincent Ferrer (12)** stands over one of his converts to self-flagellation, while the inscription below lists his miraculous achievements, including the conversion of 2500 Jews, some forty resurrections and the exorcism of seventy demons. He is joined on his pedestal, somewhat inexplicably, by Bohemia's best-loved hermit, **Saint Procopius**. If you look over the side of the bridge at this point, you'll see a nineteenth-century sculpture of **Roland (13)** – known as *Bruncvík* in Czech – brandishing his miraculous golden sword (the real thing is said to be embedded in the bridge, to be used in case of municipal emergency). The original, erected to protect the rights of the Staré Město over the full extent of the bridge, was destroyed in 1648.

The Franciscan pier – **Saint Anthony of Padua (14)**, and a lifeless nineteenth-century figure of **Saint Francis of Assisi**, accompanied by two angels (15) – is worth passing over to reach the bridge's earliest and most popular sculpture, **Saint John of Nepomuk (16)**. The only bronze statue on the bridge, it's now green with age, the gold-leaf halo of stars and palm branch gently blowing in the breeze. Saint John's appearance in 1683, on the bridge from which he was thrown to his death, was part of the Jesuits' persistent campaign to have him canonized; the statue later inspired hundreds of copies, which adorn bridges throughout central Europe. On the base, there's a bronze relief depicting his martyrdom, the figure of John now extremely worn through years of being touched for good luck. Facing Saint John is Bohemia's first martyr, a rather androgenous version of **Saint Ludmila (17)**, holding the veil with which she was strangled and standing alongside her grandson, Saint Wenceslas,

For the story of Saint John of Nepomuk's martyrdom, see p.55.

here depicted as a young child; his future martyrdom is recounted in the base relief (for more on Wenceslas and co, see p.55).

With the exception of the Jesuit general **Saint Francis Borgia (19)**, the next two piers are glum nineteenth-century space-fillers: a trio of Bohemian saints – **Norbert, Sigismund** and, for the third time, **Wenceslas (18)** – followed by **John the Baptist (20)** and **Saint Christopher (21)**. Between the piers (18 & 20), on the north side, a small bronze cross is set into the wall marking the spot where John of Nepomuk was dumped in the river (see above); touch it and, according to the locals, you're guaranteed to return to the city. In 1890, the two Jesuit statues on the next pier were swept away by a flood: the statue of the founder of the order, Saint Ignatius Loyola, was replaced with the most recent additions to the bridge (completed in 1938), **saints Cyril and Methodius (22)**, the ninth-century missionaries who first introduced Christianity to the Slavs; the other, the Jesuit missionary **Saint Francis Xavier (23)**, survived the order's unpopularity and was replaced by a copy. This is one of the more unusual sculptural groups on the bridge: the saint, who worked in India and the Far East, is held aloft by three Moorish and two "Oriental" converts; Brokof placed himself on the saint's left side.

Next in line are Jesus, Mary, and Mary's mother, **Saint Anne (24)** and, facing them, with a slightly older Jesus at his feet, **Joseph (25)**, a nineteenth-century replacement for another Brokof, this time destroyed by gunfire during the 1848 revolution. The **Crucifixion** scene **(26)** is where the original fourteenth-century crucifix stood alone on the bridge for two hundred years. The gold-leaf, Hebrew inscription, "Holy, Holy, Holy" was added in 1696, paid for by a Prague Jew who was ordered to do so by the city court, having been found guilty of blasphemy before the cross. Apart from Christ himself, all the figures, and the **Pietà** opposite **(27)**, were added by the Max brothers.

On the penultimate pier, the Dominicans placed their founder, **Saint Dominic**, and their other leading light, **Saint Thomas Aquinas**, beside the **Madonna (28)**; in amongst the cherubs is the order's emblem, a dog with a burning torch in his mouth. Opposite, **Saint Barbara**, the patron saint of miners, whose beautifully sculpted hands so impressed Kafka, is accompanied by **Saint Margaret** and **Saint Elizabeth (29)**. There's one final Madonna **(30)**, this time presiding over the kneeling figure of Saint Bernard, and a bubbling mass of cherubs mucking about with the instruments of the Passion – the cock, the dice and the centurion's gauntlet. Lastly, **Saint Ivo (31)**, patron saint of lawyers, flanked by Justice and a prospective client, stands with an outstretched hand, into which Prague law students traditionally place a glass of beer after their finals.

Charles IV (1346–78)

There may be more legends and intrigue associated with the reign of Rudolf II (see p.61), but it was under **Emperor Charles IV** (Karel IV to the Czechs) that Prague enjoyed its true golden age. In just over thirty years, Charles transformed Prague into the effective capital of the Holy Roman Empire, establishing the city's archbishopric, its university, a host of monasteries and churches, an entire new town (Nové Město), plus several monuments which survive to this day, most notably St Vitus Cathedral, and, of course, the Charles Bridge (**Karlův most**).

Born in 1316 (and christened Václav), Charles was the only son of King John of Luxembourg and Queen Eliška, daughter of Přemysl King Václav II. Suspecting his wife of plotting to dethrone him, King John imprisoned her and Charles, keeping his three-year-old son in a dungeon with only "a little light coming in from a hole in the ceiling". In 1323, the young Charles was despatched to the fashionable French court to keep him out of any further trouble and complete his education – he never saw his mother again. In France he was given the name Charles (after Charlemagne) by the French king and married off to Blanche de Valois, the first of his four wives.

In 1346, his father (by then totally blind) was killed at the Battle of Crécy, and Charles, who escaped with just a wound, inherited the Czech crown. He immediately busied himself with building up his Bohemian power base, and within two years had got himself elected Holy Roman Emperor. Fluent in Czech, French, German, Latin and Italian, Charles used his international contacts to gather together a whole host of foreign artists to his new capital, most famously persuading the Italian man of letters, Petrarch, to pay a visit.

Though later chroniclers tried to paint Charles as chaste and pure, even he admitted in his autobiography that he had strayed in his youth; "seduced by the perverted people, we were perverted by the perverts", he wrote of his Italian sojourn. And just as Rudolf II created his *Kunst- und Wunderkammer*, Charles also spent much of his spare time amassing a bizarre collection of relics to ensure a smooth passage into the after-life. He cajoled and blackmailed his way into obtaining part of the whip used in the Passion, two thorns from Christ's crown, a few drops of milk from the Virgin Mary and one of Mary Magdalene's breasts, all beautifully encased in reliquaries designed by Prague's finest goldsmiths.

The Staré Město bridge tower

From the Karlův most to Malé náměstí

On the Staré Město side is arguably the finest **bridge tower** of the lot: the western facade was trashed in the battle of 1648 but the eastern facade is still encrusted in Gothic cake-like decorations from Peter Parler's workshop, plus a series of mini-sculptures. The central figures are Saint Vitus, flanked by Charles IV on the right and his son, Václav IV, on the left; above stand two of Bohemia's patron saints, Adalbert and Sigismund. The severed heads of twelve of the Protestant leaders were suspended from the tower in iron baskets following their execution on Staroměstské náměstí in 1621, and all but one remained there until the Saxons passed through the capital ten years later. The tower now contains a small display of antique musical instruments, and allows you access onto the roof for another aerial perspective on the bridge.

The bridge tower is open daily April–Oct 9am–5.30pm.

Křižovnické náměstí to Malé náměstí

Pass under the Staré Město bridge tower and you're in **Křižovnické náměstí**, an awkward space hemmed in by its constituent buildings, and – with traffic hurtling across the square – a dangerous spot for unwary pedestrians. Hard by the bridge tower is a nineteenth-century cast-iron statue of **Charles IV (32)**, erected on the 500th anniversary of his founding of the university, and designed by a German, Ernst Julius Hähnel, in the days before the reawakening of Czech sculpture. To his left is an unusual plaque commemorating a Czech who was shot by mistake by the Red Army during the liberation on May 9, 1945.

The two churches facing onto the square are both quite striking and definitely worth exploring. The half-brick church of **sv František z Assisi** (St Francis of Assisi) was built in the 1680s to a design by Jean-Baptiste Mathey for the Order of Knights of the Cross with a Red Star, the original gatekeepers of the old Judith Bridge. The order was founded by Saint Anežka in the thirteenth century, and reached the zenith of its power in the seventeenth century, during which its monks supplied most of the archbishops of Prague. The design of the church's interior, dominated by its huge dome, decorated with a fresco of *The Last Judgement* by Václav Vavřinec Reiner, and rich marble furnishings, served as a blueprint for numerous subsequent Baroque churches in Prague. The **Galerie Křižovníků** (Tues–Sun 10am–5pm), next door, houses the church's treasury, a stunning collection of gold monstrances, reliquaries and chalices dating from the sixteenth to the early nineteenth century.

Over the road is the church of **sv Salvátor**, its facade prickling with saintly statues which are lit up enticingly at night. Founded in 1593, but not completed until 1714, sv Salvátor marks the beginning of the Jesuits' rise to power and, like many of their churches, its design copies that of the Gesù church in Rome. It's worth a quick look, if only for the frothy stucco plasterwork and delicate ironwork in its triple-naved interior.

Along Karlova

Running from Křižovnické náměstí all the way to Malé náměstí is the
narrow street of **Karlova**, packed with people winding their way
towards Staroměstské náměstí, their attention divided between
checking out the souvenir shops, and not losing their way. While
much of what's on offer in Karlova is eminently missable, there is one
sight worth seeking out, and that's the **Muzeum loutek** (Puppet
Museum), in the cool Gothic cellars of Karlova 12. Despite the
appalling lack of information in either Czech or English, the museum,
run by the international puppetry organization UNIMA, which has its
headquarters here, has an impressive display of historic Czech puppets, both string and rod, mostly dating from the late nineteenth and
the early twentieth centuries. Some of the most appealing figures are
the wonderfully malevolent devils, and there's a great miniature theatre from 1933, complete with backcloth scenery changes.

*The Muzeum
loutek is open
daily
9am–8pm in
summer, and
Sat & Sun only
in winter.*

At the first wiggle in Karlova, you come to the **Vlašská kaple**
(Italian Chapel), which served the community of Italian masons,
sculptors and painters who settled in Prague during the Renaissance
period, and is still, strictly speaking, the property of the Italian state.
The present Vlašská kaple is a tiny oval Baroque chapel completed in
1600, though sadly it's rarely open except for services.

You may have more luck with the adjacent church of **sv Kliment**,
accessible from the same portal. It's a minor gem of Prague Baroque
by Dientzenhofer with statues by Braun, a spectacular set of frescoes
depicting the life of Saint Clement (whose fate was to be lashed to an
anchor and hurled into the Black Sea), and an unusual modern
screen added by its new owners, the Greek-Catholic church, who
observe Orthodox rites but, confusingly, belong to the Roman
Catholic church.

On the opposite side of Karlova, at the junction with Liliová, is U
zlatého hada (The Golden Serpent), where the Armenian Deomatus
Damajan opened the city's first coffee house in 1708. According to
legend, the café was always full, not least because Damajan had a
red-wine fountain inside. It is now a Chinese restaurant, though sadly
minus the fountain and its original furnishings.

The Klementinum

As they stroll down Karlova, few people notice the **Klementinum**, the
former Jesuit College on the north side of the street, which covers an
area second in size only to the Hrad. In 1556, Ferdinand I summoned
the Jesuits to Prague to help bolster the Catholic cause in Bohemia,
giving them the church of sv Kliment (see above), which
Dientzenhofer later rebuilt for them. Initially, the Jesuits proceeded
with caution, but once the Counter-Reformation set in, they were put
in control of the entire university and provincial education system.
From their secure base at sv Kliment, they began to establish space
for a great Catholic seat of learning in the city by buying up the sur-

rounding land, demolishing more than thirty old town houses, and, over the next two hundred years, gradually building themselves a palatial headquarters. In 1773, soon after the Klementinum was completed, the Jesuits were turfed out of the country and the building handed over to the university authorities.

Nowadays the Klementinum houses the National Library's collection of over five million volumes, but much of the original building has been left intact. The **entrance**, inconspicuously placed just past the church of sv Kliment, lets you into a series of rather plain courtyards. The entrance to the **Zrcadlová kaple** (Mirrored Chapel) is immediately to the left after passing through the archway on the far side of the first courtyard; its interior of fake marble, gilded stucco and mirror panels boasts fine acoustics and is regularly used for concerts.

The Zrcadlová kaple is open only for concerts and special exhibitions.

The Klementinum hides several other attractions inside, but the authorities are none too keen to let the public inside. The most spectacular sight – not officially open to the public – is the **Hudební oddělení** (Music Library) on the first floor to the west of the chapel, a stunning Rococo reading room filled with leather tomes, ancient globes and frescoes. In the same wing there are temporary exhibitions (Mon–Fri 9am–9pm) of some of the library's prize possessions, which include the world's largest collection of works by the early English reformer, Yorkshireman John Wycliffe, whose writings had an enormous impact on the fourteenth-century Czech religious community, inspiring preachers like Hus to speak out against the social conditions of the time.

At roughly the centre of the Klementinum complex is the Jesuits' **observatory tower** which is the only place in the world that has being monitoring and recording meteorological date since 1775. Too late, though, for Prague's most illustrious visiting scientist, Johannes Kepler, who did his planet-gazing in the Belvedér. A religious exile from his native Germany, Kepler succeeded Tycho Brahe as court astronomer to Rudolf II, and lived at no. 4 Karlova for a number of years, during which time he drew up the first heliocentric laws on the movement of the planets.

Mariánské náměstí and around

Where the Klementinum ends, the Renaissance corner house U **zlaté studné** (The Golden Well), now a wine bar and *pension* (see p.199), stands out like a wedge of cheese; its thick stucco reliefs of assorted saints were commissioned in 1701 by the owner in gratitude for having been spared the plague.

A short diversion here, down Seminářská, brings you out onto **Mariánské náměstí**, generally fairly deserted compared to Karlova. It's hard to believe that the rather severe **Nová radnice** (New Town Hall), on the east side of the square, was built by Osvald Polívka, architect of the exuberant Art-Nouveau Obecní dům (see p.135). Its

From the
Karlův most
to Malé
náměstí

*For the full
story of Rabbi
Löw, see p.115.*

most striking features are the two gargantuan figures which stand guard at either corner, by the sculptor of the Hus Monument, Ladislav Šaloun. The one on the left, looking like Darth Vader, is the "Iron Knight", mascot of the armourers' guild; to the right is the somewhat grotesquely caricatured sixteenth-century Jewish sage and scholar, Rabbi Löw, who was visited by Death on several occasions, but allowed to live to the ripe old age of 96, provided he did not stray from his religious studies – here, a naked woman tries unsuccessfully to attract his attentions.

To get back to Karlova, head down Husova, past the Baroque **Clam-Gallasův palác** (not open to the public), which, despite its size – it takes up a good five or six old houses – is easy to overlook in this narrow space. It's a typically lavish affair by the Viennese architect Fischer von Erlach, with big and burly *Atlantes* supporting the portals.

Malé náměstí

After a couple more shops, boutiques, hole-in-the-wall bars and a final twist in Karlova, you emerge onto **Malé náměstí**, a square originally settled by French merchants in the twelfth century. The square was also home to the first apothecary in Prague, opened by a Florentine in 1353, and the tradition is continued today by the pharmacy U **zlaté koruny** (The Golden Crown), at no. 13, which boasts chandeliers and a restored Baroque interior. The square's best-known building, though, is the russet-red, neo-Renaissance **Rott Haus**, originally an ironmongers' shop founded by V. J. Rott in 1840, whose facade is smothered in agricultural scenes and motifs inspired by the Czech artist Mikuláš Aleš. The building is currently home to Prague's largest delicatessen, Dům lahůdek (see p.24).

Staroměstské náměstí

East of Malé náměstí is **Staroměstské náměstí** (Old Town Square), easily the most spectacular square in Prague, and the traditional heart of the city. Most of the brightly coloured houses look solidly eighteenth-century, but their Baroque facades hide considerably older buildings. From the eleventh century onwards, this was the city's main marketplace, known simply as Velké náměstí (Great Square), to which all roads in Bohemia led, and where merchants from all over Europe gathered. When the five towns that made up Prague were united in 1784, it was the Old Town Square's town hall that was made the seat of the new city council, and for the next two hundred years the square was the scene of the country's most violent demonstrations and battles. For a long time now, the whole place has been closed to traffic, and the cafés spread out their tables in summer, while tourists pour in to watch the town hall clock chime, to sit on the steps of the Hus Monument, and to drink in this historic showpiece.

The Hus Monument

Staroměstské
náměstí

For a brief
biography of
Jan Hus, see
p.107.

The most recent arrival in the square is the colossal **Jan Hus Monument**, a turbulent sea of blackened bodies – the oppressed to his right, the defiant to his left – out of which rises the majestic moral authority of Hus himself, gazing into the horizon. For the sculptor Ladislav Šaloun, a maverick who received no formal training, the monument was his life's work, commissioned in 1900 when the Art Nouveau style Viennese Secession was at its peak, but strangely old-fashioned by the time it was completed in 1915. It would be difficult to claim that it blends in with its Baroque surroundings, yet this has never mattered to the Czechs, for whom its significance goes far beyond aesthetic merit.

The Austrians refused to hold an official unveiling; in protest, on July 6, 1915, the 500th anniversary of the death of Hus, Praguers smothered the monument in flowers. Since then it has been a powerful symbol of Czech nationalism: in March 1939, it was draped in swastikas by the invading Nazis, and in August 1968, it was shrouded in funereal black by Praguers, protesting at the Soviet invasion. The inscription along the base is a quote from *The Will of Comenius*, one of Hus's later followers, and includes Hus's most famous dictum, *Pravda vítězí* (Truth Prevails), which has been the motto of just about every Czech revolution since then.

The Staroměstská radnice

It wasn't until the reign of King John of Luxembourg (1310–46) that Staré Město was allowed to build its own town hall, the **Staroměstská radnice**. Short of funds, the citizens decided against an entirely new structure, buying a corner house on the square instead and simply adding an extra floor; later on, they added the east wing, with its graceful Gothic oriel and obligatory wedge-tower. Gradually, over the centuries, the neighbouring merchants' houses to the west were incorporated into the building, so that now it stretches all the way across to the richly sgraffitoed **Dům U minuty**, which juts out into the square.

On May 8, 1945, on the final day of the Prague Uprising, the Nazis still held on to Staroměstské náměstí, and in a last desperate act set fire to the town hall – one of the few buildings to be irrevocably damaged in the old town. The tower and oriel chapel were rebuilt immediately, but of the neo-Gothic **east wing**, which stretched almost to the church of sv Mikuláš, only a crumbling fragment remains; the rest of it is marked by the stretch of grass to the north. Embedded in the wall of the tower is a plaque marked "Dukla", and a case containing a handful of earth from the Slovak pass where some 80,000 Soviet and Czechoslovak soldiers lost their lives in the first (and most costly) battle to liberate the country in October 1944.

Below, set into the paving, are 27 **white crosses** commemorating the Protestant leaders who were condemned to death on the orders of the Emperor Ferdinand II, following the Battle of Bílá hora. They were publicly executed in the square on June 21, 1621 by the Prague executioner, Jan Mlydář: 24 enjoyed the nobleman's privilege and had their heads lopped off; the three remaining commoners were hung, drawn and quartered. Mlydář also chopped off the right hand of three of the nobles, and hacked off the tongue of the rector of Prague University, Johannes Jessenius, which he then nailed to their respective severed heads for public display on the Charles Bridge.

The astronomical clock chimes daily 8am–8pm.

Today, the town hall's most popular feature is its *orloj* or **Astronomical Clock** – on the hour, a crowd of tourists and Praguers gather in front of the tower to watch a mechanical dumbshow by the clock's assorted figures. The Apostles shuffle past the top two windows, bowing to the audience, while perched on pinnacles below are the four threats to the city as perceived by the medieval mind: Death carrying his hourglass and tolling his bell, the Jew with his moneybags (since 1945 minus his stereotypical beard), Vanity admiring his reflection, and a turbaned Turk shaking his head. Beneath the moving figures, four characters representing virtues stand motionless throughout the performance. Finally, a cockerel pops out and flaps its wings to signal that the show's over; the clock then chimes the hour.

The clock itself has been here since the beginning of the fifteenth century; the working figures were added in 1490 by a **Master Hanuš** who, legend has it, was then blinded with a red-hot poker by the town councillors, to make sure he couldn't repeat the job for anyone else. In retaliation, he groped his way around the clock, succeeded in stopping it, and then promptly died of a heart attack – the clock stayed broken for over eighty years. The complex clock face tells not only the current time, but also Old Bohemian time and Babylonian time, as well as charting – as the medieval astrologer saw it – the movements of the sun and planets around the earth, and of course, the movement of the sun and moon through the signs of the zodiac. The revolving dial below the clock face is decorated with bucolic paintings of the "cycle of twelve idylls from the life of the Bohemian peasant" by Josef Mánes, a leading light in the Czech national revival.

The Staroměstská radnice is open Mon 10am–5pm & Tues–Sun 9am–6pm.

The powder-pink facade on the south side of the town hall now forms the **entrance** to the whole complex. A twenty-minute guided tour of the four rooms that survived the last war sets off every hour, when the clock has finished striking (more frequently in summer). It was in these rooms that the Bohemian kings were elected until the Habsburgs established hereditary rule, and in 1422 Jan Želivský, the fiery Hussite preacher and inspiration behind Prague's first defenestration (see p.141), was executed here. Despite being steeped in history, there's not much of interest here, apart from a few decorated ceilings, striped with chunky beams, and a couple of Renaissance portals. You'll probably get more enjoyment from climbing the tower – with access for the disabled – for the panoramic sweep across Prague's spires.

The church of sv Mikuláš

The destruction of the east wing of the town hall in 1945 rudely exposed Kilian Ignaz Dientzenhofer's church of sv Mikuláš, built in just three years between 1732 and 1735. The original church was founded by German merchants in the thirteenth century, and served as Staré Město's parish church until the Týn Church (see below) was completed. Later, it was handed over to the Benedictines, who commissioned Dientzenhofer to replace it with the present building. His hand is obvious: the south front is decidedly luscious – painted creamy white, with Braun's blackened statuary popping up at every cornice – promising an interior to surpass even its sister church of sv Mikuláš in Malá Strana, which Dientzenhofer built with his father immediately afterwards (see p.75). Inside, however, it's a curious mixture. Although caked in the usual mixture of stucco and fresco and boasting an impressive dome, the church has been stripped over the years of much of its ornament and lacks the sumptuousness of its namesake on the left bank. This is partly due to the fact that Joseph II closed down the monastery and turned the church into a storehouse, and partly because it's now owned by the very "low", modern, Czech Hussite Church.

The rest of the square

The largest secular building on the square is the Rococo **palác Goltz-Kinských**, designed by Kilian Ignaz Dientzenhofer and built by his son-in-law Anselmo Lurago. In the nineteenth century it became a German *Gymnasium*, which was attended by, among others, Franz Kafka (whose father ran a haberdashery shop on the ground floor). The palace is perhaps most notorious, however, as the venue for the fateful speech by the Communist prime minister, Klement Gottwald, who walked out on to the grey stone balcony one snowy February morning in 1948, flanked by his Party henchmen, to address the thousands of enthusiastic supporters who packed the square below. It was the beginning of *Vitězná února* (Victorious February), the bloodless coup which brought the Communists to power and sealed the fate of the country for the next 41 years. The top floor now hosts top-flight exhibitions of graphic art put on by the National Gallery.

The palace is open Tues–Sun 10am–6pm.

Gottwald's appearance forms the opening to Milan Kundera's novel The Book of Laughter and Forgetting; *see Books, p.272.*

Until recently, the adjacent **Dům U kamenného zvonu** (House at the Stone Bell) was much like any other of the merchant houses that line Staroměstské náměstí – covered in a thick icing of Baroque plasterwork and topped by an undistinguished roof gable. In the process of restoration in the 1970s, however, it was controversially stripped down to its Gothic core, uncovering the original honey-coloured stonework and simple wedge roof, and it now serves as a central venue for cutting-edge modern art exhibitions, lectures and concerts.

Dům U kamenného zvonu is open Tues–Sun 10am–6pm.

The south side of the square boasts a fine array of facades, mostly Baroque, with the notable exception of the neo-Renaissance **Štorchův dům**, adorned with a late nineteenth-century sgraffito painting of Saint Wenceslas by Mikuláš Aleš. Next door, **U bílého jednorožce** (The White Unicorn) – the sixteenth-century house sign actually depicts a one-horned ram – was Prague's one and only *salon*, run by Berta Fanta. An illustrious membership, including Kafka, Max Brod and Franz Werfel, came here to attend talks given by, among others, Albert Einstein and Rudolf Steiner.

The Týn church and Ungelt

Staré Město's most impressive Gothic structure, the mighty **Týn church** (Matka boží před Týnem), whose two irregular towers, bristling with baubles, spires and pinnacles, rise like giant antennae above the arcaded houses which otherwise obscure its facade, is a far more imposing building than sv Mikuláš. Like the nearby Hus monument, the Týn church, begun in the fourteenth century, is a source of Czech national pride. In an act of defiance, George of Poděbrady, the last Czech and the only Hussite King of Bohemia, adorned the high stone gable with a statue of himself and a giant gilded *kalich* (chalice), the mascot of all Hussite sects. The church remained a hotbed of Hussitism until the Protestants' crushing defeat at the Battle of Bílá hora, after which the chalice was melted down to provide the newly ensconced statue of the Virgin Mary with a golden halo, sceptre and crown.

Despite being one of the main landmarks of Staré Město, it's well-nigh impossible to appreciate the church from anything but a considerable distance, since it's boxed in by the houses around it, some of which are actually built right against the walls. To reach the entrance, take the third arch on the left, which passes under the Venetian gables of the former Týn School. By the time you read this, the church's **interior** should be restored and open once more to the public. Of the church's furnishings, only the north portal and canopy, which bears the hallmark of Peter Parler's workshop, and the fifteenth-century pulpit, whose panels are enhanced by some sensitive nineteenth-century icons, stand out from the dark morass of black and gold Baroque altarpieces.

The pillar on the right of the chancel steps contains the red marble **tomb of Tycho Brahe**, the famous Danish astronomer who arrived in Prague wearing a silver and gold false nose, having lost his own in a duel over a woman in Rostock. Court astronomer to Rudolf II for just two years, Brahe laid much of the groundwork for Johannes Kepler's later discoveries – Kepler getting his chance of employment when Brahe died of a burst bladder after one of Petr Vok's notorious binges in 1601 – hence the colloquial expression *nechci umřít jako Tycho Brahe* ("I don't want to die like Tycho Brahe", in other words, I need to go to the toilet).

Behind the Týn Church lies the Týn courtyard, better known by its German name, **Ungelt** (meaning "No Money", a pseudonym used to deter marauding invaders), which, as the trading base of German merchants, was one of the first settlements on the Vltava. A hospice, church and hostel were built for the use of the merchants, and by the fourteenth century the area had become an extremely successful international marketplace; soon afterwards the traders moved up to the Hrad, and the court was transformed into a palace. Part of the complex now serves as a luxury hotel, the Dominicans have reclaimed another section, while the rest has recently undergone a very lengthy restoration.

Staroměstské náměstí

From Celetná to the Anežský klášter

Celetná, whose name comes from the bakers who used to bake a particular type of small loaf (*calty*) here in the Middle Ages, leads east from Staroměstské náměstí direct to the Prašná brána, one of the original gateways of the old town. It's one of the oldest streets in Prague, lying along the former trade route from the old town market square, as well as on the *králová cesta*. Its buildings were smartly refaced in the Baroque period, and their pastel shades are now crisply maintained. Most of Celetná's shops veer towards the chic end of the Czech market, making it a popular place for a bit of window-shopping. Dive down one of the covered passages to the left and into the backstreets, however, and you'll soon lose the crowds, and eventually end up at the atmospheric ruins of Anežsky klášter, now home to the National Gallery's nineteenth-century Czech art collection.

Dům U černé Matky boží

Two-thirds of the way along Celetná, at the junction with Ovocný trh, is the **Dům U černé Matky boží** (House at the Black Madonna), built as a department store in 1911–12 by Josef Gočár and one of the best examples of Czech Cubist architecture in Prague. It was a short-lived style, whose most surprising attribute, in this instance, is its ability to adapt existing Baroque motifs: Gočár's house sits much more happily amongst its eighteenth-century neighbours than, for example, the functionalist shop opposite – one of Gočár's later designs from the 1930s.

Happily, the building has recently been renovated and now houses, among other things, the **České muzeum výtvarných umění** (Czech Museum of Fine Arts). The top two floors contain a small, but excellent permanent exhibition of Czech Cubist art: everything from sofas and sideboards by Gočár himself, to porcelain and paintings, plus some wonderful sculptures by Otto Gutfreund. To whet your appetite further, there are photographs of the Cubist villas in

The museum is open Tues– Sun 10am– 6pm.

Vyšehrad (covered on p.153) and of the Cubist café which originally graced the first floor, and which the curators hope one day to rebuild. In the meantime, the first, second and third floors are currently given over to temporary exhibitions of twentieth-century art, while the basement has been converted into a cheap café/restaurant.

The church of sv Jakub

Celetná ends at the fourteenth-century Prašná brána (see p.135), beyond which is náměstí Republiky, at which point, strictly speaking, you've left Staré Město behind. Back in the old town, head north from Celetná into the backstreets which conceal the Franciscan church of **sv Jakub**, with its distinctive bubbling, stucco portal on Malá Štupartská. The church's massive Gothic proportions – it has the longest nave in Prague after the cathedral – make it a favourite venue for organ recitals, Mozart masses and other concerts. After the great fire of 1689, Prague's Baroque artists remodelled the entire interior, adding huge pillasters, a series of colourful frescoes and over twenty side altars. The most famous of these is the tomb of the Count of Mitrovice, in the northern aisle, designed by Fischer von Erlach and Prague's own Maximilian Brokof.

The church has close historical links with the butchers of Prague, who were given a chapel in gratitude for their defence of the city in 1611 and 1648. Hanging from the west wall, on the right as you enter, is a thoroughly decomposed human forearm. It has been there for over four hundred years now, ever since a thief tried to steal the jewels of the Madonna from the high altar. As the thief reached out, the Virgin supposedly grabbed his arm and refused to let go. The next day the congregation of butchers had no option but to lop it off, and it has hung there as a warning ever since.

Anežský klášter

The Anežský klášter is open Tues–Sun 10am–6pm.

Further north through the backstreets, the **Anežský klášter** (Convent of St Agnes), Prague's oldest surviving Gothic building, stands within a stone's throw of the river as it loops around to the east. It was founded in 1233 as a Franciscan convent for the Order of the Poor Clares, and takes its name from Agnes (Anežka), youngest daughter of Přemysl Otakar I, who left her life of regal privilege to become the convent's first abbess. Agnes took her vows seriously, living on a diet of raw onions and fruit with long periods of fasting, and in 1874 she was beatified to try and combat the spread of Hussitism amongst the Czechs. There was much speculation about the wonders that would occur when she was officially canonized, an event which finally took place on November 12, 1989, when Czech Catholics were invited to a special mass at St Peter's in Rome. Four days later the Velvet Revolution began: a happy coincidence, even for agnostic Czechs.

The convent itself was turned into an arsenal under the Hussites, and eventually closed down in 1782 by Joseph II, who turned into a place where the Prague poor could live and set up their own workshops. The whole neighbourhood remained a slum area until well into this century, and its restoration only finally took place in the 1980s. The convent now houses the Národní galerie's **nineteenth-century Czech art collection**, and if the art inside is not always of the highest quality, it has recently been attractively rehung, with fullsome descriptions in Czech and English, and is at least interesting in terms of the Czech national revival. The building itself is also worth inspecting, and the gallery's temporary exhibitions are now among the best in the capital.

The well-preserved cloisters and the three remaining chapels on the ground floor are used for special exhibitions; for the permanent collection, you need to go up to the first floor. The collection kicks off in room 1 with Ludvík Kohl's fantasy paintings: the one of Vienna's Stephansdom shows the cathedral with two complete towers (instead of one); his imaginary completion of Prague's St Vitus Cathedral was eventually fulfilled more or less to the letter by nineteenth-century architects. Rooms 2 and 3 focus on the work of the **Mánes family**: father Antonín gave birth to romantic Czech landscape painting, and three of his offspring – Quido, Josef and Amálie – took up the brush. Josef Mánes was the most successful of the trio, much in demand as a portrait artist among the newly emerging Czech bourgeoisie, and one of the leading exponents of patriotically uplifting depictions of events of national significance (Mánes himself took part in the 1848 disturbances in Prague). Favourite themes – on display in several works in rooms 3 and 5 – range from legendary figures such as Břetislav and Jitka to the real-life tragedy of the Battle of Bílá hora.

The first six rooms can be taken at a steady canter, for the cream of the collection's late nineteenth-century works are reserved for the gallery's final double room (7 & 8). Some of the most eye-catching works are **Jaroslav Čermák**'s paintings of Yugoslavia, where he was decorated for his bravery by the Montenegran prince Nicholas I. With a dark, treacle-brown palette and an eye for drama, Čermák displays an unhealthy obsession with the depiction of white Slav women being captured by swarthy Ottoman Turks. **Antonín Chittussi**'s Corot-esque landscapes proved very popular in the Parisian salons of the 1880s, not so his most influential and uncharacteristic work, *Paris seen from Monmartre*, whose flat colours and precise lines were deemed beyond the pale.

Mikuláš Aleš, whose designs can be seen in the sgraffito on many of the city's nineteenth-century buildings, provides a few wonderfully decorative historical moments, such as the meeting between George of Poděbrady and Matthias Corvinus. Prize for most striking portrait goes to Václav Brožík's portrayal of his wife, the daughter of

From
Celetná to
the Anežský
klášter

The National Gallery's modern art collection (both foreign and Czech) can be found in the Veletržní palác (see p.164).

a wealthy Parisian art dealer. There are several other crowd pleasers, including Josef Schusser's *Lady with a Red Parasol* and G. C. Max's *Saint Julia*, which features a woman being crucified. And the collection ends with a bevy of decadent Art Nouveau nudes by Maximilián Pirner, and several of Jakub Schikaneder's misty, moody streetscapes.

Southern Staré Město

The southern half of Staré Město is bounded by the *králová cesta* (the coronation route; see p.85) to the north, and the curve of Národní and Na příkopě, which follow the course of the old fortifications, to the south. There are no showpiece squares like Staroměstské náměstí here, but the complex web of narrow lanes and hidden passageways, many of which have changed little since medieval times, make this an intriguing quarter to explore, and one where it's easy to lose the worst of the crowds.

Ovocný trh

Heading southwest from the Dům U černé Matky boží (see above), you enter **Ovocný trh**, site of the old fruit market, its cobbles recently restored along with the lime-green and white **Stavovské divadlo** (Estates Theatre), which lies at the end of the marketplace. Built in the early 1780s by Count Nostitz (after whom the theatre was originally named) for the entertainment of Prague's large and powerful German community, the theatre is one of the finest Neoclassical buildings in Prague, reflecting the enormous self-confidence of its patrons. The theatre also has a place in Czech history too, for it was here that the Czech national anthem, *Kde domov můj* (Where is My Home), was first performed, as part of the comic opera *Fidlovačka*, by J. K. Tyl (after whom the theatre was later renamed). It is also something of a mecca for Mozart fans, since it was here, rather than in the hostile climate of Vienna, that the composer chose to première both *Don Giovanni* and *La Clemenza di Tito*. This is, in fact, one of the few opera houses in Europe which remains intact from Mozart's time, though it underwent major refurbishment during the nineteenth century – it was here the Miloš Forman filmed the concert scenes for his Oscar-laden *Amadeus* here.

For more on Mozart's time in Prague, see p.74.

On the north side of the Stavovské divadlo is the home base of the **Karolinum** or Charles University, named after its founder Charles IV, who established it in 1348 as the first university in this part of Europe. Although it was open to all nationalities, with instruction in Latin, it wasn't long before disputes arose between the various "nations" came to a head. In 1408, Václav IV issued the Decree of Kutná Hora, which gave the Bohemian "nation" – both Czech- and German-speaking – a majority vote in the university. In protest, the

The former Gottwald Museum

One block west of the Stavovské divadlo, at no. 29 Rytířská, is the former
Prague Savings Bank, a large, pompous neo-Renaissance building designed
in the 1890s by Osvald Polívka, before he went on to erect some of Prague's
most flamboyant Art Nouveau structures. The building currently serves as
a branch of *Česká spořitelna*, and is definitely worth a quick peek inside;
go up the monumental staircase and check out the main banking hall.

For over thirty years it housed the museum all Praguers loved to hate
– dedicated to Klement Gottwald, the country's first Communist president. A joiner by trade, a notorious drunkard and womanizer by repute,
he led the Party with unswerving faith from the beginnings of Stalinism in
1929 right through to the show trials of the early 1950s. He died shortly
after attending Stalin's funeral in 1953 – either from grief or, more plau-
sibly, from drink.

Remarkably, his reputation survived longer than that of any other East
European leader. While those whom he had wrongfully sent to their
deaths were posthumously rehabilitated, and the figure of Stalin deni-
grated, Gottwald remained sacred, his statue gracing every town in the
country for the last forty-odd years. As late as October 1989, the
Communists were happily issuing brand new 100kčs notes emblazoned
with his bloated face, only to have them withdrawn from circulation a
month later, when the regime toppled.

other "nations" upped and left for Leipzig, the first of many ethnic
problems which continued to bubble away throughout the university's six-hundred-year history until the forced and extremely violent
expulsion of all German-speakers after World War II.

To begin with, the university had no fixed abode; it wasn't until
1383 that Václav IV bought the present site. All that's left of the
original fourteenth-century building is the Gothic oriel window
which emerges from the south wall; the rest was trashed by the
Nazis in 1945. The new main entrance is a peculiarly ugly red-brick
curtain wall building by Jaroslav Fragner, set back from the street
and inscribed with the original Latin name *Universitas Karolina*.
Only a couple of small departments and the chancellor's office and
administration are now housed here, with the rest spread over the
length and breadth of the city. The heavily restored Gothic vaults,
on the ground floor of the south wing, are now used as a contemporary **art gallery**.

Around sv Havel

The junction of Melantrichova and Rytířská is always teeming with
people pouring out of Staroměstské náměstí and heading for
Wenceslas Square. Clearly visible from Melantrichova is Santini's
undulating Baroque facade of the church of **sv Havel**, sadly no relation to the playwright-president but named after the Irish monk, Saint
Gall. It was built in the thirteenth century to serve the local German
community who had been invited to Prague partly to replace the

Jewish traders killed in the city's 1096 pogrom. After the expulsion of the Protestants, the church was handed over to the Carmelites who redesigned the interior, now only visible through an iron grille.

Straight ahead of you as you leave sv Havel is Prague's last surviving **open-air market** – a poor relation of its Germanic predecessor, which stretched all the way from Ovocný trh to Uhelný trh. Traditionally a flower and vegetable market, it runs the full length of the arcaded Havelská, and sells everything from celery to CDs, with plenty of souvenirs and wooden toys in between; the stalls on V kotcích, the narrow street parallel to Havelská, sell mainly clothes.

Uhelný trh, sv Martin ve zdi and Bartolomějská

Both markets run west into Uhelný trh, which gets its name from the *uhlí* (coal) that was sold here in medieval times. Nowadays however it's Prague red-light district – you'll see little evidence during the day, but at night it can get busy, though the local authorities are contantly drawing up plans to move the trade elsewhere.

South of Uhelný trh, down Martinská, the street miraculously opens out to make room for the twelfth-century church of **sv Martin ve zdi** (St Martin-in-the-Walls), originally built to serve the Czech community of the village of sv Martin, until it found itself the wrong side of the Gothic fortifications when they were erected in the fourteenth century. It's still essentially a Romanesque structure, adapted to suit Gothic tastes a century later, and thoroughly restored at the beginning of this century by its present owners, the Czech Brethren, who added the creamy neo-Renaissance tower. For them, it has a special significance as the place where communion "in both kinds" (ie bread and wine), one of the fundamental demands of the Hussites, was first administered to the whole congregation, in 1414.

Around the corner from sv Martin ve zdi is the gloomy lifeless street of **Bartolomějská**, dominated by a tall, grim-looking building on its south side, which served as the main interrogation centre of the universally detested Communist secret police, the *Státní bezpečnost*, or *StB*. Although now officially disbanded, the *StB* continues to be one of the most controversial issues of the post-revolutionary period. As in the rest of Eastern Europe, the accusations (often unproven) and revelations of who exactly collaborated with the *StB* have caused the downfall of a number of leading politicians right across the political spectrum. The building is now back in the hands of the Franciscan nuns who occupied the place prior to 1948, and its former police cells now serve as rooms for a small *pension*.

It's possible to stay the night in Havel's old cell; see p.199 for details.

Betlémské náměstí

After leaving the dark shadows of Bartolomějská, the brighter aspect of **Betlémské náměstí** comes as a welcome relief. The square is named after the **Betlémská kaple** (Bethlehem Chapel), whose high wooden gables face on to the square. This was founded in 1391 by religious reformists, who, denied the right to build a church, proceeded instead to build the largest chapel in Bohemia, with a total capacity of 3000. Sermons were delivered not in the customary Latin, but in the language of the masses – Czech. From 1402 to 1413, **Jan Hus** preached here (see box below), regularly pulling in more than enough commoners to fill the chapel. Hus was eventually excommunicated for his outspokenness, found guilty of heresy and burnt at the stake at the Council of Constance in 1415.

The chapel continued to attract reformists from all over Europe for another two centuries – the leader of the German Peasants' Revolt, **Thomas Müntzer**, preached here in the sixteenth century – until the advent of the Counter-Reformation in Bohemia. Inevitably, the chapel was handed over to the Jesuits, who completely altered the original building, only for it to be demolished after they were expelled by the Habsburgs in 1773. Of the original building, only the three outer walls remain, with patches of their original decoration – biblical scenes which were used to get the message across to the illiterate congregation. The rest is a scrupulous reconstruction of the fourteenth-century building by Jaroslav Fragner, using the original plans and a fair amount of imaginative guesswork. The initial reconstruction work was carried out after the war by the Communists, who were keen to portray Hus as a Czech nationalist and social critic as much as a religious reformer, and, of course, to dwell on the revolutionary Müntzer's later appearances here.

Southern Staré Město

The Betlémská kaple is open daily 9am–6pm.

Jan Hus

The legendary preacher – and Czech national hero – **Jan Hus** (often anglicized to John Huss) was born in the small village of Husinec in South Bohemia around 1372. From a childhood of poverty, he enjoyed a steady rise through the Czech education system, taking his degree at the Karolinum in the 1390s, and eventually being ordained as a deacon and priest around 1400. Although without doubt an admirer of the English religious reformer, John Wycliffe, Hus was by no means as radical as many of his colleagues who preached at the Betlémská kaple. Nor did he actually advocate many of the more famous tenets of the heretical religious movement that took his name: Hussitism. In particular, he never advocated giving communion "in both kinds" (bread and wine) to the general congregation.

In the end, it wasn't the disputes over Wycliffe, whose books were burned on the orders of the archbishop in 1414, that proved Hus's downfall, but an argument over the sale of indulgences to fund the papal wars that prompted his unofficial trial at the Council of Constance in 1415. Having been guaranteed safe conduct by Emperor Sigismund himself, Hus naïvely went to Constance to defend his views, and was burnt at the stake as a heretic. The Czechs were outraged, and Hus became a national hero overnight, inspiring thousands to rebel against the authorities of the day. In 1965, the Vatican finally overturned the sentence, and the anniversary of his death is now a national holiday.

At the western end of the square stands the **Náprstkovo muzeum**, whose founder, Czech nationalist Vojta Náprstek, was inspired by the great Victorian museums of London while in exile following the 1848 revolution. On his return, he turned the family brewery into a museum, initially intending it to concentrate on the virtues of industrial progress. Náprstek's interests gradually shifted towards anthropology, however, and the museum now displays just his fantastic American, Australasian and Oceanic ethnographic collections; the original technological exhibits are now housed in Prague's Národné technické muzeum (see p.163).

The Náprstkovo muzeum is open Tues–Sun 9am–noon & 12.45–5.30pm.

Husova and around

Between Betlémské náměstí and Karlova lies a confusing maze of streets, passageways and backyards, containing few sights as such, but nevertheless a joy to explore. One building that might catch your eye is the church of **sv Jiljí** (St Giles), on Husova, whose outward appearance suggests another Gothic masterpiece, but whose interior is decked out in the familiar black excess of the eighteenth century, with huge gilded acanthus leaf capitals and barley-sugar columns galore. The frescoes by Václav Vavřinec Reiner (who is buried in the church) are full of praise for his patrons, the Dominicans, who took over the church after the Protestant defeat of 1620. They were expelled, in turn, after the Communists took power, only to return following the events of 1989.

Reiner's paintings also depict the unhappy story of Giles himself, a ninth-century hermit who is thought to have lived somewhere in Provence. Out one day with his pet deer, Giles and his companion were chased by the hounds of King Wanda of the Visigoths. The hounds were rooted to the spot by an invisible power, while the arrow from the hunters struck Giles in the foot as he defended his pet – the hermit was later looked upon as the patron saint of cripples.

The house is open May–Sept Tues–Sun 10am–noon & 1–6pm.

A short step away, just off Husova on Řetězová, is the **Dům pánů z Kunštátu a Poděbrad** (House of the Lords of Kunštát and Poděbrady), the home of George of Poděbrady before he became the Czechs' first and last Hussite king in 1458. It's not exactly gripping, but it does give you a clear impression of the antiquity of the houses in this area, and illustrates the way in which the new Gothic town was built on top of the old Romanesque one. Thus the floor on which you enter was originally the first floor of a twelfth-century palace, whose ground floor has been excavated in the cellars.

To the waterfront

Continuing west along Řetězová and Anenská brings you eventually to the waterfront. On Anenské náměstí, just before you reach the river, is the **Divadlo na zábradlí** (Theatre on the Balustrade). This was at the centre of Prague's absurdist theatre scene in the 1960s, with Havel himself working first as a stagehand and later as resident playwright, and is currently enjoying something of a renaissance.

The gaily decorated neo-Renaissance building at the very end of Novotného lávka, on the riverfront itself, was once the city's water-works but now houses *Lávka*, a pleasant riverside café and nightclub (see p.213) and theatre on the ground floor and, on the first floor, the **Muzeum Bedřicha Smetany**, currently closed and facing an uncertain future. Smetana, despite being a German-speaker, was without doubt the most nationalist of all the great Czech composers, taking an active part in the 1848 revolution and the later national revival movement. Towards the end of his life he went deaf, and eventually died of syphilis in a mental asylum. Outside, beneath the large weeping willow that droops over the embankment, the statue of the seated Smetana is rather unfortunately placed, with his back towards one of his most famous sources of inspiration, the River Vltava (Moldau in German).

Chapter 4

Josefov

It is crowded with horses; traversed by narrow streets not remarkable for cleanliness, and has altogether an uninviting aspect. Your sanitary reformer would here find a strong case of overcrowding.

Walter White,
"A July Holiday in Saxony, Bohemia and Silesia" (1857)

L
ess than half a century after Walter White's comments, all that was left of the former ghetto of **JOSEFOV** were six synagogues, the town hall and the medieval cemetery. At the end of the nineteenth century, a period of great economic growth for the Empire, it was decided that Prague should be turned into a beautiful bourgeois city, modelled on Paris. The key to this transformation was the "sanitization" of the ghetto, a process, begun in 1893, which reduced the notorious malodorous backstreets and alleyways of Josefov to rubble and replaced them with block after block of luxurious five-storey mansions. The Jews, the poor, the gypsies and the prostitutes were cleared out so that the area could become a desirable residential quarter, rich in Art Nouveau buildings festooned with decorative murals, doorways and sculpturing. This building frenzy marked the beginning of the end for a community which had existed in Prague for almost a millennium.

In any other European city occupied by the Nazis in World War II, what little was left of the old ghetto would have been demolished. But although Prague's Jews were transported to the new ghetto in Terezín, by a grotesque twist of fate the ghetto itself was preserved by Hitler himself in order to provide a site for his planned "Exotic Museum of an Extinct Race". With this in mind, Jewish artefacts from all over central Europe were gathered here, and now make up one of the richest collections of Judaica in Europe, and one of the most fascinating sights in Prague. Also included in this chapter, at the end, are the sights around náměstí Jana Palacha, adjacent to, but strictly speaking outside of, the Jewish quarter, most notably the city's excellent Decorative Arts Museum (or UPM).

A brief history of Jewish settlement in Prague

Jews probably settled in Prague as early as the tenth century and, initially at least, are thought to have settled on both sides of the river. In 1096, at the time of the first crusade, the first recorded pogrom took place, an event which may have hastened the formation of a much more closely knit "Jewish town" within Staré Město during the twelfth century. It wasn't until much later that Jews were actually herded into a **walled ghetto** (and several centuries before the word "ghetto" was actually first coined in Venice), sealed off from the rest of the town and subject to a curfew. Jews were also subject to laws restricting their choice of profession to usury and the rag trade; in addition, some form of visible identification, a cap or badge, remained a more or less constant feature of Jewish life until the Enlightenment.

In 1262, Přemysl King Otakar II issued a *Statuta Judaeorum*, which granted the Jews their own religious and civil self-administration. In effect, however, the Jews were little more than the personal property of the king, and though Otakar himself appears to have been genuine in his motives, later rulers used the *Statuta* as a form of blackmail, extorting money whenever they saw fit. During one of the worst pogroms, in 1389, 3000 Jews were massacred over Easter, some while sheltering in the Old-New Synagogue – an event commemorated every year thereafter on Yom Kippur. In 1541, a fire ripped through Hradcany and Malá Strana and a Jew was tortured into confessing the crime. The Bohemian Estates immediately persuaded the Emperor Ferdinand I to expel the Jews from Prague. In the end, however, a small number of families were allowed to remain.

By contrast, the reign of Rudolf II (1576–1612) was a time of economic and cultural prosperity for the community, which is thought to have numbered up to 10,000, making it by far the largest Jewish community in the Diaspora. The Jewish mayor, **Mordecai Maisel**, Rudolf's minister of finance, became one of the richest men in Bohemia and the success symbol of a generation; his money bought and built the Jewish quarter its town hall, a bath house, pavements and several synagogues. This was the "golden age" of the ghetto: the time of **Rabbi Löw**, the severe and conservative chief rabbi of Prague, who is now best known as the legendary creator of the Jewish Frankenstein or "golem", though, in fact, the story of Rabbi Löw and the golem first appeared only in the nineteenth century (see box on p.115).

Amidst the violence of the Thirty Years' War, the Jews enjoyed an unusual degree of protection from the emperor, who was heavily dependent on their financial acumen. In 1648, the Jews, along with the city's students, repaid their imperial bosses by repelling the marauding Swedes on the Charles Bridge, for which they won the lasting respect of Ferdinand III (1637–57). Things went into reverse again during the eighteenth century, until in 1744, Empress Maria Theresa used the community as a scapegoat for her disastrous war against the Prussians, and ordered the expulsion of all Jews from Prague. She allowed them to return in 1748, though only after much pressure from the guilds, who were missing Jewish custom. It was the enlightened **Emperor Joseph II** (1780–90) who did most to lift the restrictions on Jews. His 1781 Toleration Edict ended the dress codes, opened up education to all non-Catholics, and removed the gates from the ghetto. In 1850, the community paid him homage by officially naming the ghetto Josefov, or Josefstadt.

The downside to Joseph's reforms was that he was hellbent on assimilating the Jews into the rest of the population. The use of Hebrew or Yiddish in business transactions was banned, and Jews were ordered to Germanize their names (the list of permitted names comprised 109 male ones and 35 female). It wasn't until the social upheavals of 1848 that Jews were given equal status within the Empire and allowed officially to settle outside the confines of the ghetto – concessions which were accompanied by a number of violent anti-Semitic protests on the part of the Czechs.

From 1848 to the present day

From 1848, the ghetto went into terminal decline. The more prosperous Jewish families began to move to other districts of Prague, leaving behind only the poorest Jews and strictly Orthodox families, who were rapidly joined by the underprivileged ranks of Prague society: gypsies, beggars, prostitutes and alcoholics. By 1890, only twenty percent of Josefov's population was Jewish, yet it was still the most densely populated area in Prague, with a staggering 186,000 people crammed into its streets. The ghetto had become a carbuncle in the centre of bourgeois Prague, a source of disease and vice: in the words of Gustav Meyrink, a "demonic underworld, a place of anguish, a beggarly and phantasmagorical quarter whose eeriness seemed to have spread and led to paralysis".

The ending of restrictions, and the destruction of most of the old ghetto, increased the pressure on Jews to assimilate, a process which brought with it its own set of problems. Prague's Jews were split roughly half and half between predominantly German- or Yiddish-speakers and Czech-speakers. Yet since some two-thirds of Prague's German population were Jewish, and all Jews had been forced to take German names by Josef II, all Jews were seen by Czech nationalists as a Germanizing influence. Tensions between the country's German-speaking minority and the Czechs grew steadily worse in the run-up to World War I, and the Jewish community found itself caught in the firing line – "like powerless stowaways attempting to steer a course through the storms of embattled nationalities", as one Prague Jew put it.

Despite several anti-Semitic riots in the first few years following the war, the foundation of the new republic in 1918, and, in particular, its founder and first president, T. G. Masaryk, whose liberal credentials were impeccable, were welcomed by most Jews. For the first time in their history, Jews were given equal rights as a recognized ethnic minority, though only a small number opted to be registered as Jewish. The interwar period was probably the nearest Prague's Jewish community came to a second "golden age", a time most clearly expressed in the now famous flowering of its *Deutsche Prager Literatur*, led by German-Jewish writers such as Franz Werfel, Franz Kafka, Max Brod and Egon Erwin Kisch.

After Nazi troops occupied Prague on March 15, 1939, the city's Jews were subject to an increasingly harsh set of regulations, which saw them barred from most professions, placed under curfew, and compelled to wear a yellow Star of David. In November 1941, the first transport of Prague Jews set off for the new ghetto in Terezín, 60km northwest of Prague. Of the estimated 55,000 Jews in Prague at the time of the Nazi invasion, over 36,000 died in the camps. Many survivors emigrated to Israel and the USA. Of the 8000 who registered as Jewish in the Prague census of 1947, a significant number joined the Communist Party, only to find themselves victims of Stalinist anti-Semitic wrath during the 1950s.

It's difficult to calculate exactly how many Jews now live in Prague – around a thousand were officially registered as such prior to 1989 – though their numbers have undoubtedly been bolstered by a new generation of Czech Jews who have rediscovered their roots, and by the new influx of Jewish Americans and Israelis. Another positive development has been the appointment of a new rabbi, former dissident Karel Sidon, after the previous incumbent was accused of being an *StB* informer. In addition, the controversy over Jewish property – most of which was seized by the Nazis, and therefore not covered by the original restitution law – has finally been resolved, allowing the community to reclaim at least some of its buildings, most importantly the six synagogues, town hall and cemetery of Josefov itself.

The former ghetto

Geographically, Josefov lies to the northwest of Staroměstské náměstí, between the main square and the Vltava river. The warren-like street plan of the old ghetto has long since disappeared, and through the heart of Josefov the ultimate bourgeois avenue, **Pařížská**, now runs, a riot of turn-of-the-century sculpturing, spikes and turrets, its ground floor premises home to a parade of international airline offices and boutiques. If Josefov can still be said to have a main street, it is really the parallel street of **Maiselova**, named after the community's sixteenth-century leader. The sheer volume of tourists – over a million a year – that visit Josefov has brought with it the inevitable rash of souvenir stalls, flogging dubious "Jewish" souvenirs, and, it is has to be said, the whole area is now something of a tourist trap. Yet to skip this part of the old town is to miss out on a whole slice of the city's cultural history.

> All the "sights" of Josefov, bar the Staronová synagóga, are covered by just one 250kč ticket, available from any of the quarter's ticket offices. Opening hours vary but are basically daily except Sat: April–Oct 9.30am–6pm; Nov–March 9.30am–4.30pm. In order to try and regulate the flow of visitors, the authorities have introduced a timed entry system, giving you around twenty minutes at each sight, though don't worry if you don't adhere rigidly to your timetable.

The synagogue is open April–Oct Mon–Thurs & Sun 9am–6pm, Fri 9am–5pm; Nov–March Mon–Thurs & Sun 9am–5pm, Fri 9am–2pm.

Staronová synagóga and Židovská radnice

Walking down Maiselova, it's impossible to miss the steep, sawtooth brick gables of the **Staronová synagóga** or Altneuschul (Old-New Synagogue), so called because when it was built it was indeed very new, though it eventually became the oldest synagoe in Josefov. Begun in the second half of the thirteenth century, it is, in fact, the oldest functioning synagogue in Europe, one of the earliest Gothic buildings in Prague and still the religious centre for Prague's Orthodox Jews. Since Jews were prevented by law from becoming architects, the synagogue is thought to have been constructed by the

Franciscan builders working on the convent of sv Anežka. Its five-ribbed vaulting is unique for Bohemia; the extra, purely decorative rib was added to avoid any hint of a cross.

To enter the synagogue, you must buy a separate ticket (200kč) from the ticket office opposite the synagogue's entrance on Červená (or from one of the other ticket offices). Men are asked to cover their heads out of respect – paper *kippahs* are handed out at the ticket office. To get to the **main hall**, you must pass through one of the two low vestibules from which women watch the proceedings through narrow slits. Above the entrance is an elaborate tympanum covered in the twisting branches of a vine tree, its twelve bunches of grapes representing the tribes of Israel. The low glow from the chandeliers is the only light in the hall, which is mostly taken up with the elaborate wrought-iron cage enclosing the *bimah* in the centre. In 1357, Charles IV allowed the Jews to fly their own municipal standard, a

The former ghetto

Prague's other working synagogue is in Nové Město (see p.137).

The Golem

Legends concerning the animation of unformed matter (which is what the Hebrew word **golem** means), using the mystical texts of the Kabbala, were around long before Frankenstein started playing around with corpses. Two hungry fifth-century rabbis may have made the most practical golem when they sculpted a clay calf, brought it to life and then ate it; but the most famous is undoubtedly **Rabbi Löw**'s giant servant made from the mud of the Vltava, who was brought to life when the rabbi placed a *shem* in its mouth, a tablet with a magic Hebrew inscription.

There are numerous versions of the tale, though the earliest invoking Rabbi Löw only appeared in the nineteenth century. In some, Yossel, the golem, is a figure of fun, flooding the rabbi's kitchen rather in the manner of Disney's *Sorcerer's Apprentice*; others portray him as the guardian of the ghetto, helping Rabbi Löw in his struggle with the anti-Semites at Rudolf II's court. In almost all versions, however, the golem finally runs amok. One particularly appealing tale is that the golem's rebellion was because Löw forgot to allow his creature to rest on the Sabbath. He was conducting the service when news of its frenzy arrived, and he immediately ran out to deal with it. The congregation, reluctant to continue without him, merely repeated the verse in the psalm the rabbi had been reciting until Löw returned. This explains the peculiarity at the Staronová synagóga where a line in the Sabbath service is repeated even today. In all the stories, the end finally comes when Löw removes the *shem* once and for all, and carries the remains of his creature to the attic of the Old-New Synagogue, where they have supposedly resided ever since (a fact disputed by the pedantic journalist Egon Erwin Kisch, who climbed in to check).

The legends are amended at each telling, and have proved an enduringly popular theme for generations of artists and writers. Paul Wegener's German expressionist film version and the dark psychological novel of Gustav Meyrink are probably two of the most powerful treatments. Meyrink's golem lives in a room which has no windows and no doors, emerging to haunt the streets of Prague every 33 years. By which reckoning, it's slightly overdue to make a reappearance.

moth-eaten remnant of which is still on show, bearing the Star of David (Prague's Jewish community were the first to adopt the Star as their official symbol). The other flag – a tattered red banner – was a gift to the community from Emperor Ferdinand III for helping fend off the Swedes in 1648. On the west wall a glass cabinet, shaped like Moses' two tablets of stone, is filled with tiny personalized light bulbs, which are paid for by grieving relatives and light up on the anniversary of the person's death (there's even one for Kafka).

Just south of the synagogue is the **Židovská radnice** (Jewish Town Hall), one of the few such buildings to survive the Holocaust. Founded and funded by Maisel in the sixteenth century, it was later rebuilt as the creamy-pink Baroque house you now see, housing an overpriced kosher restaurant. The belfry, permission for which was granted by Ferdinand III, has a clock on each of its four sides, plus a Hebrew one stuck on the north gable which, like the Hebrew script,

---

On Kafka's trail

Prague never lets go of you . . . this little mother has claws. We ought to set fire to it at both ends, on Vyšehrad and Hradčany, and maybe then it might be possible to escape.

Franz Kafka "Letter to Oskar Polak" (December 2, 1902)

Franz Kafka was born on July 3, 1883, above the *Batalion* Schnapps bar on the corner of Maiselova and Kaprova (the original building has long since been torn down, but a gaunt-looking modern bust now commemorates the site). He spent most of his life in and around Josefov. His father was an upwardly mobile small businessman from a Czech-Jewish family of kosher butchers (Kafka himself was a vegetarian), his mother from a wealthy German-Jewish family of merchants. The family owned a haberdashery shop, located at various premises on or near Staroměstské náměstí. In 1889, they moved out of Josefov and lived for the next seven years in the beautiful Renaissance Dům U minuty, next door to the Staroměstská radnice, during which time Kafka attended the *Volksschule* on Masná (now a Czech primary school), followed by a spell at an exceptionally strict German *Gymnasium*, located on the third floor of the palác Goltz-Kinských.

At 18, he began a law degree at the German half of the Karolinum, which was where he met his lifelong friend and posthumous biographer and editor, Max Brod. Kafka spent most of his working life as an accident insurance clerk, until he was forced to retire through ill health in 1922. Illness plagued him throughout his life and he spent many months as a patient at the innumerable spas in *Mitteleuropa*. He was engaged three times, twice to the same woman, but never married, finally leaving home at the age of 31 for bachelor digs on the corner of Dlouhá and Masná, where he wrote the bulk of his most famous work, *The Trial*. He died of tuberculosis at the age of 40 in a sanatorium just outside Vienna, on June 3, 1924, and is buried in the Nový židovský hřbitov in Žižkov (see p.157).

goes "backwards". On the other side of the synagogue is one of the many statues in Prague that were hidden from the Nazis for the duration of the war: an anguished statue of Moses by František Bílek, himself a committed Protestant.

Pinkasova synagóga

Jutting out at an angle on the south side of the cemetery, with its entrance on Široká, the **Pinkasova synagóga** was built in the 1530s for the powerful Pinkas family, and has undergone countless restorations over the centuries. In 1958, the synagogue was transformed into a chilling memorial to the 77,297 Czech Jews killed during the Holocaust. The memorial was closed shortly after the Six Day War – due to damp, according to the Communists – and remained so, allegedly due to problems with the masonry, until 1991.

As a German among Czechs, a Jew among Germans, and an agnostic among believers, Kafka had good reason to live in a constant state of fear, or *Angst*. Life was precarious for Prague's Jews, and the destruction of the Jewish quarter throughout his childhood – the so-called "sanitization" – had a profound effect on his psyche, as he himself admitted. It comes as a surprise to many Kafka readers that anyone immersed in so beautiful a city could write such claustrophobic and paranoid texts; and that as a member of the café society of the time, he could write in a style so completely at odds with his verbose, artistic friends. It's also hard to accept that Kafka could find no publisher for *The Castle* or *The Trial* during his lifetime.

After his death, Kafka's works were published in Czech and German and enjoyed brief critical acclaim, before the Nazis banned them, first within Germany, then across Nazi-occupied Europe. Even after the war, Kafka, along with most German-Czech authors, was deliberately overlooked in his native country, since he belonged to a community and a culture which had been exiled. In addition, his account of the terrifying brutality and power of bureaucracy over the individual, though not in fact directed at totalitarian systems as such, was too close to the bone for the Communists. The 1962 Writers' Union conference at Liblice finally broke the official silence on Kafka, and, for many people, marked the beginning of the Prague Spring. In the immediate aftermath of the 1968 Soviet invasion, the Kafka bust was removed from Josefov, and his books remained unpublished in Czechoslovakia until 1990.

Thanks to his popularity with western tourists, Kafka has now become an extremely marketable commodity. Today, it's almost impossible to avoid his image, which is plastered across T-shirts, mugs and postcards all over the city centre. A small **Expozice Franze Kafky** (Tues–Fri 10am–6pm, Sat 10am–5pm), next door to the church of sv Mikuláš, retells Kafka's life simply but effectively with pictures and quotes (in Czech, German and English), and flogs souvenirs. It's run by the Kafka Society, as is the Franz Kafka bookshop and *Café Milena*, situated opposite the town hall on Staroměstské náměstí.

The former ghetto

Of all the sights of the Jewish quarter, the Holocaust memorial is perhaps the most moving, with every bit of wall space taken up with the carved stone list of victims, stating simply their name, date of birth and date of transportation to the camps. It is the longest epitaph in the world, yet it represents a mere fraction of those who died in the Nazi concentration camps. All that remains of the synagogue's original decor is the ornate *bimah* surrounded by a beautiful wrought-iron grille, supported by barleysugar columns.

Starý židovský hřbitov (Old Jewish Cemetery)

The Nový židovský hřbitov (New Jewish Cemetery), where Kafka, among others, is buried, is in Žižkov (see p.157).

At the heart of Josefov is the **Starý židovský hřbitov**, known as *Bet Hayyim* in Hebrew, meaning "House of Life". Established in the fifteenth century, it was in use until 1787, by which time there were an estimated 100,000 buried here, one on top of the other, as many as twelve layers deep. The enormous numbers of visitors has meant that the graves themselves have been roped off to protect them, and a one-way system introduced: you enter from the Pinkasova synagóga, on Široká, and leave by the Klausová synagóga. The oldest grave, dating from 1439, belongs to the poet Avigdor Karo, who lived to tell the tale of the 1389 pogrom. Get there before the crowds – a difficult task for much of the year – and the cemetery can be a poignant reminder of the ghetto, its inhabitants subjected to inhuman overcrowding even in death. The rest of Prague recedes beyond the sombre lime trees and cramped perimeter walls, the haphazard headstones and Hebrew inscriptions casting a powerful spell.

For a full account of Terezín (Theresienstadt), see p.180.

Each headstone bears a symbol denoting the profession or tribe of the deceased: a pair of hands for the Cohens; a jug for the Levis; scissors for a tailor; a violin for a musician, etc. On many graves you'll see pebbles, some holding down *kvittleh* or small messages of supplication. The greatest number of these sits on the grave of Rabbi Löw, creator of the "golem", who is buried by the wall directly opposite the entrance; followed closely by the rich Renaissance tomb of Mordecai Maisel, some ten metres to the southeast.

Obřadní síň and Klausova synagóga

Immediately on your left as you leave the cemetery is the **Obřadní síň**, a grim neo-Renaissance house built in 1906 as a ceremonial hall by the Jewish Burial Society. It's now devoted to a harrowing exhibition of drawings from the Jewish ghetto in Terezín; the most disturbing section contains naive drawings by children, most of whom later perished in the camps.

Close to the entrance to the cemetery is the **Klausová synagóga**, a late seventeenth-century building, founded in the 1690s by Mordecai Maisel on the site of several medieval prayer halls (*klausen*), in what was then a notorious red-light district of Josefov.

The ornate Baroque interior contains a rich display of religious objects from embroidered *kippah* to *Kiddush* cups, and explains the very basics of Jewish religious practice.

The former ghetto

The other synagogues

Founded and paid for entirely by Mordecai Maisel, the neo-Gothic **Maiselova synagóga**, set back from the neighbouring houses on Maiselova, was, in its day, one of the most ornate synagogues in Josefov. Nowadays, its whitewashed interior is almost entirely bare apart from the rich offerings of its glass cabinets, which contain gold and silverwork, *hanuka* candlesticks, *torah* scrolls and other religious artefacts.

Adjacent to the town hall it was once part of is the **Vysoká synagóga** (High Synagogue), whose rich interior stands in complete contrast to its dour, grey facade. The huge vaulted hall was, until recently, used to display a selection of the hundreds of Jewish textiles, dating from the sixteenth to the early twentieth century, which were gathered here by the Nazis for their infamous museum. The building has now been restored as a working, non-Orthodox synagogue, and is closed to the general public.

East of Pařížská, up Široká, just past the church of sv Duch, stands the **Španělská synagóga** (Spanish Synagogue), on the spot once occupied by Prague's Alt Schul or Old Synagogue. The current building, begun in 1868, is by far the most ornate synagogue in Josefov, its gilded Moorish interior deliberately imitating the Alhambra (hence its name). Closed "for electrical rewiring" in 1980, the synagogue is due to re-open for services, and to the public, sometime in 1998.

Around náměstí Jana Palacha

As Kaprova and Široká emerge from Josefov, they meet at the newly christened **náměstí Jana Palacha**, previously called náměstí Krasnoarmejců (Red Army Square) and embellished with a flowerbed in the shape of a red star, in memory of the Soviet dead who were temporarily buried here in May 1945. It was probably this, as much as the fact that the building on the east side of the square is the Faculty of Philosophy, where Palach was a student, that prompted the new authorities to make the first of the street name changes here in 1989 (there's a bust of Palach on the corner of the building). By a happy coincidence, the road which intersects the square from the north is called 17 listopadu (17 November), originally commemorating the day in 1939 when the Nazis closed down all Czech institutions of higher education, but now equally good for the 1989 march (see p.132).

Palach is also honoured at the memorial to victims of Communism on Wenceslas Square (see p.128).

The north side of the square is taken up by the **Rudolfinum** or Dům umělců (House of Artists), designed by Josef Zítek and Josef

Schulz. One of the proud civic buildings of the nineteenth-century Czech national revival, it was originally built to house an art gallery, museum and concert hall for the Czech-speaking community. In 1918, however, it became the seat of the new Czechoslovak parliament, until 1938 when it was closed down by the Nazis. According to Jiří Weil, the Germans were keen to rid the building's balustrade of its statue of the Jewish composer Mendelssohn. However, since none of the statues was actually named, they decided to remove the one with the largest nose; unfortunately for the Nazis, this turned out to be Wagner, Hitler's favourite composer. In 1946, the building returned to its original artistic purpose and in the last couple of years it's been sandblasted back to its original woody-brown hue. It's now one of the capital's main exhibition and concert venues (it's home to the Czech Philharmonic), with a wonderfully grand café (see p.213), open to the general public on the first floor.

UPM (Decorative Arts Museum)

The UPM is open Tues–Sun 10am–6pm.

A short way down 17 listopadu from the square is the **UPM** (Umělecko-průmyslové muzeum), installed in another of Schulz's worthy nineteenth-century creations, richly decorated in mosaics, stained glass and sculptures. Literally translated, this is a "Museum of Decorative Arts", though the translation hardly does justice to what is one of the most fascinating museums in the capital. From its foundation in 1885 through to the end of the First Republic, the UPM received the best that the Czech modern movement had to offer – from Art Nouveau to the avant-garde – and judging from previous catalogues and the various short-term exhibitions mounted in the past, its collection is unrivalled.

Unfortunately, the permanent exhibition consists of just a sample from each of the main artistic periods from the Renaissance to the 1930s, giving only the vaguest hints at the wealth of exhibits stored away in the museum's vaults. Worse still, the top floor, which covers the period from the 1880s to the 1930s, has been closed for years. As a consolation, the museum's ground and first floors (and occasionally the nearby Rudolfinum) are used for some of the best temporary exhibitions in Prague, mostly taken from its turn-of-the-century and early twentieth-century collections. There's also a **public library** in the building, specializing in catalogues and material from previous exhibitions, and an excellent café on the ground floor (see p.213).

The public library is open Mon noon–6pm, Tues–Fri 10am–6pm; closed July & Aug.

Chapter 5

Nové Město

Although it comes over as a sprawling late nineteenth-century bourgeois quarter, **NOVÉ MĚSTO** was actually founded way back in 1348 by Charles IV as an entirely new town – three times as big as Staré Město – intended to link the southern fortress of Vyšehrad with Staré Město to the north. Large market squares, wide streets, and a level of town-planning far ahead of its time were employed to transform Prague into the new capital city of the Holy Roman Empire. Instead, however, Nové Město remained incomplete when Charles died, and quickly became the city's poorest quarter after Josefov, fertile ground for Hussitism and radicalism throughout the centuries. In the second half of the nineteenth century, the authorities set about a campaign of slum clearance similar to that inflicted on the Jewish quarter; only the churches and a few important historical buildings were left standing, but Charles' street layout survived pretty much intact. The leading architects of the day began to line the wide boulevards with ostentatious examples of their work, which were eagerly snapped up by the new class of status-conscious businessman – a process that has continued into this century, making Nové Město the most architecturally varied part of Prague.

Today, Nové Město remains the city's main commercial and business district, housing most of its hotels, nightclubs, cafés, fast-food outlets and department stores. The obvious starting point, and prob-

---

An Art-Nouveau hit list

Prague's Art Nouveau (the term is *secesní* in Czech) ranges from the vivacious floral motifs of the Paris metro to the more restrained style of the Viennese Secession. The following are some of the more striking examples covered in this chapter:

NOVÉ MĚSTO

ably the only place in Prague most visitors can put a name to, is Wenceslas Square or **Václavské náměstí**, hub of the modern city, and somewhere you're bound to find yourself passing through again and again. The two principal partially pedestrianized streets which lead off it are **Národní třída** and **Na příkopě**, which together form the *zlatý kříž* or golden cross, Prague's commercial centre and for over a century the most expensive slice of real estate in the capital. The *zlatý kříž* and the surrounding streets also contain some of Prague's finest late nineteenth-century, Art-Nouveau and twentieth-century architecture.

The rest of Nové Město, which spreads out northeast and southwest of Wenceslas Square, is much less explored, and for the most part heavily residential; unusually for Prague, using the tram and metro systems to get around here will save some unnecessary legwork. A few specific sights are worth singling out for attention – the **Dvořák** museum on Ke Karlovu, the **Mánes** art gallery on the waterfront, and the memorial to the Czechoslovak parachutists off Karlovo náměstí, for example – but the rest is decidedly less exciting than all that's gone before. However, if your ultimate destination is Vyšehrad, you can easily take in some of the more enjoyable bits of southern Nové Město en route.

Václavské náměstí (Wenceslas Square) and around

The natural pivot around which modern Prague revolves, and the focus of the events of November 1989, is **Václavské náměstí** (Wenceslas Square), more of a wide, gently sloping boulevard than a square as such. It's scarcely a conventional – or even convenient – space in which to hold mass demonstrations, yet night after night following the November 17 *masakr* in 1989 (see p.132), more than 250,000 people crammed into the square, often enduring subzero temperatures to call for the resignation of the Party leaders and demand free elections. On November 27, the whole of Prague came to a standstill, a bigger crowd than ever converging on the square to show their support for the two-hour nationwide general strike called by the opposition umbrella group, Občanské fórum (Civic Forum), who led the revolution. It was this last mass mobilization that proved decisive – by noon the next day, the Communist old guard had thrown in the towel.

The square's **history of protest** goes back to the 1848 revolution, whose violent denouement began here on June 12 with a peaceful open-air mass organized by the Prague students. On the crest of the nationalist disturbances, the square – which had been known as Koňský trh (Horse Market) since its foundation as such by Charles IV – was given its present name. Naturally enough, it was one of the natural rallying points for the jubilant crowds on October 28, 1918, when Czechoslovakia's independence was declared. Thirty years later, in 1948, the square was filled to capacity once more, this time with Communist demonstrators enthusiastically supporting the February coup. Then in August 1968, it was the scene of some of the most violent confrontations between the Soviet invaders and the local Czechs, during which the Národní muzeum came under fire – according to the Czechs, the Soviet officer in charge mistook it for the Parliament building, though they were most probably aiming for the nearby Radio Prague building, which was transmitting news of the Soviet invasion out to the West. And, of course, it was at the top of the square, on January 16, 1969, that Jan Palach set fire to himself in protest at the continuing occupation of the country by Russian troops.

Despite the square's medieval origins, its oldest building dates only from the eighteenth century, and the vast majority are much younger. As the city's money moved south of Staré Město during the industrial revolution, so the square became the architectural showpiece of the nation, and it is now lined with self-important six- or seven-storey buildings, representing every artistic trend of the last hundred years, from neo-Renaissance to Socialist Realism. Even if you've no interest in modern architecture, there's plenty to keep you occupied in the shops, arcades, cinemas, theatres and general hubbub of the square.

Wenceslas Square has always been the place to be seen, and, at its bottom end, to participate in the Prague version of the *passeggiata*. This is also the one place in the city where streetlife and nightlife continue long after midnight – the hotels and tacky nightclubs buzzing with tourists and mafiosi, while the police, the pimps and the prostitutes patrol the pavements. Access to the square by car is restricted to those who are staying at one of the square's hotels, so this has traditionally been the place to inspect the latest flash cars. However, the days when unfamiliarity with western vehicles meant that even a Vespa was looked on as if it were a recently landed intergalactic spaceship, have long since gone.

Around Můstek

The busiest part of Wenceslas Square and a popular place to meet up before hitting town is around **Můstek**, the city's most central metro station, at the northern end of the square. The area is dominated by the **Palác Koruna (a)**, a hulking wedge of sculptured concrete and gold, built for an insurance company in 1914 by Antonín Pfeiffer, one of Jan Kotěra's many pupils. The building is a rare mixture of heavy constructivism and gilded Secession-style ornamentation, but the *pièce de résistance* is the palace's bejewelled crown which lights up at night.

Opposite Palác Koruna, adjacent to one another, are two functionalist buildings designed by Ludvík Kysela in the late 1920s, billed at the time as the first glass curtain-wall buildings. Along with the Hotel Juliš (see below), they represent the perfect expression of the optimistic mood of progress and modernism that permeated the interwar republic. The building on the right as you face them (**b**), built for the chocolate firm, Lindt, was the first to be erected; the **Baťa store (c)**, on the left, followed a few years later. The latter was built for the Czech shoe magnate, Tomáš Baťa, one of the greatest patrons of avant-garde Czech art, who fled the country in 1948, when the Communists nationalized the shoe industry; the store was returned to the family, along with a number of their shoe factories, after 1989. Even if you've no intention of buying a pair of Baťa boots, it's worth taking the lift to the top floor for a bird's-eye view onto the square.

Twenty-five years earlier, Czech architecture was in the throes of its own version of Art Nouveau, one of whose earliest practitioners was Jan Kotěra. The **Peterkův dům (d)**, a slender essay in the new style, was his first work, undertaken at the tender age of 28. Kotěra, a pupil of the great architect of the Viennese Secession, Otto Wagner, eventually moved on to a much more brutal constructivism. Another supreme example of Czech functionalism, a few doors further up at no. 22, is the **Hotel Juliš (e)**, designed by Pavel Janák, who had already made his name as one of the leading lights of the short-lived Czech Cubist (and later Rondo-Cubist) movement (see p.153). Another point of interest, on the corner of Jindřišská, is the neo-Baroque **Assicurazione Generali (f)** – now home to the Polish Cultural Institute. It was designed by Osvald Polívka and Bedřich Ohmann, and was where the young Kafka worked for a couple of years as an insurance clerk.

Beyond Jindřišská

One of the Communists' most miserable attempts to continue the square's tradition of grand architecture was the **Družba**

(Friendship) department store, now **Krone** (g), which stands like a 1970s reject on the other side of Jindřišská, its only redeeming feature its rooftop café *Fromin*. Diagonally opposite is the **Melantrich** publishing house (h), whose first floor is occupied by the offices of the former Socialist Party newspaper, *Svobodné slovo* (The Free Word). For forty years, the Socialist Party was a loyal puppet of the Communist government, but on the second night of the November 1989 demonstrations, the newspaper handed over its well-placed balcony to the opposition speakers of Občanské fórum (Civic Forum), and later witnessed the historic appearance of Havel and Dubček.

Melantrich House faces probably the most famous and the two most ornate buildings on the entire square, the Art Nouveau **Grand Hotel Evropa** (i), and its slim neighbour, the Hotel Meran, both built in 1903–05 by two of Ohmann's disciples, Bendelmayer and Dryák. They represent everything the Czech modern movement stood against: chiefly, ornament for ornament's sake, not that this has in any way dented the *Evropa*'s popularity. The café terrace has always had a reputation for low-key cruising and a great deal of posing, but it's worth forgoing the sunlight for the sumptuous interior, with its symbolist art and elaborate brass fittings and light fixtures, unchanged since the hotel first opened.

Opposite the hotel is the vast **Palác Lucerna** (j), one of the more appealing of the square's numerous dimly lit shopping arcades (see box). Designed in the early part of this century in Moorish style by, among others, Havel's own grandfather, it was returned to Havel and his brother after 1989, and has been the focus of much family squabbling ever since. Apart from a brief glance at the **Hotel Jalta** (k), built in the Stalinist aesthetic of the 1950s, there's nothing

---

Prague's pasáže

Prague has an impressive array of old **shopping arcades** or *pasáže*, as they're known in Czech, the majority of which are located in and around Wenceslas Square and date from the first half of this century. Compared with the chic *passages* off the Champs-Élysées, Prague's *pasáže* offer more modest pleasures: a few shops, the odd café and, more often than not, a cinema. The king of the lot is the lavishly decorated Lucerna *pasáž*, which stretches all the way from Štěpánská to Vodičkova and contains an equally ornate cinema, café and vast concert hall. You can continue your indoor stroll on the other side of Vodičkova through the Světozor *pasáž*, which boasts another cinema, and a wonderful stained-glass mosaic advertising the old state electronics company Tesla. The first of the *pasáže* to receive a 1990s' facelift was the marble-clad Koruna *pasáž*, on the corner of Na příkopě, now lined with swanky shops including Prague's largest music store, Bonton Megastore. There have also been renewed attempts to continue the tradition, but judging by the Myslbek *pasáž*, a typically limp modern imitation opened in 1997 and fronted by Marks & Spencer on the other side of Na příkopě, the glory days are over.

*For a brief
biography of
Wenceslas, see
p.55.*

more to stop for, architecturally speaking, until you get to the
Wenceslas Monument.

The Wenceslas Monument

A statue of Saint Wenceslas (sv Václav) has stood at the top of the
square since 1680 but the present **Wenceslas Monument** (1), by the
father of Czech sculpture, Josef Václav Myslbek, was not finally
unveiled until 1912, after thirty years on the drawing board. The
Czech patron saint sits astride his mighty steed, surrounded by small-
er-scale representations of four other Bohemian saints – his mother
Ludmila, Procopius, Adalbert and Agnes – added in the 1920s. In
1918, 1948, 1968, and again in 1989, the monument was used as a
national political notice board, festooned in posters, flags and slogans
and even now, it remains the city's favourite soapbox venue.

Two of Prague's most famous martyrs were fatally wounded close
by. On October 28, 1939, during the demonstrations against the Nazi
occupation, the medical student Jan Opletal was fatally wounded
when troops opened fire on protesters. And on January 16, 1969, the
21-year-old philosophy student Jan Palach set himself alight in
protest against the continuing occupation of his country by the
Soviets; he died from his wounds three days later. Several others followed Palach's example, including Jan Zajíc, who set fire to himself
on the same spot on February 25, the anniversary of the Communist
coup. Attempts to lay flowers on this spot on the anniversary of
Palach's protest provided an annual source of confrontation; Václav
Havel received the last of his many prison sentences for just such an
action in January 1989. An impromptu martyrs' shrine of candles and
messages, set up in the aftermath of the November 1989 revolution,
has now been formalized as a simple memorial to *obětem komunis-
mu* (the victims of Communism), adorned with flowers and photos of
Palach and Zajíc.

Národní muzeum (National Museum)

*The Národní
muzeum is
open daily:
May–Sept
10am–6pm;
Oct–April
9am–5pm;
closed first
Tuesday of the
month.*

At the top, southern, end of Wenceslas Square sits the broad,
brooding hulk of the **Národní muzeum**, built by Josef Schulz.
Deliberately modelled on the great European museums of Paris and
Vienna, it dominates the view up the square like a giant golden
eagle with outstretched wings. Along with the National Theatre
(see below), this is one of the great landmarks of the nineteenth-
century Czech *národní obrození*, sporting a monumental gilt-
framed glass cupola, worthy clumps of sculptural decoration and
narrative frescoes from Czech history.

Unless you're a geologist or a zoologist, however, you're unlikely
to be excited by most of the exhibits – room after room of stuffed animals and skeletons, plus endless display cases full of rocks – but it's
worth taking at least a quick look at the ornate marble entrance hall,

and the **Pantheon** of Czech notables at the top of the main staircase. Arranged under the glass-domed hall are 48 busts and statues of distinguished Czech men (plus a couple of token women and Slovaks), including the universally adored T. G. Masaryk, the country's founding president, whose statue was removed by the Communists from every other public place. Since the revolution, the appeal of the museum's temporary exhibitions (on themes ranging from Masaryk to dinosaurs) has increased dramatically, so it's always worth checking to see what's on.

Wilsonova

At the southern end of Wenceslas Square is some of the worst blight that Communist planners inflicted on Prague; above all, the six-lane highway that now separates Nové Město from the residential suburb of Vinohrady to the east and south, and effectively cuts off the Národní muzeum from Wenceslas Square. Previously known as Vitězného února (Victorious February) after the 1948 Communist coup, the road was renamed **Wilsonova** in honour of US President Woodrow Wilson (a personal friend of the Masaryk family), who effectively gave the country its independence from Austria-Hungary in 1918.

The Prague stock exchange building alongside the Národní muzeum, only completed in the 1930s but rendered entirely redundant by the 1948 coup, was another victim of postwar "reconstruction". The architect Karel Prager was given the task of designing a new "socialist" **Federal Assembly** building on the same site, without destroying the old bourse: he opted for a supremely unappealing bronze-tinted plate-glass structure, supported by concrete stilts and sitting uncomfortably on top of its diminutive predecessor. Since the break-up of the country, the building has lost its *raison d'être* and now provides a home for, among other things, Radio Free Europe's headquarters.

Next to the Parliament building, the grandiose **Státní opera** (State Opera), built by the Viennese duo Helmer and Fellner, looks stunted and deeply affronted by the traffic which now tears past its front entrance. It was opened in 1888 as the *Neues Deutsches Theater*, shortly after the Czechs had built their own national theatre on the waterfront. Always second fiddle to the Stavovské divadlo, though equally ornate inside, it was one of the last great building projects of Prague's once all-powerful German minority. The velvet and gold interior is still as fresh as it was when the Bohemian-born composer Gustav Mahler brought the traffic to a standstill, conducting the première of his *Seventh Symphony*.

The last building on this deafening freeway is **Praha hlavní nádraží**, Prague's main railway station, and one of the final glories of the dying Empire, designed by Josef Fanta and officially opened in 1909 as the *Franz-Josefs Bahnhof*. Trapped in the overpolished subterranean modern section, it's easy to miss the station's surviving Art Nouveau parts. The original entrance on Wilsonova still exudes

imperial confidence, with its wrought-iron canopy and naked fig-
urines clinging to the sides of the towers; on the other side of the
road, two great glass protrusions signal the new entrance in the
Vrchlického sady.

Národní třída and Na příkopě

Národní třída and **Na příkopě** trace the course of the old Staré
Město moat, which was finally filled in in 1760. Their boomerang
curve still marks the border between Staré Město and Nové Město,
though strictly speaking, the dividing line runs down the middle of
the street. At the turn of the century, these two partly pedestrianized
streets formed the chief venue for the weekend *passeggiata*, and
even today they are among the most crowded expanses of pavement
in Prague. Along with a variety of stylish shops, banks, restaurants
and clubs, you'll also discover some of the city's most flamboyant
Art-Nouveau buildings.

Jungmannovo náměstí and around

Before you hit Národní třída proper, you must pass through
Jungmannovo náměstí, named for Josef Jungmann (1772–1847), a
prolific writer, translator and leading light of the Czech national
revival, whose pensive, seated statue was erected here in 1878. This
small, ill-proportioned square boasts an unrivalled panoply of Czech
architectural curiosities, ranging from Emil Králíček and Matěj
Blecha's unique **Cubist streetlamp** (and seat) from 1912, hidden
away beyond the Jungmann statue in the far eastern corner of the
square to the gleaming, functionalist facade of the ARA department
store (now the Investiční banka), built in the late 1920s on the corner of Perlova and ulica 28 října (October 28 Street, commemorating the foundation of the First Republic).

*There's an
earlier, purer
example of
Rondo-Cubism
at
Jungmannovo
náměstí 4, dec-
orated in the
Czech national
colours of red
and white, and
you'll find
another exam-
ple of the style
on p.137.*

The Palác Adria

Diagonally opposite the ARA department store is the square's most
imposing building, the chunky charcoal-coloured, vigorously sculptured **Palác Adria**, on the south side of the square. It was designed in
the early 1920s by Pavel Janák and Josef Zasche, with sculptural
extras by Otto Gutfreund and a central *Seafaring* group by Jan
Štursa. Janák was a pioneering figure in the short-lived, prewar
Czech Cubist movement; after the war, he and Josef Gočár attempted to create a national style of architecture appropriate for the newly
founded republic. The style was dubbed "Rondo-Cubism" – semi-cir-
cular motifs are a recurrent theme – though the Palác Adria owes as
much to the Italian Renaissance as it does to the new national style.

Originally built for the Italian insurance company *Reunione
Adriatica di Sicurità* – hence its current name – the basement of

the Palác Adria was until recently a studio theatre for the multimedia *Laterna magika* (Magic Lantern) company. In 1989, it became the underground nerve centre of the Velvet Revolution, when Civic Forum found temporary shelter here shortly after their inaugural meeting on the Sunday following the November 17 demonstration. Against a stage backdrop for Dürenmatt's *Minotaurus*, the Forum thrashed out tactics in the dressing rooms and gave daily press conferences in the auditorium during the crucial fortnight before the Communists relinquished power. Since then, *Laterna magika* have moved to much bigger venues, and the *Divadlo za branou III* is now based here instead.

Národní
třída and
Na příkopě

The Church of Panna Maria Sněžná

Right beside the Cubist streetlamp is the medieval gateway of the church of **Panna Maria Sněžná** (St Mary-of-the-Snows), one of the great landmarks of Wenceslas Square, towering over the backs of the two-storey houses that once lined the square, but now barely visible from any of the surrounding streets. If the gates are shut, try going through the unpromising courtyard back near the Jungmann statue.

Like most of Nové Město's churches, the Panna Maria Sněžná was founded by Charles IV, who envisaged a vast coronation church on a scale comparable with the St Vitus Cathedral, on which work had just begun. Unfortunately, the money ran out shortly after completion of the chancel; the result is curious – a church which is short in length, but equal to the cathedral in height. The 100ft-high vaulting – which collapsed on the Franciscans who inherited the half-completed building in the seventeenth century – does little to stave off claustrophobia, further compounded by an overbearing Baroque altar which touches the ceiling. To get an idea of the intended scale of the finished structure, take a stroll through the **Františkánská zahrada**, to the south of the church; these gardens make a lovely hideaway from Nové Mesto's bustle, marred only by the intrusive modern garden furniture.

Prague's wax museums

A short walk down ulica 28 října, which connects Jungmannovo náměstí with Wenceslas Square, is one of Prague's newest attractions, the **Muzeum voskových figurín** (Wax Museum), laid out on the ground floor of the Art Nouveau palác Rapid at no. 13. Though by no means Prague's first private museum, it is by far the most ambitious to date. The current entrance fee of 120kč is steep for most Czechs, yet the museum is aimed primarily at a domestic audience. For anyone familiar with London's Madame Tussaud's, the formula is predictable enough, but unless your grasp of Czech history is pretty good, many of the wax tableaux will remain slightly baffling. The most popular section with the locals is the podium of Commie stooges ranging from Lenin to the Czechs' home-grown Stalinist,

*Both wax
museums are
open daily
10am–8pm.*

The masakr – November 17, 1989

On the night of Friday, November 17, 1989, a 50,000-strong, officially sanctioned student demonstration, organized by the students' union, SSM (League of Young Socialists), worked its way down Národní with the intention of reaching Wenceslas Square. Halfway down the street they were confronted by the *bílé přilby* (white helmets) and *červené barety* (red berets) of the hated riot-police. For what must have seemed like hours, there was a stalemate as the students sat down and refused to disperse, some of them handing flowers out to the police. Suddenly, without any warning, the police attacked and what became known as the **masakr** (massacre) began. In the end, no one was actually killed, though it wasn't for want of trying by the police. Under the arches of the Kaňkův dům, Národní 16, there's a small symbolic bronze relief of eight hands reaching out for help, a permanent shrine in memory of the hundreds who were hospitalized in the violence.

Klement Gottwald, followed by today's generation of Czech politicians dressed in bad suits, sat amidst naff office furniture.

Within a few months of the Muzeum voskových figurín opening, a second wax museum, the **Pražské panoptikum**, opened up just down the street at Národní 25, in the *pasáž* of the palác Metro. It's equally professional and slick, with ticket prices (99kč) similarly inflated, and follows pretty much the same formular, with many of the same historical characters, from Hus to Havel, appearing again. If anything, you'll need an even better knowledge of Czech history and culture to enjoy the *panoptikum*, though you do get the added extra of a short miniature dance show cleverly projected onto a three-dimensional stage.

Národní třída

The eastern end of **Národní** is taken up with shops, galleries and clubs, all of which begin to peter out as you near the river. At the last crossroads before the waterfront is the new **British Council** building, which formerly belonged to the East German cultural institute. On the outside, the original constructivist facade, designed in the 1930s by Osvald Polívka, has been kept intact, while the light interior has been thoroughly and imaginatively modernized in an interesting synthesis of central European and British architectural styles, using ample helpings of the country's surplus glass. There's a window gallery on the ground floor overlooking Národní, which is run by the British Council, and you're free to walk in and take a peek at the lobby – the entrance is up Voršilská – where you can pick up information on the latest cultural offerings sponsored by the BC.

Further down Národní, on the right-hand side, is an eye-catching duo of much earlier Art Nouveau buildings, designed by Polívka in 1907–08. The first, at no. 7, was built for the **pojišťovna Praha** (Prague

Savings Bank), hence the beautiful mosaic lettering above the windows advertizing *život* (life insurance) and *kapital* (loans), as well as help with your *důchod* (pension) and *věno* (dowry). Next door, the slightly more ostentatious **Topičův dům**, headquarters of *Československý spisovatel*, the official state publishers, provides the perfect accompaniment, with a similarly ornate wrought-iron and glass canopy.

Opposite, the convent and church of **sv Voršila** (St Ursula) are distinguished by the rare sight (in this part of town) of a tree sticking out of its white facade. When it was completed in 1678, this was one of the first truly flamboyant Baroque buildings in Prague, and its white stucco and frescoed interior have recently been restored to their original state. The Ursuline nuns were booted out by the Communists, but have returned post-1989 to found one of the first ecclesiastical schools in the country.

Národní divadlo and Café Slavia

At the western end of Národní, overlooking the Vltava, is the gold-crested **Národní divadlo** (National Theatre), proud symbol of the Czech nation. Refused money from the Habsburg state coffers, Czechs of all classes dug deep into their pockets to raise funds for the venture themselves. The foundation stones, gathered from various historically significant sites in Bohemia and Moravia, were laid in 1868 by the historian and politician, František Palacký, and the composer, Bedřich Smetana; the architect, Josef Zítek, spent the next thirteen years on the project. In June 1881, the theatre opened with a première of Smetana's *Libuše*. In August of the same year, fire ripped through the building, destroying everything except the outer walls. Within two years the whole thing was rebuilt – even the emperor contributed this time – under the supervision of Josef Schulz (who went on to design the National Museum), and it opened once more to the strains of Smetana's opera *Libuše*. The grand portal on the north side of the theatre is embellished with suitably triumphant allegorical figures, and, inside, every square inch is taken up with paintings and sculptures by leading artists of the Czech national revival. Tickets are relatively cheap but most productions are in Czech, so unless there's an opera or ballet on, content yourself with a quick peek at the decor prior to a performance.

See p.231 for details of Prague's theatres and box offices.

Standing behind the Národní divadlo, and in dramatic contrast with it, is the theatre's state-of-the-art extension, the ultra-modern glass box of the **Nová scéna**, designed by Karel Prager, the leading architect of the Communist era, and completed in 1983. It's one of those buildings most Praguers love to hate – it was described by one Czech as looking like "frozen piss" – though compared to much of Prague's Communist-era architecture, it's not that bad. Just for the record, the lump of molten rock in the courtyard is a symbolic evocation of *My Socialist Country*, by Malejovský.

Národní
třída and
Na příkopě

For more on
Jaroslav
Seifert, see
p.158.

The **Café Slavia**, opposite the theatre, has been a favourite haunt of the city's writers, dissidents and artists (and, inevitably, actors) since the days of the First Republic. The Czech avant-garde movement, *Devětsil*, led by Karel Teige, used to hold its meetings here in the 1920s; the meetings are recorded for posterity by another of its members, the Nobel prize-winner Jaroslav Seifert, in his *Slavia Poems*. The café has been carelessly modernized since those arcadian days, and only re-opened in 1997 after being closed for over five years – much to the annoyace of its regulars.

Na příkopě

Heading northeastwards from Můstek at the bottom end of Wenceslas Square, you can join the crush of bodies ambling down **Na příkopě** (literally "On the moat"). The street was once lined on both sides with grandiose buildings, like the former *Haas* department store at no. 4, built in 1869–71 by Theophil von Hansen, the architect responsible for

A new
museum
dedicated to
Alfons Mucha
has opened on
Panská, see
p.146.

much of the redevelopment of the Ring in Vienna. Many of the finest buildings, though – like the *Café Corso* and the *Café Français*, once the favourite haunts of Prague's German-Jewish literary set – were torn down and replaced during the enthusiastic construction boom of the interwar republic. The Art Nouveau U **Dörflerů**, at no. 7, from 1905, is one of the few survivors along this stretch, its gilded floral curlicues gleaming in the midday sun. Further along, on the same side of the street, the brand new **Pasáž Myslbek**, fronted by Marks & Spencers, is one of the few contemporary works of architecture in central Prague, and probably for that reason alone, demands attention.

Prague's main
tourist office is
at no. 22.

There are another couple of interesting buildings on the opposite side of the street, at nos. 18 and 20, designed by Polívka over the course of a twenty-year period for the *Zemská banka* and connected by a kind of Bridge of Sighs suspended over Nekázanka. The style veers between 1890s neo-Renaissance and later Art Nouveau elements, such as Jan Preisler's gilded mosaics and Ladislav Saloun's attic sculptures. It's worth nipping upstairs to the main banking hall of what is now the **Živnostenka banka**, at no. 20, to appreciate the financial might of Czech capital in the last decades of the Austro-Hungarian Empire. Yet more financial institutions, this time from the dour 1930s, line the far end of Na příkopě, as it opens up into náměstí Republiky.

Northern Nové Město

Náměstí Republiky is worth pausing at, if only to admire the Obecní dům – Prague's most alluring Art Nouveau structure – but this aside, there's nothing in the northern or eastern part of Nové Město that merits a special trip. Nevertheless, you may find yourself in this part of town by dint of its shops, restaurants and hotels, or perhaps en route to Prague's main domestic train station, Masarykovo nádraží.

Tourists rarely venture this far east, and for that reason alone, it makes an interesting diversion, revealing a side to central Prague that few visitors see.

Náměstí Republiky

Náměstí Republiky is an unruly space, made more so since the construction of its metro station and the ugly brown *Kotva* department store, built by Swedish architects in the 1970s. The oldest structure on the square is the **Prašná brána** (Powder Gate), one of the eight medieval gate-towers that once guarded Staré Město. The present tower was begun by King Vladislav Jagiello in 1475, shortly after he'd moved into the royal court, which was situated next door at the time. Work stopped when he retreated to the Hrad to avoid the wrath of his subjects; later on, it was used to store gunpowder – hence the name and the reason for the damage incurred in 1757. The small historical exhibition inside traces the tower's architectural metamorphosis over the centuries, up to its present remodelling courtesy of the nineteenth-century restorer, Josef Mocker. Most people, though, ignore the displays, and climb straight up for the modest view from the top.

*The Prašná
brána is open
daily
10am–6pm.*

Obecní dům

Attached to the tower, and built on the ruins of the old royal court, the **Obecní dům** (Municipal House) is by far the most exciting Art-Nouveau building in Prague, one of the few places that still manages to conjure up the atmosphere of Prague's turn-of-the-century café society. Conceived as a cultural centre for the Czech community, it's probably the finest architectural achievement of the Czech national revival, designed by Osvald Polívka and Antonín Balšánek, and extravagantly decorated inside and out with the help of almost every artist connected with the Czech Secession. From the lifts to the cloakrooms, just about all the furnishings remain as they were when the building was completed in 1911, and every square inch of the interior and exterior has recently been lovingly renovated. Appropriately enough, it was here that Czechoslovakia's independence was declared on October 28, 1918.

The simplest way of soaking up the interior – peppered with mosaics and pendulous brass chandeliers – is to have a coffee in the cavernous café, or a full meal in the equally spacious *Francouská restaurace* or the *Plzenská restaurace* in the basement. For a more detailed inspection of the building's spectacular interior (which includes paintings by Alfons Mucha, Jan Preisler and Max Švabinský, among others), you can sign up for a **guided tour**; tickets are available from the new information and ticket centre on the ground floor, beyond the main foyer. Several rooms on the second floor are given over to temporary art exhibitions, while the building's **Smetanova**

*The ticket
office and
information
centre at the
Obecní dům
are open daily
10am–6pm.*

síň, Prague's largest concert hall, stages numerous concerts, including the opening salvo of the *Pražské jaro* (Prague Spring Festival) – traditionally a rendition of Smetana's *Má vlast* (My Country) – which takes place in the presence of the president.

Hybernská and Senovážné náměstí

Large exhibitions – occasionally worth a look – are held in U hybernů (The Hibernians), a haughty Neoclassical building opposite the Obecní dům, built as a customs office in the Napoleonic period, on the site of a Baroque church which belonged to the order of Irish Franciscans who fled Tudor England (hence its name). If you walk down **Hybernská** from here, you'll pass the Art Nouveau **Hotel Central** on the right. Designed by Dryák and Bendelmayer (who built the Grand Hotel Evropa) and dating from 1900, its newly restored gilded decoration stands out amidst its dour nineteenth-century neighbours.

Opposite the hotel is the **American Center for Culture and Commerce**, formerly the headquarters of the Social Democratic Party, which was forcibly amalgamated with the Communist Party shortly after the 1948 coup. The party regained its independence in 1989, and, after a shaky start, looks set to be the next party in government when Václav Klaus finally falls from power. In January 1912, a small backroom in the building was given over to a congress of the Russian Social Democratic Labour Party. The party was deeply divided, and the meeting poorly attended, with only fourteen voting delegates present (all but two of them Bolsheviks), and **Lenin** himself in the chair. It was this meeting which pushed through the formal takeover of the party by the Bolsheviks, to the exclusion of the Mensheviks and others, and gave the Czech Communists the perfect excuse for turning the whole place into a vast museum dedicated to Lenin, of which there is now, not surprisingly, absolutely no trace.

Around Masarykovo nádraží and Senovážné náměstí

A little further down Hybernská, a wrought-iron canopy marks the entrance to Prague's first railway station, **Masarykovo nádraží**, opened in 1845 – a modest, almost provincial affair compared to the Art Nouveau Praha hlavní nádraží. On the opposite side of Hybernská is the **Café Arco**, once a favourite of Kafka (who worked nearby), and the circle of Prague-German writers known as the *Arconauts*. The current incumbents make nothing of its literary associations, and have filled the place with slot machines and pool tables.

South of Masarykovo nádraží, down Dlážděná, is the old hay market, **Senovážné náměstí**, packed out with parked cars and a couple of market stalls. Its most distinguished feature is the freestanding fifteenth-century belfry of the church of **sv Jindřich** (St Henry); both have undergone several facelifts, most recently by the ubiquitous Gothic restorer, Josef Mocker.

Northern
Nové Město

A short way up Jeruzalémská, you'll find the **Jubilejní synagóga**, named in honour of the sixtieth year of the Emperor Franz-Josef I's reign in 1908. Built in a colourful Moorish style similar to that of the Španělská synagóga in Josefov, the Hebrew inscription on the facade strikes a note of liberal optimism: "Do we not have one father? Were we not created by the same God?" The synagogue holds regular Sabbath services; at all other times, it's usually closed.

*Prague's other
synagogues
are covered in
Chapter 4.*

North of Masarykovo nádraží

Running roughly parallel with Hybernská, to the north of Masarykovo nádraží, is the much busier street of **Na poříčí**, an area that, like sv Havel in Staré Město, was originally settled by German merchants. Kafka spent most of his working life as a frustrated and unhappy clerk for the *Arbeiter-Unfall-Versicherungs-Anstalt* (Workers' Accident Insurance Company), in the grand nineteenth-century building at no. 7. Further along on the right is a much more unusual piece of corporate architecture, the **Banka legií**, one of Pavel Janák's rare Rondo-Cubist efforts from the early 1920s. Set into the bold smoky-red moulding is a striking white marble frieze by Otto Gutfreund, depicting the epic march across Siberia undertaken by the Czechoslovak Legion and their embroilment in the Russian Revolution. You're free to wander into the main banking hall on the ground floor, which, though marred by the current bank fittings, retains its curved glass roof and distinctive red-and-white marble patterning. The glass curtain-walled **Bílá labuť** (White Swan) department store, opposite, is a good example of the functionalist style which Janák and others went on to embrace in the late 1920s and 1930s.

*The Banka
legií is open
Mon–Fri
8am–5pm; for
more on Janák
and the
Cubists, see
p.153.*

As a lively shopping street, Na poříčí seems very much out on a limb, as do the cluster of hotels at the end of the street, and around the corner in **Těšnov**. The reason behind this is the now defunct Těšnov train station, which was demolished in the 1960s to make way for the monstrous Wilsonova flyover. Antonín Balšánek's purpose-built neo-Renaissance mansion, housing the **Muzeum Prahy** (Prague Museum), on the other side of the flyover, is the lone survivor of this redevelopment. Inside, there's an ad hoc collection of the city's art, a number of antique bicycles, and usually an intriguing temporary exhibition on some aspect of the city. The museum's prize possession, though, is Antonín Langweil's paper model of Prague which he completed after eleven years in 1837. It's a fascinating insight into early nineteenth-century Prague – predominantly Baroque, with the cathedral incomplete and the Jewish quarter "unsanitized" – and, consequently, has served as one of the most useful records for the city's restorers. The most surprising thing, of course, is that so little has changed.

*The museum
is open Tues,
Wed &
Fri–Sun
10am–6pm,
Thurs
10am–8pm.*

Northern
Nové Město

*The Poštovní
muzeum is
open
Tues–Sun
9am–4.30pm.*

Nábřeží Ludvika Svobody and around

North of Na poříčí, close to the river bank, nábřeží Ludvika Svobody, there's another museum which might appeal to some: the **Poštovní muzeum** (Postage Museum), housed in the Vávra mill on Nové mlýny, near one of Prague's many water towers. The first floor contains a series of jolly nineteenth-century wall paintings of Romantic Austrian landscapes, and a collection of drawings on postman themes. The real philately is on the ground floor – a vast international collection of stamps arranged in vertical pull-out drawers. The Czechoslovak issues are historically and artistically interesting, as well as of appeal to collectors. Stamps became a useful tool in the propaganda wars of this century; even such short-lived ventures as the Hungarian-backed Slovak Socialist Republic of 1918–19 and the Slovak National Uprising of autumn 1944 managed to print special issues. Under the First Republic, the country's leading artists, notably Alfons Mucha and Max Švabinský, were commissioned to design stamps, some of which are exceptionally beautiful.

As you leave the museum, look across to your left towards Revoluční: the statue of **Jan Šverma** is one of the few Communist-era monuments to have survived the post-1989 iconoclasm that brought countless statues tumbling down. Šverma, who joined the Communist Party shortly after it was formed in 1921 and died fighting against the Nazis in 1944, has been targeted by the Prague branch of the Confederation of Political Prisoners who want him removed from his pedestal, and the nearby bridge (currently Švermův most) renamed. Further east along the embankment is another monument of the Communist era, the former headquarters of the Party's Central Committee, now the **Ministry of Tranport**, where Dubček and his fellow reformers were arrested in August 1968, before being spirited away to Moscow for "frank and fraternal" discussions.

Southern Nové Město

The streets south of Národní and Wenceslas Square still run along the medieval lines of Charles IV's town plan, though they're now lined with grand, late nineteenth- and twentieth-century buildings. Such is their scale, however, that some of these broad boulevards – like Žitná and Ječná – have become the main arteries for Prague's steadily increasing traffic. Together with the large distances involved, this makes southern Nové Město one part of the city where hopping on a tram can be a good way of getting about. Three tram routes worth knowing about are: tram #24, which goes along Vodičkova, up the side of Karlovo náměstí and past the Botanická zahrada; tram #3, which follows a similar route but heads off to Palackého náměstí and south along the riverfront; and tram #18, which heads south from Národní down Spálená, up the side of Karlovo náměstí and past the Botanická zahrada.

South to Karlovo náměstí

Of the many roads which head down towards Karlovo náměstí, Vodičkova is probably the most impressive, running southwest for half a kilometre from Wenceslas Square. You can catch several trams along this route, though there are a handful of buildings worth checking out on the way, so you may choose to walk. The first, U Nováků, is impossible to miss, thanks to Jan Preisler's mosaic of bucolic frolicking (its actual subject, *Trade and Industry*, is confined to edges of the picture), and Polívka's curvilinear window frames and delicate, ivy-like ironwork. Originally built for the *Novák* department store in the early 1900s, for the last sixty years it has been a cabaret hall, restaurant and café all rolled into one; however, the original fittings have long since been destroyed.

Halfway down the street, at no. 15, the *McDonald's* "restaurant" – the first to open in the Czech Republic in March 1992 – must qualify

---

Milena Jesenská

The most famous "Minervan" was **Milena Jesenská**, born in 1896 into a Czech family whose ancestry stretched back to the sixteenth century. Shortly after leaving school, she was confined to a mental asylum by her father when he discovered that she was having an affair with a Jew. On her release, she married the Jew and moved to Vienna, where she took a job as a railway porter to support the two of them. While living in Vienna, she sent a Czech translation of one of Kafka's short stories to his publisher; Kafka wrote back himself, and so began their platonic, mostly epistolary, relationship. Kafka described her later as "the only woman who ever understood me", and with his encouragement she took up writing professionally. Tragically, by the time Milena had extricated herself from her disastrous marriage, Kafka, still smarting from three failed engagements with other women, had decided never to commit himself to anyone else; his letters alone survived the war, as a moving testament to their love.

Milena returned to Prague in 1925, and moved on from writing exclusively fashion articles to critiques of avant-garde architecture, becoming one of the city's leading journalists. She married again, this time to the prominent functionalist architect Jaromír Krejcar, but later, a difficult pregnancy and childbirth left her addicted to morphine. She overcame her dependency only after joining the Communist Party, but was to quit after the first of Stalin's show trials in 1936. She continued to work as a journalist in the late 1930s, and wrote a series of articles condemning the rise of fascism in the Sudetenland.

When the Nazis rolled into Prague in 1939, Milena's Vinohrady flat had already become a centre for resistance. For a while, she managed to hang on to her job, but her independent intellectual stance and provocative gestures – like wearing a yellow star as a mark of solidarity with her Jewish friends – soon attracted the attentions of the Gestapo, and after a brief spell in the notorious Pankrác prison, she was sent to Ravensbrück, the women's concentration camp near Berlin, where she died of nephritis (inflammation of the kidneys) in May 1944.

---

as a landmark of sorts. It occupies the site of the *Akademická kavárna*, one of the many lost literary cafés of turn-of-the-century Prague. Directly opposite stands the imposing neo-Renaissance **Minerva girls' school**, covered in bright-red sgraffito. Founded in 1866, it was the first such institution in Prague, and was notorious for the antics of its pupils, the "Minervans", who shocked bourgeois Czech society with their experimentations with fashion, drugs and sexual freedom (see box p.139). As Vodičkova curves left towards Karlovo náměstí, Lazarská, meeting point of the city's night trams, leads off to the right. At the bottom of this street is **Diamant**, another of Prague's Cubist buildings, completed in 1912 by Emil Králíček. It's grubby with pollution now, but the geometric sculptural reliefs on the facade, the main portal and the frame enclosing a Baroque statue of St John of Nepomuk on Spálená, remain worth viewing none the less.

Karlovo náměstí

Once Prague's biggest square, **Karlovo náměstí**'s impressive proportions are no longer so easy to appreciate, obscured by a tree-planted public garden and cut in two by the busy thoroughfare of

---

The Assassination of Reinhard Heydrich

The assassination of Reinhard Heydrich in 1942 was the only attempt the Allies ever made on the life of a leading Nazi. It's an incident which the Allies have always billed as a great success in the otherwise rather dismal seven-year history of the Czech resistance. But, as with all acts of brave resistance during the war, there was a price to be paid. Given that the reprisals meted out to the Czech population were entirely predictable, it remains a controversial, if not suicidal, decision to have made.

The target, **Reinhard Tristan Eugen Heydrich**, was a talented and upwardly mobile anti-Semite (despite rumours that he was partly Jewish himself), a great organizer and a skilful concert violinist. He was a late recruit to the Nazi Party, signing up in 1931, after having been dismissed from the German Navy for dishonourable conduct towards a woman. However, he swiftly rose through the ranks of the SS to become second in command after Himmler, and in the autumn of 1941, he was appointed *Reichsprotektor* of the puppet state of *Böhmen und Mähren* – effectively, the most powerful man in the Czech Lands. Although his rule began with brutality, it soon settled into the tried and tested policy which Heydrich liked to call *Peitsche und Zucker* (literally, "whip and sugar").

On the morning of May 27, 1942, as Heydrich was being driven by his personal bodyguard, *Oberscharführer* Klein, in his open-top Mercedes from his manor house north of Prague to his office in Hradčany, three Czechoslovak agents (parachuted in from England) were taking up positions in the northeastern suburb of Libeň. As the car pulled into Kirchmayer Boulevard (now V Holešovičkách), one of them, a Slovak called Gabčík, pulled out a Sten gun and tried to shoot. The gun jammed, at which Heydrich, rather than driving out of the situation, ordered Klein

---

Ječná. It was created by Charles IV as Nové Město's cattle market (Dobytčí trh) and used by him for the grisly annual public display of his impressive collection of saintly relics (see p.92), though now it actually signals the southern limit of the city's main commercial district and the beginning of resdiential Nové Město.

Southern
Nové Město

The **Novoměstská radnice** (New Town Hall), at the northeastern corner of the square, sports three impressive triangular gables embellished with intricate blind tracery. It was built, like the one on Staroměstské náměstí, during the reign of King John of Luxembourg, though it has survived rather better, and thanks to its recent facelift, is now one of the finest Gothic buildings in the city. After the amalgamation of Prague's separate towns in 1784, however, it was used solely as a criminal court and prison, and even today the public are only allowed to visit the building's small art gallery, which puts on temporary art exhibitions (Tues–Sun 10am–6pm). It was here that Prague's **first defenestration** took place on July 30, 1419, when the radical Hussite preacher Jan Želivský and his penniless religious followers stormed the building, mobbed the councillors and burghers and threw twelve or thirteen of them (including the mayor) out of the town hall win-

For details of Prague's second defenestration, see p.57.

to stop the car and attempted to shoot back. At this point, another agent, Kubiš, threw a bomb at the car. The blast injured Heydrich and Kubiš, who immediately leapt out and began firing at Kubiš who, with blood pouring down his face, jumped on his bicycle and fled downhill. Gabčík meanwhile pulled out a second gun and exchanged shots with Heydrich, until the latter collapsed from his wounds. Gabčík fled into a butcher's, shot Klein – who was in hot pusuit – in the legs and escaped down the backstreets.

Meanwhile back at the Mercedes, a baker's van was flagged down by a passer-by, but refused to get involved. Eventually, a small truck carrying floor polish was commandeered and Heydrich taken to the Bulovka hospital. Heydrich died eight days later from shrapnel wounds and was given full Nazi honours at his Prague funeral; the cortège passed down Wenceslas Square, in front of a crowd of thousands. As the home resistance had forewarned, revenge was quick to follow. The day after Heydrich's funeral, the village of **Lidice** (see p.191) was burnt to the ground and its male inhabitants murdered; two weeks later the village of Ležáky suffered a similar fate.

The plan to assassinate Heydrich had been formulated in the early months of 1942 by the Czechoslovak government-in-exile in London, without consultation with the Czech Communist leadership in Moscow, and despite fierce opposition from the resistance within Czechoslovakia. Since it was clear that the reprisals would be horrific – thousands were executed in the aftermath – the only logical explanation for the plan is that this was precisely the aim of the government-in-exile's operation – to forge a solid wedge of resentment between the Germans and Czechs. In this respect, if in no other, the operation was ultimately successful.

dows onto the pikes of the Hussite mob below, who clubbed any survivors to death. Václav IV, on hearing the news, suffered a stroke and died just two weeks later. So began the long and bloody Hussite Wars.

Following the defeat of Protestantism two centuries later, the Jesuits were allowed to demolish 23 houses on the east side of the square to make way for their college (now one of the city's main hospitals) and the accompanying church of **sv Ignác** (St Ignatius), begun in 1665 by Carlo Lurago and Paul Ignaz Bayer. The latter has recently been restored and is modelled, like so many Jesuit churches, on the Gesù in Rome; it's worth looking in if only for the wedding-cake stucco on the ceiling.

Nos. 40–41, at the southern end of the square, is the so-called **Faustův dům** (Faust House), a late Baroque building with a long and diabolical history of alchemy. An occult priest from Opava owned the house in the fourteenth century, and, two hundred years later, the English alchemist and international con-man Edward Kelley was summoned here by the eccentric Emperor Rudolf II to turn base metal into gold. The building is also the traditional setting for the Czech version of the Faust legend, with the arrival one rainy night of a penniless and homeless student, Jan Šťastný (meaning lucky, or *Faustus* in German). Finding money in the house, he decided to keep it – only to discover that it was put there by the Devil, who then claim his soul in return. Seemingly unperturbed by the historical fate of the site, a new pharmacy now plies its trade on the ground floor.

The Orthodox cathedral of sv Cyril and Metoděj

West off Karlovo náměstí, down Resslova, the noisy extension of Ječná, is the Orthodox cathedral of **sv Cyril and Metoděj**, originally constructed for the Roman Catholics by Bayer and Dientzenhofer in the eighteenth century, but since the 1930s, the main base of the Orthodox church in the Czech Republic. Amid all the traffic, it's extremely difficult to imagine the scene here on June 18, 1942, when seven of the Czechoslovak secret agents involved in the most dramatic assassination of World War II (see box above) were besieged in the church by over seven hundred members of the Waffen SS. Acting on the basis of a tip-off by one of the Czech resistance who turned himself in, the Nazis surrounded the church just after 4am and fought a pitched battle for over six hours, trying explosives, flooding and any other method they could think of to drive the men out of their stronghold in the crypt. Eventually, all seven agents committed suicide rather than give themselves up. There's a plaque at street level on the south wall commemorating those who died, and an exhibition on the whole affair situated in the crypt itself, which has been left pretty much as it was; the entrance is underneath the church steps on Na Zderaze.

The church crypt is open Tues–Sun 10am–4pm.

Along the embankment

Magnificent turn-of-the-century mansions line the Vltava's right
bank, almost without interruption, for some two kilometres from the
Charles Bridge south to the rocky outcrop of Vyšehrad. It's a long
walk, even just along the length of **Masarykovo** and **Rašínovo
nábřeží**, though there's no need to do the whole lot in one go: you
can hop on a tram (#17 or #21) at various points, drop down from
the embankments to the waterfront itself, or escape to one of the two
islands connected to them, Střelecký or Slovanský ostrov, better
known as Žofín.

Access to either of the two islands in the central section of the
Vltava is from close to the Národní divadlo. The first, **Střelecký
ostrov**, or Shooters' Island, is where the army held their shooting
practice, on and off, from the fifteenth until the nineteenth century.
Closer to the other bank, and accessible via most Legií (Legion's
Bridge) it became a favourite spot for a Sunday promenade and it's
still popular, especially in summer. The first *Sokol* festival took place
here in 1882 (see p.82), the first May Day demonstrations in 1890,
and, one hundred years on, having been used and abused by the
Communists for propaganda purposes, the traditional low-key
Májales celebrations have returned.

The second island, Slovanský ostrov, more commonly known as
Žofín (after the island's concert hall, itself named for Sophie, the
mother of the Emperor Franz -Josef I), came about as a result of the
natural silting of the river in the eighteenth century. By the late nineteenth century it had become one of the city's foremost pleasure
gardens, where, as the composer Berlioz remarked, "bad musicians
shamelessly make abominable music in the open air and immodest
young males and females indulge in brazen dancing, while idlers and
wasters . . . lounge about smoking foul tobacco and drinking beer".
On a good day, things seem pretty much unchanged from those
heady times. Concerts, balls and other social gatherings take place
here in the newly renovated and very yellow cultural centre, built in
1835, and there are rowing boats for hire from May to October.

At the southern tip of Slovanský ostrov stands the onion-domed
Šítek water tower, which provided a convenient look-out post for the
Czech secret police, whose job it was to watch over Havel's Prague
flat (see below). Close by, spanning the narrow channel between the
island and the river bank, is the striking white functionalist box of
the **Mánes** art gallery. Designed in open-plan style by Otakar
Novotný in 1930, the gallery is named after Josef Mánes, a traditional nineteenth-century landscape painter and Czech nationalist, and
puts on consistently interesting exhibitions; in addition there's a café
and an upstairs restaurant, suspended above the channel. Most of the
ornate apartment buildings along the waterfront itself are private,
and therefore inaccessible. One exception is the Art Nouveau concert
hall, **Hlahol**, at Masarykovo nábřeží 16, built for the Hlahol men's

*The Mánes art
gallery is open
Tues–Sun
10am–6pm.*

choir in 1903–06, and designed by the architect of the main railway station, Josef Fanta, with a pediment mural by Mucha and statues by Šaloun – check the listings magazines or the posters outside the hall for details of forthcoming concerts.

Fred and Ginger, Havel and Palackého náměstí

If the Mánes gallery seems at odds with the turn-of-the-century architecture along the embankment, it is as nothing to what stands at the beginning of **Rašínovo nábřeží** (named after the interwar Minister of Finance, Alois Rašín, who was assassinated by a non-card-carrying Communist in the 1920s). Designed by the Canadian-born Frank O. Gehry and the Yugoslav-born Vlado Milunić, the building has been nicknamed "**Fred and Ginger**", after the shape of one of the building's towers, which look vaguely like a couple ball-room dancing. The site is all the more controversial as it stands next door to an apartment block built at the turn of the century by Havel's grandfather, where, until the early 1990s, Havel, and his first wife, Olga, lived in the top-floor flat.

Further along the embankment, at **Palackého náměstí**, the build-ings retreat for a moment to reveal an Art Nouveau sculpture to rival Šaloun's monument in Staroměstské náměstí (see p.97): the **Monument to František Palacký**, the great nineteenth-century Czech historian, politician and nationalist, by Stanislav Sucharda. Like the Hus Monument, which was unveiled three years later, this mammoth project – fifteen years in the making – had missed its moment by the time it was finally completed in 1912, and found uni-versal disfavour. The critics have mellowed over the years, and nowa-days it's appreciated for what it is – an energetic and inspirational piece of work. Ethereal bronze bodies, representing the world of the imagination, shoot out at all angles, contrasting sharply with the plain stone mass of the plinth, and below, the giant seated figure of Palacký himself, representing the real world.

Vyšehradská and Ke Karlovu

Behind Palackého náměstí, on **Vyšehradská**, the twisted concrete spires of the **Emauzy monastery** are an unusual modern addition to the Prague skyline. The monastery was one of the few important his-torical buildings to be damaged in the last war, in this case by a stray Anglo-American bomb. Charles IV founded the monastery for Croatian Benedictines, who used the Old Slavonic liturgy (hence its Czech name, na Slovanech, or "at the Slavs"), but after the Battle of Bílá hora it was handed over to the more mainstream Spanish Benedictines. The cloisters contain some extremely valuable Gothic frescoes, but since the return of the monks from their forty-year exile, access has become unpredictable.

Rising up behind Emauzy, is one of Kilian Ignaz Dientzenhofer's little gems, the church of **sv Jan Nepomucký na skalce** (St John of

Nepomuk-on-the-rock), perched high above Vyšehradská, with a facade that displays the plasticity of the Bavarian's Baroque style in all its glory. Heading south, Vyšehradská descends to a junction, where you'll find the entrance to the university's **Botanická zahrada** (Botanical gardens), laid out in 1897 on a series of terraces up the other side of the hill. Though far from spectacular – the 1930s' greenhouses are a bit sad – they're one of the few patches of green in this part of town.

Southern Nové Město

The Botanical gardens are open daily April–Oct 9am–6pm, Nov–March 10am–4pm.

On the far side of the gardens, Apolinářská runs along the south wall and past a grimly Gothic red-brick maternity hospital, with steeply sided stepped gables, before joining up with **Ke Karlovu**. Head left up here and the first street off to the right is Na bojišti, which is usually packed with tour coaches. The reason for this is the U **kalicha** pub, on the right, which was immortalized in the opening passages of the consistently popular comic novel *The Good Soldier Švejk*, by Jaroslav Hašek. In the story, on the eve of the Great War, Švejk (*Schweik* to the Germans) walks into *U kalicha*, where a plain-clothes officer of the Austrian constabulary is sitting drinking and, after a brief conversation, finds himself arrested in connection with the assassination of Archduke Ferdinand. Whatever the pub may have been like in Hašek's day (and even then, it wasn't his local), it's now unashamedly oriented towards reaping in the Deutschmarks, and about the only authentic thing you'll find inside – albeit at a price – is the beer.

Vila Amerika (Dvořak Museum)

Further north along Ke Karlovu, set back from the road behind wrought-iron gates, is a more rewarding place of pilgrimage, the rus-set-coloured **Vila Amerika** (named after the local pub), now a muse-um devoted to Czech composer, **Antonín Dvořák**, who lived for a time on nearby Žitná. Even if you've no interest in Dvořák, the house itself is a delight, built as a Baroque summer palace around 1720 and one of Kilian Ignaz Dientzenhofer's most successful secular works. Dvořák, easily the most famous of all Czech composers, for many years had to play second fiddle to Smetana in the orchestra at the Národní divadlo, where Smetana was the conductor. In his forties, Dvořák received an honorary degree from Cambridge before leaving for the "New World", and his gown is one of the very few items of memorabilia to have found its way into the museum, along with the programme of a concert given at London's Guildhall in 1891. But the tasteful period rooms with the composer's music wafting in and out, and the tiny garden dotted with Baroque sculptures compensate for what the display cabinets may lack.

The Dvořák Museum is open Tues–Sun 10am–5pm.

Muzeum Policie and Na Karlově church

I. P. Pavlova metro station is not far from Vila Amerika, but if you've got a few hundred more metres left in you, head south down Ke

**Southern
Nové Město**

*The Muzeum
Policie is open
Tues–Sun
10am–5pm.*

Karlovu. At the end of the street, the former Augustinian monastery of Karlov is now the **Muzeum Policie** (Police Museum), formerly the Museum of the Security Forces – and, in the heyday of "normalization" in the 1970s, one of the most fascinating museums in the city. Works by Trotsky, photos of Bob Dylan, plays by Havel and contraband goods were all displayed in the grand room of dissidence; closed-circuit TV watched over your every move; and the first thing you saw on entry were two hundred pistols confiscated from western secret agents pointing at you from the wall. But the most famous exhibit was undoubtedly a stuffed German shepherd dog called Brek, who saw twelve years' service on border patrols, intercepted sixty "law-breakers", was twice shot in action and eventually retired to an old dogs' home.

With the barbed wire and border patrols all but disappeared, and the police at the nadir of their popularity, the new exhibition concentrates on road and traffic offences, and the force's latest challenges: forgery, drugs and murder. It's not what it used to be, but it's still mildly diverting, with several participatory displays, including a quiz on the Highway Code (in Czech) and a particularly gruesome section on forensic science.

*Na Karlově is
open Sundays
2–5.15pm.*

Attached to the museum is **Na Karlově** church, founded by Charles IV (of course), designed in imitation of Charlemagne's tomb in Aachen, and quite unlike any other church in Prague. If it's open, you should take a look at the dark interior, which was remodelled in the sixteenth century by Bonifaz Wohlmut. The stellar vault has no central supporting pillars – a remarkable feat of engineering for its time, and one which gave rise to numerous legends about the architect being in league with the devil.

From outside the church, there's a great view south across the Botič valley, to the twin delights of the skyscraper *Hotel Forum* and the low-lying **Palác kultury** (Palace of Culture), originally used for party congresses and now the country's biggest concert venue; to the right of the Palác kultury is Vyšehrad (see p.147). Vyšehrad metro is on the other side of the Nuselské most; alternatively, you can walk down to the the bottom of the valley and catch a tram (#7, #18 or #24).

Mucha Museum

February 1998 saw the opening of a new **museum** devoted to the life and work of **Alfons Mucha** (1860–1939), probably the most famous of all Czech artists. Mucha made his name in fin-de siècle-Paris, where he shared a studio with Gauguin, and designed Art-Nouveau posters for Sarah Bernhardt. The artist himself came to despise this "commercial" period of his work, and in 1918, Mucha moved back to his homeland and threw himself into the national cause, designing patriotic stamps, banknotes and posters. The **Mucha Museum** (daily 10am–6pm) is located in the Kaunicky palác, Panská 7.

Chapter 6

Vyšehrad and the eastern suburbs

B y the end of his reign in 1378, Charles IV had laid out his city on such a grand scale that it wasn't until the industrial revolution hit Bohemia in the mid-nineteenth century that Prague began to spread beyond the boundaries of the medieval town. The first of the suburbs, industrial Karlín, was rigidly planned, with public parks and grid street plans strictly laid out to the east of the old town; twentieth-century suburbs have tended to grow with less grace, trailing their tenements across the hills, and swallowing up existing villages on the way. **Vinohrady** and **Žižkov**, which are covered in this chapter, still retain their individual late nineteenth-century identities, which makes them worth checking out on even a short visit to the city; they also contain one or two specific sights to guide your wandering. **Vyšehrad**, which was actually one of the earliest points of settlement in Prague, is something of an exception to all the above, and is by far the most enticing of the outlying areas. Its cemetery contains the remains of Bohemia's artistic elite; the ramparts afford superb views over the river; and below its fortress, there are several examples of Czech Cubist architecture.

Vyšehrad

At the southern tip of Nové Město, around 3km south of the city centre, the rocky red-brick fortress of **VYŠEHRAD** (literally "High Castle") has more myths attached to it per square inch than any other place in Bohemia. According to Czech legend, this is the place where the Slav tribes first settled in Prague, where the "wise and tireless chieftain" Krok built a castle, and whence his youngest daughter Libuše went on to found *Praha* itself. Alas, the archeological evidence doesn't bear this claim out, but it's clear that Přemyslid Vratislav II (1061–92), the first Bohemian ruler to bear the title "king", built a royal palace here to get away from his younger broth-

VYŠEHRAD AND THE EASTERN SUBURBS

er who was lording it in the Hrad. Within half a century the royals had moved back to Hradčany, into a new palace, and from then on Vyšehrad began to lose its political significance.

The fortress enjoyed something of a renaissance under the Emperor Charles IV, who wished to associate his own dynasty with that of the early Přemyslids. A system of walls was built to link the fortress to the newly founded Nové Město, and it was decreed that the *králová cesta* (the coronation route) should begin from here. These fortifications were destroyed by the Hussites in 1420, but the hill was settled again over the next two hundred years. In the mid-seventeenth century, the Habsburgs turfed everyone out and rebuilt the place as a fortified barracks, only to tear it down in 1866 to create a public park. By the time the Czech national revival movement became interested in Vyšehrad, only the red-brick fortifications were left as a reminder of its former strategic importance; they rediscovered its history and its legends, and gradually transformed it into a symbol of Czech nationhood. Today, Vyšehrad makes for one of the most rewarding trips away from the human congestion of the city, a perfect afternoon escape and a great place from which to watch the evening sun set behind the Hrad.

The fortress

The nearest metro is Vyšehrad.

There are several **approaches to the fortress** (see map on pp.148–149): from Vyšehrad metro station, walk west past the modern Palác kultury, and enter through the Leopoldova brána (**a**); if you've come by tram #3, #7, #17 or #21, which trundle along the waterfront, you can either wind your way up Vratislavova and enter through the Cihelná brána (**b**), or take the steep stairway from Rašínovo nábřeží that leads up through the trees to a small side entrance in the west wall. Vysehrad is perfect for a picnic, but **food and drink** can also be had at *Na Vyšehradě* (daily 10am–10pm), a reasonably priced *vinárna* (wine bar) opposite the church of sv Petr and Pavel. In addition, there are several good pubs and restaurants in the streets below the fortress (see p.218).

The last approach brings you out right in front of the blackened sandstone church of **sv Petr and Pavel** (**c**), rebuilt in the 1880s by Josef Mocker in neo-Gothic style (with further, even more ruthless, additions completed in the 1900s) on the site of an eleventh-century basilica. The twin open-work spires are now the fortress's most familiar landmark; however, the church's polychrome interior is often closed to the public to protect against vandalism and to allow archeologists to search for the remains of the eleventh-century royal palace, discovered here some time ago.

Vyšehradský hřbitov (Vyšehrad Cemetery)

One of the first initiatives of the national revival movement was to establish the **Vyšehradský hřbitov**, which spreads out to the north and east of the church. It's a measure of the part that artists and intellectuals played in the foundation of the nation, and the regard in which they are still held, that the most prestigious graveyard in the city is given over to them: no soldiers, no politicians, not even the Communists managed to muscle their way in here. Sheltered from the wind by its high walls, lined on two sides by delicate arcades, it's a tiny cemetery (reflecting, as it were, the size of the nation) filled with well-kept graves, many of them designed by the country's leading sculptors.

To the uninitiated only a handful of figures are well known, but for the Czechs the place is alive with great names (there's a useful plan of the most notable graves at the entrance nearest the church). Ladislav Šaloun's grave for **Dvořák**, situated under the arches, is one of the more showy ones, with a mosaic inscription, studded with gold stones, glistening behind wrought-iron railings. **Smetana**, who died twenty years earlier, is buried in comparatively modest surroundings near the Slavín monument (see below). The *Pražské jaro* festival begins with a procession from his grave to the Obecní dům, on the anniversary of his death (May 12).

Other graves that attract (mostly Czech) pilgrims are those of the nineteenth-century writer Božena Němcová, by the east end of the

Vyšehrad

The cemetery is open daily March, April & Oct 8am–6pm; May–Sept 8am–7pm; Nov–Feb 9am–4pm.

church; and playwright Karel Čapek, whose grave faces the arcades – he coined one of the two Czech words to have entered the English language, "robot" (the other was "pistol"). Several graves of lesser-known individuals stand out artistically, too: in particular, František Bílek's towering statue of *Sorrow* on the grave of V. B. Třebizský, which aroused a storm of protest when it was first unveiled; Bohumil Kafka's headstone for Dr J. Kaizl, with a woman's face peeping out from the grave; and Karel Hladík's modern *Cathedral* sculpture, which sits above his own grave.

The focus of the cemetery, though, is the **Slavín monument (d)**, a big, bulky stele designed by Antonín Wiehl, covered in commemorative plaques and topped by a sarcophagus and a statue representing Genius. It's the communal resting place of more than fifty Czech artists, including the painter Alfons Mucha, the sculptors Josef Václav Myslbek and Ladislav Šaloun, the architect Josef Gočár, and the opera singer Ema Destinová.

Mácha's remains were brought here from a cemetery in Litoměřice in 1938, when the Nazis took over the Sudetenland.

The grave of the Romantic poet **Karel Hynek Mácha** was the assembly point for the demonstration on November 17, 1989, which triggered the Velvet Revolution. This was organized to commemorate the 50th anniversary of the Nazi attack on Czech higher education institutions in 1939. Student protests against the German occupation reached a peak on October 28, 1939, when violent clashes resulted in the death of medical student, **Jan Opletal**; his funeral, on November 11, was accompanied by more violent disturbances. On November 17, the Nazis took the initiative, executing various student leaders, packing thousands off to the camps and shutting down all Czech higher education institutes. Fifty years later, in 1989, the cemetery was the gathering point for a 50,000-strong crowd who attempted to march from here to Wenceslas Square, only to be stopped short in Národní, where the infamous *masakr* took place (see box, p.132).

The rest of the fortress

The rest of the deserted fortress makes for a pleasant afternoon stroll; you can walk almost the entire length of the ramparts, which give some superb views out across the city. The small museum of historical drawings in the hradební věž (e) and the exhibition in the neo-Gothic Nové děkanství (f) are both pretty dull, though you might want to head for the latter to buy some postcards. The heavily restored rotunda of sv Martin (g) – one of a number of Romanesque rotundas scattered across Prague – is the sole survivor of the medieval fortress built by Vratislav II in the eleventh century.

Time is better spent lounging on the patch of grass to the south of the church, where you'll come across the gargantuan statues by Myslbek that used to grace the city's Palackého most. Four couples are dotted across the green, all taken from Prague legends: *Přemysl and Libuše* (h), the husband and wife team who founded Prague and started Bohemia's first royal dynasty, the Přemyslids; *Lumír and Píseň* (i), the legendary Czech singer and his muse, Song; *Záboj and Slavoj* (j), two mythical Czech warriors; and *Ctirad and Šárka* (k), for whose story, see p.171.

Czech Cubism in Vyšehrad

Even if you harbour only a passing interest in modern architecture, it's worth seeking out the cluster of **Cubist villas** below the fortress in Vyšehrad. Whereas Czech Art Nouveau was heavily influenced by the Viennese Secession, it was Paris rather than the imperial capital that provided the stimulus for the short-lived but extremely productive Czech Cubist movement. In 1911, the *Skupina výtvarných umělců* or SVU (Group of Fine Artists) was founded in Prague, and quickly became the movement's organizing force. **Pavel Janák** was the *SVU*'s chief theorist, **Josef Gočár** its most illustrious exponent, but **Josef Chochol** was the most successful practitioner of the style in Prague.

Cubism is associated mostly with painting, and the unique contribution of its Czech offshoot was to apply the theory to **furniture** (some of which is now on permanent display at the Dům U černé Matky boží; see p.101) and **architecture**. In Vyšehrad alone, Chochol completed three buildings, close to one another below the fortress, using prismatic shapes and angular lines to produce the sharp geometric contrasts of light and dark shadows characteristic of Cubist painting. Outside the Czech Republic, only the preparatory drawings by the French architect Duchamp-Villon for his *Maison Cubiste* (never realized), can be considered remotely similar.

The SVU's plans were cut short by World War I, after which Janák and Gočár attempted to establish a specifically Czechoslovak style of architecture incorporating prewar Cubism. The style was dubbed **Rondo-Cubism** since the prismatic moulding had been replaced by semicircular motifs, but only a few projects got off the ground before Czech architects turned to the functionalist ideals of the international modernist movement.

The buildings

The most impressive example of Czech Cubist architecture, brilliantly exploiting its angular location, is Chochol's **nájemný obytný dům** (l), an apartment block at Neklanova 30, begun in 1913 for František Hodek and now housing a restaurant on its ground floor. Further along Neklanova at no. 2, there's Antonín Belada's **nájemný obytný dům (m)**, with its Cubist facade, and around the corner is the most ambitious project of the lot – Chochol's **Kovařovicova vila (n)**, which backs onto Libušina. The front, on Rašínovo nábřeží, is presently concealed behind some overenthusiastic shrubs, but it's still possible to appreciate the clever, slightly askew layout of the garden, designed right down to its zigzag garden railings. Further

---

Cubist and Rondo-Cubist buildings in Prague

Prague's unique Cubist and Rondo-Cubist buildings, most of which are covered in the text, are scattered right across the city. Here is a checklist of where to find the best examples of the style.

Staré Město		Vyšehrad	
Gočár's Dům U černé		Chochol's nájemný obytný	
Matky boží	p.101	dům	p.153
		Belada's nájemný obytný	
Nové Město		dům	p.153
Janák & Zasche's		Chochol's Kovařovicova	
Palác Adria	p.130	vila	p.153
Blecha & Králíček's		Chochol's Rodinný trojdům	p.154
lamppost	p.130		
Gočár's Banka legií	p.137	**The suburbs**	
Králíček's Diamant	p.140	Gočár's Rodinný dvojdům	p.160

---

along the embankment is Chochol's largest commission, the **Rodinný trojdům** (o), a large building complex with a heavy mansard roof, a central "Baroque" gable with a pedimental frieze, and room enough for three families.

For details of cafés, pubs and restaurants in Vinohrady, see p.215, p.218 and p.224.

Vinohrady

Southeast of Nové Město is the well-to-do late nineteenth-century suburb of **VINOHRADY**, home over the years to many of the country's most notable personages. Under the Communists, the suburb became decidedly run-down, but with the re-emergence of the property market, Vinohrady has once more become a desirable part of town to live in, with two spacious parks – **Riegrovy sady**, to the north, and **Havlíčkovy sady**, to the south – and a fabulous array of turn-of-the-century apartment buildings. In terms of conventional sightseeing, however, the area is definitely low priority, but there are a few places here (and in neighbouring Žižkov) worth a visit, most of them quick and easy to reach by metro.

If Vinohrady has a centre, it's the leafy square of **náměstí Míru**, a good introduction to the aspirations of this confident, bourgeois neighbourhood. At its centre stands the brick-built basilica of **sv Ludmila**, designed by Josef Mocker in the 1880s in a severe neo-Gothic style, though the interior furnishings have the odd flourish of Art Nouveau. In front of the church is a recently erected statue commemorating the **Čapek brothers**, writer Karel and painter Josef, who together symbolized the golden era of the interwar republic. Karel died in 1938, shortly after the Nazi invasion, while Josef perished in Belsen seven years later; their influence was deliberately underplayed by the Communists, hence the delay in erecting an appropriate memorial. Two more buildings on the square deserve attention, the most flamboyant being the **Divadlo na Vinohradech**, built in 1907, using Art Nouveau and neo-Baroque elements in equal measure. More subdued, but equally ornate inside and out, is the district's former **Národní dům**, a grandiose neo-Renaissance edifice housing a ballroom/concert hall and restuarant.

Vinohrady

The nearest metro is náměstí Míru.

From náměstí Míru, block after block of decaying tenements, each clothed in its own individual garment of sculptural decoration, form a grid plan of grand bourgeois avenues stretching eastwards to the city's great cemeteries (see below). If the weather's nice, you could stroll your way to Plečnik's church (see below), dropping in at *U knihomola* (The Bookworm), Mánesova 79, one of Prague's best foreign-language **bookshops** (see p.241). However, distances are greater than you think, and you may prefer to take the metro.

Plečník's church

Vinohrady's other main square, **náměstí Jiřího z Poděbrad**, halfway between náměstí Míru and the cemeteries, contains Prague's most celebrated modern church, **Nejsvětější Srdce Páně** (Most Sacred Heart of Our Lord), built in 1928 by Josip Plečník, the Slovene architect responsible for much of the remodelling of the Hrad (see box on p.50). It's a marvellously eclectic and individualistic work, employing a sophisticated potpourri of architectural styles: a Neoclassical pediment and a great slab of a clock tower with a giant transparent face in imitation of a Gothic rose window, as well as the bricks and mortar of contemporary constructivism. Plečník also had a sharp eye for detail; look out for the little gold crosses inset into the brickwork like stars, inside and out, and the celestial orbs of light suspended above the heads of the congregation. If you can collar the priest, it may be possible to climb the clock tower.

The nearest metro is Jiřího z Poděbrad.

Janák and Gočár's functionalist churches

Further afield are two more uncompromisingly modernist churches. The first is the **Husův sbor** (Hussite Church), three blocks south of Plečník's church down U vodárny, on the corner of Dykova. Built in the early 1930s by Pavel Janák, the church's most salient feature is its freestanding hollow tower, which encloses a corkscrew spiral staircase and is topped by a giant copper chalice, symbol of the Hussite faith. A memorial on the wall commemorates the church's pioneering role in the Prague Uprising against the Nazis in May 1945, when it served as a clandestine Czech resistance headquarters.

Josef Gočár's equally severe, functionalist church of **sv Václav**, built around the same time, lies a kilometre or so southeast on náměstí Svatopluka Čecha; take tram #4 or #22 from náměstí Miru or the bottom of U vodárny. Here it forms the centrepiece of a sloping green square, with a distinctive stepped roof rising up from a slender, smoothly rendered 80m-high tower.

Žižkov

Though they share much the same architectural heritage, ŽIŽKOV, unlike Vinohrady, is a traditionally working-class area, and was a Communist Party stronghold even before the war, earning it the nickname "Red Žižkov". Nowadays its peeling turn-of-the-century tenements are home to a large proportion of Prague's Romany community, and boast more pubs per head than any other district in Prague, and some of its roughest nightlife. The main reason for venturing into Žižkov is to visit its two landmarks – ancient (Žižkov hill) and modern (the television tower) – and the city's main cemeteries, at the eastern end of Vinohradská.

The Žižkov TV tower

The TV tower is open daily 10am–11pm.

At over 100m in height, the Žižkov TV tower (Televizní vysílač), is the tallest (and the most unpopular) building in Prague. Close up, though, it's difficult not to be impressed by this truly intimidating piece of futuristic architecture, its smooth grey exterior giving no hint of humanity. Begun in the 1970s in a desperate bid to jam West German television transmission, the tower has only become fully operational within the last few years. In the course of its construction, however, the Communists saw fit to demolish part of a nearby Jewish cemetery, that had served the community between 1787 and 1891; a small section survives to the northwest of the tower. If you're lucky, you should be able to take a lift to the viewing platform on the eighth floor to enjoy a spectacular view across Prague, but it's as well to check with the tourist office before setting out. To get to the tower, take the metro to Jiřího z Poděbrad and walk northeast a couple of blocks – it's difficult to miss.

The cemeteries

The cemeteries are open daily dawn to dusk: the nearest metro to the Olřany cemeteries is Flora; the nearest metro to the War cemetary is Pelivského.

Approaching from the west, the first and the largest of Prague's vast cemeteries – each of which is bigger than the entire Jewish quarter – are the Olšanské hřbitovy, originally created for the victims of the great plague epidemic of 1680. The perimeter walls are lined with glass cabinets, stacked like shoe-boxes, containing funereal urns and mementoes, while the graves themselves are a mixed bag of artistic achievements, reflecting the funereal fashions of the day as much as the character of the deceased. The cemeteries are divided into districts and crisscrossed with cobbled streets; at each gate there's a map, and an aged janitor ready to point you in the right direction.

The cemeteries' two most famous incumbents are an ill-fitting couple: Klement Gottwald, the country's first Communist president, whose ashes were removed from the mausoleum on Žižkov hill after 1989 and reinterred here, and Jan Palach, the philosophy student who set light to himself in January 1969 in protest at the Soviet occupation. More than 750,000 people attended Palach's funeral in January 1969, and in an attempt to put a stop to the annual vigils at his graveside, the secret police removed his body in 1973 and reburied him in his home town, 60km outside Prague. His place was taken by an unknown woman, Maria Jedličková, who for the next seventeen years had her grave covered in flowers instead. Finally, in 1990, Palach's body was returned to Olšany; you'll find it just to the east of the main entrance on Vinohradská.

To the east of Olšany cemeteries, and usually totally deserted, is the **Vojenský hřbitov** (Military Cemetery); the entrance is 200m up Jana Želivského, on the right. Its centrepiece is the monument to the 436 Soviet soldiers who lost their lives on May 9, 1945 in the liberation of Prague, surrounded by a small, tufty meadow dotted with simple white crosses. Nearby, the graves of Czechs who died fighting for the Habsburgs on the Italian front in World War I are laid out in a semicircle.

Nový židovský hřbitov (New Jewish Cemetery)

Immediately south of the war cemetery is the **Nový židovský hřbitov**, founded in the 1890s, when the one by the Žižkov TV tower was full (see opposite), and designed to last for a century, with room for 100,000 graves. It's a melancholy spot, particularly so in the east of the cemetery, where large empty allotments wait in vain to be filled by the generation who perished in the Holocaust. In fact, the community is now so small that it's unlikely the graveyard will ever be full. Most people come here to visit **Franz Kafka**'s grave, 400m east along the south wall and signposted from the entrance. He is buried, along with his mother and father (both of whom outlived him), beneath a plain headstone; the plaque below commemorates his three sisters who died in the camps.

Žižkov hill

Žižkov hill (also known as Vítkov) is the thin green wedge of land that separates Žižkov from Karlín, a grid-plan industrial district to the north. From its westernmost point, which juts out almost to the edge of Nové Město, is the definitive panoramic view over the city centre. It was here, on July 14, 1420, that the Hussites enjoyed their first and finest victory at the **Battle of Vítkov**, under the inspired leadership of the one-eyed general, Jan Žižka (hence the name of the district). Ludicrously outnumbered by more than ten to one, Žižka and his fanatically motivated troops thoroughly trounced Emperor Sigismund and his papal forces.

Despite its overblown totalitarian aesthetics, the giant concrete **Žižkov monument** which graces the crest of the hill, was actually built between the wars as a memorial to the Czech nation – the gargantuan equestrian statue of the mace-wielding Žižka, which fronts the monument, is reputedly the world's largest. The building was

Žižkov

There's a memorial to Palach and other victims of the Communist era on Wenceslas Square (see p.128), and a box on Gottwald on p.105.

The cemetery is open daily except Sat: April–Aug 8am–5pm; Sept–March 8am–4pm. For more on Kafka's associations with Prague, see p.116.

Žižkov

later used by the Nazis as an arsenal, and eventually became a Communist mausoleum: presidents Gottwald, Zápotocký and Svoboda were all buried here, along with the Unknown Soldier and various other Party hacks. Žižkov was an ideal resting place, lying as it does in the heart of "Red Žižkov", from where the Communists drew so much of their pre-1948 working-class support. Gottwald himself was originally pickled and embalmed (à la Lenin) but a fire damaged his corpse so much, the leader had to be cremated in 1963. In 1990, the remaining bodies were cremated and quietly reinterred in Olšany, and at present there's an ongoing legal battle over what should happen next with the monument.

To get to the monument, take the metro to Florenc, walk under the railway lines, and then up the steep lane U památníku. On the right as you climb the hill is the **Armádní muzeum** (Army Museum), guarded by a handful of unmanned tanks, howitzers and armoured vehicles. Before 1989, this museum was a glorification of the Warsaw Pact, pure and simple; its recent overhaul has produced a much more evenly balanced account of both world wars, particularly in its treatment of the previously controversial subjects of the Czechoslovak Legion, the Heydrich assassination (see p.140) and the Prague Uprising. The collection now covers only the period from 1914 to 1945.

The Armádní muzeum is open Mon–Fri 9am–5pm; see p.65 for the pre-1914 military museum.

Chapter 7

Holešovice and the western suburbs

T he northern and western **suburbs** on the left bank of the Vltava are spread over a much larger area than those to the east of the river. They are also far more varied: some, like Holešovice and parts of Smíchov, date from the time of the industrial revolution, whereas Dejvice and Střešovice were laid out between the wars as well-to-do garden suburbs. The left bank also boasts a great deal more greenery, including the city's largest public park,

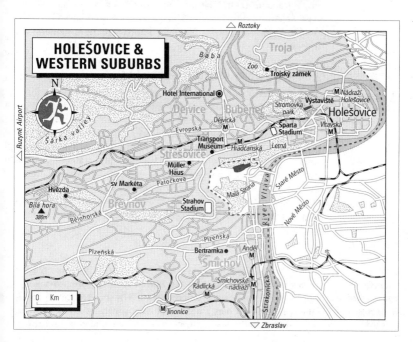

Stromovka. All this goes to make up a fascinating patchwork of communities, which few tourists bother to see. It's worth the effort, though, if only to remind yourself that Prague doesn't begin and end at the Charles Bridge.

There are several specific sights in each suburb that can lend structure to your meanderings. The single most important sight is the **Veletržní palác** in **Holešovice**, the long-awaited home for the nation's modern art collection. Another popular destination is the **Bertramka** (Mozart Museum) in **Smíchov**. Other sights – like the functionalist villas in **Dejvice** and **Střešovice** – are of more specialized interest; and some are simply unknown to most visitors, like the exquisite Renaissance chateau of **Hvězda**.

Holešovice and Bubeneč

The late nineteenth- and early twentieth-century districts of **HOLEŠOVICE** and **BUBENEČ**, tucked into a huge U-bend in the Vltava, have little in the way of truly magnificent architecture, but they make up for it with two huge splodges of green: to the south **Letná**, overlooking the city centre, and to the north **Stromovka**, bordering the Výstaviště funfair and international trade fair grounds. Holešovice also has a couple of excellent museums: the city's **Národní technické muzeum**, which shows off the Czechs' past scientific and industrial achievements, and the aforementioned **Veletržní palác**, Prague's impressive new modern art museum.

Chotkovy sady and the Bílkova vila

These first two sights are strictly speaking part of the Hradčany that lies to the northeast of the castle, but for convenience, they begin this chapter. The easiest way to this part of town is to take tram #22 one stop from Malostranská metro to the Belvedér, or the metro to Hradčanská metro and head up Tychonova, a street flanked on one side by a military barracks and training ground, and on the other by a series of semi-detached houses. These include **Josef Gočár**'s rodinný dvojdům at nos. 4 & 6, built with a traditional mansard roof in a restrained Cubist style, similar to that employed on the Dům U černé Matky boží in Staré Město (see p.101).

The Belvedér and the Královská zahrada are both covered in Chapter 1 (see p.63).

Chotkovy sady

At the top of Tychonova, the leafy avenue of Marianské hradby slopes down to the left, past the Belvedér, to the **Chotkovy sady**, Prague's first public park, founded in 1833 by the ecologically minded city governor, Count Chotek. The atmosphere here is a lot more relaxed than in the nearby Královská zahrada, and you can happily

stretch out on the grass and soak up the sun, or head for the south wall, which enjoys an unrivalled view of the bridges and islands of the Vltava. At the centre of the park there's a bizarre, melodramatic grotto-like memorial to the nineteenth-century Romantic poet Julius Zeyer, an elaborate monument from which life-sized characters from Zeyer's works, carved in white marble, emerge from the blackened rocks amid much drapery.

Bílkova vila

*The Bílkova
vila is open
mid-May to
mid-Oct
Tues–Sun
10am–6pm;
mid-Oct to
mid-May Sat
& Sun
10am–5pm.*

Across the road from the park, hidden behind its overgrown garden at Mieckiewiczova 1, the **Bílkova vila** honours one of the most original of all Czech sculptors, František Bílek (1872–1941). Born in a part of South Bohemia steeped in the Hussite tradition, Bílek lived a monkish life, spending years in spiritual contemplation, reading the works of Hus and other Czech reformers. The Bílkova vila was built in 1911 to the artist's own design, intended as both a "cathedral of art" and the family home. At first sight, it appears a strangely mute red-brick building, out of keeping with the extravagant Symbolist style of Bílek's sculptures: from the outside, only the front porch, supported by giant sheaves of corn, and the sculptural group, the fleeing Comenius and his followers, in the garden, give a clue as to what lies within.

Inside, the brickwork gives way to bare stone walls lined with Bílek's religious sculptures, giving the impression that you've walked into a chapel rather than an artist's studio: "a workshop and temple", in Bílek's own words. In addition to his sculptural and relief work in wood and stone, often wildly expressive and spiritually tortured, there are also ceramics, graphics and a few mementoes of Bílek's life. His work is little known outside his native country, but his contemporary admirers included Franz Kafka, Julius Zeyer, and Otokar Březina, whose poems and novels provided the inspiration for much of Bílek's art. Bílek's living quarters have also been restored and opened to the public, with much of the original wooden furniture, designed and carved by Bílek himself, still in place. Check out the dressing table for his wife, shaped like some giant church lectern, and the wardrobe decorated with a border of hearts, a penis, a nose, an ear, an eye plus the sun, stars and moon.

Letná

A high plateau hovering above the city, the flat green expanse of the **Letná** plain has long been the traditional assembly point for invading and besieging armies. It was laid out as a public park in the mid-nineteenth century, but its main post-1948 function was as the site of the May Day parades. For these, thousands of citizens were dragooned into marching past the south side of the city's main football ground, the Sparta stadium, where the old Communist cronies would take the salute from a giant red podium.

On November 26, 1989, the park was the scene of a more genuine expression of popular sentiment, when over 750,000 people gathered here to join in the call for a general strike against the Communist regime. Unprecedented scenes followed in April 1990, when a million Catholics came to hear Pope John Paul II speak on his first visit to an Eastern Bloc country other than his native Poland.

The former Stalin monument

Letná's – indeed Prague's – most famous monument is one which no longer exists. The **Stalin monument**, the largest in the world, was once visible from almost every part of the city: a thirty-metre-high granite sculpture portraying a procession of Czechs and Russians being led to Communism by the Pied Piper figure of Stalin, but popularly dubbed *tlačenice* (the crush) because of its resemblance to a Communist-era bread queue. Designed by Jiří Štursa and Otakar Švec, it took 600 workers 500 days to erect the 14,200-tonne monster. Švec, the sculptor, committed suicide shortly before it was unveiled, as his wife had done three years previously, leaving all his money to a school for blind children, since they at least would not have to see his creation. It was eventually revealed to the cheering masses on May 1, 1955 – the first and last popular celebration to take place at the monument. Within a year, Khrushchev had denounced his predecessor and, after pressure from Moscow, the monument was blown to smithereens by a series of explosions spread over a fortnight in 1962.

All that remains above ground is the statue's vast concrete platform and steps, on the southern edge of the Letná plain, now graced with David Černý's symbolic giant red metronome (which is lit up at night); it's also a favourite spot for skateboarders and another good viewpoint, with the central stretch of the Vltava glistening in the afternoon sun. Built into the hillside below is Prague's one and only nuclear bunker, intended to preserve the Party elite, post-armageddon. For years, it was actually used to store the city's slowly rotting potato mountain; more recently it has been sporadically squatted and used as a nightclub venue.

If you're in need of some refreshment, head for the **Hanavský pavilón**, a café and restaurant (see p.225) housed in the nearby to the metronome originally built for the 1891 Prague Exhibition and looking rather like a Russian Orthodox church. It was devised by Count Hanavský as a showpiece of wrought-ironwork, in a flamboyant style which anticipated the arrival of Art Nouveau a few years later.

Národní technické muzeum

Despite its dull title, the **Národní technické muzeum** (National Technical Museum), on Kostelní, is a surprisingly interesting museum, with an interactive gallery or two, and even the odd English caption appearing here and there. Its showpiece hanger-like main hall

*The Národní
technické
muzeum is
open
Tues–Sun
9am–5pm.*

contains an impressive gallery of motorbikes, Czech and foreign, and a wonderful collection of old planes, trains and automobiles, from Czechoslovakia's industrial heyday between the wars, when the country's Škoda cars and Tatra soft-top stretch limos were really something to brag about. The oldest car in the collection is Laurin & Klement's 1898 *Präsident*, more of a motorized carriage than a car; the museum also boasts the oldest Bugatti in the world. Upstairs, there are interactive displays (a rarity in a Czech museum) tracing the development of early photography, and a collection of some of Kepler's and Tycho Brahe's astrological instruments. Below ground, a mock-up of a coal mine offers guided tours every other hour, at 11am, 1pm and 3pm.

Veletržní palác

*The Veletržní
palác is open
Tues–Sun
10am–6pm,
Thurs until
9pm.*

After several decades of bureaucratic and political wrangling, Prague's most ambitious museum to date, the **Veletržní palác** (Trade Fair Palace), has finally opened its doors, allowing the public to see the Národní galerie's vast collection of twentieth-century Czech art on permanent display for the first time in years. In addition, there's a small but judiciously chosen selection of European art from the late nineteenth and early twentieth centuries. And last but not least, there's the building itself, Prague's ultimate functionalist masterpiece, a seven-storey building constructed in 1928 by Oldřich Tyl and Josef Fuchs. The building doesn't look that great from the outside, but inside, its gleaming white vastness is suitably awesome. Even the normally hypercritical Le Corbusier, who visited the building the year it was completed, was impressed: "Seeing the Trade Fair Palace, I realised how to make large buildings, having so far built only several relatively small houses on a low budget."

Despite the fact that the Národní galerie doesn't even use the main exhibition hall, but confines itself to the north wing of the building, the museum is both big and bewildering. Special exhibitions occupy the first, fourth and ground floors; from the ground floor you can stare up at the glass-roofed atrium, overlooked by six floors of balconies. The permanent collection occupies the second and third floors, but there is no easy way to follow it chronologically. The best approach is to take the lift to the third floor and start with the Czech art from 1900 to 1960 (as the account below does), since this was

---

Situated at the corner of Dukelských hrdinů and Veletržní, some distance from the nearest metro station, the Veletržní palác gets nothing like the number of visitors it should. **To get there** by public transport, catch tram #5 from náměstí Republiky, tram #12 from Malostranská metro, tram #17 from Staroměstská, or tram #5, #12 or #17 from Nádraží Holešovice.

the museum's original *raison d'être*. On each floor, there's a side room, with an art studio or library, where you (and your kids) can relax and read or draw.

Czech modern art (České moderní umění), 1900–60

The collection of **Czech modern art from 1900 to 1960**, on the third floor, begins with a whole series of works by **František Kupka**, a Czech by birth, but an artist who lived and worked in Paris from 1896 on. In international terms, Kupka is by far the most important Czech painter of this century, having secured his place in the history of art by being (possibly) the first artist in the western world to exhibit abstract paintings. *Fugue in Two Colours (Amorpha)*, one of the two abstract paintings Kupka exhibited at the Salon d'Automne in 1912, is displayed here. Alongside this seminal work are earlier, pre-abstract paintings such as the very normal double portrait of himself and his wife; an Expressionist portrait of a Parisian cabaret actress; and *Piano Keys – Lake*, a strange, abstracted, though by no means abstract, work from 1909. You'll come across more of Kupka's later abstract and cosmic works elsewhere in the collection.

While Kupka is thought of by many as a French artist, **Jan Preisler** couldn't be more thoroughly Czech. His mosaics and murals, which can be found on Art Nouveau buildings all over Prague, tend to be ethereal and slightly detached, whereas his oil paintings, like the cycle of *Black Lake* paintings displayed here, are more typically melancholic. Several wood sculptures by **František Bílek**, one of the country's finest sculptors, offer a taste of his anguished style, but for a more comprehensive insight into his art, you should visit the Bílkova vila (see p.160).

The Edvard Munch retrospective held in Prague in 1905 prompted the formation in 1907 of the first Czech modern art movement, Osma (The Eight), three of whose members feature in **Bohumil Kubišta**'s defiant *Triple Portrait* from the same year. Works like Kubišta's *Card Players*, and **Emil Filla**'s *Reader of Dostoyevsky* (in which the subject appears to have fallen asleep) are both firmly within the Expressionist genre. However, it wasn't long before several of the Osma group were beginning to experiment with Cubism. Filla eventually adopted the style wholesale, helping found the Cubist SVU in 1911; Kubišta refused to follow suit, instead pursuing his own unique blend of Cubo-Expressionism, typified by the wonderful self-portrait, *The Smoker*.

Josef Čapek, brother of the playwright, is another Czech clearly influenced by Cubism, as seen in works such as *Accordion Player*, but like Kubišta, Čapek found Filla's doctrinaire approach difficult to take, and he left SVU in 1912. Look out, too, for the sculptures of **Otto Gutfreund**, a member of SVU, whose works range from his Cubo-Expressionist *Anxiety* to the more purely Cubist *Sitting Woman* (1915). After World War I, during which he joined the Foreign Legion but was interned for three years for insubordination, Gutfreund switched to depicting everyday folk in technicolour, as in *Trade* and *Industry*, in a style that prefigures Socialist Realism. His life was cut short in 1927, when he drowned while swimming in the Vltava.

Devětsil, founded in 1920 and the driving force of the Czech avant-garde between the wars, is represented here by the movement's two leading artists: **Toyen** (Marie Cermínová) and her life-long companion **Jindřich Štyrský**, whose abstract works – they dubbed them "Artificialism" – reveal the couple's interest in the French Surrealists. Predictably enough, however, there are no examples of Štyrský's pornographic photomontages, or Toyen's sexually charged drawings, which form an important part of their work. One Czech artist who had already enthusiastically embraced Surrealism was **Josef Šíma**, who settled permanently in Paris in the 1920s; several of his trademark floating torsoes and cosmic eggs can be seen here. Lastly, be sure to check out the wild kinetic-light sculpture (1936) by **Zdeněk Pešánek**, a world pioneer in the use of neon in art, who created a stir the following year at the Paris Expo with a neon fountain.

Nineteeth- and twentieth-century French art

By far the most popular section of the gallery is the **nineteenth- and twentieth-century French art section** (*Francouzské umění 19. a 20. století*), on the second floor, featuring anyone of note who hovered around Paris in the fifty years from 1880 onwards. There are few masterpieces here, but it's all high-quality stuff, most of it either purchased for the gallery in 1923, or bequeathed by art dealer Vincenc Kramář in 1960, and until the mid-1990s displayed in the Šternberský palác in Hradčany.

The collection kicks off with several works by **Auguste Rodin**, particularly appropriate given the ecstatic reception given to the Prague exhibition of his work in 1902. Rodin's sculptures are surrounded by works from the advance guard of Impressionism: Courbet, Delacroix, Corot and early Monet and Pissarro. Beyond, the loose brushwork, cool turquoise and emerald colours of **Auguste Renoir**'s *Lovers* are typical of the period of so-called High Impressionism. There's also a surprisingly good collection of works by **Pablo Picasso**, including several paintings and sculptures from his crucial early Cubist period (1907–08); his still-life from 1909 uses precisely the kind of prisms and geometric blocks of shading that influenced the Czech Cubist architects.

Among the other works here, there's a characteristically sunny, Provençal *Green Wheat* by **Vincent van Gogh**, a couple of paintings by Paul Cézanne and Georges Seurat, and the only known self-portrait by **Henri Rousseau**, at once both confident and comical, the artist depicting himself, palette in hand, against a boat decked with bunting and the recently erected Eiffel Tower. *Bonjour Monsieur Gauguin* is a tongue-in-cheek tribute to Courbet's painting of similar name, with Gauguin donning a suitably bohemian beret and overcoat. Another first-rate portrait is *Joaquina*, painted in 1910–11 by **Henri Matisse**, in which both Fauvist and Oriental influences are evident.

Twentieth-century European art

If the French art section is modest, the collection of **twentieth-century European art** (Evropské umění 20. století) is minuscule. It does, however, contain a couple of minor gems, beginning with **Gustav Klimt**'s mischievous *Virgins*, a mass of naked bodies and tangled limbs painted in psychedelic colours. Although none of the artists here is Czech, many of them had close connections with Bohemia: **Egon Schiele**'s mother came from Český Krumlov, the subject of a gloomy autumnal canvas, *Dead City*; and the handful of typically vigorous landscapes by **Oskar Kokoschka** date from his brief stay here in the 1930s, when the political temperature got too hot in Vienna. Perhaps the most influential artist on show is **Edvard Munch**, whose one canvas, *Dance at the Seaside*, hardly does justice to the considerable effect he had on a generation of Czech artists after his celebrated 1905 Prague exhibition.

Czech art, 1960–95

The collection of **Czech art from 1960 to 1995** sits rather uncomfortably on the same floor as the French and European art. Most visitors approach it the wrong way round, chronologically speaking, since the section which abuts twentieth-century European art displays Czech works from the 1980s. Still, whichever way you come at it, this is an interesting enough collection, taken at a canter.

Coming from the European art section, Ivan Kafka's *On Potent Impotence* installation should raise a smile, whereas Jiří Sozansky's photos and videos of the destruction of the town of Most to make way for an open-cast lignite mine is chilling (metaphorically and literally). Surprisingly there's very little overtly political art here, with the exception of Květoslava Válová's *Recognition and Amazement*, featuring a pair of Big Brother eyes, and *Great Dialogue* by Karel Nepraš, in which two red figures lambast each other at close quarters with loudspeakers.

As with the 1900–60 gallery, there is a total absence of Socialist Realist works. Instead, the gallery concentrates on artists like **Mikuláš Medek**, whose surrealist and abstract works were more or less banned from public galleries throughout the Communist period. Still, you do get a rare chance to see a couple of pieces by **Jiří Kolář** (pronounced "collage") who, as his name suggests, specializes in collages of random words and reproductions of other people's paintings. The collection of 1990s works spills over onto the balcony, and includes an entire, hermetically sealed office, by Milan Knížák, which you can peek into.

Výstaviště

Výstaviště is
open Tues–Fri
2–10pm, Sat &
Sun
10am–10pm.

Five minutes' walk north from the Veletržní palác, up Dukelských hrdinů, takes you right to the front gates of the **Výstaviště** (Exhibition Grounds), a motley assortment of buildings, originally created for the 1891 Prague Exhibition, which have served as the city's main trade fair arena and funfair ever since. From 1948 until the late 1970s, The Communist Party held its rubber-stamp congresses in the flamboyant glass and iron **Průmyslový palác** at the centre of the complex, and more recently several brand new permanent structures were built for the 1991 Prague Exhibition, including a circular theatre, **Divadlo Spirála**.

The
Planetarium is
open
Mon–Thurs
8am–noon &
1–6pm, Sat &
Sun
9.30am–noon
& 1–5pm.

The grounds are at their busiest on summer weekends, when hordes of Prague families descend on the place to down hot dogs, drink beer and listen to traditional brass band music. Apart from the annual fairs and lavish special exhibitions, there are a few permanent attractions, such as the city's **Planetarium**, the **Maroldovo panorama** (Tues–Fri 1–5pm, Sat & Sun 11am–5pm), a giant diorama of the 1434 Battle of Lipany (see p.253), and the **Dětský svět** (Tues–Fri 2–5pm, Sat & Sun 11am–5pm), a run-down funfair and playground for kids. In the long summer evenings, there's also an open-air cinema (*letní kino*), and regular performances by the **Křižíkova fontána**, dancing fountains devised for the 1891 Exhibition by the Czech inventor František Křižík, which perform a music and light show to packed audiences; ask at the tourist office, or check the listings magazines, for the current schedule.

The
Lapidárium is
open Tues–Fri
noon–6pm, Sat
& Sun
10am–6pm.

Lastly, Výstaviště also contains the Národní muzeum's **Lapidárium** – on the right as you enter – official depository for the city's sculptures, which are under threat either from demolition or from the weather. It's actually a much overlooked art collection, ranging from the eleventh to the nineteenth centuries, that includes works such as the plague column from Staroměstské náměstí, rescued from marauding Czech nationalists in 1918, and many of the original Charles Bridge sculptures.

Stromovka

To the west of Výstaviště lies the *královská obora* or royal enclosure, more commonly known as **Stromovka**, originally laid out as hunting grounds for the noble occupants of the Hrad, and – again thanks to Count Chodek – now Prague's largest and leafiest public park. If you're heading north for Troja and the city zoo (see below), a stroll through the park is by far the most pleasant approach. If you want to explore a little more of the park, head west sticking to the park's southern border and you'll come to a water tunnel, built by the surrealist court painter Giuseppe Arcimboldo as part of Rudolf II's ambitious horticultural scheme to carry water from the Vltava to the lakes he created a little to the north.

Further west still is Stromovka's main sight, the **Místodržitelský letohrádek**, one of the earliest neo-Gothic structures in the city, begun way back in 1805. Originally conceived as a royal hunting chateau, it served as the seat of the Governor of Bohemia until 1918, and now houses the Národní muzeum's periodicals collection (closed to the public). To continue on to Troja and the zoo, head north under the railway, over the canal, and on to the Císařský ostrov (Emperor's Island) – and from there to the right bank of the Vltava.

Troja

Though still well within the municipal boundaries, the suburb of TROJA, across the river to the north of Holešovice and Bubeneč, still has a distinctly country feel to it. Its most celebrated sight is Prague's only genuine **chateau** or **zámek**, perfectly situated against a hilly backdrop of vines. Troja's other attraction is the city's slightly dilapidated, but still enormously popular **zoo**.

To get to Troja, you can either **walk** from Výstaviště (taking the route described above); catch **bus** #112, which runs roughly every fifteen minutes from metro Nádraží Holešovice; or, from April to September you can reach Troja by boat from the boat launch between Jiráskův and Palackého most (see Nové Město map on pp.122–123).

Trojský zámek

The **Trojský zámek** (Troja chateau) was designed by Jean-Baptiste Mathey for the powerful Šternberg family towards the end of the seventeenth century. Despite a recent renovation and rusty red repaint, its plain early Baroque facade is no match for the action-packed, blackened figures of giants and titans who battle it out on the chateau's monumental balustrades. To visit the **interior**, you'll have to join one of the guided tours. The star exhibits are the gushing frescoes depicting the victories of the Habsburg Emperor Leopold I (who reigned from 1657 to 1705) over the Turks, which cover every inch of the walls and ceilings of the grand hall; ask for the *anglický text* when you enter. Alternatively, you can simply take a wander through the chateau's pristine trend-setting French-style formal **gardens** (open all year), the first of their kind in Bohemia.

The chateau is open April–Sept Tues–Sun 10am–5pm.

The zoo

On the other side of U trojského zámku, which runs along the west wall of the chateau, is the city's capacious but underfunded **zoo** (zoologická zahrada), founded in 1931 on the site of one of Troja's numerous hillside vineyards. Despite its rather weary appearance, all the usual animals are on show here, and kids, at least, have few problems enjoying themselves. Thankfully, a programme of moderniza-

The zoo is open daily: March & April 9am–5pm; May 9am–6pm; June–Sept 9am–7pm; Oct–Feb 9am–4pm.

tion is currently under way, though only the new lion and tiger building, to the south, has so far been completed. In the summer, you can take a "ski-lift" (lanová dráha) from the duck pond to the top of the hill, where the prize exhibits – a rare breed of miniature horse known as Przewalski – hang out.

Dejvice, Střešovice and beyond

Spread across the hills to the northwest of the city centre are the leafy garden suburbs of **Dejvice** and **Střešovice**, peppered with fashionable modern villas, built between the wars for the upwardly mobile Prague bourgeoisie and commanding magnificent views across the north of the city. Both districts are short on conventional sights, but interesting to explore all the same. Some distance further west, the valley of **Šárka** is about as far as you can get from an urban environment without leaving the city. To the south of Šárka is the battlefield of **Bílá hora**, and **Hvězda**, a park containing a pretty star-shaped chateau that's well worth the effort to see.

Dejvice

DEJVICE was planned and built in the early 1920s for the First Republic's burgeoning community of civil servants and government and military officials. Its unappealing main square, **Vítězné náměstí** (metro Dejvická), is unavoidable if you're planning to explore any of the western suburbs, since it's a major public transport interchange.

To get to the Hotel International take tram #20 or #25 from metro Dejvická.

There's nothing much of note in this central part of Dejvice, though you can't help but notice the **Hotel International** at the end of Jugoslávských partyzánů, a Stalinist skyscraper that is disturbingly similar to the universally loathed Palace of Culture in Warsaw. For followers of Socialist Realist chic, its workerist motifs merit closer inspection – somewhat incredibly, it's now part of the Holiday Inn hotel chain (see p.201).

Baba

To get to Baba, take bus #131 from metro Hradčanská.

Dejvice's most intriguing villas are located to the north in **Baba**, a model neighbourhood of 33 functionalist houses, each individually commissioned and built under the guidance of one-time Cubist and born-again functionalist, Pavel Janák. A group of leading architects affiliated to the Czech Workers' Alliance, inspired by a similar project in Stuttgart, initiated what was, at the time, a radical housing project to provide simple, single-family villas. The idea was to use space and open-plan techniques rather than expensive materials to create a luxurious living space.

Despite the plans of the builders, the houses were mostly bought up by Prague's artistic and intellectual community. Nevertheless, they have stood the test of time better than most utopian architecture, not least because of the fantastic site – facing south and overlooking the city. Some of them remain exactly as they were when first built, others have been thoughtlessly altered, but as none of them is open to the public you'll have to be content with surreptitious peeping from the following streets: Na ostrohu, Na Babě, Nad Paťankou and Průhledová.

Dejvice,
Střešovice
and beyond

Střešovice

STŘEŠOVICE, southwest of Dejvice, has no central square and is dominated rather by its wealthy villa quarter, **Ořechovka**, where Havel now lives – his villa, at Dělostřelecká 1, cost more than 1.5 million dollars. The most famous of the villas, though, is the **Müller Haus** (Loosova vila) at Nad hradním vodojemem 14, designed by the Brno-born architect, Adolf Loos. Completed in 1930 (after planning permission had been refused ten times), it was one of Loos' few commissions, a typically uncompromising white box, wiped smooth with concrete rendering. Now grey with pollution, it's nothing to look at from the outside, but then Loos believed that "a building should be dumb on the outside and reveal its wealth only on the inside". However, since you can't get inside, there's no way to appreciate the careful choice of rich materials and minimal furnishings that were Loos' hallmark. There are plans to turn the house into a museum to Loos – regarded by many as one of the founders of modern architecture – but for the moment,

To reach the Müller Haus, take tram #1 or #18 from metro Hradčanská.

Střešovice is also home of the city's Transport Museum (Muzeum MHD), on Patočka, for more on which see p.243.

Šárka and Ctirad

The Šárka valley takes its name from the Amazonian **Šárka**, who, according to Czech legend, committed suicide here sometime back in the last millennium. The story begins with the death of Libuše, the founder and first ruler of Prague. The women closest to her, who had enjoyed enormous freedom and privilege in her court, refused to submit to the new patriarchy of her husband, Přemysl. Under the leadership of a woman called Vlasta, they left Vyšehrad and set up their own proto-feminist, separatist colony called Děvín, on the opposite bank of the river.

They scored numerous military victories over the men of Vyšehrad, but never managed to finish off the men's leader, a young warrior called **Ctirad**. In the end they decided to ensnare him and tied one of their own warriors naked to a tree, sure in the knowledge that Ctirad would take her to be a maiden in distress and come to her aid. Šárka offered to act as the decoy, luring Ctirad into the ambush, after which he was tortured and killed. However, in her brief meeting with Ctirad, Šárka fell madly in love with him and, overcome with grief at what she had done, threw herself off the aforementioned cliff. And just in case you thought the legend has a feminist ending, it doesn't. Roused by the cruel death of Ctirad, Přemysl and the lads had a final set-to with Vlasta and co, and butchered the lot of them.

---

surrounded by hundreds of similarly boxy houses, you may well wonder what all the fuss is about.

Šárka

If you've had your fill of postcards and crowds, take tram #20 or #26 from metro Dejvice to the last stop and walk north down into the **Šárka valley**, a peaceful limestone gorge that twists eastwards back towards Dejvice. The first section (Divoká Šárka) is particularly dramatic, with grey-white crags rising up on both sides – it was here that Šárka plunged to her death (see box above). Gradually the valley opens up, with a grassy meadow to picnic on, and an open-air swimming pool nearby, both fairly popular with Czechs on summer weekends. There are various points further east from which you can pick up a city bus back

---

The Battle of Bílá hora

The **Battle of Bílá hora** (White Mountain) may have been a skirmish of minor importance in the Thirty Years' War, but, for the Czechs, it was to have devastating consequences. The victory of the Catholic forces of Habsburg emperor Ferdinand II in 1620 set the seal on the Czech Lands for the next three hundred years. It prompted an emigration of religious and intellectual figures that relegated the country to a cultural backwater for most of modern history. The defeat also unleashed a decimation of the Bohemian and Moravian aristocracy, which meant that, unlike their immediate neighbours, the Poles and Hungarians, the Czechs had to build their nineteenth-century national revival around writers and composers, rather than counts and warriors.

The 28,000 Catholic soldiers – made up of Bavarians, Spanish, German and French troops (among them the future philosopher, Réné Descartes) – outnumbered the 21,000-strong Czech, Hungarian and German Protestant army, though the latter occupied the strategic chalky hill to the west of Prague. Shortly after noon on November 8 the imperial troops (under the nominal command of the Virgin Mary) began by attacking the Protestants' left flank, and, after about an hour, prompted a full-scale flight. The Protestant commander, Christian von Anhalt, went hot-foot back to the Hrad, where he met the Czech king, Frederick of Palatinate, who was late for the battle, having been delayed during lunch with the English ambassador.

Frederick, dubbed the "Winter King" for his brief reign, had once tossed silver coins to the crowd, and entertained them by swimming naked in the Vltava, while his wife, Elizabeth, daughter of James I of England, had shocked Prague society with her expensive dresses, her outlandish hairdo, and her plunging décolletage. Now, abandoned by their allies, the royal couple gathered up the crown jewels and left Prague in such a hurry they almost forgot their youngest son – later to become the dashing Prince Rupert of the English Civil War – who was playing in the nursery. The city had no choice but to surrender to the Catholics, who spent a week looting the place, before executing 27 of the rebellion's leaders on Staroměstské náměstí (see p.98).

---

into town, depending on how far you want to walk. The full walk to where the Šárka stream flows into the Vltava, just north of Baba, is about 6–7km all told, though none of it is particularly tough going.

Dejvice,
Střešovice
and beyond

Hvězda, Bílá hora and Břevnov

A couple of kilometres southwest of Dejvice, trams #1, #2 and #18 terminate close to the main entrance to the hunting park of Hvězda, one of Prague's most beautiful and peaceful parks. Wide, soft, green avenues of trees radiate from a bizarre star-shaped building (*hvězda* means "Star") that was designed by the Archduke Ferdinand of Tyrol for his wife in 1555. Recently restored, it houses a worthy but dull **museum**, devoted to the writer Alois Jirásek (1851–1930), who popularized old Czech legends during the national revival, and the artist Mikuláš Aleš (1852–1913), whose drawings were likewise inspired by Czech history. There's also a small exhibition on the Battle of Bílá hora (see box opposite) on the top floor. It's the building itself, though – decorated with delicate stucco work and frescoes – that's the real reason for venturing inside; it makes a perfect setting for the chamber music concerts occasionally staged here.

The museum is open Tues–Sat 9am–4pm, Sun 10am–5pm.

A short distance southwest of Hvězda is the once entirely barren limestone summit of **Bílá hora** (White Mountain), accessible from Hvězda through one of the many holes in the park's southern perimeter wall. It was here in 1620, that the first battle of the Thirty Years' War took place, sealing the fate of the Czech nation for the following three hundred years. In little more than an hour, the Protestant forces of the "Winter King" Frederick of Palatinate were roundly beaten by the Catholic troops of the Habsburg Emperor Ferdinand. As a more or less direct consequence, the Czechs lost their aristocracy, their religion, their scholars and, most importantly, the remnants of their sovereignty. There's nothing much to see now, apart from the small monument (*mohyla*), and a pilgrims' church, just off Nad višňovkou. This was erected by the Catholics to commemorate the victory, which they ascribed to the timely intercession of the Virgin Mary – hence its name, **Panna Maria Vítězná** (St Mary the Victorious).

To get to Bílá hora, take tram #8 from metro Hradčanská or #22 from metro Malostranská to the western terminus, then walk up Nad višňovkou and across the field.

If you've time to spare before heading back into town, it's only five minutes' walk east of the park, down Zeyerova alej, to the idyllic Baroque monastery of **sv Markéta** in Břevnov. Founded as a Benedictine abbey by Saint Adalbert, tenth-century bishop of Prague, it was worked over in the eighteenth century by both Christoph and Kilian Ignaz Dientzenhofer, and bears their characteristic interconnecting ovals, inside and out. The monks have now returned, which has made it easier to gain access to the church. To get back into town, take tram #8 or #22 from just below the monastery.

There are guided tours of the monastery on Sat 9 & 10.30am, 2 & 4pm, Sun 10.30am, 2 & 4pm; at other times it's possible to peek inside through the glass doors.

Smíchov

SMÍCHOV is for the most part a late nineteenth-century working-class suburb, home to the city's largest brewery, which produces the ubiquitous Staropramen, and a large community of Romanies, its skyline peppered with satanic chimneys dutifully belching out smoke. To the west, as the suburb gains height, the run-down tenements give way to another of Prague's sought-after villa quarters. To the north, Smíchov borders with Malá Strana, and, officially at least, takes in a considerable part of the woods of Petřín, south of the Hladová zeď (see p.83).

Anděl and náměstí 14 října

There's only one important sight in Smíchov – the Bertramka (see below) – but a stroll around the busy streets of Smíchov is rewarding in its own way. As you leave Anděl metro station, the modern hub of Smíchov, note the Soviet-designed Socialist Realist marble **mosaic**, a relic from the days when the station was called Moskevská. Another monument to a lost era is the disused **synagogue**, adjacent to the station, up Plzeňská. Built in 1863 to serve the wealthy Jewish business folk, it was remodelled in the 1930s in functionalist style, and sports unusual crenellations on the roof – only the Hebrew inscription on the ground floor gives any indication of its former use.

If you're looking for a café to relax in, head for the Apostrof, housed in a renovated Baroque chateau by the church (see p.215).

The district's traditional heart is **náměstí 14 října**, a short walk from metro Anděl up Štefánikova. The Art Nouveau Národní dům, and the adjacent market hall (now converted into a bland supermarket), both erected around 1906, have seen better days, but the neo-Renaissance **church of sv Václav**, built in the 1880s and overlooking the square, is worth a visit. Inside, the church is a jewel box of rich Byzantine decoration, with gilded mosaics, huge Ionic pillars of red Swedish granite, a coffered ceiling and a wonderfully Turkish-looking gilded pulpit.

Bertramka (Mozart Museum)

Bertramka is open April–Sept Tues–Fri 2–5pm, Sat & Sun 10am–noon & 2–5pm; Oct–March Tues–Fri 1–4pm, Sat & Sun 10am–noon & 1–4pm. For more on Mozart's links with Prague, see box on p.74.

Mozart stayed with the Dušeks at their newly acquired **Bertramka villa** on several occasions – it was here that he put the finishing touches to his *Don Giovanni* overture, the night before the premiere at the Stavovské divadlo (see p.104). It was the sort of household that would have appealed to Mozart, musical and slightly rakish: František Dušek was a well-respected pianist in his own right, while his wife, Josefa Dušková, a popular singer seventeen years younger than her husband, was one of Prague's most fashionable hostesses. As long ago as 1838, the villa was turned into a shrine to Mozart, though very little survives of the house he knew, thanks to a fire on New Year's Day, 1871 – not that this has deterred generations of Mozart lovers from flocking here. These days, what the museum lacks in memorabilia, it makes up for with its Rococo ambience, a

The Pink Tank

Smíchov's greatest claim to fame is the episode of the **pink tank**. Until 1991, Tank 23 sat proudly on its plinth in náměstí Sovětských tankistů (Soviet tank drivers' square), one of a number of obsolete tanks generously donated by the Soviets after World War II to serve as monuments to the 1945 liberation. Tank 23 was special, however, as it was supposedly the first tank to arrive to liberate Prague, on May 9, hotfoot from Berlin.

The real story of the liberation of Prague was rather different, however. When the Prague uprising began on May 5, the first offer of assistance actually came from a division of the anti-Communist Russian National Liberation Army (KONR), under the overall command of a renegade general, Andrei Vlasov. Vlasov was a high-ranking Red Army officer, who was instrumental in pushing the Germans back from the gates of Moscow, but switched sides after being captured by the Nazis in 1942. The Germans were (rightly, as it turned out) highly suspicious of the KONR, and, for the most part, the renegade Russians were kept well away from the real action. In the war's closing stages, however, the KONR switched sides once more and agreed to fight alongside the Czech resistance, making a crucial intervention against the SS troops who were poised to crush the uprising in Prague. Initially, the Czechs guaranteed Vlasov's men asylum from the advancing Soviets in return for military assistance. In reality, the Czechs were unable to honour their side of the bargain and the KONR finally withdrew from the city late on May 7 and headed west to surrender themselves to the Americans. When the Red Army finally arrived in Prague, many of Vlasov's troops were simply gunned down by the Soviets. Even those in the hands of the Americans were eventually passed over to the Russians and shared the fate of their leader Vlasov who was tried *in camera* in Moscow and hanged with piano wire on August 2, 1946.

The unsolicited reappearance of Soviet tanks on the streets of Prague in 1968 left most Czechs feeling somewhat ambivalent towards the old monument. And in the summer of 1991, situationist artist David Černý painted the tank bubble-gum pink, and placed a large phallic finger on top of it, while another mischievous Czech daubed "Vlasov" on the podium. Since the country was at the time engaged in delicate negotiations to end the Soviet military presence in Czechoslovakia, the new regime, despite its mostly dissident leanings, roundly condemned the act as unlawful. Havel, in his characteristically even-handed way, made it clear that he didn't like tanks anywhere, whether on the battlefield or as monuments.

In the end, the tank was hastily repainted khaki green and Černý was arrested under the familiar "crimes against the state" clause of the penal code, which had been used by the Communists with gay abandon on several members of the then government. In protest at the arrest of Černý, twelve members of the federal parliament turned up the following day in their overalls and, taking advantage of their legal immunity, repainted the tank pink. Finally, the government gave in, released Černý and removed the tank from public view. There's now no trace of tank, podium or plaque, and even the square has been renamed náměstí Kinských.

lovely garden and regular Mozart recitals. To get to Bertramka, take the metro to Anděl, walk a couple of blocks west up Plzeňská, then left up Mozartova.

Chapter 8

Out from the city

F ew capital cities can boast such extensive unspoilt tracts of woodland so near at hand as Prague. Once you leave the half-built high-rise estates of the outer suburbs behind, the traditional provincial feel of **Bohemia** (Čechy) immediately makes itself felt. Many towns and villages still huddle below the grand residences of their former lords, their street layout little changed since medieval times.

To the north, several such chateaux grace the banks of the Vltava, including the wine-producing town of **Mělník**, on the Labe (Elbe) plain. Further away, but well served by public transport, is **Terezín**, the wartime Jewish ghetto that is a living testament to the Holocaust. One of the most obvious day-trip destinations is to the east of

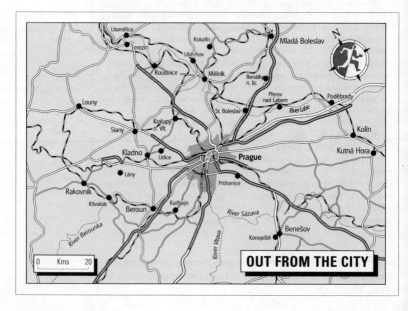

OUT FROM THE CITY

Prague: **Kutná Hora**, a medieval silver-mining town with one of the most beautiful Gothic churches in the country, and a macabre gallery of bones in the suburb of Sedlec.

Further south the **Konopiště** chateau boasts exceptionally beautiful and expansive grounds. Southwest of Prague, a similar mix of woods and rolling hills surrounds the popular castle of **Karlštejn**, a gem of Gothic architecture, dramatically situated above the River Berounka. West of Prague, there are two places of pilgrimage: **Lány** is the resting place of the founder of modern Czechoslovakia, and summer residence of the president; and **Lidice**, razed to the ground by the SS, is another town which recalls the horror of Nazi occupation.

Getting around

Transport throughout Bohemia is fairly straightforward, thanks to a comprehensive network of railway lines and regional bus services, though connections can be less than smooth, and journeys slow. If you're planning to try and see more than one or two places outside Prague, or one of the more difficult destinations to reach, it might be worth considering renting a car.

For details of car rental firms, see p.44; for bike rental, see p.45.

By train

The most relaxing way to day-trip from Prague is by **train**; the antiquated rolling stock of Czech Railways, České dráhy (ČD), is a pleasure to travel in. However, the system, which has changed little since it was bequeathed to the country by the Habsburgs in 1918, is often a lot slower than the buses. It's also currently entering a period of crisis, with the threat of closure hanging over something like one third of the railway system.

ČD run two main **types of train**: *rychlík* (or *spěšný*) trains are the faster ones which stop only at major towns, while *osobní* (or *zastavkový*) trains stop at just about every station, averaging as little as 30kph. It's also worth knowing about the existence of fast trains known as either SuperCity (SC), EuroCity (EC) or InterCity (IC), for which you need to pay a supplement. However, for the purposes of the day-trips described below, you won't need to take these fast services.

To buy a ticket, simply state your destination – if you want a return ticket (*zpáteční*), you must say so. First-class carriages (*první třída*) exist only on fast trains. There are half-price **discount fares** for children under 12, and you can take two children under 5 for free (providing they don't take up more than one seat). There are even some "crèche carriages" on the slower trains, where those with children under 10 have priority over seats.

With very few English-speakers employed on the railways, it can be difficult getting **train information**. The larger stations have a simple airport-style arrivals and departures board, which includes information on delays under the heading *zpoždění*. Many stations have poster-style displays of arrivals (*příjezd*) and departures (*odjezd*), the former on white paper, the latter on yellow, with fast trains printed in red. All but the smallest stations also have a comprehensive display of **timings and route information** on rollers. These timetables may seem daunting at first, but with a little practice they should become decipherable. First find the route you need to take on the diagrammatic map and make a note of the number printed beside it; then follow the timetable rollers through until you come to the appropriate number. The only problem now is language since everything will be written in Czech. A platform, or *nástupiště*, is usually divided into two *kolej* on either side. Some of the more common notes at the side of the timetable are *jezdí jen v* (only running on), or *nejezdí v* or *nechodí v* (not running on), followed by a date or a symbol: a cross or an "N" for a Sunday, a big "S" for a Saturday, two crossed hammers for a workday, "A" for a Friday and so on. Small stations may simply have a board with a list of departures under the title *směr* (direction) followed by a town.

By bus

Travelling by **bus** (*autobus*) tends to be quicker, and marginally cheaper, but a lot less scenic than by train. Bear in mind, though, that timetables are often designed with the working and/or school day in mind. This means that services are at their most frequent between 6am and 8am and between 4pm and 6pm during the week, with few or no services at weekends; so always check return times before you set out.

Most routes are still run by the state bus company, ČSAD, though private companies such as Čebus are making inroads into the more popular routes. In places outside Prague, the **bus station** is often adjacent to the train station, though you may be able to pick up the bus from the centre of town, too. The bigger terminals in Prague, like Praha-Florenc, are run with train-like efficiency, though finding the right departure stand (*stání*) can be a daunting task. For most minor routes, simply buy your ticket from the driver.

Bus **timetables** are even more difficult to figure out than train ones, as there are no maps at any of the stations. In the detailed timetables, each service is listed separately, so you may have to scour several timetables before you discover when the next bus is. A better bet is to look at the departures and arrivals board. Make sure you check on which day the service runs, since many run only on Mondays, Fridays or at the weekend (see the above section on trains for the key phrases). Minor bus stops are marked with a rusty metal sign saying *zastávka*. If you want to get off, ask *já chci vystoupit?*; "the next stop" is *příští zastávka*.

Mělník and around

Occupying a spectacular, commanding site at the confluence of the Vltava and Labe rivers, **MĚLNÍK**, 33km north of Prague, lies at the heart of Bohemia's tiny wine-growing region. The town's history goes back to the ninth century, when it was handed over to the Přemyslids as part of Ludmila's dowry when she married Prince Bořivoj. And it was here, too, that she introduced her heathen grandson Václav (later to become Saint Wenceslas, aka "Good King") to the joys of Christianity. Viticulture became the town's economic mainstay only after Charles IV, aching for a little of the French wine of his youth, introduced grapes from Burgundy (where he was also king).

The old town

Mělník's greatest monument is its Renaissance **chateau**, perched high above the flat plains and visible for miles around. The present building, its courtyard covered in familiar sgraffito patterns, has recently been returned to its last aristocratic owners, the Lobkowicz family, who are in the process of restoring the chateau's magnificently proportioned rooms, which also provide great views out over the plain. Visits are by guided tour only, and you've a choice between exploring seven beautifully painted rooms of the castle interior, filled with artefacts and Old Masters returned to the family since 1989, or touring the wine museum in the cellars, finishing up with free samples of plonk; alternatively you can do both tours. In addition, there's a museum of prams, strollers and baby carriages which forms part of the local **museum** on the first floor of the chateau.

The chateau is open daily March–Dec 10am–5pm; the museum is open May–Oct Tues–Sun 9am–5pm.

Below the chateau, vines cling to the south-facing terraces, as the land plunges into the river below. From beneath the great tower of Mělník's onion-domed church of **sv Petr and Pavel**, next door to the chateau, there's an even better view of the rivers' confluence, and the subsidiary canal, once so congested with vessels that traffic lights had to be introduced to avoid accidents. The church itself contains a compellingly macabre **ossuary** or *kostnice*, filled with more than 10,000 bones of medieval plague victims, fashioned into weird and wonderful skeletal shapes by students in the early part of this century.

The ossuary is open Tues–Sun 10.30am–4pm.

The rest of the old town is pretty small, but it's pleasant enough for a casual stroll. One half of the main square, náměstí Míru, is arcaded Baroque and typical of the region, and there's an old medieval gateway nearby, the Pražská brána, which has been converted into an art gallery.

Practicalities

There's no direct train service to Mělník from Prague, but there is a regular **bus service** which leaves from metro Nádraží Holešovice and stand 18 at Florenc, and takes under an hour. On arrival at Mělník bus station, to reach the older part of town, simply head up Krombholcova in the direction of the big church tower. If your next destination is Terezín, you have the choice of either the bus or the train; the **train station** is still further from the old town, a couple of blocks northeast of the bus station, down Jiřího z Poděbrad.

As for **food and drink**, the *Zámecká restaurace* is as good (and cheap) a place as any to sample some of the local wine (and enjoy the view): the red Ludmila is the most famous of Mělník's wines, and there's even a rare Czech rosé produced by the castle vineyards, but if you prefer white, try a bottle of Tramín. Equally good views can be had from *Stará škola* restaurant, behind the church; otherwise, you could try *Na hradbách*, on náměstí Míru, which serves up big portions, local wines, not to mention Guinness and Kilkenny, in a cosy brick and wood-panelled interior.

Terezín

The road from Prague to Berlin passes right through the fortress town of **TEREZÍN** (Theresienstadt), just over 60km northwest of the capital. Purpose-built in the 1780s by the Habsburgs to defend the northern border against Prussia, it was capable of accommodating 14,500 soldiers and hundreds of prisoners. In 1941, the population was ejected and the whole town turned into a **Jewish ghetto**, and used as a transit camp for Jews whose final destination was Auschwitz.

Although the **Hlavní pevnost** (Main Fortress) has never been put to the test in battle, Terezín remains a garrison town. Today, it's an eerie, soulless place, built to a dour eighteenth-century grid plan, its bare streets still ringing with the sounds of soldiers and military police. As you enter, the red-brick fortifications are still an awesome sight, though the huge moat has been put out of action by local gardening enthusiasts.

A brief history of the ghetto

In October 1941, Reinhard Heydrich and the Nazi high command decided to turn the whole of Terezín into a Jewish ghetto. It was an obvious choice: fully fortified, close to the main Prague–Dresden railway line, and with an SS prison already established in the **Malá pevnost** (Small Fortress) nearby. The original inhabitants of the town – less than 3500 people – were moved out, and transports began arriving at Terezín from many parts of central Europe. Within a year, nearly 60,000 Jews were interned here in appallingly overcrowded conditions; the monthly death rate rose to 4000. In October 1942, the first transport left for Auschwitz. By the end of the war, 140,000 Jews had been deported to Terezín; fewer than 17,500 remained when the ghetto was finally liberated on May 8, 1945.

One of the perverse ironies of Terezín is that it was used by the Nazis as a cover for the real purpose of the *Endlösung* or "final solution",

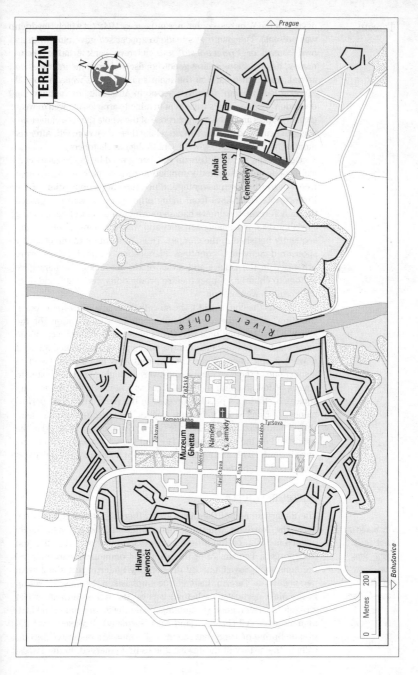

TEREZÍN

△ Prague

N

Malá
pevnost

Cemetery

River Ohře

Pražská

Komenského

Žižkova

Muzeum
Ghetta

B. Němcové

Náměstí

Čs. armády

Havlíčkova

28. října

Palackého

Tyršova

Hlavní
pevnost

Metres

0   200

▽ Bohušovice

devised at the Wannsee conference in January 1942 (at which Heydrich was present). The ghetto was made to appear self-governing, with its own council or *Freizeitgestaltung*, its own bank printing ghetto money, its own shops selling goods confiscated from the internees on arrival, and even a café on the main square. For a while, a special "Terezín family camp" was even set up in Auschwitz, to continue the deception. The deportees were kept in mixed barracks, allowed to wear civilian clothes and – the main purpose of the whole thing – send letters back to their loved ones in Terezín telling them they were OK. After six months' "quarantine", they were sent to the gas chambers.

Despite the fact that Terezín was being used by the Nazis as cynical propaganda, the ghetto population turned their unprecedented freedom to their own advantage. Since the entire population of the Protectorate (and Jews from many other parts of Europe) passed through Terezín, the ghetto had an enormous number of outstanding Jewish artists, musicians, scholars and writers (many of whom subsequently perished in the camps). Thus, in addition to the officially sponsored activities, countless clandestine cultural events were organized in the cellars and attics of the barracks: teachers gave lessons to children, puppet theatre productions were held, and literary evenings were put on.

Towards the end of 1943, the so-called *Verschönerung* or "beautification" of the ghetto was implemented, in preparation for the arrival of the International Red Cross inspectors. Streets were given names instead of numbers, and the whole place was decked out as if it were a spa town. When the International Red Cross asked to inspect one of the Nazi camps, they were brought here and treated to a week of Jewish cultural events. A circus tent was set up in the main square; a children's pavilion erected in the park; numerous performances of Hans Krása's children's opera, *Brundibár* (Bumble Bee), staged; and a jazz band, called the Ghetto Swingers, performed in the bandstand on the main square. The Red Cross visited Terezín twice, once in June 1944, and again in April 1945; both times the delegates filed positive reports.

Muzeum Ghetta

The museum is open daily: April–Sept 9am–6pm; Oct–March 9am–5.30pm.

The unnerving feel of the place apart, there's just one thing to see here, the **Muzeum Ghetta** (Ghetto Museum), which was finally opened in 1991, on the fiftieth anniversary of the arrival of the first transports in Terezín. After the war, the Communists had followed the consistent Soviet line by deliberately underplaying the Jewish perspective on Terezín. Instead, the emphasis in the museum set up in the Malá pevnost (see below) was on the war as an anti-fascist struggle, in which good (Communism and the Soviet Union) had triumphed over evil (Fascism and Nazi Germany). It wasn't until the Prague Spring of 1968 that the idea of a museum dedicated specifically to the history of the Jewish ghetto first emerged. In the 1970s, however, the intended building was turned into a Museum of the Ministry of the Interior instead.

Now that it's finally open, this extremely informative and well-laid-out exhibition at last attempts to do some justice to the extraordinary and tragic events which took place here between 1941 and 1945, including background displays on the measures which led inexorably to the *Endlösung*. There's also a fascinating video (with English subtitles) showing clips of the Nazi propaganda film shot in Terezín – *Hitler Gives the Jews a Town* – intercut with harrowing interviews with survivors.

Malá pevnost

On the other side of the River Ohře, east down Pražská, lies the **Malá pevnost** (Small Fortress), built as a military prison in the 1780s, at the same time as the main fortress. The prison's most famous inmate was the young Bosnian Serb, Gavrilo Princip, who succeeded in assassinating Archduke Ferdinand in Sarajevo in 1914, and was interned and died here during World War I. In 1940 it was turned into an SS prison by Heydrich and, after the war, it became the official memorial and museum of Terezín. The vast cemetery laid out by the entrance to the fortress is now dominated by a large Christian cross, an insensitive recent addition given that the vast majority of Terezín's victims were Jewish.

The Malá pevnost is open daily: April–Sept 9am–6pm; Oct–March 9am–4pm.

There are guides available (often survivors from Terezín), or else you can simply buy the brief broadsheet guide to the prison in English, and walk around yourself. The infamous Nazi refrain *Arbeit Macht Frei* (Work Brings Freedom) is daubed across the entrance on the left, which leads to the exemplary washrooms, still as they were when built for the Red Cross tour of inspection. The rest of the camp has been left empty but intact, and graphically evokes the cramped conditions under which the prisoners were kept half-starved and badly clothed, subject to indiscriminate cruelty and execution. The main **exhibition** is housed in the smart eighteenth-century mansion set in the prison gardens, which was home to the camp *Kommandant*, his family and fellow SS officers. A short documentary, intelligible in any language, is regularly shown in the cinema that was set up in 1942 to entertain the prison officers.

Practicalities

Terezín is about an hour's **bus** ride from Prague's Florenc terminal (buses leave from stand 17) and therefore easy to visit on a day trip. The nearest train station is at Bohušovice nad Ohří (slow trains from Prague's Masarykovo nádraží), 2km south of the fortress. Another alternative, albeit a more expensive one, is to sign up for one of the guided tours of Terezín that leave from Prague. The Matana travel agency, Maiselove 15, Josefov (☎232 1954) charges 1000kč for a day trip with a guide and lunch thrown in. Foodwise, if you're on your own, you're best off either bringing a picnic or heading for *U hojtašů*, a restaurant on Komenského.

Kutná Hora

For 250 years or so, **KUTNÁ HORA** (Kuttenberg) was one of the most important towns in Bohemia, second only to Prague. At the end of the fourteenth century its population was equal to that of London, its shantytown suburbs straggled across what are now green fields, and its ambitious building projects set out to rival those of the capital itself. Today, Kutná Hora is a small provincial town with a population of just over 20,000, but the monuments dotted around it, the superb Gothic cathedral, and the remarkable monastery and ossuary in the suburb of **Sedlec**, make it one of the most enjoyable of all possible day trips from Prague.

A brief history

Kutná Hora's road to prosperity began in the late thirteenth century with the discovery of **silver deposits** in the surrounding area. German miners were invited to settle and work the seams, and around 1300 Václav II founded the royal mint here and sent for Italian craftsmen to run it. Much of the town's wealth was used to fund the beautification of Prague, but it also allowed for the construction of one of the most magnificent churches in central Europe and a number of other prestigious Gothic monuments in Kutná Hora itself.

At the time of the Hussite Wars, the town was mostly German-speaking, and staunchly Catholic; local miners used to throw captured Hussites into the deep mine shafts and leave them to die of starvation. Word got out, and the town was besieged and eventually taken by Žižka's fanatical Táborites in 1421, only to be recaptured by Sigismund and his papal forces shortly afterwards, and again by Žižka, the following year.

While the silver stocks remained high the town was able to recover its former prosperity, but at the end of the sixteenth century the mines dried up and Kutná Hora's wealth and importance came to an abrupt end – when the Swedes marched on the town during the Thirty Years' War, they had to be bought off with beer rather than silver. The town has never fully recovered, shrivelling to less than a third of its former size, its fate emphatically sealed by a devastating fire in 1770.

The Town

The small, unassuming houses that line the town's main square, Palackého náměstí, and medieval lanes give little idea of Kutná Hora's former glories. A narrow alleyway on the south side of the square, however, leads to the more appealing, leafy Havlíčkovo náměstí, on which stands the **Vlašský dvůr** (Italian Court), originally conceived as a palace by Václav II, and for three centuries the town's bottomless purse. It was here that Florentine minters produced the Prague Groschen (*pražské groše*), a silver coin widely used throughout central Europe until the nineteenth century. The building itself has been mucked about with over the years, most recently – and most brutally – by nineteenth-century restorers, who left only the chestnut trees, a fourteenth-century oriel window (capped by an unlikely looking wooden onion dome) and the statue of a miner unmolested. The original workshops of the minters have been bricked in, but the outlines of their little doors and windows are still visible in the courtyard. The short **guided tour** of the old chapel, treasury and royal palace gives you a fair idea of the building's former importance.

Outside the court is a statue of the country's founder and first president, T. G. Masaryk, twice removed – once by the Nazis and once by the Communists – but now returned to its pride of place. Before you leave, take a quick turn in the court gardens, which climb down in steps to the Vrchlice valley below. This is undoubtedly Kutná Hora's best profile, with a splendid view over to the cathedral of sv Barbora (see below).

Kutná Hora

The Vlašský dvůr is open daily 10am–6pm.

Kutná Hora

Behind the Vlašský dvůr is **sv Jakub** (St James), the town's oldest church, begun a generation or so after the discovery of the silver deposits. Its grand scale is a clear indication of the town's quite considerable wealth by the fourteenth century, though in terms of artistry it pales in comparison with Kutná Hora's other ecclesiastical buildings. The leaning tower is a reminder of the precarious position of the town, the church's foundations being prone to subsidence from the disused mines below. If you want to see some of these, head for the **Hrádek**, an old fort which was used as a second mint and now serves as a **Mining Museum** (Muzeum a středověké důlní dílo). Here you can pick up a white coat, miner's helmet and torch, and visit some of the medieval mines that were discovered beneath the fort in the 1960s.

The museum is open April–Oct Tues–Sun 9am–noon & 1–5pm.

Cathedral of sv Barbora

Kutná Hora's cathedral of **sv Barbora** is arguably the most beautiful church in central Europe. Not to be outdone by the great monastery at Sedlec (see overleaf) or the St Vitus Cathedral in Prague, the miners of Kutná Hora began financing the construction of a great Gothic cathedral of their own, dedicated to Saint Barbara, the patron saint of miners and gunners. The foundations were probably laid by Parler in the 1380s, but work was interrupted by the Hussite wars, and the church remains unfinished, despite a flurry of building activity at the beginning of the sixteenth century by, among others, Benedikt Ried (who built the Vladislavský sál in Prague Castle).

The cathedral is open summer Tues–Sun 8am–noon & 1–5pm; winter 9–11.30am & 2–3.30pm.

The approach road to the cathedral, Barborská, is lined with a parade of gesticulating Baroque saints and cherubs that rival the sculptures on the Charles Bridge; on the right-hand side is the palatial former Jesuit College. The church itself bristles with pinnacles, finials and flying buttresses which support its most striking feature, a roof of three tent-like towers, culminating in unequal needle-sharp spires. Inside, cold light streams through the plain glass windows, illuminating a playful vaulted nave whose ribs form branches and petals stamped with coats of arms belonging to Václav II and the local miners' guilds. The wide spread of the five-aisled nave is remarkably uncluttered: a Gothic pulpit – half wood, half stone – creeps tastefully up a central pillar, and black and gold Renaissance confessionals hide discreetly in the north aisle. On the south wall is the Minters' Chapel, decorated with fifteenth-century wall frescoes showing the Florentines at work, while in the ambulatory chapels some fascinating paintings – unique for their period – depict local miners at work.

The rest of the town

There are a few minor sights worth seeking out in the rest of the town. On Rejskovo náměstí, the squat, many-sided **Kašna** (fountain) by Matouš Rejsek strikes an odd pose – anything less like a fountain would be hard to imagine. At the bottom of the sloping Šultysova is a particularly fine **Morový sloup** (Plague Column), giving thanks for the end of the plague of 1713; while just around the corner, at the top of Lierova, is one of the few Gothic buildings to survive the 1770 fire, the **Kamenný dům** built around 1480 and covered in an ornate sculptural icing. This used to contain an unexceptional local museum, which has now been moved a couple of blocks down Jiřího z Poděbrad, to Kilian Ignaz Dientzenhofer's unfinished **Voršilský klášter** (**Ursuline convent**). Only three sides of the convent's ambitious pentagonal plan were completed, its neo-Baroque church added in the late nineteenth century while sv Barbora was being restored.

The convent is open April & Oct Sat & Sun 9am–4pm; May–Sept daily 9am–5pm.

Sedlec

Buses #1 and #4 run 3km northeast to **SEDLEC**, once a separate village but now a suburb of Kutná Hora. Adjoining Sedlec's defunct eighteenth-century Cistercian monastery (now the largest tobacco factory in Europe, owned by Phillip Morris) is the fourteenth-century church of **Panna Maria** (St Mary), imaginatively redesigned in the eighteenth century by Giovanni Santini, who specialized in melding Gothic with Baroque. Here, given a plain French Gothic church gutted during the Hussite wars, Santini set to work on the vaulting, adding his characteristic sweeping stucco rib patterns, relieved only by the occasional Baroque splash of colour above the chancel steps. For all its attractions, however, the church seems to be permanently covered in scaffolding, and closed except for the occasional service.

Cross the main road, following the signs, and you come to the monks' graveyard, where an ancient Gothic chapel leans heavily over the entrance to the macabre subterranean **kostnice** or ossuary, full to overflowing with human bones. When holy earth from Golgotha was scattered over the graveyard in the twelfth century, all of Bohemia's nobility wanted to be buried here and the bones mounted up until there were more than 40,000 complete sets. In 1870, worried about the ever-growing piles, the authorities commissioned František Rint to do something creative with them. He rose to the challenge and moulded out of bones four giant bells, one in each corner of the crypt, designed wall-to-ceiling skeletal decorations, including the Schwarzenberg coat of arms, and, as the centrepiece, put together a chandelier made out of every bone in the human body. Rint's signature (in bones) is at the bottom of the steps.

The ossuary is open daily: summer 8am–noon & 1–5pm; winter 9am–noon & 1–4pm.

Practicalities

The simplest way to get to Kutná Hora is to take a **bus** from stand 56 at Praha-Florenc or from metro Želivského (1hr 15min). Fast **trains** from Prague's Masarykovo nádraží take around an hour (there's only one in the morning); slow ones take two hours; trains from Praha hlavní nádraží involve a change at Kolín. The main **train sta-**

tion (Kutná Hora hlavní nádraží) is a long way out of town, near Sedlec; bus #1 or #4 will take you into town, or there's an occasional shuttle train service to Kutná Hora město train station, near the centre of town.

The town has a highly efficient system of orientation signs, and at almost every street corner a pictorial list of the chief places of interest keeps you on the right track. Having said that, the train station signposted is not the main one. As for **eating and drinking**, *U Bakaláře*, at the junction of Husova and Šultysova, is one of the best restaurants in town, with a wide choice for vegetarians; *U Jakuba*, near the church of the same name, has an outdoor patio and a good fish menu; while *Piazza Navona*, on Palackého náměstí, is a real Italian pizzeria. There are plenty of good pubs, too, where you can get more simple fare: try *U anděla*, at the beginning of Jiřího z Poděbrad, which serves *Bernard* beer, or *U havířů on* Šultysova, which offers a variety of brews including the local *Kutnohorské* beer.

Konopiště

The popularity of **Konopiště**, with a quarter of a million visitors passing through its portcullis every year, is surpassed only by the likes of Karlštejn (see p.189). Coach parties from all over the world home in on this Gothic castle, which is stuffed with dead animals, weaponry and hunting trophies. Most interesting are its historical associations: King Václav IV was imprisoned for a while by his own nobles in the castle's distinctive round tower, and the Archduke Franz Ferdinand, heir to the Habsburg throne, lived here with his wife, Sophie Chotek, until their assassination in Sarajevo in 1914. The archduke shared his generation's voracious appetite for hunting, eliminating all living creatures foolish enough to venture into the grounds. However, he surpassed all his contemporaries by recording, stuffing and displaying a significant number of the 171,537 birds and animals he shot between the years 1880 and 1906, the details of which are recorded in his *Schuss Liste* displayed inside.

There's a choice of two **guided tours**, both of which you'll be relieved to know include the hunting trophies. The forty-minute tour of the *Zámecké sbírky* takes you through the chapel, past the stuffed bears and deer teeth, to the assorted lethal weapons of one of the finest armouries in Europe, displayed as they were in Franz Ferdinand's time. The tour of the *Zámecké salony* is slightly less gruesome but ten minutes longer, exploring the period interiors, which contain some splendid Renaissance cabinets and lots of Meissen porcelain. Occasionally there are tours in English, French and German, too, so ask at the box office before you sign up. Much the best reason to come to Konopiště, though, is to explore its 555-acre **park**, which boasts several lakes, sundry statuary, an unrivalled rose garden and a deer park.

To get to Konopiště take a fast (50min) or slow (1hr 5min) **train** from Praha hlavní nádraží to Benešov u Prahy; the castle is a two-kilometre walk or a short but infrequent bus ride west of the railway station.

Karlštejn

KARLŠTEJN is a small ribbon village, strung out along one of the tributaries of the Berounka – pretty, but not attractive enough to warrant a coach park the size of a football pitch. It's the **castle**, occupying a defiantly unassailable position above the village, which draws in the mass of tourists (over quarter of a million a year). Designed in the fourteenth century by Matthias of Arras for Emperor Charles IV as a giant safe-box for the imperial crown jewels and his large personal collection of precious relics, it quickly became Charles' favourite retreat from the vast city he himself had masterminded. Women were strictly forbidden to enter the castle, and the story of his third wife Anna's successful break-in (in drag) became one of the most popular Czech comedies of the nineteenth century.

The village of Karlštejn has been transformed over the last decade, with every other house offering rooms to rent or selling souvenirs. Most of what you see is eminently missable, with the exception of the **Muzeum Betlémů** (times as for the castle, but without a lunch break), which occupies the ground floor of a house towards the top of the village. For a modest entrance fee, you can admire an impressive array of nativity scenes dating back to the early nineteen century. They range in size from complex mechanical set-ups to miniature affairs that can fit into small sea shells – there's even one in gingerbread.

If only the castle itself – a stunning sight from a distance – had such memorable treats in store. Sadly, centuries of neglect and generations of over-zealous restorers have taken their toll on the interior. Most of the rooms visited on the guided tour contain only the barest of furnishings, the empty spaces taken up by uninspiring displays on the history of the castle. Theoretically, the top two chambers would make the whole trip worthwhile: unfortunately, you can only look into (but not enter) the emperor's residential **Mariánská věž**. It was here that Charles shut himself off from the rest of the world, with any urgent business passed to him through a hole in the wall of the tiny ornate chapel of **sv Kateřina**.

As for the castle's finest treasure, the **Holy Rood Chapel** (*Kaple svatého kříže*), connected by a wooden bridge that leads on from here to the highest point of the castle, the **Velká věž**, this has been closed now since 1980 and it looks like it will remain so in the future as the sheer number of visitors would damage the decor irrevocably. Traditionally, only the emperor, the archbishop and the electoral princes could enter this gilded treasure house, whose six-metre-thick walls contain 2200 semiprecious stones and 128 painted panels, the

The castle is open Tues–Sun: April & Oct 9am–noon & 1–5pm; May, June & Sept closes 6pm; July & Aug closes 7pm; Nov–March closes 4pm. Tours start from the main inner court-yard.

KARLŠTEJN

N

1 Entrance
2 Voršilská brána
3 Second gateway
4 Studniční
5 Courtyard
6 Imperial Palace
7 Chapel of sv Mikuláš
8 Chapel of sv Kateřina
9 Mariánská věž
10 Wooden bridge

Outer Bailey

Velká
věž

0   Metres   50

A small selection of Master Theodoric's panels are exhibited in Prague's Jiřský klášter (see p.59).

work of Master Theodoric, Bohemia's greatest fourteenth-century painter. The imperial crown jewels, once secured here behind nineteen separate locks, were removed to Hungary after an abortive attack by the Hussites, while the Bohemian jewels are now stashed away in the cathedral in Prague.

Practicalities

Slow *osobní* or *zastavkový* **trains** leave Prague's Smíchovské nádraží for Karlštejn roughly every hour, and take about 35 minutes to cover the 28km from Prague. The village is ten minutes' walk across the river from the station, and it's a further fifteen- to twenty-minute climb up to the castle entrance. If you're looking for somewhere to grab a beer and a bite to **eat**, try *U Janů*, which has an outdoor terrace, or the *Koruna*, both on the main street. Alternatively, bring a picnic with you and eat by the banks of the river.

If you're feeling energetic, or have your own wheels, you could go to the popular flooded quarry, **Malá Amerika**. Getting there is tricky, however: either take the red-marked path from near the castle, and head off northwest through the woods at U dubu (you may need to ask a Czech to point you in the right direction), or head west down the track, which comes off the road between Mořina and Bubovice.

Lidice

The small mining village of **LIDICE**, 18km northwest of Prague, hit world headlines on June 10, 1942, at the moment when it ceased to exist. On the flimsiest pretext, it was chosen as scapegoat for the assassination of the Nazi leader Reinhard Heydrich. All 173 men from the village were rounded up and shot by the SS, the 198 women were sent to Ravensbrück concentration camp, and the 89 children either went to the camps, or, if they were Aryan enough, were packed off to "good" German homes, while the village itself was burnt to the ground.

Knowing all this as you approach Lidice makes the modern village seem almost perversely unexceptional. At the end of the straight tree-lined main street, 10 června 1942 (June 10, 1942), there's a dour concrete memorial with a small but horrific **museum** where you can watch a short film about Lidice, including footage shot by the SS themselves as the village was burning. The spot where the old village used to lie is just south of the memorial, now merely smooth green pasture punctuated with a few simple reminders and a new bronze memorial to the 82 local children who were gassed in the camps.

After the massacre, the "Lidice shall live" campaign was launched and villages all over the world began to change their name to Lidice. The first was Stern Park Gardens, Illinois, soon followed by villages in Mexico and other Latin American countries. From Coventry to Montevideo, towns twinned themselves with Lidice, so that rather than "wiping a Czech village off the face of the earth" as Hitler had hoped, the Nazis created an international symbol of anti-fascist resistance.

For a detailed account of Heydrich's assassination, see p.140.

The museum is open daily; April–Oct 8am–5pm; Nov–March 8am–4pm.

There are regular buses from Florenc bus station, which pass by Lidice en route to Kladno; the journey takes 45 minutes.

Prague: Listings

Chapter 9

Accommodation

Finding a place to stay in Prague is no longer the nightmare it was back in the early 1990s when the city simply couldn't cope with the influx of new visitors. That said, the market is still top heavy with overpriced hotels and there is a chronic shortage of decent, inexpensive hotels. Those who don't mind forgoing the pleasures of staying in a hotel, will encounter few problems getting a private room, except perhaps in July and August. All in all, though, accommodation is still likely to be by far the largest chunk of your daily expenditure, with private rooms starting at around 500kč per person. At the extreme ends of the

---

Accommodation agencies in Prague

AVE
☎ 24 22 35 21, fax 24 22 34 63; daily 7am–10pm.
AVE is the largest agency in Prague, with offices at the airport and both international train stations, and are therefore excellent last-minute fall-backs. They can book private rooms from 500kč.

City of Prague Accommodation Service
Haštalská 7, Staré Město; metro náměstí Republiky; ☎ 231 02 02, fax 231 66 40; daily 9am–1pm, 2–6pm.
More upmarket outfit with a good selection of centrally located private rooms from 600kč per person.

Hello Travel
Senovážné náměstí 3, Nové Město; metro Hlavní nádraží; ☎ & fax 24 21 26 47; daily 9am–9pm.
A short walk from the main train station. Hostels for 250kč per person; private rooms from 500kč; private apartments from 600kč per person.

Pragotur
Za Poříčskou bránou 7, Karlín; metro Florenc; ☎ 231 11 16, fax 24 81 61 72; Mon–Fri 9am–6pm.
Their main office is situated just across the road from Florenc bus station, but they also operate through the various PIS offices. They can book anything from private rooms from 400kč per person to hotels and hostels.

Top Tour
Rybná 3, Staré Město; metro náměstí Republiky; ☎ 232 10 77, fax 24 81 14 00; winter daily 10am–7pm; summer daily 9am–8pm.
Private rooms from 500kč per person, and en suite apartments from 800kč per person; reductions for longer stays.

Accommodation

spectrum, you could spend as little as 250kč per person for the cheapest youth hostel bed, or 5000kč and upwards in the more salubrious hotels. It's worth asking about any special deals, or reduced rates, though, quite honestly, unless you're in the city during a particularly slack period, demand for beds keeps prices buoyant. If you're going to Prague during high season (from Easter to September, and over the Christmas holidays), it's sensible to arrange accommodation before you arrive through one of the specialist

---

If you're thinking of taking a private room or hotel somewhere in Prague, it's as well to know a little about the merits, or otherwise, of the various **postal districts** in the city (see map on p.36).

Prague 1

Prague 1 covers all of the old city on both sides of the river, and half of Nové Město, and consequently is the most expensive part of the capital in which to stay. Anything in this area will be within easy walking distance of the main sights, and will save you a lot of hassle, though you'll pay a higher rate for the privilege.

Prague 2

Prague 2 is another prime central area, taking in the southern half of Nové Město and western half of Vinohrady, a nineteenth-century des. res. with good metro connections.

Prague 3

The less salubrious, eastern half of Vinohrady in Prague 3 is nevertheless well served by the metro; Žižkov, on the other hand, is a crumbling, working-class district, connected to the centre only by trams.

Prague 4

Covers a wide area in the southeast of the city, stretching from half-decent, predominantly nineteenth-century sub-urbs such as Nusle, Podolí and Braník to the grim high-rise *panelák* buildings of Chodov and Háje. If you find yourself in either of the latter two areas, you can at least be sure of quick metro connections to the city centre.

Prague 5

Vast area in the hilly southwest of the city, with clean air and attractive family villas predominating and a metro line running through some of it. The area closest to the city, however, is Smíchov,

a polluted, working-class district, with correspondingly cheap rooms.

Prague 6

The perfect, hilly villa district to the north of the centre, a favourite with for-eign embassies and their staff (not to mention Havel himself). The metro only goes as far as Dejvická, however, which means that only Dejvice and Bubeneč enjoy really fast connections with the centre.

Prague 7

The nineteenth-century suburb of Holešovice in the northeast is served by the metro and has become something of a favourite ex-pat haunt. Troja, home to numerous ad hoc campsites, is almost bucolic and correspondingly difficult to get to.

Prague 8

The grid-plan streets of nineteenth-cen-tury Karlín are close to the centre and well served by the metro, which extends as far as Libeň; the rest of the area is neither aesthetically pleasing, nor easy to reach.

Prague 9

This is a real last resort area in the northeast of the city – dominated by fac-tories, and difficult to get to (Vysočany is the only district with metro connec-tions) – avoid if at all possible.

Prague 10

Beware of Prague 10, which extends right into the countryside, though areas like Strašnice and Vršovice in the southeast of the city are closer to the centre of things and served, in part, by the metro.

agencies listed on p.4 and p.11. As for camping, the main sites are a fair trek from the centre of town, and have only minimal facilites; but cheapness is their virtue: for two people and a tent pitch prices start at around 250kč.

Private rooms

Renting a **private room** remains by far the most popular way to stay in Prague. Most Czechs keep their places very tidy and clean, but before agreeing to part with any money, be sure you know exactly where you're staying and check about transport to the centre – some places can be a long way out of town. Private rooms start at around 500kč per person, and, like as not, you'll be sharing bathroom, cooking facilities, etc with your host family. This can be a great way to meet the locals, though Czech hospitality can be somewhat over-whelming and such arrangements may not suit everyone. Most places also offer self-contained apartments, though you'll pay significantly more per person for the privilege .

The enormous supply of private accommodation in Prague means it's not really necessary to book in advance – although it can be worth doing so to save time, and for some peace of mind, especially if you're arriving in July or August (see p.4 & p.11 for lists of travel agencies that specialize in booking accommodation in Prague). If you arrive without a room reservation, the easiest thing to do is head for one of the many **accommodation agencies** at the airport or main train stations, or, if the queues are long, one of the other agencies in town (see box on p.195). Alternatively, you're almost certain to be approached by a tout at the station, airport or some-times outside one of the agencies. Most offers are genuine, but make sure you ask for a receipt before you pass over any money. Again, check exactly how far out of the centre you're going to be (and preferably see the room) before commit-ting yourself.

Accommodation

Hotels and pensions

Pre-1989, Prague's **hotels** were much of a muchness: 1950s decor, a radio per-manently tuned to the state news chan-nel (very 1984) and sporadically hot showers. Matters have improved enor-mously since then, with almost all hotels now modernized to some degree, and more and more guaranteeing en-suite bathrooms, TVs and breakfast. The latter is usually included in the price of your room, and though more often than not little more than coffee and rolls, it's worth grabbing given the lack of any great alternatives out on the streets of Prague. **Pensions** are a new phenome-non and, though they tend to be smaller and less expensive, you can't guarantee it. Over all, standards still vary wildly, and don't always keep up with prices.

Since demand still exceeds supply, there's really no point in trekking around

---

Accommodation prices

The accommodation lists below are divided according to area; within each section the lists are arranged alphabetically. After each entry you'll find a symbol which corresponds to one of nine price categories:

① Under 1000 kč	④ 2000–2500 kč	⑦ 3500–4000kč
② 1000–1500 kč	⑤ 2500–3000kč	⑧ 4000–5000kč
③ 1500–2000 kč	⑥ 3000–3500 kč	⑨ 5000kč and upwards

All prices are for the cheapest double room available in high season, which usually means without private bath or shower in the less expensive places. For a single room or a double in low season, expect to pay around two-thirds of the price.

Accommodation

any of the hotels listed below on the off chance that they will have vacancies. Besides, Prague's cheaper hotels and pensions are scattered throughout the city, with few in the older quarters of Hradčany, Malá Strana and Staré Město. The best policy is to contact the hotel by fax or phone before you leave for Prague and attempt to make a reservation that way, or use one of the agencies listed on p.195. The sub-headings used below correspond with the chapter headings in the guide. The price codes (for more on which, see box above), are followed by a grid reference to make it easy to locate the right street; the introductory notes under the sub-heading tell you which map to consult.

Hradčany

Hradčany is obviously a great area to stay in, right by the castle. The only problem is there are just two places to stay, and neither is particularly cheap. The grid references after the price codes refer to the map on pp.46–47.

Savoy, Keplerova 6; ☎24 30 24 30, fax 24 30 21 28; tram #22 from metro Malostranská. Austrian-owned super-luxury hotel on the western edge of Hradčany, concealed behind a pretty Art Nouveau facade and famous for its marble bathrooms. Pretty prices too, with doubles starting at over 7000kč. ⑨. A4.

U raka, Černínská 10; ☎20 51 11 00, fax 20 51 05 11; tram #22 from metro Malostranská. The perfect hideaway, six rooms in a little half-timbered cottage in Nový Svět. No children or dogs. ⑧. C1.

Malá Strana

Malá Strana is a beautiful area, and, with the exception of a few key streets, relatively traffic-free and quiet. It's also a pricey area; most places are in the higher price categories, but there are one or two bargains, for which it's worth booking ahead. The nearest **metro** station for all the places listed below is Malostranská, though some will require a further tram ride on tram #12 or #22.

The grid references after the price codes refer to the map on pp.72–73.

Dientzenhofer, Nosticova 2; ☎53 88 96, fax 24 51 11 93. Birthplace of its namesake, and a very popular pension due to its price and the fact that it's one of the few reasonably priced places (anywhere in Prague) to have wheelchair access. Just seven rooms on offer. ⑤. G7.

Hoffmeister, Pod Bruskou 9; ☎561 81 55, fax 53 09 59. If you're looking for a large luxury hotel, this place, just a step away from Malostranská metro, has got to be a better bet than many of the more modern monstrosities in the outskirts. ⑨. J1.

Hotel pod věží, Mostecká 2; ☎53 37 10, fax 53 18 59. Even nicer than the Hoffmeister, this tiny luxury hotel is right by the Charles Bridge with just twelve rooms and every possible facility you could think of. ⑨. H5.

Kampa – Stará zbrojnice, Všehrdova 16; ☎24 51 04 09, fax 24 51 03 77. Wonderful backstreet location on Kampa island, close to the Charles Bridge, but not quite as appealing as some of the hotels in Malá Strana, hence the price. ⑥. F9.

Rippl, Vlašská 30; ☎57 31 11 07, fax 53 35 46. The sheer anonymity of this pension from the outside is one of its draws (ring the top bell marked Rippl). A series of characterful, tastefully modernized rooms – some without en suite, some with – run by a very friendly, English-speaking couple. ③. D3.

Sax, Jánský vršek 3; ☎53 84 22, fax 53 84 98. Fancy designer hotel tucked away in the backstreets off Tržiště, and a relative bargain given the location. ⑥. E3.

Sidi, Na Kampě 10; ☎55 61 35, fax 53 14 44. Just two apartments situated above a small gay bar, just beneath the Charles Bridge, run by a charming owner. ⑧. H7.

U kiliána, Všehrdova 13; ☎57 31 09 50, fax 73 41 10. One plain en suite double and one triple above a snack bar down a quiet side street on Kampa. ③.

U krále Karla, Úvoz 4; ☎53 88 05, fax 53 88 11. Possibly the most tastefully exquisite of all the small luxury hotels in Malá Strana, with beautiful antique furnishings and stained-glass windows. ⑨. D1.

U kříže, Újezd 20; ☎53 33 26, fax 53 34 43. No airs and graces at this modernized hotel on a busy street in the south of Malá Strana; B&B prices reduced in July and August. ⑤. E9.

U páva (The Peacock), U lužického semináře 32; ☎24 51 09 22, fax 53 33 79. Lovely little eight-room luxury hotel in a quiet part of Malá Strana; it's worth forking out for a room on the third floor, where you get an unrivalled view over the Vojanovy sady and up to the Hrad. ⑨. I5.

U tří pštrosů (The Three Ostriches), Dražického náměstí 12; ☎24 51 07 79, fax 24 51 07 83. Exquisite Renaissance house adjacent to the Charles Bridge, with rooms for around 6000kč a double, some with original ceiling frescoes and views across the river. ⑨. H5.

Staré Město

Staré Město is right in the centre of things, with lots of pubs and restaurants to choose from, all within easy walking distance. Inexpensive places to stay are few and far between, but there are a few moderately priced options – again, it's worthwhile booking ahead if possible. The grid references after the price codes refer to the map on pp.86–87.

Betlém Club, Betlémské náměstí 9; ☎24 21 68 72, fax 24 21 80 54; metro Národní třída. Small rooms, slightly tacky decor, but a perfect location and a Gothic cellar for breakfast. ⑥. D7.

Centrál, Rybná 8; ☎24 81 10 13, fax 232 84 04; metro náměstí Republiky. One of the very few reasonably priced hotels in Staré Město – no work of art, but true to its name and surprisingly reasonably priced. ⑤. I4.

Paříž, U Obecního domu 1; ☎24 22 21 51, fax 24 22 54 75; metro náměstí Republiky. The turn-of-the-century decor here is less flamboyant than at the *Evropa*, though equally pleasing to the eye, but at over 6000kč a double, you might expect better service. ⑨. J4.

U klenotníka, Rytířská 3; ☎24 21 16 99, fax 26 17 82; metro Můstek. Pension offering ten small, reasonably well-appointed rooms in a former jewellery factory. ⑥. F7.

U krále Jiřího, Liliová 10; ☎24 22 20 13, fax 24 22 19 83; metro Staroměstská. Eight cosy attic rooms above an "Irish" pub, hidden in the network of lanes which characterize this part of Staré Město. ④. D6.

U mědvídků, Na Perštýně 7; ☎24 21 19 16, fax 24 22 09 30; metro Národní třída. Eight plainly furnished rooms (doubles and triples only) above a famous Prague pub; booking ahead essential. ②–③. E8.

Unitas, Bartolomějská 9 ; ☎232 12 89, fax 232 77 09; metro Národní třída. Gloomy doubles, triples and quads in converted prison cells and rooms once used by the secret police (Havel stayed in P6), now owned by Fransiscan nuns. No smoking, no drinking and a 1am curfew, but unbelievably cheap. ②. D8.

U zlaté studny, Karlova 3; ☎& fax 24 21 05 39; metro Staroměstská. Three apartments overlooking the tourist thoroughfare of Karlova, decked out in High Baroque style. ⑦. D6.

Nové Město

Nové Město covers a large area of the city, and some of its main thoroughfares are badly blighted by traffic. Some places listed here are literally walking distance from the old town, but in its nether regions, you'll need to hop on a tram or metro to get into the centre of town.

The grid references after the price codes refer to the map on pp.122–123.

Albatros, nábřeží Ludvíka Svobody; ☎24 81 05 47, fax 24 81 12 14; tram #5, #14 or #26 from metro náměstí Republiky. Double cabins for rent on a moored boat at the end of Revoluční. Not quite as romantic as it sounds, but the best of the city's three floating

Accommodation

Accommodation

Price codes

① *Under*
1000kč

② *1000–*
1500 kč

③ *1500–*
2000 kč

④ *2000–*
2500 kč

⑤ *2500–*
3000kč

⑥ *3000–*
3500 kč

⑦ *3500–*
4000kč

⑧ *4000–*
5000kč

⑨ *5000kč and*
upwards

"botels" – watch out for the on-board disco which keeps going until the early hours. ④. G1.

Atlantic, Na poříčí 9; ☎ 24 81 10 84, fax 24 81 23 78; metro náměstí Republiky. Modern and conveniently located, with reasonable facilities. ⑤. H2.

Axa, Na poříčí 40; ☎ 24 81 25 80, fax 24 81 20 67; metro Florenc. Partially refurbished hotel with adjacent swimming pool and gym, just ten minutes' walk from náměstí Republiky – make sure you see your room before booking in, as standards in each can vary. ⑥. I2.

Březina, Legerova 41; ☎ 96 18 88 88, fax 29 84 82; metro I. P. Pavlova. Seven truly inexpensive rooms, some en suite, some shared facilities, but within walking distance of Wenceslas Square. ③. H7.

Grand Hotel Evropa, Václavské náměstí 25; ☎ 24 22 81 17, fax 24 22 45 44; metro Můstek/Muzeum. Without doubt, the most beautiful hotel in Prague, built in the 1900s and sumptuously decorated in Art Nouveau style; the rooms are slowly being modernized, as are the prices, but it still has some cheap doubles with shared facilities. ④. G5.

Hlávkova kolej, Jenštejnská 1; ☎ 29 21 39, fax 29 27 05; metro Karlovo náměstí. Ornate late nineteenth-century hotel on the outside; former student hostel on the inside, with spartan but clean en suite doubles. ③. C7.

Hotel 16, Kateřinská 16; ☎ 29 53 29, fax 29 39 56; metro Karlovo náměstí. Really friendly little hotel offering small en suite rooms with TV in a quiet backstreet of southern Nové Mesto. ⑤. F8.

Koruna, Opatovická 16; ☎ 24 91 51 74, fax 29 24 92; metro Národní třída. Great location in the backstreets just south of Národní, though the hotel itself is no great shakes. ⑤. D6.

Legie, Sokolská 33; ☎ 29 11 18, fax 24 91 44 41; metro I. P. Pavlova. Former military R-and-R centre, just one stop or a short stroll from Wenceslas Square. It looks bad from the outside, but the rooms are fine inside (the cheaper ones have shared facilities). ②. G7.

Opera, Těšnov 13; ☎ 231 56 09, fax 231 14 77; metro Florenc. Moderately priced nineteenth-century hotel and remarkably pleasant considering it's right by the fly-over. ⑥. I1.

Palace, Panská 12; ☎ 24 09 31 11, fax 24 22 12 40; metro Můstek. While all the other luxury hotels in Prague try their best, the *Palace*, located just off Wenceslas Square, really is the best in terms of service and facilities – but then what else would you expect at over 9000kč a double? ⑨. G4.

Salvator, Truhlářská 10; ☎ 231 22 34, fax 231 63 55; metro náměstí Republiky. Ad hoc lift in courtyard takes you up to this fourth-floor pension with small, but clean en suite rooms. Good price for the location. ③. H2.

Standard, Rašínovo nábřeží 38; ☎ & fax 29 87 97; metro Karlovo náměstí. An apt name for this riverside hotel; the modernized rooms are en suite and all have TVs but there's absolutely nothing special about them. ④. C10.

Vyšehrad and the eastern suburbs

Vinohrady is a pleasant nineteenth-century suburb, a few metro or tram stops east of Wenceslas Square, while Pižkov is a more run-down area, best known for its riotous pubs, and large Romany population. The grid references after the price codes refer to the map on pp.148–149.

Anna, Budečská 17, Vinohrady; ☎ & fax 24 23 93 34; metro náměstí Míru. Tastefully decorated and renovated rooms in a nice part of Vinohrady, close to Wenceslas Square. ⑤. E5.

Ametyst, Jana Masaryka 11, Vinohrady; ☎ 691 17 58, fax 691 17 90; metro náměstí Míru. Refurbished, purple (though not quite the right purple), neo-Rennaissance pile with a wonderful view overlooking the Botič valley. ⑦. D6.

Golden City, Táboritská 3, Žižkov; ☎ 27 54 24, fax 27 27 45; tram #5, #9 or #26 from metro Hlavní nádraží. Hospitable owner with eight en suite doubles and triples with TV/telephone;

three self-catering apartments also available. ③. H4.

Kafka, Cimburkova 24, Žižkov; ☎27 31 01, fax 27 29 84; tram #5, #9 or #26 from metro Hlavní nádraží. TVs, en suite shower and toilet, but only sporadic hot water – stilll better than what the residents on the other side of the courtyard can expect. ②. G3.

Luník, Londýnská 50, Vinohrady; ☎24 25 39 74, fax 24 25 39 86; metro I. P. Pavlova. Unpretentious modernized hotel in a fairly peaceful location, just a short walk from Wenceslas Square. ④. D5.

Ostaš, Orebitská 8, Žižkov; ☎& fax 627 93 86; tram #5, #9 or #26 from metro Hlavní nádraží. Rather soulless place just off Kostnické náměstí, but offering clean, modern rooms with en suite facilities and TVs. ④. F3.

Pension City, Belgická 10, Vinohrady; ☎& fax 691 13 34; metro náměstí Míru. Quiet locale, cheap, clean en suite rooms with TVs and within walking distance of Wenceslas Square. ③. D6.

U tří korunek, Cimburkova 28, Žižkov; ☎27 21 09, fax 27 22 09; tram #5, #9 or #26 from metro Hlavní nádraží. One of Žižkov's better hotels, with en suite facilities and TVs in all rooms. ⑤. G3.

Villa Voyta, K Novému dvoru 124, Lhotka; ☎472 55 11, fax 472 94 26; bus #113, #171, #189 or #215 from metro Kačerov. Twelve rooms tastefully furnished in a modernized Art Nouveau garden villa right out in the southern burbs. To really get the most of this place, you need to be able to afford to eat in the superb, but pricey restaurant, and get taxis to and from town. ⑧. Off the map.

Holešovice and the western suburbs

Holešovice is another pleasant late-nineteenth-century residential suburb, within easy walking distance of a lot of greenery, and with good metro and tram connections. Střešovice is a highly sought-after garden villa suburb, but its public transport connections aren't great.

Smíchov, rather like Pižkov, has a reputation as a bit of a rough, industrial suburb, but it's well connected by metro, and, naturally enough, fairly inexpensive.

The grid references after the price codes refer to the map on pp.34–35.

Accommodation

Balkán, Svornosti 28, Smíchov; ☎& fax 54 06 70; metro Anděl. One of the cheapest hotels in Prague; like Smíchov itself, no frills, but clean and comfortable. ②. D9.

Coubertin, Atletická 4, Strahov; ☎35 28 51, fax 20 51 32; bus #217, #149 or #143 to the Strahov stadión from metro Dejvická. Modern hotel attached to the south side of the Strahov stadium; only really worth it if you're coming for a sporting event. ④. B7.

Gay Vila David, Holubova 5; ☎90 01 12 93, fax 54 98 20; tram #14 from metro Anděl. Friendly gay, lesbian pension (complete with sauna) in the hills above Smíchov; advance booking essential. ④. B10.

Digital's, Na Petynce 106, Střešovice; ☎& fax 24 31 35 83; bus #108 or #174 from metro Hradčanská. Nine en suite rooms, located in the villa quarter fifteen to twenty minutes' walk from the Hrad. ③. A5.

Henry, U papírny 11, Holešovice; ☎80 77 54, fax 80 12 57; metro Nádraží Holešovice. The purple theme is a bit worrying, but the rooms are plainly modernized, and have shower/toilet and TV; a stone's throw from Výstavištšě. ③. G1.

International, Koulova 15, Dejvice; ☎24 39 31 11, fax 24 31 06 16; tram #20 or #25 from metro Dejvická. Classic 1950s Stalinist hotel with plenty of dour social realist friezes and large helpings of marble, now somewhat unbelievably part of the *Holiday Inn* hotel chain. ⑧. B1.

Julián, Elišky Peškové 11, Smíchov; ☎53 51 37, fax 54 75 25; tram #6, #9 or #12 from metro Anděl. Big hotel on the very edge of Malá Strana. Slightly dodgy decor, but all the usual facilities. ⑤. D8.

Petr, Drtinova 17; ☎57 31 40 68, fax 57 31 00 67; tram #6, #9 or #12 from

Accommodation

metro Anděl. Newly refurbished hotel situated at the foot of Petřín hill, close to Malá Strana. ③. C7.

Petynka, Na Petynce 100, Střešovice; ☎& fax 24 31 70 81; bus #108 or #174 from metro Hradčanská. Five rooms with shared facilities, just a few doors down from the *Digital's*. ②. A5.

Praha, Sušická 20, Dejvice; ☎24 34 11 11, fax 24 31 12 18; tram #2, #20 or #26 from metro Dejvická. The old Party VIP hotel, where the likes of Ceaușescu once stayed; an appropriately grotesque concrete palace with wonderful views over to the Hrad. Inconveniently placed for public transport, so most guests take a taxi. ⑧. A2.

Pyramida, Bělohorská 24, Břevnov; ☎311 32 41, fax 311 32 91; tram #8 or #22. V-shaped Communist-era high-rise hotel, that's not a pretty sight from the outside, but it's only a short hop by tram to the Hrad, and there's an art cinema close by. All rooms en suite with TVs. ③. A6.

Splendid, Ovenecká 33, Bubeneč; ☎37 33 51; tram #1, #8, #25 or #26 (stop Letenské náměstí). Situated in a pleasant part of town, right by the Stromovka park. ④. F2.

Větrník, U Větrníku 40, Střešovice; ☎20 51 33 90, fax 36 14 06; tram #1 or #18 from metro Hradčanská. Six rooms in a converted eighteenth-century windmill, with private tennis courts and nice proprietor – book early. ⑤. West of A4.

Hostels

There are a fair few **hostels** in Prague which cater for the large number of backpackers who hit the city all year round – and these are supplemented further by a whole host of more transient, high-season-only hostels. **Prices** in hostels range between 150kč to 250kč for a bed, usually in a dormitory. Some hostels operate **curfews** – it's worth asking before you commit yourself – and, although some rent out blankets and sheets, it's as well to bring your own sleeping bag. Note that some of the accommodation agencies in Prague also deal with hostels; see p.195 for details.

The chief Czech organisation affiliated to *Hostelling International* is *Cestovní kancelář mládeže* (*CKM*), whose head office is at Žitná 12, Nové Město (☎24 91 57 67; metro Karlovo náměstí). They run a hostel at the same address, and can book you into the **Domov mládeže**; you can also buy *HI* membership from them.

Prague's university, the *Karolinum*, rents out over a thousand **student rooms** from June to mid-September, starting at 200kč for a bed. Go to the head booking office at Voršilská 1, Nové Město (☎24 31 11 05, fax 24 31 11 07; metro Národní třída).

Another organization specializing in summer-only dorms is *Traveller's Hostels*, a chain of centrally located youth hostels which are very poular with US students. Their main booking office is round the corner at Mikulandská 5, Nové Město (☎& fax 24 91 07 39); dorm beds go for 200kč and upwards per person and are available from mid-June to mid-Sept.

CKM, Žitná 12, Nové Město; ☎29 29 84, fax 24 22 39 11; metro Karlovo náměstí. Official HI hostel in the same building as *Juniorhotel* (④). No curfew and no lockout; four-bed dorms 400kč per person, 500kč without an HI card. E7.

Clown and Bard, Bořivojova 102, Žižkov; ☎27 24 36; tram #5, #9 or #26 from metro Hlavní nádraží. So laid-back it's horizontal, and not a place to go if you don't like hippies, but it's clean, undeniably cheap, and rents out doubles (①) as well as dorm beds for under 200kč per person. Open all year.

Domov mládeže, Dykova 20, Vinohrady; ☎25 06 88, fax 25 14 29; metro Jiřího z Poděbrad. Big nineteenth-century mansion with eighty beds separated into dorms sleeping up to five people at around 300kč per person. Open all year.

ESTEC Hostel, Vaníčkova 5, Strahov; ☎52 73 44; bus #217, #149 or #143 to the Strahov stadión from metro Dejvická. This is a chaotic, but cheap hostel in the midst of student land, but only a fifteen-minute walk from Hradčany through Petřín. To find the hostel, head for block 5, opposite the east stand of the Strahov stadium. Dorms 180kč for a bed; doubles 280kč per person; singles 400kč. Open all year with no curfew.

Kolej J. A. Komenského, Parléřova 6, Břevnov; ☎35 03 32, fax 35 20 10; tram #8 or #22. You can turn up on spec, but it's best to book through *Universitas Tour*, Opletalova 38, Nové Město (☎26 04 26, fax 24 21 22 90). Good location, just ten minutes walk from the Hrad; dorm beds as well as doubles for around 300kč per person. Open all year.

Hotel Standart, Přístavní 2, Holešovice; ☎87 52 58, fax 80 67 52; tram #12 or #25 from metro Nádraží Holešovice. Despite the name this is an official HI hostel. It's not conveniently located, though tram #3 will get into the centre of town quickly enough. Dorm beds (and breakfast) from around 300kč per person (with an HI card); ask about doubles too. Open all year.

Libra Q, Senovážné náměstí 21; ☎24 10 55 36, fax 24 22 15 79; metro Hlavní nádraží. Friendly, centrally located, inexpensive hostel with dorm beds from 300kč per person, and cheap doubles (①–②). Open all year.

Pension Florida, Křenická 56, Strašnice; ☎781 38 75; metro Skalka. Shambolic, hippy-strewn hostel in a none too picturesque part of town, but within easy walking distance of the metro and run by an eccentric and extremely welcoming Czech woman in her sixties. Dorm

beds from just 250kč per person. Open all year.

TJ Sokol Karlín, Malého 1, Karlín; ☎22 20 09; metro Florenc. Situated in the unsalubrious locale of the Praha-Florenc bus station. Reception opens at 6pm and you'll be turfed out at 8am the next morning – a definite last resort. Open all year.

Campsites

Prague abounds in **campsites** – there's a whole rash of them in Troja (see below) – and most are relatively easy to get to by public transport. Facilities, on the whole, are rudimentary and badly maintained, but the prices reflect this, starting at around 200kč for a tent and two people. Note that most Prague campsites are closed from November to March.

Autocamp Trojská, Trojská 375, Troja; ☎688 60 36, fax 854 29 45; bus #112 from metro Nádraží Holešovice. Good location, in someone's large back garden 3km north of the centre, on the road to the Troja chateau. Open April–Nov.

Intercamp Kotva, U ledáren 55, Braník; ☎46 60 85, fax 46 61 10; tram #3 or #17 from metro Karlovo náměstí. Prague's oldest campsite (and one of its nicest) situated beside the River Vltava in the far south of the city. Bike rental available. Open April–Oct.

Kemp Džbán, Nad lávkou 3, Vokovice; ☎36 90 06, fax 36 13 65; tram #20 or #26 from metro Dejvická. Large field with tent pitches, bungalows and basic facilities, 4km west of the centre, near the Šárka valley. Open all year.

Accommodation

Chapter 10

Eating and drinking

The good news is that you can eat and drink very cheaply in Prague: the food is filling and the beer is divine. The bad news is that Czechs have little concern for their cholesterol levels, and almost no interest in fresh vegetables or side salads. That said, things have improved over the last few years, with the appearance of some very good pizzerias, and even the odd authentic ethnic restaurant. In addition, there's a whole range of new, slightly more expensive restaurants aimed at the palettes (and wallets) of the passing tourist, the expat community, wealthy Czechs and the diplomatic crowd.

The biggest mistake most first-time visitors make is to confine their eating and drinking to the obvious sightseeing areas, where prices are generally much higher, quality lower, and, in summer, packed to the gunnels. It's worth venturing instead into the backstreets of Staré Město and Nové Město, where good-value restaurants tend to hide; or to suburbs like Vinohrady and Holešovice, just ten minutes' travel by metro from the centre.

It's as well to remember that traditionally Czechs eat their main meal of the day at lunchtime, between noon and 2pm. In *pivnice* and other more traditional Czech restaurants, you'll get the widest choice of dishes around this time of day, with progressively fewer available as the day goes on – kitchens in pubs can close as early as 9pm. The majority of restaurants cater for more international habits, however, with the evening sitting usually more important than the lunchtime slot.

Czech cuisine

Forty years of culinary isolation under the Communists introduced few innovations to the Germanic-influenced **Czech cuisine**, with its predilection for pork, gravy, dumplings and pickled cabbage. Fresh vegetables (other than potatoes) are a rare sight on traditional Czech menus, and salads are still waiting for their day.

Most menus start with **soup** (*polévka*), one of the country's culinary strong points, served mainly at lunchtimes. Some places will have a selection of starters such as *uzený jazyk* (smoked tongue) or *tresčí játra* (cod's liver). *Šunková rolka* is another favourite, consisting of ham topped with whipped cream and horseradish, but you're more likely to find yourself skipping the starters, which are often little more than a selection of cold meats.

Main courses are overwhelmingly based on **meat** (*maso*), usually pork, sometimes beef. The Czechs are experts on these meats, and although the quality could often be better, the variety of sauces and preparative techniques beats traditional Anglo-American cooking hands down. The difficulty lies in decoding names such as *klašterny tajemství* ("mystery of the monastery") or even a common dish like *Moravský* *vrabec* (literally "Moravian sparrow", but actually just roast pork).

Fish (*ryby*) are generally listed, along with chicken and other fowl like duck, under a separate heading. Trout and carp (the traditional dish at Christmas) are the cheapest and most widely available fish, and although their freshness may be questionable, they are usually served, grilled or roasted, in delicious buttery sauces.

Dumplings (*knedlíky*), though German in origin and name, are now the mainstay of Bohemian cooking. The term itself is misleading for English-speakers, since they resemble nothing like the English dumpling – more like a heavy white bread. *Houskové knedlíky* are made from flour and come in large slices (four or five to a dish), while *bramborové knedlíky* are smaller and made from potato and flour. Occasionally, you may be treated to *ovocné knedlíky* (fruit dumplings), the king of *knedlíky*. **Fresh salads** rarely rise above tomato, cucumber or cabbage (*zelí*), often swimming in a slightly sweet, watery dressing.

With the exception of *palačinky* (pancakes) filled with chocolate or fruit and cream, **desserts**, where they exist at all,

can be pretty unexciting. Often the ice cream and cakes on offer in restaurants aren't really up to the standards of the stuff sold on the street, so go to a café or *cukrárna* (confectioners) if you want a dose of sugar; for more on which see p.211.

Alcohol

Alcohol consumption among Czechs has always been high, and in the decade following the events of 1968 it doubled. A whole generation found solace in drinking, mostly beer; the Czechs topped the world league table of beer consumption some time ago. However, it's a problem which seldom spills out onto the streets; violence in pubs is uncommon and you won't see that many drunks in public.

Czech **beer** ranks among the best in the world and the country remains the true home of most of the lager drunk around the world today. It was in the Bohemian city of Plzeň (Pilsen) that the first **bottom-fermented** beer was introduced in 1842, after complaints from the citizens about the quality of the top-fermented predecessor. The new brewing

---

Vegetarian eating

Czech meat consumption remains one of the highest in the world – around half a kilo a day per head of the population – it's hardly suprisingly that **vegetarianism** is a minority sport. Nevertheless, you're better off in Prague than anywhere else in the country. For a start, places which cater mostly for ex-pats usually have one or two veggie options, and there are plenty of pizzerias.

Even in Czech places, most menus have a section called *bezmasa* (literally "without meat") – don't take this too literally, though, for it simply means the main ingredient is not dead animal; dishes like *omeleta se šunkou* (ham omelette) regularly appear under these headings, so always check first. Emergency standbys which most Czech chefs will knock up for you without too much fuss include *knedlíky s vejci* (dumplings and egg), *omeleta s hráškem* (pea omelette), or *smažený sýr*, a slab of melted cheese (and, more often than not, ham) deep-fried in breadcrumbs. Other common deep-fried dishes include *smažené žampiony* (mushrooms) and *smažený květák* (cauliflower).

The only exclusively veggie places are *Country Life* (see p.210), *Góvinda* (see p.223), *Lotos* (see p.222), *Radost FX* (see p.215), and *U Bakaláře* (see p.210). Veggie phrases to remember are *"jsem vegeterián/vegeteriánka. máte nejaké bezmasa?"* (I'm a vegetarian. Is there anything without meat?); for emphasis, you could add *"nejím maso nebo ryby"* (I don't eat meat or fish).

Eating and Drinking

style quickly spread to Germany, and is now blamed for the bland rubbish served up in the English-speaking world as lager or Pils.

The distinctive flavour of Czech beer comes from the famous Bohemian hops, Žatec (Saaz) Red, still hand-picked and then combined with the soft local water and served with a high content of absorbed carbon dioxide – hence the thick, creamy head. Under the Communists, brewing methods in the Czech Republic remained stuck in the old ways, but the 1990s have seen many breweries opt for modernization: pasteurization, de-oxidization, rapid maturation and carbon dioxide injections – all of which mean less taste, more fizz. It's a development against which the Czech Beer Party and Britain's own Campaign for Real Ale (CAMRA) are fighting hard.

Beer (*pivo*) is served by the half-litre; if you want anything smaller, you must specifically ask for a *malé pivo* (0.3l). The average jar is medium strength, usually about 1050 specific gravity or 4.2 per-

cent alcohol. Somewhat confusingly, the Czechs class their beers using the Balling scale, which measures the original gravity, calculated according to the amount of malt and dissolved sugar present before fermentation. The most common varieties are 10° (*desítka*), which are generally slightly weaker than 12° (*dvanáctka*). Light beer (*světlé*) is the norm, but many pubs also serve a slightly sweeter dark variety (*černé*) – or, if you prefer, you can have a mixture of the two (*řezané*).

Czech **wine** will never win over as many people as its beer, but since the import of French and German vines in the fourteenth century, it has produced a modest selection of medium-quality wines. The main wine region is South Moravia, though a little is produced around the town of Mělník (see p.179). Suffice to say that most domestic wine is pretty drinkable – Frankovka is a perfectly respectable, though slightly sweet, red; Tramín a good, dry white – and rarely much more than £1/$1.60 a bottle in shops, while the best stuff can only be had from the private wine cellars, hundreds of which still exist out in the regions. A Czech speciality to look out for is burčák, a very young, misty wine of varying (and often very strong) alcoholic content, which appears on the streets in the vine harvest season in September.

All the usual **spirits** are on sale and known by their generic names, with rum and vodka dominating the market. The home production of brandies is a national pastime, which results in some almost terminally strong liquors. The most renowned of the lot is **slivovice**, a plum brandy originally from the border hills between Moravia and Slovakia. You'll probably also come across borovička, a popular Slovak firewater, made from pine trees; myslivec is a rough brandy with a firm following. There's also a fair selection of intoxicating herbal concoctions: fernet is a dark-brown bitter drink, known as bavorák (Bavarian beer) when it's mixed with tonic, while becherovka is a supposedly healthy herbal spirit from the Bohemian spa town of Karlovy Vary, with a very unusual, almost medicinal taste.

The Czech Republic is also one of the few countries in the world where **absinthe** is still legal. The preferred poison of Parisian painters and poets in the 1920s, absinthe is a nasty green spirit made from fermented wormwood – it even gets a mention in Revelations: "and the name of the star is called Wormwood: and the third part of the waters became wormwood; and many men died of the waters, because they were made bitter". St John wasn't wrong: at 170 degrees proof, it's dangerous stuff and virtually undrinkable neat. To make it vaguely palatable, you need to set light to an absinthe-soaked spoonful of sugar, and then mix the caramalized mess with the absinthe.

There's not much to say about Czech **soft drinks**, with the exception of the high-energy drink Semtex, a can of which will amuse friends back home. Last of all, if you're looking for a decent **mineral water** (minerální voda), ask for the ubiquitous Mattoni, a mild and not too fizzy option.

Breakfast, snacks and fast food

Many Czechs get up so early in the morning (often around 5 or 6am) that they don't have time to start the day with anything more than a quick cup of coffee. As a result, the whole concept of **breakfast** (snídaně) as such is alien to the Czechs. Most hotels will serve the "continental" basics, but it's cheaper and often more enjoyable to go hunting for your own. Bear in mind, too, that if you get up much past 10am, you might as well join Prague's working population for lunch.

Pastries (pečivo) are available from Prague's bakeries (pekářství or pekárna), but rarely in bars and cafés, so you'll most likely have to eat them on the go. Traditional Czech pastry (koláč) is more like sweet bread, dry and fairly dense with only a little condiment to flavour it, such as almonds (oříškový), poppy seed jam (mákový), plum jam (povidlový) or a kind of sour-sweet curd cheese (tvarohový). Recently, French- and Viennese-style bakeries have started to appear in Prague, selling croissants (loupáky) and lighter cream cakes.

Czech **bread** (chléb) is some of the tastiest around when fresh. The standard loaf is domácí or šumava, a dense mixture of wheat and rye, which you can buy whole, in halves (půl) or quarters (čtvrtina). Český chléb is a mixture of rye, wheat and whey, with distinctive slashes across the top; kmínový chléb is the same loaf packed full of caraway seeds. Moskva is a national favourite, despite the name – a moist, heavy, sour-dough loaf that lasts for days. Rolls come in two basic varieties: rohlík, a plain white finger roll, and houska, a rougher, tastier round bun.

Prague's stand-up **bufets** are open from as early as 6am and offer everything from light snacks to full meals. A cross between a British greasy spoon and an American diner, they're usually self-service (samoobsluha) and non-smoking, and occasionally have rudimentary seats. The cheapest of the tired-looking meat

Eating and Drinking

Eating and Drinking

A FOOD AND DRINK GLOSSARY

Basics

chléb	bread	*nápoje*	drinks	*sklenice*	glass
chlebíček	(open) sandwich	*nůž*	knife	*snídaně*	breakfast
cukr	sugar	*oběd*	lunch	*sůl*	salt
hořčice	mustard	*obloha*	garnish	*šálek*	cup
houska	round roll	*ocet*	vinegar	*talíř*	plate
knedlíky	dumplings	*ovoce*	fruit	*tartarská*	
křen	horseradish	*pečivo*	pastry	*omáčka*	tartare sauce
lžíce	spoon	*pepř*	pepper		
maso	meat	*polévka*	soup	*večeře*	supper/ dinner
máslo	butter	*předkrmy*	starters		
med	honey	*přílohy*	side dishes	*vejce*	eggs
mléko	milk	*rohlík*	finger roll	*vidlička*	fork
moučník	dessert	*ryby*	fish	*volské oko*	fried egg
		rýže	rice	*zeleniny*	vegetables

Soups

boršč	beetroot soup	*kapustnica*	sauerkraut, mushroom and meat soup
bramborová	potato soup		
čočková	lentil soup		
fazolová	bean soup	*kuřecí*	thin chicken soup
hovězí vývar	beef broth	*rajská*	tomato soup
hrachová	pea soup	*zeleninová*	vegetable soup

Fish

kapr	carp	*pstruh*	trout	*treska*	cod
losos	salmon	*rybí filé*	fillet of fish	*zavináč*	herring/ rollmop
makrela	mackerel	*sardinka*	sardine		
platys	flounder	*štika*	pike		

Meat dishes

bažant	pheasant	*ledvinky*	kidneys
biftek	beef steak	*řízek*	steak
čevapčiči	spicy meat balls	*roštěná*	sirloin
drštky	tripe	*salám*	salami
drůbež	poultry	*sekaná*	meat loaf
guláš	goulash	*skopové maso*	mutton
hovězí	beef	*slanina*	bacon
husa	goose	*svíčková*	fillet of beef
játra	liver	*šunka*	ham
jazyk	tongue	*telecí*	veal
kachna	duck	*vepřový*	pork
klobásy	sausages	*vepřové řízek*	breaded pork cutlet or schnitzel
kotleta	cutlet		
kuře	chicken	*zajíc*	hare
kýta	leg	*žebírko*	ribs

Vegetables

brambory	potatoes	*hranolky*	chips, french	*lilek*	aubergine
brokolice	broccoli		fries	*okurka*	cucumber
celer	celery	*hrášek*	peas	*pórek*	leek
cibule	onion	*karot*	carrot	*rajče*	tomato
česnek	garlic	*květák*	cauliflower	*ředkev*	radish
chřest	asparagus	*kyselá*	pickled	*řepná bulva*	beetroot
čočka	lentils	*okurka*	gherkin	*špenát*	spinach
fazole	beans	*kyselé zelí*	sauerkraut	*zelí*	cabbage
houby	mushrooms	*lečo*	ratatouille	*žampiony*	mushrooms

Fruit and cheese and nuts

banán	banana	*oříšky*	peanuts
borůvky	blueberries	*ostružiny*	blackberries
broskev	peach	*oštěpek*	heavily smoked, curd
brusinky	cranberries		cheese
bryndza	goat's cheese in brine	*parenica*	rolled strips of lightly
citrón	lemon		smoked, curd cheese
grejp	grapefruit	*pivní sýr*	cheese flavoured with
hermelín	Czech brie		beer
hrozny	grapes	*pomeranč*	orange
hruška	pear	*rozinky*	raisins
jablko	apple	*švestky*	plums
jahody	strawberries	*třešně*	cherries
kompot	stewed fruit	*tvaroh*	fresh, curd cheese
maliny	raspberries	*urda*	soft, fresh, whey cheese
mandle	almonds	*uzený sýr*	smoked cheese
meruňka	apricot	*vlašské ořechy*	walnuts
niva	semi-soft, crumbly, blue cheese		

Common terms

čerstvý	fresh	*s.m. (s máslem)*	with butter
domácí	home-made	*sladký*	sweet
dušený	stew/casserole	*slaný*	salted
grilovaný	roast on the spit	*smažený*	fried in breadcrumbs
kyselý	sour	*studený*	cold
na kmíně	with caraway seeds	*syrový*	raw
na roštu	grilled	*sýrový*	cheesey
na zdraví	cheers!	*teplý*	hot
nadívaný	stuffed	*uzený*	smoked
nakládaný	pickled	*vařený*	boiled
(za)pečený	baked/roast	*znojmský*	with gherkins
plněný	stuffed		

Drinks

čaj	tea	*mléko*	milk	*svařené*	
destiláty	spirits	*pivo*	beer	*víno*	mulled wine
káva	coffee	*presso*	espresso	*tonic*	tonic
koňak	brandy	*s ledem*	with ice	*vinný*	white wine
láhev	bottle	*soda*	soda	*střik*	with soda
minerální	mineral	*suché víno*	dry wine	*víno*	wine
(voda)	(water)	*šumivý*	fizzy		

Eating and Drinking

sausages on offer is *sekaná*, bits of old meat and bread squashed together to form a meat loaf (for connoisseurs only). *Guláš* (goulash) is popular, usually *Szegedinský* (pork with sauerkraut) but sometimes *special* (with better meat and a creamier sauce). Less substantial fare boils down to *chlebíčky* – artistically presented **open sandwiches** with combinations of gherkins, cheese, salami, ham and aspic – and mountains of mayonnaise-type **salad**, bought by weight (200 grammes is a medium-sized portion).

The ubiquitous Czech street **takeaway** is the hot dog or *párek*, a dubious-looking frankfurter (traditionally two – *párek* means a pair), dipped in mustard and served in a white roll (*v rohlíku*). A greasier option is *bramborák*, a thin potato pancake with little flecks of bacon or salami in it; *felafal* is another popular takeaway, usually with pitta bread and salad. And, of course, there are now numerous western-style fast food joints (most notably *McDonalds*) all over Prague.

Staré Město

Grid references after the opening times refer to the map on pp.86–87.

Bona Vita, Dlouhá 4; metro Staroměstská. Antiseptic self-service *bufet* with daily soya-based specialities, plus some meaty dishes. *Mon–Fri 11.30am–10.30pm, Sat & Sun 11am–10pm.* G4.

Bonal, Staroměstské náměstí 4; metro Staroměstská; Václavské náměstí 57; metro Muzeum Czech-German joint venture selling sandwiches, pastries and good coffee. Staré Město branch is stand-up only; Wencelsas Square branch has seating. *Daily 9am–8pm.* F4.

Country Life, Melantrichova 15; metro Můstek. Cramped, popular stand-up buffet within a health food shop, which serves vegan snacks. *Mon–Thurs 8.30am–6pm, Fri 8.30am–2.30pm, Sun noon–6pm.* F6.

Dům lahůdek, Malé náměstí; metro Staroměstská. Big delicatessen on several levels, with great picnic fodder plus traditional *chlebíčky*, salads, coffee and cakes. *Mon–Sat 7am–7pm, Sun 10am–8pm, Sun 1–8pm.* E5.

Queenz, Havelská 12; metro Můstek. Inexpensive centrally located Middle Eastern kebab and felafel outlet. *Mon–Sat 10am–8pm, Sun noon–8pm.* F7.

U Bakaláře, Celetná 13; metro Staroměstská/náměstí Republiky. Self-service veggie hole-filler, serving typical Czech fry-up food to hungry tourists.

Ice cream

Whatever the season, Czechs have to have their daily fix of **ice cream** (*zmrzlina*), dispensed from window kiosks in the sides of buildings, and, more frequently now, from more substantial outlets, some with seating.

Dánská zmrzlina, Spálená 49, Nové Město; metro Národní třída. None-too-cheap option, but you're paying for the delicious cones, baked fresh on the premises. *Daily 10am–8pm.*

Dolce Vita, Vězenská, 15, Staré Město; metro Staroměstská. A real sit-down café in the old town, which also serves excellent ice cream. *Daily 10am–11pm.*

Ovocný bar, Václavské náměstí 52, Nove Město; metro Můstek/Muzeum. Very Czech, very *Clockwork Orange*

bilberry-coloured milk bar serving ice cream and huge fruit salads; located on the first floor above a grocery store on the corner of Ve Smečkách. *Mon–Sat 9.30am–9.30pm, Sun noon–9pm.*

Světozor, Vodičková 39, Nové Město; metro Můstek. Sit-down or takeaway, this reasonably priced *lahůdky* in the *pasáž* of the same name, has over twenty varieties of ice cream, plus pastries, cakes, the lot; it's situated in the Světozor cinema passage. *Mon–Sat 9am–8pm, Sun noon–8pm.*

Mon–Fri 9am–7pm, Sat & Sun
11am–7pm. H5.

Nové Město

Grid references after the opening times
refer to the map on pp.122–123.

Adonis, Jungmannova 21; metro Národní
třída. Cheap Middle Eastern fare – stuffed
vine leaves, *felafal, taboule* and a salad
bar – sit-in or takeaway. *Daily
11am–8pm.* E5.

Cornucopia, Jungmannova 10; metro
Národní třída. Simple, cheap sandwich
bar with a few hot dishes on offer, soup
of the day and seating inside.
*Mon–Thurs 9.30am–10pm, Fri–Sun
10am–8pm.* E5.

McDonald's, Vodičková 15; metro
Národní třída. The first in the country, on
the site of the famous *fin-de-siècle*
Akademická kavárna, its main virtue is
that it sells draught beer and has a children's play area. *Daily 8am–11pm.* F5.

Poříčská pekárna, Na poříčí 30; metro
náměstí Republiky. Viennese-style bakery
selling coffee and pastries. *Mon–Fri
7am–7pm, Sat until 1pm.* I2.

Rybařská bufet, Václavské náměstí 43;
metro Můstek/Muzeum. Stand-up buffet
with fish in batter and fishy salads on
offer. *Mon–Fri 9am–8pm.* G5.

U české koruny, Vodičkova 30; metro
Národní třída. Classic Czech stand-up
bufet, inside the arcade at no. 30, with a
sit-down restaurant section tacked on.
*Mon–Fri 10am–11pm, Sat & Sun
11am–8pm.* F5.

U rozvařilů, Na poříčí 26; metro náměstí
Republiky/Florenc. New old-style *bufet*
where everything is under 50kč, you
perch at zinc-top tables and the beer
flows freely. *Mon–Fri 8am–7.30pm, Sat
8am–7pm, Sun 10am–5pm.* I2.

Cafés

Prague can no longer boast a café society to rival that of Vienna or Paris, as it
could at the beginning of this century
and between the wars, as only a handful of classic haunts survive.

Nevertheless, many Praguers still spend
a large part of the day smoking and
drinking in the cafés, particularly in the
summer, when the tables spill out onto
the streets and squares. The cafés listed
below are a mixed bunch. The majority
serve just coffee and cakes, and more
often than not, alcohol; others also serve
up cheap and filling (though by no
means gourmet) meals.

Like the Austrians who once ruled over
them, the Czechs have a grotesquely
sweet tooth, and the coffee-and-cake hit is
part of the daily ritual. The more traditional
cafés offer a wide range of **cakes**: *dort*, like
the German *Torte*, consist of a series of
custard cream, chocolate and sponge layers, while *řez* are lighter, square cakes,
usually containing a bit of fruit. A *věneček*,
filled with "cream", is the nearest you'll get
to an éclair; a *větrník* is simply a larger version with a bit of fresh cream added. One
speciality to look out for is *rakvička*, which
literally means "little coffin", an extended
piece of sugar with cream, moulded
vaguely into the shape of a coffin.

Coffee is drunk black and in its most
basic form is described as *turecká*
(Turkish) – it's really just hot water
poured over coffee grains. Espresso
(*presso*) is becoming more and more
common, in Prague at least, though its
quality varies considerably. Downmarket
*bufet*s sell *ledová káva*, a weak, cold
black coffee, while at the other end of
the scale *Vídeňská káva* (Viennese coffee) is a favourite with the older generation, served with a dollop of whipped
cream. Another rather rich option is a
mix with advocaat, *Alžírská káva*. **Tea** is
drunk weak and without milk, although
you'll usually be given a glass of boiling
water and a tea bag so you can do your
own thing.

Malá Strana

Grid references after the opening times
refer to the map on pp.72–73. The nearest **metro** for all the following places is
Malostranská.

Baraka, Míšenská 2. A smoky little
gallery/café conveniently hidden away

Eating and
Drinking

Eating and Drinking

Prague's tea-houses

According to local legend, the Russian anarchist Mikhail Bukanin entered a Prague café in 1848 and ordered tea. When the owner said that he'd never heard of the drink, Bakunin marched into the kitchen and made the city's first cup of tea. Eighty years later, there were an estimated 150 tea-houses or *čajovny* in Prague, but the culture died out under the Communists. Today's **tea-houses** are a 1990s' phenomenon, though they have their historical roots in the First Republic. Partly a reaction to the smoke-filled, alcohol-driven atmosphere of the ubiquitous Czech pub, and partly a reaction against the multinational, fast-food culture that has recently arrived in Prague, tea-houses are non-smoking, slightly hippified places to enjoy a quiet cuppa and chill out. The tea drinking is taken very seriously, and several of the places listed below stock a staggering array of leaves.

Čajovna, Záhořanského 6, Nové Město; metro Karlovo náměstí. Minimalist, ascetic tea house with a lovely striped wooden floorboard and a nice mixed assortment of chairs. *Mon–Fri 10am–10pm.*

Čajovna Dátá Santóš, Žitná 42, Nové Město; metro Muzeum. A haven of eastern calm in the Sokol building on traffic-clogged Žitná, serving decent Indian snacks with an admirable range of teas. *Mon–Fri 3–10pm, Sat 3–8pm.*

Dobrá čajovna, Boršov 6, Staré Město; metro Staroměstská. Probably the most successful of all the tea-houses at re-creating a distinctively mellow, rarified atmosphere, with hookah smoking permitted. An astonishing variety of teas (and a few Middle Eastern snacks) are served by young male proto-Buddhist waiters who slip by silently in their sandals. This place is very difficult to find (it's off Karoliny Světlé) and the door is frequently locked, so you'll need to ring the bell to find out if there's any space available (or if they like the look of you). *Daily 8am–noon & 4–10pm.*

Dobrá čajovna, Václavské náměstí 14, Nové Město; metro Můstek/Muzeum. The pioneering tea house with a slightly less rarified but equally relaxing ambience. It's set back from the square, has world music wafting through it, floor seating and a vast range of teas. *Daily 10am–11.30pm.*

Růžová čajovna, Růžová 8, Nové Město; metro Můstek/Muzeum. The "pink tea-house" is a lighter, more modern version that caters for a less hippified clientele, and doesn't play exclusively non-western music. *Mon–Fri 10am–9pm, Sat 11am–10pm, Sun 11am–9pm.*

U zeleného čaje, Nerudova 19, Malá Strana; tram #12 or #22 from metro Malostranská. The "green tea" is a great little stop-off for a pot of tea or a veggie snack en route to or from the Hrad; the only problem is getting a place at one of the four tables. *Daily 10am–7pm.*

Zapomentá čajovna, Janský vršek 8, Malá Strana; tram #12 or #22 from metro Malostranská. The "forgotten tea-house" is housed in a hidden courtyard in the backstreets of Malá Strana, at U osla v kolébce (Donkey in a Cradle), the house where many folk reckon the alchemist Edward Kelley once lived. *Daily 10am–10pm.*

beside the Charles Bridge. *Daily 10am–midnight.* H5.

Bílý orel, Malostranské náměstí 28. Just round the corner from the *Malostranské kavárna* (see below), without the pedigree or quite the ambience, but it has more space and a wider range of food. *Daily 8.30am–1am.* G4.

Chiméra, Lázeňská 6. Coffee, toast and cigarettes are the defining features of this pleasant art gallery/café which has a few comfy armchairs to crash out in. *Daily 10am–10pm.* G5.

Malostranská kavárna, Malostranské náměstí 28. A time-honoured café founded in 1874 in a late eighteenth-century palace, and despite its prime position still a very pleasant place inside. *Daily 9am–11pm.* G4.

St Nicholas Café, Tržiště 10. Basement café/bar that pulls in wealthy, posey, beautfiul Czechs and the diplomatic crowd in some numbers. *Mon–Fri noon–1am, Sat & Sun 4pm–1am.* F4.

Savoy, Vítězná 5. Renovated nineteenth-century café with high, gilded ceiling, but rather unfortunate modern fittings and little atmosphere. *Daily 9am–midnight.* F10.

U zavěšenýho kafe, Radnické schody 7. A "hanging coffee" is one that has been paid for by the haves for the have-nots who drop in. That apart, this place is a pleasant smokey cross-over café/pub, serving cheap *Měšťan* beer and traditional Czech food. *Daily 11am–midnight.* D1.

Staré Město

Grid references after the opening times refer to the map on pp.86–87.

Barock, Parízská 24; metro Staroměstská. Deeply fashionable, candle-lit and popular French-style café in russet with framed photos of supermodels on the walls. The Thai, Japanese and Chinese is good, but pricey. *Daily 8.30am–1am.* E3.

Blatouch, Vězenská 7; metro Staroměstská. Smoky, literary café, frequented mostly by Czech students. Olives, snacks, jazz and alcoholic/non-alcoholic cocktails available. *Mon–Thurs 11am–midnight, Fri 11am–1am, Sat 2pm–1am, Sun 2pm–midnight.* F3.

Café Érra, Konviktská 11; metro Národní třída. Golden brown designer café in the backstreets off Betlémské náměstí that's proving popular with Prague's young arty professional mobile phone users. Tasty salads and snacks on offer too. *Daily 9am–11pm.* C8.

Café Milena, Staroměstské náměstí 22; metro Staroměstská. Fair attempt at a 1920s'-style café, situated opposite the astronomical clock, named after Kafka's famous and talented lover, Milena

Jesenská (see p.139), and by far the nicest café in this part of the old town. *Daily 10am–10pm.* F5.

Chez Marcel, Haštalská 12; metro náměstí Republiky. Effortlessly chic French café. A good place to grab a coffee, a *tarte tatin*, read a French mag or eat some moderately priced bistro-style food. *Mon–Fri 8am–1am, Sat & Sun 9am–1am.* I2.

Gulu Gulu, Betlémské náměstí 8; metro Národní třída. Popular café/pub with bare floorboards, Miró-style murals, newspapers and friendly bar staff. Radegast beer is on offer. *Mon–Thurs noon–midnight, Fri & Sat 10am–3am, Sun 10am–2am.* D7.

Hogo Fogo, Salvátorská 4; metro Staroměstská. Monochrome café tucked into the backstreets off Pařížská serving cheap, filling student-style pasta and meat dishes – very popular with young Czechs. *Mon–Thurs 11.30am–midnight, Fri & Sat noon–2am, Sun noon–midnight.* F4.

Konírna, Anenská 11; metro Staroměstská. Very popular vaulted stable building, with cheap drinks and salad bar. *Mon–Fri noon–midnight, Sat & Sun 6pm–midnight.* C6.

Lávka, Novotného lávka; metro Staroměstská. Tiny riverside café, with tables outside in summer, a superb view of the castle, and adjacent nightclub. *Daily noon–2am.* B6.

O' Ché's, Liliová 14; metro Staroměstská. Prague's premier Irish-run Cuban-themed café/bar. *Daily 10am–1am.* D7.

Paříž, U obecního domu 1; metro náměstí Republiky. The prices are sky-high for Prague, but there's a certain rather formal elegance about this hotel's Art Nouveau *kavárna*. *Daily 8am–1am.* J4.

Reno, UPM, 17 listopadu; metro Staroměstská. Great place to relax after taking in the treasures of the Applied Art Museum (see p.120). *Mon–Fri 10am–6pm, Sat & Sun 11am–6pm.* C3.

Rudolfinum, Alšovo nábřeží 12; metro Staroměstská. Gloriously grand nineteenth-century café on the first floor of the old parliament building (see p.120). *Daily 10am–6pm.* C3.

Eating and Drinking

Eating and Drinking

Nové Město

Grid references after the opening times refer to the map on pp.122–123.

Archa, Na poříčí 26; metro náměstí Republiky/Florenc. Designer café belonging to the avant-garde venue of the same name, with big fishbowl windows for street-watching. *Mon–Fri 9am–9pm, Sat 10am–8pm, Sun 1–8pm.* I2.

Fromín, Václavské náměstí 21; metro Můstek. Very posey, loud café/bar above a decent restaurant of the same name on top of the Krone department store (take the lift at the side). Glass-floored balcony, central dance floor, video screens, plus big windows and a small outdoor terrace overlooking Wenceslas Square. *Daily 11am–2am.* G5.

Gany's, Národní 20; metro Národní třída. High ceiling, mirrors, daily papers, lots of cakes, a billiard hall and window seats overlooking Národní make this a popular re-fuelling spot for tourists and shoppers alike. *Daily 8am–11pm.* E5.

Grand Hotel Evropa, Václavské náměstí 25; metro Můstek/Muzeum. To truly appreciate the sumptuous Art Nouveau decor, you'll have to forsake the terrace and step inside – still worth it even if the coffee and staff are below par, and they slap a surcharge on for the music. *Daily 7am–midnight.* G5.

Institut Français, Štěpánská 35; metro Muzeum. Housed in the French cultural centre – great coffee and superb French pastries, plus of course the chance to pose with a French newspaper, make this one of Prague's best cafés. *Mon–Fri 9am–6pm.* F6.

Obecní dům, náměstí Republiky; metro náměstí Republiky. The *kavárna*, with its famous fountain, is in the more restrained south hall of this huge Art Nouveau complex, and has recently been glitteringly restored – an absolute aesthetic treat. *Daily 8am–11pm.* G3.

Paris-Praha, Jindřišská 7; metro Můstek. Small café serving good French coffee, adjacent to the French delicatessen of the same name. *Mon–Fri 10.30am–7.30pm.* G4.

Praha-Roma, V jámě 5; metro Muzeum. Small *pasticceria* with dubious pink decor, serving authentic Italian pastries, coffee and ice cream. *Daily 9.30am–10pm.* F6.

Slavia, Národní 1; metro Národní třída. An enduring and endearing Prague institution (see p.134), that has finally re-opened after being closed for the last five years. *Daily 8am–midnight.* C5.

U sv Vojtěcha, Vojtěšská 14; metro Karlovo náměstí. Lively coffee place not far from the Národní divadlo and Žofín, with big windows that open out on to the street in summer. *Mon–Fri 8am–10pm, Sat 10am–10pm, Sun 10am–8pm.* C6.

Velryba (The Whale), Opatovická 24; metro Národní třída. One of the most determinedly cool cafés in Prague, not intended as an ex-pat joint (and not keen to entice tourists), serving cheap, post-revolutionary Czech food (several veggie options) and a stunning range of malt whiskies. *Daily 11am–2am.* D6.

Vyšehrad and the eastern suburbs

Grid references after the opening times refer to the map on pp.148–149.

Medúza, Belgická 17, Vinohrady; metro náměstí Míru. Trendy young crowd hang out in this deliberately faded, inexpensive café, which serves breakfast until 3pm and gets packed out most evenings. *Mon–Sat 11am–1am, Sun noon–1am.* D5.

Radost FX Café, Bělehradská 120, Vinohrady; metro I. P. Pavlova. Without doubt the best vegetarian restaurant in town (okay, so there's not much competition), with imaginative dishes using fresh produce that draw in a large ex-pat posse, particularly for the Sunday brunch. *Daily 11.30am–6am.* D6.

U knihomola (The Bookworm), Mánesova 79, Vinohrady; metro Jiřího z Poděbrad. Basement café in one of Prague's main ex-pat bookstores, with foreign papers to browse and art exhibitions to admire. *Mon–Thurs 10am–11pm, Fri & Sat 10am–midnight, Sun 11am–8pm.* F5.

Holešovice and the western suburbs

Grid references after the opening times refer to the map on pp.34–35.

Café Apostrof, Matoušova, Smíchov. Smart café in a pristinely renovated Dientzenhofer palace on náměstí 28 října, with lots of violins and art on the walls. A positive oasis in Smíchov. *Daily 11am–11pm.* D8.

The Globe, Janovského 14, Holešovice; metro Vltavská. This laid-back café – like the adjoining bookstore of the same name – is one big ex-pat hang-out, but enjoyable nevertheless. *Daily 10am–midnight.* G2.

Terasy na Barrandově, Hlubočepy; bus #105, #120, #128, #246, #247, #248 from metro Smíchovské nádraží. Prewar functionalist classic perched above the Vltava close to the famous Barrandov film studios. A fashionable place in the 1930s, now just a little too far out to draw any kind of crowd –

still worth a trip though. *Daily 11am–11pm.* Off the map.

U panáků, Letohradská 44, Holešovice; tram #1 from metro Vltavská. Puppet theatre café hung with marionettes, close to the Národní technické muzeum. *Tues, Thurs & Fri 4pm–midnight, Wed 3pm–midnight, Sat & Sun 2pm–midnight.* F3.

Pubs and bars

Traditional Czech *pivnice* are smoky, male-dominated places, where 99 percent of the customers are drinking copious quantities of Czech beer by the half-litre. Pubs with a more youthful clientele, and ex-pat bars, tend to be a bit more mixed, but if you're not interested in drinking (and preferably smoking), you're going to have a hard time having a good time. Still, as with British pubs, whatever their faults, they remain deeply embedded in the local culture, and to sample that, you'll need to sample the amber nectar. Food is almost always of the traditional Czech variety (for more on Czech cuisine, see p.204) – cheap and filling, but ultimately it could shorten your life by a couple of years.

Hradčany

Grid references after the opening times refer to the map on pp.46–47.

U černého vola (The Black Ox), Loretánské náměstí 1; tram #22 from metro Malostranská. Great pub doing a brisk business providing the popular light beer *Velkopopovický kozel* in huge quantities to thirsty local workers. *Daily 10am–10pm.* C4.

Malá Strana

Grid references after the opening times refer to the map on pp.72–73. The nearest metro is Malostranská, followed either by a short walk or a stop or two on tram #12 or #22.

Baráčnická rychta, Na tržiště 22 (down a narrow passageway leading south off Nerudova). A real survivor – a small backstreet *pivnice* squeezed in between

Eating and Drinking

Eating and Drinking

the embassies, with a cheap and filling menu. *Mon–Sat 11am–11pm.* E3.

Jo's Bar, Malostranské náměstí 7. A narrow bar in Malá Strana that is a perennially popular ex-pat/backpacker hang-out. Tex-Mex food served all day, bottled beer only and a heaving crowd guaranteed most evenings. *Daily 11am–2am.* F4.

Scarlett O'Hara's, Mostecká 21. One of Prague's many Irish-theme pubs. This one's better than the *James Joyce*, but not as cosy as *Molly Malone's*. *Daily noon–2am.* G5.

U bílé kuželky (The White Bowling Pin), Míšeňská 12. Not a bad pub considering its touristy location right by the Charles Bridge; reasonably priced *Pilsner Urquell* and Czech pub food. *Daily noon–10pm.* H5.

U černého orla (The Black Eagle), Újezd 33. Popular student pub with cheap food and Staropramen 10° beer, across the bridge from the Národní divadlo. *Mon–Fri 10am–10pm, Sat & Sun 11am–10pm.* E9.

U dvou slunců (The Two Suns), Nerudova 47. Recently resurrected old pub on prime tourist route up to the castle, serving *Krušovice* beer and Czech grub. *Daily 11am–11pm.* E2.

U hrocha (The Hippo), Thunovská 10. A genuine Czech pub in the heart of Malá Strana, difficult to believe but true – cheap grub and beer. *Daily noon–11pm.* G3.

U kocoura (The Cat), Nerudova 2. One of the few surviving pubs on Nerudova,

owned by the Beer Party, but, for the most part, abandoned by its old clientele. Some of the best *Pilsner Urquell* in town; but little to eat beyond sausages. *Daily 11.30am–midnight.* G3.

U malého Glena, Karmelitská 23. Smart-looking pub/jazz bar that attracts a fair few ex-pats thanks to its better-than-average food and live music. *Daily 7.30am–2am.* F5.

U staleté báby (Old Granny), Na Kampě 15. Round the corner from the formal restaurant of the same name is this friendly (and even child-friendly) pub offering tasty beer snacks; you can sit outside or wander down to the riverside with your Pilsner Urquell. *Daily noon–midnight.* H7.

Staré Město

Grid references after the opening times refer to the map on pp.86–87.

Banana Café, Štupartská 9; metro náměstí Republiky. Strange kitsch disco bar above *La Provence* restaurant deep in the heart of ex-pat territory. Worth experiencing once (perhaps). *Daily 5pm–1am.* H4.

Chapeau Rouge, Malá Štupartská; metro náměstí Republiky. Loud, posey, ex-pat boozer with wooden floorboards and red hat on door in the heart of the so-called French Quarter or "Bermuda Triangle". *Daily 4pm–4am.* H4.

James Joyce, Liliová 10; metro Staroměstská. A soulless and expensive re-creation of an Irish pub, with prices that only foreign businessmen think are reasonable – go to *U krále Jiřího* or *Molly Malone's* instead (see below). *Mon–Sat 10.30am–1am, Sun noon–1am.* D7.

Konvikt, Bartolomějská 11; metro Národní třída. New, but very normal smokey Czech pub serving *pilsner* and Czech food. *Mon–Fri 9am–11pm, Sat & Sun 11am–11pm.* D8.

Krušovická pivnice, Široká 20; metro Staroměstská. Josefov watering hole with a mostly Czech clientele, lashings of *Krušovice* beer and inexpensive pub grub. *Daily 11am–midnight.* F3.

Marquis de Sade, Templová 8; metro náměstí Republiky. Great space: huge high ceiling, big comfy sofas, and a mostly ex-pat crowd. Crap beer and limited snacks, but a good place to start the evening, before the live band kicks in. *Daily 4pm–2am.* I4.

Molly Malone's, U obecního dvora 4; metro Staroměstská. Best of Prague's Irish pubs with real Irish staff (who speak very little Czech), an open fire and draught *Kilkenny* and *Guinness* (neither of them very cheap). *Mon–Thurs & Sun noon–12.45am, Fri & Sat noon–1.45am.* G2.

Na Ovocném trhu, Ovocný trh 17; metro náměstí Republiky. New pub behind the Stavovské divadlo – perfect for a pre-theatre bite and a jar of *Velkopopvický kozel. Mon–Sat 10am–10pm, Sun 11.30am–10pm.* H5.

Radegast, Templová 2; metro náměstí Republiky. Typically boozy pub divided into booths, serving its namesake plus decent Czech food. Attracts Czechs and ex-pats. *Daily 11am–midnight.* I4.

Taz-Pub, U obecniho domu 3; metro náměstí Republiky. The latest in a series of rough and rowdy pubs in the vicinity of the *Hotel Paříž*, though this one is less fun than its predecessors. *Mon–Fri noon–2am, Sat & Sun 2pm–2am.* J4.

U krále Jiřího (The King George), Liliová 10; metro Staroměstská. Forget the more visible *James Joyce* (see above), and head down the steps to this nice Czech pub serving south Bohemian *Platan* beer instead. *Daily 3pm–1am.* D7.

U medvídků (The Little Bears), Na Perštýně 7; metro Národní třída. A Prague institution going back to the thirteenth century: the food isn't great, and the *Budvar* not always what it should be, but it's central, unpretentious and roomy. *Mon–Sat 11.30am–11pm, Sun 11.30am–10pm.* E8.

U milosrdných, Kozí 21; metro Staroměstská. Refurbished pub far enough away from the tourist crowds, serving typical Czech food and Plzeň beers. *Daily 10am–10pm.* G2.

U pivrnce, Maiselova 3; metro Staroměstská. No-frills basic Czech food and Radegast beer, which is something of a boon in the heart of Josefov; shame about the unfunny cartoons on the walls. *Daily 11am–11.30pm.* E4.

U Vejvodů, Vejvodova 2; metro Národní třída. Classic medieval *pivnice* in the warren of streets south of Karlova, permanently covered in scaffolding. The usual inexpensive, filling Czech dishes are on offer, washed down with *Smíchov*'s best. *Daily 11am–11pm.* E7.

U zlatého tygra (The Golden Tiger), Husova 17; metro Staroměstská. Small *pivnice* with nearly every seat taken by regulars. Once frequented by Prague's literary in-crowd – the late writer and bohemian, Bohumil Hrabal, was a semi-permanent resident – but better known now for having been visited by President Clinton. *Daily 3–11pm.* D6.

Žíznivý pes (Thirsty Dog), Elišky Krásnohorské 5; metro Staroměstská. The previous incarnation of this pub was a much loathed/loved ex-pat joint that shook the foundations of the Obecní dům. It remains to be seen whether this reincarnation can live up to its legend. *Daily noon–2am.* F3.

Nové Město

Grid references after the opening times refer to the map on pp.122–123.

Branický sklípek, Vodičkova 26; metro Můstek. One of the few places in the

Eating and Drinking

Eating and Drinking

centre where you can down Prague's Braník beers. *Mon–Fri 9am–11pm, Sat & Sun 11am–11pm.* F5.

Jáma (The Hollow), V jámě 7; metro Můstek/Muzeum. Loud ex-pat pub with lots of cocktails and a range of passable attempts at Tex-Mex and Chinese dishes. *Daily 11am–1am.* F6.

John Bull, Senovážná 8; metro náměstí Republiky. A real imitation British pub, serving indifferent John Bull ale and cheap Czech food; popular with the local bank clerks. *Mon–Fri 11am–10pm, Sat 11am–9pm.* G3.

Novoměstský pivovar, Vodičkova 20; metro Národní třída. New micro-brewery, which serves its own misty home brew, plus Czech food, in a series of bright, sprawling modern beer halls. *Mon–Sat 11.30am–11.30pm, Sun noon–10pm.* E6.

Sport Bar Praha, Ve Smečkách 30; metro Muzeum. Big, lively American-style sports bar, with pool tables and lots of screens – the beer's crap and overpriced, but it's the one place you're guaranteed to see the match you want. *Mon–Thurs & Sun 10am–2am, Fri & Sat 11am–5am.* G6.

U bubeníčků, Myslíkova 8; metro Karlovo náměstí. Good unpretentious place to down a few halves of Herold or Gambrinus and eat some simple Czech cuisine, after visiting the Mánes gallery – it even has the menu in Russian. *Daily 11am–11pm.* C6.

U Fleků, Křemencova 11; metro Karlovo náměstí. Famous medieval *pivnice* where the unique dark 13° beer, Flek, has been exclusively brewed and consumed since 1499. Seats over 500 German tourists at a go, serves short measures (0.4l) for high prices, slaps an extra charge on for the music and still you have to queue. This is a tourist trap and the only reason to visit is to sample the beer., which you're best off doing during the day. *Daily 9am–11pm.* D6.

U havrana (The Crow), Hálkova 8; metro I. P. Pavlova. Surprisingly unseedy, normal pub serving food and Měšťan and Kozel beer throughout the night. *Mon–Fri 24hr, Sat & Sun 6pm–6am.* G7.

U Pešků, Sokolská 50; metro I. P. Pavlova. Large and lively beer hall on one of Prague's most unhealthy streets, plus a smaller, more sedate *jídelna* serving some interesting Czech dishes – look out for the goose (*husa*). *Daily 11am–11pm.* G8.

U Pinkasů, Jungmannovo náměstí 15; metro Můstek. Famed as the first *pivnice* in Prague to serve Pilsner Urquell (which it still does). Despite its proximity to Wenceslas Square, it still manages to keep its Czech regulars. *Daily 9am–midnight.* F4.

U pravdu (The Truth), Žitná 15; metro Karlovo náměstí/Muzeum. Cheap Czech food, Radegast and Staropramen at this local boozer, which has a separate restaurant section and a garden out back. *Daily 11am–10pm.* F7.

U zpěváčků (The Choir Boy), Na struze 7; metro Národní třída. Loud and smoky workers/musicians' pub just around the corner from the Národní divadlo, with an ironic line in Marxist-Leninist tracts, and the local Staropramen on tap. *Mon–Thurs 10am–2am, Fri 10am–3am, Sat 11am–3am & Sun 11am–2am.* C6.

Vyšehrad and the eastern suburbs

Grid references after the opening times refer to the map on pp.148–149.

Akropolis, Kubelíkova 27, Žižkov; metro Jiřího z Poděbrad. Funkily decked out and very popular smoke-filled pub that plays half-decent music and serves cheap Czech food and *Kozel* beer. *Mon–Sat 4pm–2am, Sun 4pm–midnight.* F4.

Hostinec pod Vyšehradem, Vratislavova 4, Vyšehrad; tram #3, #7 or #17 from metro Karlovo náměstí. Neo-Gothic on the outside but perfectly normal inside, serving cheap mugs of Gambrinus. *Daily 11am–11pm.* A6.

Na zvonařce (The Bell), Šafaříkova, Vinohrady; tram #6 or #11 from metro I. P. Pavlova. Cheap Czech cuisine, Pilsner Urquell, Radegast, billiards, occasional dancing, and great views from the terrace over the Nuselské schody and Botič valley. *Daily 10am–midnight.* D6.

U Bergnerů, Slezská 134, Žižkov; metro Flora. For beer connoisseurs: one of the few pubs serving the slightly bitter unfiltered beer from the recently resurrected brewery in Kacov; good, simple Czech food available, too. *Daily 11am–midnight.* H6.

U Bulinů, Budečská 2, Vinohrady; metro náměstí Míru. Fine Czech pub with equally good pub food on offer, situated on the corner of Francouzská. *Daily 10am–10pm.* E5.

U koleje (The College), Slavíkova 24, Vinohrady; metro Jiřího z Poděbrad. Thriving local: cigarette smoke, Kozel beer, meat and dumplings all guaranteed. *Mon–Fri 11am–10pm.* F5.

U růžového sadu (The Rose Garden), Mánesova 89, Vinohrady; metro Jiřího z Poděbrad. Imaginatively decorated for a Czech pub, with old shop signs and the like, and perfectly situated if you're visiting the Plečnik Church or the Bookworm bookstore; Gambrinus and dark Purkmistr beer on tap. *Mon–Fri 10am–11.30pm, Sat 11am–11.30pm, Sun 11am–10pm.* F5.

U vystřeleného oka (The Shot-Out Eye), U božích bojovníků, Žižkov; metro Florenc. Big, loud, smoky, heavy drinking pub just south of the Žižkov Hill, off Husitská, with (unusually) good music playing and lashings of *Radegast* beer. and absinthe chasers. *Daily 3.30pm–1am.* G3.

U zlaté kotvy, Vratislavova 19, Vyšehrad; tram #3, #7 or #17 from metro Karlovo náměstí. New pub with dubious colour scheme, but excellent, cheap Gambrinus, Pilsner and Punkmistr dark beer. *Mon–Fri 9am–10pm, Sat & Sun 10am–10pm.* A6

Holešovice and the western suburbs

Grid references after the opening times refer to the map on pp.34–35.

The Derby, Dukelských hrdinů 20, Holešovice; tram #12 or #17 from metro Malostranská. Spacious, lively, British-style ex-pat pub that lays on chess, draughts and backgammon, plus big, filling pizzas and a wide range of Czech and foreign beers on draught. *Daily 11am–2am.* G2.

Jamajka, Staropramenu 23, Smíchov; metro Anděl. Unpretentious basement pub serving incredibly cheap beer from Nymburk. *Daily 4pm–1am.* D8.

Na slamníku (The Straw Bed), Schwaigrova 7, Bubeneč; bus #131 from metro Hradčanská. The perfect place to end up after a stroll in Stromovka: a *pivnice* serving good Czech grub and Krušovice beer. *Daily 4pm–midnight.* D2.

Na staré kovárně v Braníku (The Old Blacksmith's in Braník), Kamenická 17, Holešovice; tram #26 from metro náměstí Republiky. Nicely refurbished pub that's popular with the locals and a crowd of young Czechs. Small menu of meaty daily dishes, Radegast beer and good music. *Mon–Sat 11.30am–1am, Sun 11.30am–11.30pm.* F3.

Eating and Drinking

Czech menus

In pubs and inexpensive restaurants, the **menu** (*jídelní lístek*), which should be displayed outside, is often in Czech only and deciphering it without a grounding in the language can be quite a feat. Just bear in mind that the general rule is for the right-hand column to list the prices, while the far left column often gives you the estimated weight of every dish in grammes; if what you get weighs more or less, the price alters accordingly.

The menu is usually divided into various sections beginning with *předkrmy* (starters) or *polévky* (soups), followed by the main courses: *jídla na objednávku* (food to order), *hotová jídla* (ready-made food), *drůbez a ryby* (fowl and fish) and, if you're lucky, *bezmasa* (vegetarian dishes). Side dishes are listed under *přílohy*; puddings, where available, are listed under the heading *moučníky*.

Eating and Drinking

For a glossary of Czech terms for food and drink, see pp.208–209.

Nad královskou oborou (The Royal Game Preserve), Nad královskou oborou 31, Bubeneč; bus #1255 from the northern end of Revoluční. Another place to head for after a stroll in Stromovka; good Czech food, Purkmistr dark and Gambrinus light beers on tap, the world's cheapest pint of Guinness, plus live bands (Fri & Sat). *Daily noon–11pm.*

U buldoka (The Bulldog), Preslova 1, Smíchov; metro Anděl. A half-decent Smíchov pub is hard to find, so here's one, serving Gambrinus. *Mon–Thurs 11.30am–11.30pm, Fri until midnight, Sat noon–midnight, Sun 4–10pm.* D8.

U váhy (The Weight), Nádražní 88, Smíchov; metro Anděl. Right by the Staropramen brewery and therefore the unofficial brewery tap; it also does food. *Mon–Fri 10am–10pm, Sat & Sun 11am–10pm.* D8.

Restaurants

Prague's **restaurant** scene has greatly improved in the last few years in terms of both choice and quality, but the influx of tourists has pushed the prices out of the reach of many Czechs, who tend more than ever to stick to pubs when eating out. Service is gradually becoming more sophisticated, though surly staff are still no rarity, nor are unscrupulous waiters who exercise dubious arithmetics when totting up the bill. Beware of extras in the pricier restaurants, where you will be charged for everything you touch, including the almonds you thought were courtesy of the house.

Hradčany

The grid references after the opening times refer to the map on pp.46–47; the nearest **metro** for the places listed below is Malostranská, after which you can either walk up to the castle area or catch tram #22.

INEXPENSIVE

Saté Grill, Pohořelec 3. There isn't really a better place to fill your belly for very little in the vicinity of the Hrad. Simple veggie and non-veggie noodle dishes prepared, all with a vaguely Indonesian bent. *Daily 11am–10pm.* C4.

U Lorety, Loretánské náměstí 8; ☎53 13 95. Familiar Czech menu, bang next door to the Loreto chapel, and facing the monster Černínský palác – a great place to eat outside in summer. *Daily 11am–11pm.* C4.

MODERATE

U ševce Matouše (The Cobbler), Loretánské náměstí 4. The cobbler's been made redundant and the prices have quadrupled, but this is still the best steak house in Prague. *Daily noon–4pm & 6–11pm.* C4.

EXPENSIVE

U zlaté hrušky (The Golden Pear), Nový Svět 3 ☎53 11 33. Romantic, exclusive, intimate, the setting is perfect, the menu is imaginative, and the bill (after careful massaging by the management) will probably exceed 1000kč a head. *Daily 11.30am–3pm & 6.30pm–midnight.* C2.

The restaurant listings are divided into geographical areas that correspond to the chapters, and into price categories, too – inexpensive, moderate and expensive. As a rough guide, you'll be able to get a soup, main course and pudding with a couple of beers thrown in for:

Inexpensive under 250kč a head
Moderate 250–500kč a head
Expensive 500kč and upwards

While 500kč for a meal is hardly extravagant compared to meal prices in the EU or US, it's still pricey for most Czechs. Note that at restaurants where we have included phone numbers, it is advisable to book beforehand.

Malá Strana

The grid references after the opening times refer to the map on pp.72–73. The nearest **metro** for all the places listed below is Malostranská, followed by a tram ride on tram #12 or #22 or a short walk.

INEXPENSIVE

Anatolia, Újezd 5. Turkish restaurant at the southern end of Újezd, serving great grilled meats, *tzatziki*, fresh Turkish bread, real Turkish tea and coffee and sweets, too. *Daily 9am–11pm.* E9.

Bar Bar, Všehrdova 17. Arty crêperie with big cheap salads, sweet and savoury crêpes and Jamaican *palačinky* on offer. *Mon–Fri 11am–midnight, Sat & Sun noon–midnight.* F8.

Čertovka, U lužického semináře 24. Small place down an alleyway, with indifferent Czech food but a great summer terrace overlooking Charles Bridge. *Daily 11.30am–midnight.* J4.

Faros, Šporkova 5; ☎53 34 82. Cosy little Greek restaurant in the backstreets of Malá Strana; a nice change and fairly veggie-friendly. *Daily noon–11pm.* D2.

MODERATE

Avalon, Malostranské náměstí 12. Big Hockney mural as a backdrop and a California-inspired menu with everything from burgers to fresh salads, but particularly strong on shellfish and the finned variety; tables outside in the summer. *Daily 11am–1am.* F4.

Nebozízek (Little Auger), Petřínské sady 411; ☎53 79 05. Situated at the halfway stop on the funicular up Petřín. You used to go here for the view, not the food; now you can enjoy both as long as you stick to the traditional Czech dishes. *Daily 11am–6pm & 7–11pm.* C7.

Palffy palác, Valdštejnská 14. Grand candle-lit room on the first floor of the conservatoire, with indifferent food (stick to the salads and desserts) and a wonderful outdoor terrace from which to survey the red rooftops of Malá Strana. *Daily 10am–11pm.* H2.

U maltézských rytířů, Prokopská 10; ☎53 63 57. One of the cheapest gourmet spots in Prague, serving faultless local cuisine and excellent apple strudel. *Daily 11am–11pm.* G5.

U modré kachničky (The Blue Duck), Nebovidská 6; ☎06 20 38 22. Cosy little restaurant, decorated with murals and antiques, and offering a mouth-watering selection of dishes, including many Czech favourites, given the gourmet treatment. *Daily noon–3.30pm & 6.30–11.30pm.* F7

U patrona, Dražického náměstí 4. Excellent restaurant very close to the Charles Bridge, offering beautifully prepared local dishes. *Daily 11.30am–2.30pm & 5.30–11.30pm.* H5.

U tří houslíček (The Three Violins), Nerudova 10. Pleasant art-loving ambience to this Czech restaurant which boasts a good handful of veggie dishes. Just one of a number of small wine bars that line the climb up to the castle. *Daily 11am–midnight.* F3.

EXPENSIVE

Circle Line, Malostranské náměstí 12; ☎53 03 08. The fresh seafood and sumptuous salads are the main draw, though the meat and veggie courses are equally good. Approaching 1000kč a head and situated below the less expensive *Avalon* (see above). *Mon–Sat 6–11pm.* F4.

David, Tržiště 21; ☎53 93 25. Elegant restaurant which specializes in doing Bohemian cuisine full justice – around 750kč a head. *Daily 11.30am–11pm.*

Kampa Park, Na Kampě 8b; ☎53 48 00. Pink house exquisitely located right by the Vltava on Kampa Island with an international menu and tables outside in summer. *Daily 11.30am–1am.* H6.

U malířů (The Artist's), Maltézské náměstí 11; ☎24 51 02 69. Prague's most expensive French restaurant is a converted sixteenth-century house that used to belong to an artist called Jiří Šic (pronounced "Shits"). The food *can* be delicious, but your bill will head towards

Eating and Drinking

Eating and Drinking

2000kč a head regardless. *Daily 7–10.30pm*. G6.

U Mecenáše, Malostranské náměstí 10; ☎53 38 81. Vaulted Gothic *vinárna* where Václav IV used to drink (a lot) and which now pulls in hungry tourists. The menu features the usual Czech favourites, all well prepared. *Mon–Fri 5–11.30pm, Sat & Sun 1pm–11.30pm*. G4.

Staré Město and Josefov

The grid references after the opening times refer to the map on pp.86–87.

INEXPENSIVE

Klub architektů, Betlémské náměstí; metro Národní třída. Sweaty Gothic cellar by the side of the Betlémská kaple, packed full of smart and sophisticated locals enjoying the excellent choice of cheap veggie food and meat dishes; some tables outside in the summer. *Daily 11.30am–midnight*. D7.

Lotos, Platnéřská 13; metro Staroměstská. Decor's an odd mixture of tie-die and ultra-tidy sterility. Food's bizarre too: banana ragout but also veggie wholefood versions of Czech cuisine – this is your chance to have a meat-free pork and dumplings. No smoking but there is alcohol. *Daily 11am–10pm*. C5.

Modrá zahrada (Blue Garden), Pařížská 14; metro Staroměstská. Given its location, right by the Jewish sights, this is a surprisingly pleasant, stylish and inexpensive pizzeria (the entrance is on Široká) serving big portions washed down with Radegast or wine. You have to ask specifically for mozzarella, otherwise you'll get Czech Eidam. *Daily 11am–midnight*. E3.

Pizzeria Rugantino, Dušní 4; metro Staroměstská. This pizzeria, just off Dlouhá, is the genuine article: an oak-fired oven, gargantuan thin bases and nineteen toppings to choose from, Bernard on tap. *Mon–Sat 11am–11pm, Sun 6–11pm*. F3

U supa (The Vulture), Celetná 22; metro náměstí Republiky. Lively fourteenth-century pub-style restaurant serving typical Czech food and Braník beer, either inside or on the cobbles of its cool, vaulted courtyard. *Mon–Sat 11am–4pm & 6–11pm*. H5.

V Blatnici, Michalská 6; metro Můstek. Popular basement *vinárna* bang in the old town, serving Moravian wines and cheap Czech food. *Mon–Sat noon–10pm*. F6.

MODERATE

Le Saint-Jacques, Jakubská 4; metro náměstí Republiky. Excellent French cuisine on offer here in the heart of the so-called "French quarter". *Daily noon–3pm & 6–11pm*. I4.

Massada, Michalská 16; metro Můstek. Smart kosher restaurant, offering some unusual dishes such as latkes, aubergines and fruit dumplings, though I'm not sure what the Talmud says about microwaves; beer's a fair price, too, at 45kč for 0.4l. Flesh-based dishes upstairs; dairy and veggie dishes downstairs. *Daily 8am–midnight*. F6.

Red, Hot & Blues, Jakubská 12; metro náměstí Republiky. Laid-back joint deep in the heart of ex-pat territory serving chilli-hot Tex-Mex – *burritos, étoufées* and Creole food – to the sound of jazz and blues. *Daily 10am–11pm*. I4.

EXPENSIVE

Bellevue, Smetanovo nábřeží 18; ☎24 22 76 14; metro Národní třída. The view of the Charles Bridge and the Hrad is outstanding and they serve imaginative Czech-centred cuisine – hardly surprising then that it's around 1000kč a head and you need to book ahead to eat here. *Mon–Sat noon–3pm & 5.30–11pm, Sun 11am–3pm & 7–11.30pm*. B9.

Jewel of India, Pařížská 20; metro Staroměstská. Plush Tandoori restaurant for those pining for a bit of Indian cuisine. *Daily noon–2.30pm & 5.30–11.30pm*. E3.

Metamorphosis, Ungelt; metro Staroměstská/náměstí Republiky. Ground-floor café serving snacks, desserts and drinks, plus an atmospheric Gothic cellar restaurant specializing in Mediterranean dishes. The best of the swish new outfits that inhabit the restored courtyard hidden behind the Týn church. *Daily 11am–1pm.* H4.

Praha Tamura, Havelská 6; ☎ 24 23 20 56; metro Můstek. Authentic Japanese sashimi and sushi at authentic Japanese prices; fixed menus at 1200kč and 1900kč. *Daily 11am–midnight.*

Reykjavik, Karlova 20; metro Staroměstská. Prime tourist location but the owners really are Icelandic, though the cuisine is pretty international. The soups and starters are definitely worth going for, but the best feature is the wonderful variety of fresh fish, flown in from you know where. *Daily 11am–11pm.* D6.

V zátiší (Still-Life), Liliová 1; ☎ 24 22 89 77; metro Národní třída. Exquisitely prepared international cuisine with fresh vegetables and regular non-meat dishes, all served in *nouvelle cuisine* sized portions by professional waiters. *Daily noon–3pm & 5.30–11pm.* D7.

Nové Město

The grid references after the opening times refer to the map on pp.122–123.

INEXPENSIVE

Diogenes, Gorazdova 22, metro Karlovo náměstí. Genuine Greek restaurant with a seafood bent. *Mon–Sat 11am–11pm, Sun noon–11pm.* C7.

Góvinda, Soukenická 27; metro náměstí Republiky. Hare Krishna (*Haré Kršna* in Czech) restaurant serving organic Indian veggie slop for knock-down prices. *Mon–Sat 11am–5pm.* H1.

Pizzeria Coloseum, Vodičkova 32; metro Můstek. Basement pizzeria in the passage beside *Kentucky Fried Chicken*, dishing up big pizzas and pasta dishes, washed down with *Krušovice* beer and Moravian wine. *Mon–Sat 11.30am–11.30pm, Sun noon–11.30pm.* F5.

Pizzeria Kmotra (Godmother), V jirchářích 12; ☎ 24 91 58 09; metro Národní třída. This sweaty basement pizza place is cur-

rently Prague's most popular, justifiably so – if possible book a table in advance. *Daily 11am–1am.* D6.

Pizzeria Mamma Mia, Na poříčí 13; metro náměstí Republiky. The main feature here is the restaurant's very own in-house tree. Otherwise it's easier to get a seat than at *Kmotra* and not quite so stiflingly hot. *Mon–Sat 11am–11pm, Sun 5–10pm.* H2

Polská, Opatovická 3; metro Národní třída. If you're wearying of solid Czech food, why not try some solid Polish fare? Traditional Polish *pierogi* and a full belly guaranteed. *Daily noon–11.30pm.* D6.

MODERATE

Bella Napoli, V jámě 8; metro Národní třída. One of Prague's better Italian restaurants, situated above a tacky disco, offering pasta and pizza dishes, plus a great *antipasti* buffet. *Mon–Sat 11.30am–11.30pm, Sun 6–11.30pm.* F6.

Cicala, Žitná 43; metro I. P. Pavlova. Very good little Italian basement restaurant that does a good range of pasta and pizza, has an appetizing *antipasti* selection, and specializes (mid-week) in fresh seafood. *Mon–Sat 11.30am– 10.30pm.* G7.

Salammbo, Vyšehradská; metro Karlovo náměstí. Tunisian restaurant that makes a few concessions to the Czech palate – ask for the spicier dishes if you want a hotter hit. *Mon–Sat 11am–3pm & 6pm–midnight, Sun 6pm–midnight.* D10.

U bílého slona (The White Elephant), Soukenická 4; metro náměstí Republiky. Toned-down Thai cuisine at moderate prices – don't go upstairs where the food is the same but the prices are higher. *Mon–Sat 11am–11pm.* G2.

U čišků, Karlovo náměstí 34; ☎ 29 88 91; metro Karlovo náměstí. Cosy restaurant on the the east side of the square, dishing up a seriously meaty menu of beef, pork, goose, duck and anything else that moves, washed down with Plzeň beers. *Daily noon–3.30pm & 5–11pm.* E7.

Eating and Drinking

Eating and Drinking

Cerberus, Soukenická 19; ☎231 09 85; metro náměstí Republiky. Cosy, pristine little joint serving up pasta and Czech favourites, including plenty of imaginative pork dishes. *Daily noon–4pm & 5pm–midnight.* G2.

Fakhreldine, Klimentská 48; ☎232 79 70; metro Florenc. Lebanese restaurant that charges a high price for its authentic Middle Eastern cuisine, in which the starters outnumber the main courses. *Daily noon–midnight.* I1.

Francouzská restaurace, **Obecní dům**, náměstí Republiky; metro náměstí Republiky. The Art Nouveau decor in this cavernous hall is absolutely stunning; the setting is formal and therefore puts a lot of tourists off, though the food's actually not that expensive. *Daily noon–3pm & 6–11pm.* G3.

La Perle de Prague, Rašínovo nábřeží 80; ☎21 98 41 60; metro Karlovo náměstí. Very formal French restaurant with plenty of pretensions, situated on the top floor of the notorious Fred & Ginger building (see p.144) – well over 1000kč a head. *Daily 12.30–2.30pm & 7.30–10.30pm.* C7.

Vyšehrad and the eastern suburbs

The grid references after the opening times refer to the map on pp.148–149.

INEXPENSIVE

Myslivna (The Hunting Lodge), Jagellonská 21, Žižkov; metro Flora. One of Prague's best game restaurants, serving up excellent venison and quail. *Daily 11.30am–3.30pm & 6–11pm.* G5.

U Šemíka, Vratislavova 36, Vyšehrad; tram #3, #7, #17, #18 or #24 from metro Karlovo náměstí. Simple place below Vyšehrad specializing in fish in some strange sauces. *Daily 11.30am–11.30pm.* A6.

Záhřeb, Záhřebská 24, Vinohrady; metro náměstí Míru. Plain, cheap restaurant serving fish and meat dishes, expertly cooked, plus the odd Chinese-style dish, too. *Daily 11am–11pm.* D6.

MODERATE

Dolly Bell, Neklanova 20, Vyšehrad; tram #3, #7, #17, #18 or #24 from metro Karlovo náměstí. Yugoslav restaurant (named after a film – it sounds more promising in Serbo-Croat), which serves up excellent Balkan grub, and features upside-down tables stuck to the ceiling. *Daily 2–11pm.*

Il Ritrovo, Lublaňská 11, Vinohrady; tram #6 from metro I. P. Pavlova. Excellent Italian-run outfit with a wide range of pasta dishes and good salads, a great *antipasti* bar in the centre of the restaurant and delicious *tiramisu* for dessert. *Mon–Sat noon–3pm & 6pm–midnight.* C6.

Kongzi, Seifertova 18, Žižkov; tram #5, #9 or #26 from metro Hlavní nádraží. Very reasonable Chinese restaurant in deepest Žižkov. *Daily 11am–3pm & 6–11pm.*

Taj Mahal, Škrétova 10, Vinohrady; metro Muzeum. Basement Indian curry restaurant, behind the Národní muzeum, serving the real thing: poppadums, bhajees, samosas and an excellent *chicken korma*, but not so hot on veggie dishes. *Mon–Sat noon–3pm & 5.30–11.30pm.* D4.

Holešovice and the western suburbs

The grid references after the opening times refer to the map on pp.34–35.

INEXPENSIVE

La Crêperie, Janovského 4, Holešovice; tram #5, #12 or #17. Stylish French-run crêperie serving sweet and savoury pancakes, French liquers and even the rare Nová Paka beer. *Mon–Sat noon–11pm.* G3.

U Matouše, Preslova 17, Smíchov; metro Anděl. Unpretentious restaurant serving good Czech cuisine with a few surprises aside from the staples: *smažený Olomoucký sýr*, a pungent deep-fried cheese and *špekové knedlíky*, bacon and onion dumplings, to name but two. *Daily 11am–11pm.* D8.

MODERATE

Ullman, Kostelní, Holešovice; tram #1 from metro Vltavská. Convenient Letná restaurant in the Letenský zámeček, oppposite the Národní technické muzeum, serving typical slightly upgraded Czech food, including some veggie options, with *Velkopopvický kozel* on draught. *Daily 11am–11pm.* F3.

U cedru (The Cedar), Národní obrany 27, Dejvice; metro Dejvická. If you can't afford the prices at *Fakhreldine* in town, try the more reasonable, but even more delicious Lebanese fare from this joint. *Daily 11am–11pm.* C3.

EXPENSIVE

Hanavský pavilón, Letenské sady 173; ☎ 32 57 92; tram #18 or #22 from metro Malostranská. Highly ornate Art Nouveau pleasure pavilion high above the Vltava, with stunning views and a bill that is unlikely to be less than 800kč per person. *Daily 11.30am–3.30pm & 6pm–1am.* D4.

Eating and Drinking

Chapter 11

Clubs and live venues

The great thing about going out for the night in Prague is that the beer flows cheaply, entry to most late-night places is pretty negligible, and there are one or two venues open until 5 or 6am. That said, Prague has nothing like the number of **clubs** you'd expect from a European capital. The dance craze has a small, but dedicated following, and there are a few good one-off raves over the summer (a case of scouring the fly posters around), but pure dance clubs are the exception away from the tacky meat markets around Wenceslas Square, whose resistance to change is remarkable. Many nightclubs double as live music venues, with Czech bands spanning the entire range of musical tastes from (mostly white) reggae to thrash. To find out the latest on the city's up-and-coming events, check the listings sections in *Prague Post*, or the Czech listings monthly *Přehled*.

Rock, Pop and Dance Music

Major western **bands** are beginning to include Prague in their European tours and, to be sure of a full house, many offer tickets at a fraction of their price in the West. There are gigs by Czech bands almost every night in the city's clubs and discos – a selection of the better ones is listed below. Be warned that many clubs in Prague appear to be under constant threat of closure – in particular the axe was hanging over

Arkadia and *Subway* as this book went to print.

Akropolis, Kubelíkova 27, Žižkov; tram #5, #9 or #26. Decent live venue space adjacent to the café/bar of the same name, that attracts good bands and a discerning, mostly Czech crowd. *Doors open 7pm*.

Arkadia, Na příkopě 22, Nové Město; metro náměstí Republiky. A very mixed crowd, including many of Prague's African students, ascends the stairs to the top floor of the Slovanský dům for the club's reggae nights – loud, proud and very early 1980s. *Daily 10pm–5am*.

Belmondo Revival Club, Bubenská 1, Holešovice; metro Vltavská. Regular gigs at the club that championed repro bands – hence the name – plus cheap beer and a couple of pool tables. *Doors open 7.30pm*.

Klub X, Na příkopě 15, Nové Město; metro náměstí Republiky. Typical Prague nightclub that has had absolutely no decor, but if there's a fair crowd in, and you're up for it, you'll have a good time regardless. *Daily 7pm–4am*.

Lucerna, Vodičkova 36, Nové Město; metro Můstek. Without doubt the best gig venue in Prague, a gilded turn-of-the-century hall with balcony, but only worth visiting when there's an event booked in – check the listings.

Music Park, Francouzská 4, Vinohrady; metro náměstí Míru. Prague's high-tech club is the city's premier meat market away from Wenceslas Square, with naff theme nights and plenty of mafiosi. *Tues–Sat 9pm–5am.*

Radost FX, Bělehradská 120, Vinohrady; metro I. P. Pavlova. Still by far the slickest dance club in Prague, attracting a mix of clubbers and despots; great veggie café upstairs. *Daily until 6am.*

Rock Café, Národní 22, Nové Město; metro Národní třída. The *Rock Café* has had its day. It made its name in the early days of post-Communist euphoria, but is now considered passé in Prague, though it still puts on the odd worth-while gig. *Daily 6pm–6am.*

Roxy, Dlouhá 33, Staré Město; metro náměstí Republiky. The *Roxy* is a great lit-tle venue: a recently revamped interior and an interesting programme of events from arty films and exhibitions to live acts and dance nights. *Tues–Sun 6pm–late.*

Subway, Na příkopě 22, Nové Město; metro náměstí Republiky. DJs, jazz and good old rock'n'roll entertain a mixed bunch of tourists and locals, but the biggest draw is the outdoor beer court-yard. Situated on the ground floor of the Slovanský dům. *Daily 9pm–5am.*

Újezd, Újezd 18, Malá Strana; tram #12 or #22 from metro Malostranská. Like

Clubs and Live Venues

Gay and Lesbian Nightlife

Prague Post does the occasional update on **gay and lesbian nightlife** in Prague, otherwise you'll need to get hold of the the monthly gay magazine *SOHO Revue*, which has an English summary, or *Amigo*, another listings mag. You'll also find use-ful flyers at the places listed below (for more on gay life, see p.243).

"A" Klub, Milíčova 32, Žižkov; tram #5, #9 or #26. The city's only gay venue where women outnumber men – in fact Friday nights are women-only at the moment. It's small but stylish and defi-nitely worth checking out. *Daily 6pm–6am.*

Borsalino, Husitská 7, Žižkov; metro Florenc. Mixed gay/lesbian disco with a sauna and popular, occasional drag nights. *Mon–Sat noon–late.*

Drake's, Petřínská 5, Smíchov; tram #6, #9 or #12 from metro Anděl. Expensive, almost exclusively male hangout, which bills itself as a "really big cruise facility"; twenty private video booths are the biggest draw. *Open 24 hours a day.*

Fire Club, Seifertova 3, Žižkov; tram #5, #9 or #26. The latest slick dance spot to open, *Fire Club* is hoping to fill the vacuum left when the old Riviera club closed in 1997. *Fri & Sat 9pm–5am.*

G & L Club, Lublaňská 48, Vinohrady; metro I. P. Pavlova. Mixed lesbian/gay crowd at this pretty decent restaurant, which turns into a disco after 10pm. *Daily 8pm–4am.*

Mercury, Kolínská 11, Žižkov; metro Flora. A mixed gay/lesbian crowd enjoy this camp but classy place where you can eat, dance and watch strip shows and drag on the weekend. Occasional lesbian-only nights. *Daily 9pm–6am.*

Tom's Bar, Pernerova 4, Karlín; metro Florenc. Small but popular restaurant and downstairs disco frequented almost exclusively by Czech gay men. *Tues–Sat 7.30pm–3am.*

U dubu, Záhřebská 14, Vinohrady; metro náměstí Míru. Typical, cheap Czech pub with a predominantly gay male clientele. *Daily 6–11pm.*

U Petra Voka, Na bělidle 40, Smíchov; metro Anděl. Pre-1989 mixed gay/kes-bian nightspot that's recently re-opened, and features a disco and drag nights. *Daily 8pm–late.*

U střelce, Karoliny Světlé 12, Staré Město; metro Národní třída. Sweaty cel-lar club whose drag shows pull in a mixed straight/gay crowd. *Mon–Thurs & Sun 6pm–4am, Fri & Sat until 6am.*

Clubs and Live Venues

Rock Café, this place has a long pedigree, but unlike Rock Café it still hosts real low-tech Czech bands – the only problem is they're usually grim. *Open until 1am.*

Jazz

Prague has a surprisingly long indigenous tradition, and is home to a handful of good jazz clubs. With little money to attract acts from abroad, however, the artists are almost exclusively Czech – jazz flautist Jiří Stivín and the Karel Růžička Quartet are both worth catching – and do the entire round of venues each month. The one exception to all this is the annual **international jazz festival** in October, which attracts at least one big name; previous greats have included Wynton Marsalis, B. B. King and Jan Garbarek. More often than not, it's a good idea to book a table at the jazz clubs listed below – this is particularly true of *AghaRTA* and *Reduta*.

AghaRTA Jazz Centrum, Krakovská 5, Nové Město; metro Muzeum; ☎ 24 21 29 14. Probably the best jazz club in Prague, with a good mix of Czechs and foreigners and a consistently good programme of gigs; situated in a side street off the top end of Wenceslas Square. *Daily 7pm–1am.*

Malostranská beseda, Malostranské náměstí 21, Malá Strana; tram #12 or #22 from metro Malostranská; ☎ 53 90 24. Ramshackle inexpensive venue that attracts lots of Czechs, despite its location. The programme is by no means exclusively jazz. *Daily until 1am.*

Metropolitan Jazz Club, Jungmannova 14, Nové Město; metro Můstek; ☎ 24 21 60 25. Small jazz restaurant that tends to stick to a traditional menu, on stage and in the kitchen. *Daily until 1am.*

Reduta, Národní 20, Nové Město; metro Národní třída; ☎ 24 91 22 46. Prague's best-known jazz club – Bill Clinton played his sax here in front of Havel. *Live jazz daily from 9pm.*

U malého Glena, Karmelitská 23, Malá Strana; tram #12 or #22 from metro Malostranská. Tiny downstairs stage is worth checking out for its ecelctic mix of bluegrass, acid jazz, be-bop and blues. Sunday jam sessions start at 6pm; all other gigs begin at 9pm. *Daily 7.30am–3am.*

U staré paní, Michalská 9, Staré Město; metro Můstek; ☎ 26 49 20. Decent jazz restaurant that really gets going when the live music kicks in from 9pm onwards. *Daily 4pm–4am.*

Železná, Železná 16, Staré Město; metro Můstek; ☎ 24 21 25 41. Inexpensive, centrally located cellar venue that puts on a regular live programme of mostly trad jazz bands. *Daily 3pm–1am.*

Chapter 12

The arts

Alongside the city's numerous cafés, pubs and clubs, there's a rich **cultural life** in Prague. Music is everywhere in the city: especially in the summer, when the streets, churches, palaces, opera houses, concert halls and even the gardens are filled with the strains of classical music. True, there are too many Mozart concerts pandering to the tourist trade, but equally there are also some very high-quality chamber concerts. Czech theatre and film are still trying to come to terms with the loss of state subsidies and diminishing audiences – not to mention new freedom of expression. Even if you don't understand Czech, there are theatre performances worth catching – Prague has a strong tradition of mime, "black theatre" and puppetry, and many cinemas show films in their original language. Rock, pop and jazz gigs are covered in the previous chapter.

Tickets

By far the best way to obtain **tickets** is from the box office (*pokladna*) of the venue concerned. In addition, there are several **ticket agencies**, though they tend to cater for foreigners and hike up their prices accordingly. **Ticketpro** sells tickets for most events and has the largest number of branches in the city, including one at Salvátorská 10; BTI (*Bohemia Ticket International*) sells tickets for the big venues only and has several offices, including one at Na příkopě 16. Ticket **prices**, with a few notable

exceptions, are still extremely cheap for westerners (around 300kč for a concert or theatre performance), and absolute peanuts for the cinema (under 100kč). Lastly, don't despair if everything is officially sold out (*vyprodáno*), as stand-by tickets are often available at the venue's box office on the night.

Listings and information

The English-language **listings** in *Prague Post* are selective, but they do at least pick out the events which may be of particular interest to the non-Czech speaker, and list all the major venues and their addresses. Also in English is the monthly handout, *The Arts In Prague*, which, along with the bi-lingual fortnightly listings fold-out *Do města/Downtown* and the Czech monthly listings booklet *Přehled*, are available from any *PIS* office. Any additional **information** you might need can usually be obtained from one of the *PIS* offices around town: at Na příkopě 20, or in the Staroměstská radnice.

Classical Music, Opera and Ballet

Folk songs lie at the heart of Czech music and have found their way into much of the country's **classical music**, of which the Czechs are justifiably proud, having produced four composers of international stature – Dvořák, Janáček, Smetana and Martinů – and, a fifth, Mahler who, though German-speaking, was born in Bohemia. If the music of Mozart appears

The Arts

rather too often in the city's monthly concert programme, it's partly because the tourists love him, but also because of his special relationship with Prague (for more on which see p.74).

The city boasts three large-scale theatres where opera is regularly staged, and has four resident orchestras, the most famous of which are the Czech Philharmonic (*Česká filharmonie*), which is based at the Rudolfinum, and the Czech Symphony Orchestra (*Český symfonický orchestr*), whose home is the Smetanova síň in the Obecní dům. The country has also produced a host of singers, like the late Ema Destinová, and virtuoso violinists, the latest of whom play with the much praised Suk Quartet.

By far the biggest annual event is the *Pražské jaro* (Prague Spring), the country's most prestigious **international music festival**. It traditionally begins on May 12, the anniversary of Smetana's death, with a performance of *Má vlast*, and finishes on June 2 with a rendition of Beethoven's Ninth Symphony. Tickets for the festival sell out fast – try your luck by writing to the Prague Spring Festival box office at Hellichova 18, Malá Strana; *festival@login.cz*. The main venues are listed below, but keep an eye out for concerts in the city's churches and palaces, gardens and courtyards (the main ones are listed separately below); note that evening performances tend to start fairly early, either at 5 or 7pm.

The major venues

Tickets for all three of the city's opera houses can be bought from the official box office at Stavovské divadlo (see below).

Národní divadlo (National Theatre), Národní 2, Nové Město; ☎ 24 91 34 37; metro Národní třída. Prague's grandest nineteenth-century theatre is the living embodiment of the Czech national revival movement, and continues to put on a wide variety of mostly, though by no means exclusively, Czech plays, opera and ballet. Worth visiting for the decor

alone. *Box office Mon–Fri 10am–6pm, Sat & Sun 10am–12.30pm & 3–6pm.*

Státní opera Praha (Prague State Opera), Wilsonova 4, Nové Město; ☎ 24 22 76 93; metro Muzeum. A sumptuous nineteenth-century opera house, built by the city's German community, which once attracted star conductors such as Mahler and Zemlinksy. Now it's the number two venue for opera, with a repertoire that tends to focus on Italian pieces. *Box office Mon–Fri 10am–5.30pm, Sat & Sun 10am–noon & 1–5.30pm.*

Stavovské divadlo (Estates Theatre), Ovocný trh 1, Staré Město; ☎ 24 21 50 01; metro Můstek. Prague's oldest opera house, which witnessed the première of Mozart's *Don Giovanni*, puts on a mixture of opera, ballet and straight theatre (with simultaneous headphone translation available). *Box office Mon–Fri 10am–6pm, Sat & Sun 10am–12.30pm & 3–6pm.*

Concert venues

Anežký klášter (Convent of sv Anežka), U milosrdných 17, Staré Město; ☎ 24 81 08 35; metro náměstí Republiky. Regular Czech chamber concerts, often of the big four Czech composers, are given in the convent's atmospheric Gothic chapel (see p.102).

Basilika sv Jakuba (St James), Malá Štupartská, Staré Město; metro náměstí Republiky. Choral church music, sung mass and Prague's finest organ used for regular recitals (see p.102).

Bertramka, Mozartova 169, Smíchov; ☎ 54 38 93; metro Anděl. Occasional concerts given at the Mozart Museum (see p.174), mostly though not entirely of the composer's own music.

Chrám sv Mikuláše (St Nicholas), Malostranské náměstí, Mala Stráná; metro Malostranská. Prague's most sumptuous Baroque church is the perfect setting for choral concerts and organ recitals (see p.75).

Dům U kamenného zvonu (House at the Stone Bell), Staroměstské náměstí 13, Staré Město; ☎ 24 81 00 36; metro

Staroměstská. An adventurous programme of modern and classical concerts is staged at this contemporary art
gallery, housed in an old building on Old
Town Square (see p.101).

Lichtenštejnský palác (Liechtenstein
Palace), Malostranské náměstí 13, Malá
Strana; metro Malostranská. The university music department lives here and puts
on mostly Baroque music by chamber
orchestras and string quartets.

Lobkovický palác (Lobkovic Palace), Jiřská
3, Hradčany; ☎ 53 73 06; metro
Malostranská. Concerts held in the
palace's main be-frescoed hall at the
eastern edge of Prague Castle (see p.62).

Míčovna, U prašného mostu, Hradčany;
tram #22 from metro Malostranská.
Renaissance ball game court in the
Královská zahrada of Prague Castle (see
p.63).

Nostický palác (Nostitz Palace),
Maltézské náměstí 1, Malá Strana; metro
Malostranská. Chamber concerts here
start at the civilized hour of 8pm, and
include a glass of champagne as part of
the ticket price.

Pražský Hlahol, Masarykovo nábřeží 16,
Nové Město; ☎ 29 34 30; Karlovo
náměstí. Home to the Hlahol Choir, the
hall holds regular concerts on
Wednesday evenings and is decorated
by, among others, the Art Nouveau artist
Alfons Mucha.

Rudolfinum, Alšovo nábřeží 12, Staré
Město; ☎ 24 89 33 52; metro
Staroměstská. A truly stunning Neo-
Renaissance concert hall from the late
nineteenth century, and home base for
the Czech Philharmonic. The Dvořákova
síň is the large hall; the Sukova síň is the
chamber concert hall. *Box office open
Mon–Fri 10am–12.30pm & 1–6pm, plus
Sat & Sun when concerts are scheduled.*

Smetanova síň, Obecní dům, náměstí
Republiky 5, Nové Město; metro náměstí
Republiky. Fantastically ornate and
recently renovated Art Nouveau concert
hall which usually kicks off the Prague
Spring festival, and is home to the excellent Czech Symphony Orchestra.

Valdštejnská zahrada (Valdštejn
Gardens), Letenská, Malá Strana; metro
Malostranská. Probably the finest of the
summer-only outdoor venues
(see p.79).

Zrcadlová kaple, Klementinum,
Mariánské náměstí, Staré Město; metro
Staroměstská. Regular chamber and
organ concerts held in the ornate pink
Baroque Mirrored Chapel (see p.95).

The Arts

Theatre

Theatre has always had a special place
in Czech culture, one which the events
of 1989 only strengthened. Not only did
the country end up with a playwright as
president, but it was the capital's theatres that served as information centres
during those first few crucial weeks.
Nowadays, however, the whole theatre
scene, for so long heavily subsidized –
and censored – by the authorities, is
going through a difficult patch. Czech
audiences have dropped considerably
and tourists have become a lucrative
source of income at a time when
money is desperately needed – there
are several English-language theatre
companies now based in Prague. Ticket
prices have risen dramatically, though
you can still get into most theatres for
less than 250kč; tickets are available
from the venues themselves, or for considerably more from the ticket agencies
listed on p.229.

Prague also has a strong tradition of
mime and **"black light theatre"** (visual
trickery created by "invisible" actors
dressed all in black) ranging from the
classical style of the late Ladislåv Fialka
and his troupe to the more experimental
work of Boris Polívka. However, along
with Prague's long-running multimedia
company, Laterna magika, many of these
shows are deliberately geared towards
tourists, and make for disappointing
viewing. **Puppet theatre** (*loutkové divadlo*) also has a long indigenous tradition,
as an art form for both adults and children, and is currently enjoying something
of a renaissance, thanks to its accessibil-
ity to non-Czech audiences.

The Arts

Unfortunately, this has meant never-ending performances of Mozart's *Don Giovanni* in period costume specifically aimed at passing tourists. At the other end of the spectrum, few companies now maintain the traditional puppets-only set-up, instead featuring live actors in their productions, many of which can be very wordy, making the shows less accessible if you don't speak the language.

Major theatres

The Stavovské divadlo and the Národní divadlo both put on plays as well as opera and ballet, and are listed on p.230. Below is a selection of Prague's other main theatres; the phone numbers given are for box offices.

Činoherní klub, Ve Smečkách 26, Nové Město; ☎96 22 21 23; metro Muzeum. Regularly puts on good repertoire stuff from ancient to modern literary classics. *Box office daily from 3pm.*

Divadlo Kolowrat, Ovocný trh 6, Staré Město; ☎24 21 43 39; metro Můstek. The Národní divadlo puts on its more adventurous productions in its studio theatre, situated in a sweaty attic in a newly renovated Baroque palace. *Box office Mon–Fri 10am–6pm, Sat & Sun 10am–12.30pm & 3–6pm.*

Divadlo na Vinohradech, náměstí Míru 7, Vinohrady; ☎24 25 76 01; metro náměstí Míru. An ornate nineteenth-century theatre that puts on anything from the classics to comedy (in Czech), and even the occasional concert. Best known as the former home stage of Havel's current spouse, Dagmar Veškrnová. *Box office Mon–Sat 10am–7pm.*

Fringe theatre

Archa, Na poříčí 26, Nové Město; ☎232 88 00; metro Florenc. By far the most innovative venue in Prague, with two very versatile spaces, an art gallery and a café. The programming includes music, dance and theatre with an emphasis on the avant-garde. *Box office daily 9am–9pm.*

Divadlo na zábradlí, Anenské náměstí 5, Staré Město; ☎24 22 19 33; metro Staroměstská. Havel's old haunt and a centre of absurdist theatre back in the 1960s, it's still a provocative rep theatre, with a wide variety of shows (in Czech). *Box office Mon–Fri 2–7pm, Sat & Sun 5–7pm.*

Divadlo v Celetné, Celetná 17, Nové Město; ☎24 81 27 62; metro náměstí Republiky. Home of several fringe companies and a student drama venue, which puts on tourist-friendly productions (including puppetry). *Box office Mon–Fri 9am–midnight, Sat & Sun 1pm–midnight.*

Labyrint, Štefánikova 57, Smíchov; ☎54 50 27; metro Anděl. One of Prague's main arty fringe theatres, with an excellent basement studio theatre, which stages English-language productions in the summer months. *Box office Mon–Fri 1–8pm, Sat 1–6pm.*

Studio Ypsilon, Spálená 16, Nové Město; ☎29 22 55; metro Národní třída. One of the city's leading repertoire theatres, with music as well as straight drama (in Czech). *Box office Mon–Thurs 1.30–5.30pm, Fri 1–5pm.*

Black light theatre, dance, musicals and mime

Divadlo U Hasičů, Římská 45, Vinohrady; ☎25 51 41; metro náměstí Míru. This is *the* place to catch traditional Czech folk songs and dancing. *Box office Mon–Fri 10am–1pm & 3–8pm.*

Divadlo Spirála, Výstaviště, Holešovice; ☎20 10 32 14; tram #5, #12 or #17 from nádraží Holešovice. Spectacular 360-degree theatre that puts on suitably stagey shows (mostly musicals). *Box office Mon–Fri 8am–8pm, Sat 1–8pm, Sun 1–4pm.*

Hudební divadlo v Karlíně, Křižíkova 10, Karlín; ☎24 21 07 10; metro Florenc. Puts on a wide range of musicals and operettas, plus mime and the like in its studio. *Box office Mon–Sat 10am–1pm & 2–6pm.*

Laterna magika (Magic Lantern), Nová scéna, Národní 4, Nové Město; ☎24 91

41 29; metro Národní třída. The National Theatre's *Nová scéna*, one of Prague's most modern and versatile stages, is now the main base for Laterna magika, founders of multimedia theatre way back in 1958, now content just to pull in crowds of tourists. *Box office Mon–Fri 10am–8pm, Sat & Sun 3–8pm.*

Ta Fantastika, Karlova 8, Staré Město; ☎ 24 22 90 78; metro Staroměstská. Probably the best of the "black theatre" venues, albeit strategically located close to the Charles Bridge, offering dialogue-free shows specifically aimed at tourists. *Box office daily 11am–9pm.*

Puppet theatre

Divadlo minor, Senovážné náměstí 28, Nové Město; ☎ 24 21 96 75; metro náměstí Republiky. The former state puppet theatre puts on children's puppet shows most days, plus adult shows on occasional evenings – sometimes with English subtitles. *Box office open Mon–Fri 2–5pm and one hour before performance.*

Divadlo Spejbla a Hurvínka, Dejvická 38, Dejvice; ☎ 32 33 51; metro Dejvická/Hradčanská. Features the indomitable puppet duo, Spejbl and Hurvínek, created by Josef Skupa earlier this century and still going strong at one of the few puppets-only theatres in the country. *Box office Wed–Fri 3–6pm, Sat & Sun 1–5pm.*

Mezinárodní institut loutkárského umení (UNIMA), Karlova 12, Staré Město; ☎ 26 93 83; metro Staroměstská. A mouthful of an organization, Prague is UNIMA's international headquarters so the productions staged at their centrally located Divadlo na královské cestě should by rights be brilliant. *Box office open one hour before performance.*

Národní divadlo marionet (National Marionette Theatre), Žatecká 1, Staré Město; ☎ 232 34 29; metro Staroměstská. This company's traditional all-string marionette version of Mozart's *Don Giovanni* has proved extremely popular and has been running without a break for several years now, but they

also put on regular kids' shows at the weekends. *Box office open one hour before performance.*

Film

As with the theatre, **cinema** (*kino*) attendances have been going down dramatically over the last few years. The advent of video machines, more TV stations and steadily rising ticket prices are to blame for the most part. Nevertheless, the cinema remains a relatively cheap and popular form of entertainment, and although Hollywood blockbusters form a large part of the weekly fare, the Czech film industry is enjoying something a renaissance, with the likes of Jan Svěrák's *Kolja* winning an Oscar in 1997 (for more on Czech film, see p.268).

Hollywood films do tend to be shown dubbed, but there's usually at least one cinema where films are shown in their original language with subtitles (*titulky*). And thanks to Prague's large ex-pat community, some Czech films are occasionally shown with English subtitles – these are all listed in *Prague Post*, but for a comprehensive rundown of the week's films, check out the bi-lingual *Do města/Downtown*. Film titles are nearly always translated into Czech, so you'll need to have your wits about you to identify films such as *Umělcova smlouva* as *The Draughtsman's Contract.*

The city's main **cinemas** are concentrated around Wenceslas Square, while the list below is confined to the more interesting screens, plus Prague's art house film clubs, where you may need to buy a membership card (*legitimace*) in order to purchase tickets. Keep a look out, too, for films shown at the various foreign cultural institutions around town (see p.244 for addresses), and for the summer-only open-air *letní kina* which is held on the Střelecký ostrov and in Výstaviště. The city's **international film festival**, which takes place in June, has failed to dislodge Karlovy Vary's annual bash as the country's leading film festival. More interesting is the newly established annual **independent film festival**,

The Arts

The Arts

Prague Indies, which was held for the first time in mid-November 1997.

Broadway, Na příkopě 31, Nové Město; ☎21 61 32 78; metro náměstí Republiky. The second largest screen in the city, and the best sound system, Broadway is the most central of Prague's newly refurbished cinemas and shows mainstream films.

Dlabačov, Bělohorská 24, Břevnov; ☎311 53 28; tram #22 from metro Malostranská. Film club (membership 20kč) on the ground floor of the Hotel Pyramid, showing a discerning selection of new releases and plenty of other art house classics.

Illusion, Vinohradská 48, Vinohrady; ☎25 02 60; metro náměstí Míru. A regular programme of old Czech movies, though sadly without English subtitles.

Jalta, Václavské náměstí 43, Nové Město; ☎24 22 88 14; metro Můstek. Two screens here, including the only *kinokavárna* left in Prague, where you can have a drink and smoke while watching the film.

Lucerna, Vodičkova 36, Nové Město; ☎24 21 69 72; metro Můstek. Without doubt the most ornate film theatre in Prague, decked out in Moorish style by Havel's grandfather.

MAT, Karlovo náměstí 19, Nové Město; ☎24 91 57 65; metro Karlovo náměstí. Café and cinema popular with the film crowd, with an eclectic programme of shorts, documentaries and full-length features.

Multikino Galaxie, Arkalycká 874, Háje; ☎96 14 14 14; metro Háje. Prague's first-ever multiplex, boasting eight screens – including the city's largest – is located deep in the high-rise suburbs at the end of the metro line. Nevertheless, it is incredibly popular.

Ponrepo, Bartolomějská 11, Staré Město; metro Národní třída. Really old classics from the black-and-white era, dug out from the National Film Archives. Membership cards (120kč) can only be bought Mon–Fri 2–5pm.

Pražský filmový klub, Václavské náměstí 17, Nové Město; ☎26 20 35; metro Můstek. *Kino Praha* runs a very popular film club (membership 30kč) in its second screen, showing some seriously offbeat and unusual material from the archives.

The Visual Arts

The Národní galerie (National Gallery) runs the city's main **permanent art collections**, each of which is described in detail in the guide section. Most of these galleries also give over space for **temporary exhibitions**, and there are several which only ever stage special exhibitions. *Prague Post* has selective listings, and there's a list of foreign cultural institutes, which also put on regular exhibitions, on p.244, but as ever you'll find the fullest listings in the Czech monthly listings magazine *Přehled*. After years of fairly dull state-approved art, there have been some illuminating and challenging exhibitions in recent years: on previously ignored topics such as Czech Cubism, on relatively "undiscovered" artists such as Josef Váchal, on artists such as Jiří Kolář, who are better known in the West than in their own country, and even reappraisals of socialist realism and the like. Dozens of **commercial galleries** have also sprung up, only a handful of which can be relied on regularly to show interesting stuff; below is a selection of the best (the "galerie a výstavy" section of *Přehled* will have a full rundown).

Exhibitions spaces

Belvedér, Mariánské hradby 1, Hradčany; tram #22 from metro Malostranská. One of the most beautiful Renaissance buildings in Prague (see p.63), which usually shows works by contemporary artists. *Tues–Sun 10am–6pm.*

České muzeum výtvarných umění (Museum of Czech Fine Art), Husova 19–21, Staré Město; metro Staroměstská. Showcases retrospectives of twentieth-century Czech and foreign artists. *Tues–Sun 10am–noon & 1–6pm.*

Císařská konírna (Imperial Stables), druhé nádvoří, Hradčany; tram #22 from Malostranská. Temporary exhibition space in Rudolf II's stables, situated in the second courtyard of Prague Castle. *Tues–Sun 10am–6pm.*

Dům U černé Matky boží, Celetná 34, Staré Město; metro náměstí Republiky. First two floors of this Cubist museum are given over to exhibitions of twentieth-century Czech artists. *Tues–Sun 10am–6pm.*

Dům U kamenného zvonu, Staroměstské náměstí 13, Staré Město; metro Staroměstská. A real range from Baroque to avant-garde sees the light of day in the small Gothic rooms and courtyard of this ancient building (see p.99). *Tues–Sun 10am–6pm.*

Galerie Hollar, Smetanovo nábřeží 6, Nové Město; metro Národní třída. The main exhibition space for Czech graphic artists is situated on the noisy river embankment, but there are plenty of old prints for sale. *Tues–Sun 10am–1pm & 2–6pm.*

Galerie Jaroslav Fragnera, Betlémské náměstí 5a, Staré Město; metro Národní třída. Gallery space next door to the Betlémská kaple used for architectural exhibitions. *Tues–Sun 10am–6pm.*

Jízdárna pražkého hradu (Prague Castle Riding School), U prašného mostu, Hradčany; tram #22 from Malostranská. One of the Národní galerie's main temporary exhibition spaces, often used to display twentieth-century Czech art. *Tues–Sun 10am–6pm.*

Karolinum, Ovocný trh 3, Staré Město; metro Můstek. Gothic vaulted room in Prague's Charles University which puts on shows by Czech and foreign artists. *Tues–Sun 10am–6pm.*

Mánes, Masarykovo nábřeží 250, Nové Město; metro Karlovo náměstí. White functionalist building spanning a channel in the Vltava, with an open-plan gallery and a tradition of excellent exhibitions. *Tues–Sun 10am–6pm.*

Městská knihovna, Mariánské náměstí 1, Staré Město; metro Staroměstská. Slightly off the Staré Město beaten track, exhibitions at the Municipal Library's gallery space are usually devoted to Czech artists and are well worth checking out. *Tues–Sun 10am–6pm.*

Palác Goltz-Kinských (Goltz-Kinsky Palace), Staroměstské náměstí 12, Staré Město; metro Staroměstská. Prints and drawings from the Národní galerie's collection. *Tues–Sun 10am–6pm.*

Rudolfinum, Alšovo nábřeží 12, Staré Město; metro Staroměstská. One of the few galleries in Prague which can take large-scale international exhibitions. *Tues–Sun 10am–6pm.*

UPM, 17 listopadu 2, Staré Město; metro Staroměstská. The UPM, the city's museum of applied art (see p.120), owns some of the finest Czech art in the world, much of which is hidden away in the vaults due to lack of space – be sure to catch their generally excellent temporary exhibitions. *Tues–Sun 10am–6pm.*

Valdštejnská jízdárna, Valdštejnská 3, Malá Strana; metro Malostranská. Another Národní galerie's exhibitions space. *Tues–Sun 10am–6pm.*

Veletržní palác, Dukelských hrdinů 47, Holešovice; tram #5, #12 or #17. Prague's vast new modern art museum puts on excellent temporary exhibitions and retrospectives in its first-floor galleries (see p.164). *Tues–Sun 10am–6pm, Thurs until 9pm.*

Commercial galleries

Galerie Behémot, Elišky Krásnohorské 6, Josefov; metro Staroměstská. Avant-garde installations by up-and-coming Czech and Slovak contemporary artists. *Tues–Sun 1–7pm.*

Galerie jednorožec s harfou, Průchodní 4, Staré Město; metro Národní třída. The "Unicorn with a Harp" gallery is located in an alleyway off Konviktská, and showcases works in a variety of media by contemporary disabled artists. *Daily 11am–10pm.*

Galerie mladých, Vodičkova 10, Nové Město; metro Můstek. Artists' co-op, which displays works by contemporary

The Arts

The Arts

young Czech artists under Gothic vaults. *Tues–Sun 10am–1pm & 2–6pm.*

Galerie MXM, Nosticova 6, Malá Strana; metro Malostranská. Prague's pioneering and highly influential private gallery puts on consistently good shows by contemporary Czech artists in its one, small vaulted room. *Tues–Sun noon–7pm.*

Galerie Pallas, Ungelt – Týn 1, Staré Město; metro Staroměstská. The gem of Prague's private galleries, hidden in the courtyard behind the Týn church, with works by all the greats of the Czech modern art movements of the twentieth century: Alfons Mucha, Cubists Emil Filla and Bohumil Kubišta, plus contemporary artists' works. *Mon–Sat 10am–6pm.*

Galerie Petra Brandla, Na slupi 17, Nové Město; metro Vyšehrad. This is where the country's recently returned aristocrats sell off the family silver, or in this case, their Czech and foreign masters – anything from Monet to Mucha – to raise a bit of capital. *Mon 1–6pm, Tues–Fri 10am–noon & 1–6pm.*

Galerie Rob van den Doel, Jánský vršek 15, Malá Strana; metro Malostranská. Art gallery, situated just off Nerudova, devoted to glass-making, for which the Czechs have an enviable reputation. *Tues–Sun 10.30am–5.30pm.*

Gambra-surrealisticka galerie, Černínská 5, Hradčany; tram #22 from metro Malostranská. The gallery of Prague's small, but persistent surrealist movement,

past and present, hidden in the enchanted backstreets of Hradčany, also provides a window for the works of animator extraordinaire, Jan Švankmajer, and his wife, the artist Eva Švankmajerová. *Wed–Sun noon–6pm.*

Středoevropská galerie, Husova 10 & 21, Staré Město; metro Staroměstská. Czech and foreign artists' works are exhibited in two separate galleries: one, at no. 10, focuses on graphic works, while the other, at no. 21, concentrates on oil paintings. *Daily 10am–6pm.*

Photographic galleries

Galerie Josefa Sudka, Úvoz 24, Malá Strana; metro Malostranská. Confusingly there are now two photography galleries named after the father of the modern Czech art form – this one's the only photo space on the left bank. *Tues–Sun 10am–noon & 1–6pm.*

Komorní galerie domu fotografie Josefa Sudka, Maiselova 2 & U Radnice 5, Staré Město; metro Staroměstská. There are two bits to this gallery: the exhibition space is on Maiselova 2, while the commercial section, where you can buy stuff, is at U Radnice 5. *Tues–Sun 10am–7pm.*

Pražský dům fotografie, U radnice 14, Staré Město; metro Staroměstská. Prague's oldest established photographic gallery enjoys a prime location on the corner of Staroměstské náměstí. *Daily 11am–6pm.*

Chapter 13

Sports

The Czech Republic is equally famous for its world-class tennis players, its national football squad and its ice hockey players; however the sport which pulls the biggest crowds, by far, is soccer. Getting tickets to watch a particular sport is easy (and cheap) enough on the day – even big matches rarely sell out. If you want to check forthcoming sports events, read the sports pages in *Prague Post*, or ask at a *PIS* office. Participating in sports activities is more difficult – Czechs who do so all belong to local clubs and rental facilities for the general public are only slowly beginning to become established.

Spectator Sports

Prague is a great place to catch live and exciting sports action, especially soccer and ice hockey; and, somewhat unbelievably, you can still drink inexpensive and delicious beer on the terraces.

Soccer

The break-up of Czechoslovakia may have cut transport costs for clubs in half, but it has had nothing but a detrimental effect on the quality of the country's football league since the Czechoslovak league divided in the summer of 1993. The most predictable development is that the best home-grown players have, almost without exception, chosen to seek fame and fortune abroad. Another small tragedy is that the old army team, Dukla Praha – immortalized in the pop

song *All I Want for Christmas is a Dukla Prague Away-Kit* by British band Half Man Half Biscuit – has been forced to leave the capital, and is now based some 60km southwest in the town of Příbram.

For years cosseted by state backing, all the county's clubs are having to learn fast how to survive in the market. Big money has been pumped into certain clubs by local entrepreneurs, accompanied by a predictable dose of curruption scandals and wrangling over TV rights. Nevertheless, true to form, the most consistent teams in the *Českomoravská liga*, are still Sparta Praha and Slavia Praha. The season runs from August to late November and late February to early June, and matches are usually held on Sundays.

The most successful club in the country is **Sparta Praha**, who have won eight league titles in the last ten years, and look set to maintain their hold over Czech football for some time to come. That said, in 1996, they had to endure the embarassment of being saved from bankrupty by their current owners, Slovak steelworks VSŽ Košice. They play at the country's finest, and newly renovated, Sparta stadium, by the Letná plain (five minutes' walk from metro Hradčanská); international matches are also regularly played there. Sparta's closest rivals, **Slavia Praha**, majority-owned by a British investment firm, finally won the league title in 1996, for the first time in nearly fifty years; their ground is in Vršovice, just off U Slavie (tram #4 or

Sports

#22 from metro náměstí Míru). **Viktoria Žižkov**, a previously little-known club, enjoyed a brief period of glory in the mid-1990s, winning the Czech cup in 1994, thanks to self-made man, Vratislav Čekan, but those halcyon days came to an abrupt halt when Čekan pulled out in 1996 after a financial scandal. Viktoria's ground is on Seifertova (tram #5, #9 or #26 from metro Hlavní nádraží). Prague's least successful professional side, **Bohemians**, were relegated to the second division in 1997; they play just south of Vršovické náměstí (tram #4 or #22 from metro náměstí Míru).

Ice hockey

Ice hockey runs soccer a close second as the nation's most popular sport. It's not unusual to see kids playing their own form of the game in the street, rather than kicking a football around. As with soccer, the fall of communism prompted an exodus by the country's best players who left to seek fame and fortune in North America's National Hockey League (NHL). One of the NHL's top scorers, Jaromír Jágr, who currently plays for the Pittsburgh Penguins, is by far the most famous Czech player. In 1998, the Czech national team surprised everyone by taking the gold medal in the Winter Olympics.

Games are fast and physical, make for cold but compelling viewing, and can take anything up to three hours; they take place at the weekend. The season starts at the end of September and culminates in the annual World Championships the following summer, when the fortunes of the national side are subject to close scrutiny, especially if pitched against the old enemy Russia, not to mention their former bed-mate and new rival, Slovakia. A double victory against the Soviets in 1969 precipitated riots in towns across the country, culminating in the torching of the Soviet airline Aeroflot's offices in Prague.

Unlike in football, **Sparta Praha** are only one of a number of successful teams, and the *Extraliga* is usually hotly contested. Sparta's *zimní stadión* (winter stadium) is next door to the Výstaviště exhibition grounds in Holešovice (metro nádraží Holešovice). Prague's only other first division team are **Slavia Praha**, who play at the *zimní stadión* to the south of the Havlíčkovy sady in Vršovice (tram #4 or #22 from metro náměstí Míru).

Tennis

Tennis has been one of the country's most successful exports, although with both Martina Navrátilová and Ivan Lendl now retired, the glory days of Czech tennis may well be over, despite the valiant efforts of Jana Novotná and Petr Korda. (Contrary to what you might read in the western press, the Swiss player and top seed Martina Hingis is of Slovak, not Czech, descent). Any home-grown talent there is will be on domestic display only in the Škoda Czech Open, the country's only ATP event, held every August on Prague's Štvanice ostrov, the island on the Hlávkův most (metro Florenc).

Horse racing

Prague's main racecourse is at **Velká Chuchle**, 5km or so south of the city centre; bus #129, #172, #241, #244, or *osobní* train from metro Smíchovské nádraží. Steeplechases and hurdles take place on Sunday afternoons from May to October; trots all year round on Thursdays. There's a smaller trot course on **Císařský ostrov** (May–Oct only); walk through the Stromovka park and across the river to the island from metro Nádraží Holešovice.

Participatory Sports

At present there isn't a great deal to choose from, but the situation is improving; the big drawback remains the lack of facilities for renting equipment. However, anyone keen on working out will have no problems as there are now numerous public gyms.

Swimming

The waters of the Vltava, Beroun and Labe are all pretty polluted – the Sázava is marginally better – so for a clean swim it's best to head for one of the city's swimming pools, though these, too, can be of varying water quality.

Hotel Axa, Na poříčí 40, Nové Město; metro Florenc. Has a 25-metre indoor pool – the oldest and largest of the hotel pools in Prague. *Mon–Fri 7am–10pm, Sat & Sun 9am–6pm.*

Koupaliště Divoká Šárka, Divoká Šárka, Vokovice; tram #20 or #26 from metro Dejvická. Idyllically located in a craggy valley to the northwest of Prague, with two small oudoor pools filled with cold but fresh and clean water – great for a full, hot day out. Food and drink and plenty of shade available, too. *Daily 9am–7pm.*

Koupaliště Oáza, Novodvorská, Lhotka; bus #106, #121, #139 or #170 from metro Kačerov. Deep pool with sandy borders set in a park; wading pool and bouncy castle for children. Food, beer and ice cream available. *Daily 9am–7pm.*

Plavecký stadión Podolí, Podolská, Podolí; tram #3, #17 or #21 from metro Karlovo náměstí, stop Kublov. Well-heated fifty-metre indoor pool, plus two smaller outdoor ones and a children's wading pool and water slide. *Mon–Fri 6am–9.45pm, Sat & Sun 8am–7.45pm.*

Plavecký stadión Slavia, Vladivostocká 2, Vršovice; tram #7 from metro Strašnická. Clean, indoor pool in winter; outdoor only in summer. *Mon–Fri 6–8am & 6–8pm, Sat & Sun 9am–7pm.*

Ice skating

Given the nation's penchant for ice hockey, it's not surprising that **ice skating** (*bruslení*) is Prague's most popular winter activity. There's no shortage of rinks (*zimní stadión*) in the city, although public opening hours are limited, and of course there are the city's two reservoirs, Hostivář and Šárka, which regularly freeze over in winter. Most rinks don't rent out skates, and those that do have only a limited selection. Your best bet is to buy a pair from shops like Bílá labuť

or Sport YMCA, both on Na poříčí, Nové Město (metro Florenc); men's skates tend to be for ice hockey, women's for figure skating – either will set you back around £25/$40.

Nikolajka, U Nikolajky 28, Smíchov; metro Anděl. Located just below the Havlíčkovy sady, with long weekend opening hours but no skate rental. *Fri 8am–10pm, Sat & Sun 1–3.30pm.*

Štvanice, Štvanice ostrov, Holešovice; five-minute walk on to the island from metro Florenc. Skate rental is available but the rink is only open to the public for a very limited period. *Fri 7.30–10pm, Sat 1–3.30pm, Sun 8.30–11am.*

Výstaviště, U Výstaviště, Holešovice; metro Nádraží Holešovice. Skating takes place in the *malá hala* behind the big ice hockey stadium; rental is from the basement. *Sat & Sun 1–3.30pm.*

Sports

Gyms and saunas

There's no shortage of fitness centres and hotels in Prague with good gyms, saunas and masseurs. Rates are generally very low compared to the West, but hours are erratic so check before you go.

Body & Fitness Club, Bolzanova 7, Nové Město; ☎ 24 22 73 96; metro Hlavní nádraží. Small weight-training gym with modern equipment and air-conditioning; massage is also available. *Mon–Fri 10am–10pm, Sat 10am–3pm, Sun 9am–6pm.*

Cardiofitness (Hotel Axa), Na poříčí 40, Nové Město; ☎ 232 93 59; metro Florenc. Very reasonably priced gym, sauna, first-rate massage and 25-metre indoor pool (see above for swimming times). *Gym Mon–Fri 7am–10pm, Sat & Sun 9am–6pm; sauna daily 2–9pm.*

Hotel Forum Fitness, Kongresová 4, Nusle; ☎ 61 19 13 26; metro Vyšehrad. Pool, sauna, weights, solarium and massage – pricey, but luxurious, with an amazing view over Prague. *Mon–Fri 7am–10pm, Sat & Sun 9am–6pm.*

Chapter 14

Shopping

Despite enormous improvements over the past few years, service in Prague's shops is still surly, and the variety and quality of a lot of the goods suspect. The few bargains that still exist are in goods like glass, ceramics, wooden toys, cutlery, CDs, cassettes, LPs and books and, of course, smoked meats, salamis and alcohol, all of which the Czechs continue to produce at a fraction of western prices. If it's multinational goods you want, then you should encounter few problems, all the big players from Body Shop to DKNY have branches here in Prague, charging prices that are roughly the same as in the EU.

Department stores

For most basic goods, you're best off heading for a department store (*obchodní dům*), which will stock most things – including toiletries, stationery and usually an extensive food and drink selection. The prices are low, but so, often, is the quality.

Bílá labuť, Na poříčí 23, Nové Město; metro Florenc. Built in the 1930s, when its functionalist design turned more than a few heads, but nowadays in need of serious renovation. *Mon–Fri 8am–7pm, Sat 8am–6pm.*

Kotva, náměstí Republiky 8, Nové Město; metro náměstí Republiky. Ugly, Swedish-built store, spread over five floors, with a food section in the basement. *Mon–Wed & Fri 9am–7pm, Thurs 8am–8pm, Sat 9am–4pm.*

Tesco, Národní 26, Nové Město; metro Národní třída. Neo-functionalist store on four floors, selling everything from food to hi-fi goods, that bears absolutely no resemblence to its British supermarket namesake, beyond its neon sign. *Mon–Wed 8am–7pm, Thurs & Fri 8am–8pm, Sat 9am–6pm, Sun 10am–5pm.*

Markets and food stores

Prague is chronically short of good **markets** of all types, despite the introduction of free enterprise. For bread, butter, cheese, wine and beer, you should simply go to the nearest *potraviny* or supermarket. These have changed enormously since 1989 in terms of what they stock, but are still a long way from the superstores of the western world. Again, low prices are the main draw. For health-food-starved visitors, a few outlets now stock some basic items, as listed below.

Markets

Havelská, Staré Město; metro Můstek. Food, flowers and wooden toys are sold in the only open-air fruit and veg market in central Prague. *Mon–Fri 8am–6pm, Sat & Sun 8am–1pm.*

Pražská tržnice, Bubenské nábřeží, Holešovice; metro Vltavská. Prague's largest market, a sprawling mass of cheap stalls housed in a disused abattoir. *Mon–Fri 8am–6pm, Sat 8am–2pm.*

Specialist food stores

Buongiorno Italia, Soukenická 4, Nové Město; metro náměstí Republiky. Great little Italian deli that does *frittata* sandwiches, too. *Mon–Sat 9am–9pm.*

Country Life, Melantrichova 15, Staré Město; metro Můstek. All the health food staples from dried bananas to seaweed, plus freshly baked wholemeal bread. *Mon–Thurs 8.30am–6pm, Fri 8.30am–3.30pm, Sun 1–5pm.*

Dům lahůdek, Malé náměstí 3, Staré Město; metro Staroměstská. Prague's number one deli spread over several floors; the smoked fish and caviar section is particularly good. *Mon–Sat 9am–7.30pm, Sun 10am–6pm.*

Fruits de France, Jindřišská 9, Nové Město; metro Můstek. Unusually good selection of fruit and vegetables, plus various other longer-lasting delights flown in fresh from France. *Mon–Wed & Fri 9.30am–6pm, Thurs 11.30am–6.30pm, Sat 9.30am–1pm.*

Moby Dick, Zborovská 49, Smíchov; tram #6, #9 or #22. Fresh fish and seafood arrives from Belgium on Wednesdays at this fishmongers. *Mon & Wed–Sat 10.30am–7pm.*

Books, maps and graphics

Prague is now home to numerous English-language bookstores (*knihkupectví*), which thrive on the large ex-pat community. The city is also replete with second-hand bookstores (*antikvariát*), though these are often pricey antiquarian-type places rather than cheap, rambling stores; however, many also stock a good selection of old prints and posters.

Big Ben Book Shop, Malá Štupartská 5, Staré Město; metro náměstí Republiky. Bookstore that specializes in TEFL material, but also stocks cheap paperbacks, too. *Mon–Fri 9am–6pm, Sat 10am–5pm.*

Bohemian Ventures, náměstí Jana Palacha 2, Staré Město; metro Staroměstská. Located on the ground

floor of the university's philosophy faculty, this shop specializes in new English-language books, including cheap Penguin classics and heaps of dictionaries. *Mon–Fri 9am–5pm.*

Dušní, Dušní 6, Staré Město; metro Staroměstská. *Antikvariát* with big selection of second-hand Czech, German, French and English books. *Mon–Fri 10am–6pm, Sat 10am–1pm.*

The Globe, Janovského 14, Holešovice; tram #5 or #26 from metro náměstí Republiky. The ex-pat bookstore *par excellence*: both a social centre and superbly well-stocked ramshackle store, with an adjacent café and friendly staff. *Daily 10am–midnight.*

Judaica, Široká 7, Staré Město; metro Staroměstská. Probably the best-stocked of all the places flogging Jewish books to passing tourists, with books and prints, second-hand and new. *Mon–Fri 10am–6pm.*

Karel Křenek, Celetná 31, Staré Město; metro náměstí Republiky. High-quality second-hand and antiquarian dealer, with a handful of English books, and lots of old maps, graphics and art books. *Open Mon–Fri 10am–noon & 2–6pm, Sat 10am–2pm.*

U knihomola (The Bookworm), Mánesova 79, Vinohrady; metro Jiřího z Poděbrad. Much larger selection of art and coffee-table books and a classier range all round, than its rival, The Globe. The café in the basement is quiet and relaxed. *Mon–Thurs 10am–11pm, Fri & Sat 10am–midnight, Sun 11am–8pm.*

Music

Czech CDs are no longer the bargain they once were, though they are still priced a tad lower than in the West; cassettes and LPs are significantly cheaper. Classical buffs will fare best of all, not just with the Czech composers, but with cheap copies of Mozart, Vivaldi and other favourites on sale at just about every street corner.

Bonton Megastore, palác Koruna, Václavské náměstí 1; metro Můstek.

Shopping

Shopping

Prague's biggest record store in the newly renovated *pasáž* at the bottom of Wenceslas Square, with rock, folk, jazz and classical, and headphones for previews to boot. *Mon–Fri 9am–8pm, Sat & Sun 10am–7pm.*

Karel Schuss, Národní 25, Nové Město; metro Národní třída. The best second-hand record store in Prague, particularly good for jazz and folk, but also rock/pop – not much in the way of classical. *Mon–Sat 11.30am–7.30pm.*

Maximum Underground, Jilská 22, Staré Město; metro Staroměstská. The best indie record shop in town, very strong on new wave and punk, and even some ragga, rave and world music. *Mon–Sat 11am–7.30pm.*

Popron, Jungmannova 30, Nové Město; metro Můstek. Calls itself a "megastore", though it's nowhere near as big as Bonton's store – strongest on pop and rock CDs, though it does stock jazz and classical (not to mention video games). *Mon–Sat 9.30am–7pm, Sun 10am–6pm.*

Supraphon, Jungmannova 20, Nové Město; metro Můstek. Pretty good selection of classical CDs, cassettes and even LPs. *Mon–Fri 9am–7pm, Sat 9am–1pm.*

Souvenirs, toys and antiques

Tacky tourist gifts – Kafka T-shirts, Mucha merchandise and Gorby/Yeltsin matrioshka dolls – are mostly sold from market stalls set up along the main tourist thoroughfares. For better quality goods and more specialist gifts, try some of the shops listed below.

Amor, Václavské náměstí 40, Nové Město; metro Muzeum. Czech garnets are among the best in the world, and this shop has some unusually interesting pendants and brooches. *Mon–Fri 9am–8pm, Sat & Sun 9am–6pm.*

Antikva Nova Praga, Štěpánská 24, Nové Město; metro Muzeum. Lithographs, drawings, acrylic and oil paintings mostly by Czech artists. *Mon–Fri 10am–1pm & 2–6pm.*

Art Deco Galerie, Michalská 21, Staré Město; metro Můstek. Clothes, shoes, coffee sets, lamps and accessories, all dating from the turn of the century or between the wars (at a price). *Mon–Fri 2–7pm.*

Česká lidová řemesla, Karlova 12 & 26, Staré Město; metro Staroměstská. It's impossible to miss this chain of shops as they've got a branch on just about every main tourist thoroughfare in Prague. Each one stocks wooden toys and Czech folk art from painted eggshells and linen to straw and corn dolls. *Daily 10am–6pm.*

Keramika, Václavské náměstí 60, Nové Město; metro Muzeum. All kinds of glazed pottery cups, mugs and bowls at reasonable prices. *Mon–Fri 10am–7pm, Sat 10am–4pm.*

Manhartský dům, Celetná 12, Staré Město; metro náměstí Republiky. Performance-quality marionettes at high prices. *Daily 10am–6pm.*

Moser, Na příkopě 12, Nové Město; metro Můstek. The most famous glass and crystal manufacturers in the country – however, you won't find many bargains here (or anywhere else in Prague). *Mon–Fri 9am–7pm, Sat 9am–4pm.*

Sparta Praha, Betlémské náměstí 7, Staré Město; metro Národní třída. Everything from a Sparta Praha shirt to an ashtray, and even some Slavia souvenirs, too. *Mon–Thurs 10am–5pm, Fri 10am–4pm.*

Zerba, Vodičkova 37, Nové Město; metro Můstek. Come here for your Czech trams, trains and wind-up metal toys. *Mon–Fri 10am–6pm, Sat 9am–2pm.*

Chapter 15

Directory

AIRLINES British Airways, Staroměstské náměstí 10, Staré Město; ☎ 24 81 37 28; metro Staroměstská. British Midland, Washingtonova 17, Nové Město; ☎ 24 23 92 80; metro Muzeum. **Czechoslovak Airlines**, V celnici 5, Nové Město; ☎ 20 10 41 11; metro náměstí Republiky. **Delta**, Národní 32, Nové Město; ☎ 26 82 51; metro Národní třída. **KLM**, Václavské náměstí 37, Nové Město; ☎ 24 22 96 78; metro Můstek/Muzeum. **Lufthansa**, Pařížská 28, Staré Město; ☎ 24 81 10 07; metro Staroměstská.

AMERICAN EXPRESS Amex, Václavské náměstí 56, Nové Město; ☎ 24 22 98 83; metro Muzeum. Mon–Fri 9am–6pm, Sat 9am–noon; slightly longer hours in summer (exchange office open daily in the summer).

BOTTLES The Czech Republic has yet to become a fully paid-up member of the throwaway culture and many drinks still come in glass bottles with a deposit on them. For non-deposit bottles, or if you simply can't be bothered to retrieve the deposit, there are now numerous bottle banks scattered around Prague.

CHILDREN The Czech attitude to kids is generally very positive. That said, you'll see few Czech babies out in the open, unless snuggled up in their giant old-fashioned perambulators, and almost no children in pubs, cafés or even most restaurants. Czechs generally expect children to be unreasonably well behaved and respectful to their elders,

and many of the older generation may frown at over-boisterous behaviour. Nevertheless, most kids will enjoy Prague, with its hilly cobbled streets and trams, especially in the summer, when the place is positively alive with buskers and street performers. The obvious attractions for children are the Petřín hill, with its funicular and mirror maze (see p.84); the Zoo (see p.169); the Národní technické muzeum (see p.163); and the MHD Muzeum, a short walk west of Hradcany at Patočkova 4, (April–Oct Sat & Sun 9am–5pm), which houses a collection of historic trams and trolleybuses; take tram #1 or #8 from metro Hradčanská. Another year-round option is to hop aboard the regular tram #22, as it goes round some great hairpins, across the river and past a fair few city landmarks. In the summer a historic tram (#91) also criss-crosses the city; tickets are slightly more expensive than normal and they run less frequently.

CIGARETTES Loosely packed and lethal, the only virtue of Czech cigarettes is their cheapness. Top of the domestic range is **sparta**, named after the country's leading soccer team. The workers smoke Mars or Start, while the rest smoke Petra. Havel switched from the latter to Marlboro once he became president and has since given up. Duma rolling tobacco is widely available; domestic brands and their cigarette papers are worth avoiding. Matches are *zápalky*.

Directory

CONTRACEPTIVES Condoms (*kondom* or *prezervativ*) are now available in metro stations in the centre of Prague from machines marked *Men's Shop, Easy Shop* or some such euphemism. They're also on sale from pharmacies.

CULTURAL INSTITUTES

American Center for Culture and Commerce, Hybernská 7a, Nové Město; ☎ 24 23 10 85; metro náměstí Republiky. Exhibitions and video showings, plus an excellent library with books, papers and magazines. *Exhibitions Mon–Fri 9am–4.30pm; library Mon, Tues & Thurs 11am–5pm, Wed noon–5pm, Fri 11am–3pm.*

Austrian Cultural Institute (Rakouský kulturní institut), Jungmannovo náměstí 18, Nové Město; ☎ 24 23 48 75; metro Můstek. Very good exhibitions of Austrian art, plus the odd concert, film and talk. *Gallery Mon–Fri 10am–5pm; library Mon–Fri 10am–1pm & 2–4pm.*

British Council (Britská rada), Národní 10, Nové Město; ☎ 24 91 21 79; metro Národní třída. A window gallery for temporary exhibitions; newspapers and magazines in the foyer and the top-floor reading room; Sky TV in the auditorium and various films, concerts and events during the year. There's an English-language teaching library and resources centre in the basement. *Mon–Fri 9am–4pm; closed Aug.*

Goethe Institute, Masarykovo nábřeží 32, Nové Město; ☎ 24 91 57 25; metro Národní třída. Weekly film showings and more frequent lectures; small exhibition space and café. *Café Mon–Fri 9am–7pm; library Mon, Tues & Thurs 2–6pm, Wed 10am–noon & 2–6pm, Fri 10am–noon.*

Hungarian Cultural Centre (Maďarské kulturní středisko), Rytířská 25, Staré Město; ☎ 24 22 24 24; metro Můstek. Weekly film showings and regular exhibitions and concerts. *Mon–Fri 10am–6pm.*

Institut Français (Francouzský institut), Štěpánská 35, Nové Město; ☎ 24 21 66 30; metro Muzeum. Great exhibitions and a great café, with croissants and *journeaux*; also puts on more or less

daily screenings of classic French films, plus lectures and even the odd concert. *Café Mon–Fri 9am–6pm; library Mon–Fri 10am–6pm, Sat 10am–1pm.*

Polish Institute (Polský institut), Václavské náměstí 19, Nové Město; ☎ 24 21 47 08; metro Můstek. Weekly film showings, occasional concerts and lectures. *Open Mon–Fri 9am–5pm, Sat 9am–noon.*

Slovak Institute (Slovenský institut), Purkynova 4, Nové Město; ☎ 24 91 56 29; metro Národní třída. Exhibitions, talks and concerts mostly, plus a library. *Mon–Fri 10am–6pm; library Mon 12.30–3pm, Tues, Thurs & Fri 10am–noon & 12.30–6pm, Wed closes 3pm.*

ELECTRICITY This is the standard continental 220 volts AC. Most European appliances should work as long as you have an adaptor for European-style two-pin round plugs. North Americans will need this plus a transformer.

EMBASSIES/CONSULATES

Australia, Na Ořechovce 38, Sřešovice; ☎ 24 31 00 71; tram #1, #8 or #18 from metro Hradčanská.

Belgium, Valdštejnská 6, Malá Strana; ☎ 24 51 05 32; metro Malostranská.

Britain, Thunovská 14, Malá Strana; ☎ 24 54 04 39; metro Malostranská.

Canada, Mickiewiczova 6, Hradčany; ☎ 24 31 11 08; metro Hradčanská.

Denmark, U páté baterie, Střešovice; ☎ 24 31 19 46; tram #1 or #18 from metro Hradčanská.

Finland, Dřevná 2, Nové Město; ☎ 24 91 35 94; metro Karlovo náměstí.

France, Velkopřevorské náměstí 2, Malá Strana; ☎ 24 51 04 02; metro Malostranská.

Germany, Vlašská 19, Malá Strana; ☎ 24 51 03 23; metro Malostranská.

Hungary Badeniho 1, Hradčany; ☎ 36 50 41; metro Hradčanská.

Ireland, Tržiště 13, Malá Strana; ☎ 53 09 02; metro Malostranská.

Norway, Na Ořechovce 69, Střešovice; ☎35 45 26; tram #1, #8 or #18 from metro Hradčanská.

Sweden, Úvoz 13, Malá Strana; ☎24 51 04 36; metro Malostranská.

USA, Tržiště 15, Malá Strana; ☎24 51 08 47; metro Malostranská.

EXCHANGE OFFICES 24-hour service at 28 října 13, Nové Město, metro Můstek.

GAY/LESBIAN There is no great "scene" in Prague as such, but there are a few bars and clubs that have become an established part of Prague nightlife (details on p.227) and even a gay-friendly hotel (see p.201). For information and help, phone the **Gay Information Centre**; ☎26 44 08. Another good source of information is the *SOHO revue*, a monthly Czech gay magazine, with a brief section in English and some useful listings. **Lambda**, the first organization for Czech gays and lesbians which started up in 1989, is based at Truhlářská 29, Staré Město; ☎231 64 01; metro náměstí Republiky. The age of consent in the Czech Republic is 15, whatever your sexual orientation.

LANGUAGE SCHOOLS Angličtina expres, Záhřebská 32, Vinohrady (☎24 25 14 82), charges between 60–100kč an hour; **British Council**, Národní 10, Nové Město (☎24 95 11 23), charges around 100kč an hour.

LAUNDRIES Most Czechs still wash their clothes by hand or leave them at a *čistírna*, where they are washed, dried, ironed and neatly folded. If time isn't a problem, try **Čistírna oděvů**, Opletalova 16, Nové Město; metro Muzeum/Hlavní nádraží; Mon–Fri 8am–6pm. Ex-pats tend to head for self-service launderettes: **Laundry Kings**, Dejvická 16; ☎312 37 43; metro Hradčanská; Mon–Fri 6am–10pm, Sat & Sun 8am–10pm, is very much part of the ex-pat scene. Other American-style launderettes include Laundryland, Londýnská 71, Vinohrady; ☎25 11 24; metro I. P. Pavlova; daily 8am–10pm; and Prague Laundromat, Korunní 14, Vinohrady; ☎25 55 41; metro náměstí Míru; daily 8am–8pm.

LEFT LUGGAGE Most bus and train stations have lockers and/or a 24-hour left-luggage office, which officially only take bags under 15kg. If your bag is very heavy, say *promiňte, je těžký* and offer to carry it to the locker yourself – *já to vezmu*. To work the lockers, put a crown in the slot on the inside of the door and set the code (choose a number you can easily remember and make a note of it), then shut the door. To re-open it, set the code on the outside and wait a few seconds before trying the door. The lockers are usually checked every night, and the contents of any still occupied are taken to the 24-hour left-luggage office.

If you forget your number, you'll have to go through a lengthy bureaucratic procedure, involving the police, in order to retrieve your luggage.

RELIGIOUS SERVICES Anglican, Sun 11am, sv Kilment, Klimentská 18, Nové Město; metro náměstí Republiky. **Baptist**, Sun 11am, Vinohradská 68, Vinohrady; metro Jiřího z Poděbrad. **Greek/Russian Orthodox**, sv Cyril & Metoděj, Resslova 9, Nové Město. **Interdenominational**, Sun 11.15am, Czech Brethren, Vrázova 4, Smíchov; metro Anděl. **Jewish Orthodox**, Mon–Thurs & Sun 8am, Fri dusk, Sat 9am & dusk, Staronová synagóga, Červená, Josefov; metro Staroměstská. **Jewish Reform**, Jubilejní synagóga, Jeruzalemská, Nové Město; Fri dusk, Sat 8.45am; metro Hlavní nádraží. **Lutheran**, Sun 11am, sv Michal, V jirchářích 4, Nové Město; metro Národní třída. **Roman Catholic** (in English), Sun 10.30am, sv Josef, Josefská, Malá Strana; metro Malostranská.

TAMPONS Tampons (*tampóny*) and sanitary towels (*dámské vložky*) are cheap and easy to get hold of in major department stores (see p.240).

THOMAS COOK Václavské náměstí 47, Nové Město; ☎26 31 06; metro Muzeum; *Mon–Fri 9am–9pm, Sat 9am–4pm, Sun 10am–2pm*.

TIME The Czech Republic is generally one hour ahead of Britain and six hours ahead of EST, with the clocks going for-

Directory

ward as late as May and back again some time in September – the exact date changes from year to year. Generally speaking, Czechs use the 24-hour clock.

TOILETS Apart from the automatic ones in central Prague, toilets (*záchody, toalety* or *WO*) are few and far between. In some, you still have to buy toilet paper (by the sheet) from the attendant, whom you will also have to pay as you enter. Standards of hygiene can be low.

WOMEN The Czech Republic remains a deeply conservative and patriarchal society, despite the upheaval of 1989. The atmosphere in Prague is slightly more liberated than in the rest of the country, however, and street-level sexual harassment rarely approaches levels experienced in some western countries. Pubs are about the only places where men always predominate; the usual common-sense precautions apply here and elsewhere. Feminism and women's issues keep a very low profile in the Czech Republic. The city's main feminist organization is the **Centre for Gender Studies**, Národní dům, náměstí 14 října 16, Smíchov; metro Anděl; ☎ 54 42 25.

Metric Weights and Measures

1 ounce = 28.3 grammes (g)

1 inch = 2.54 centimetres (cm)

1 pound = 454g

1 foot = 0.3 metres (m)

2.2 pounds = 1 kilogramme

1 yard = 0.91m

1 pint = 0.47 litres (l)

1.09 yards = 1m

1 quart = 0.94l

1 mile = 1.61 kilometres (km)

1 gallon = 3.78l

0.62 miles = 1km

The Contexts

A History of Prague

The famous pronouncement (attributed to Bismarck) that "he who holds Bohemia holds mid-Europe" gives a clear indication of the pivotal role the region has played in European history. As the capital of Bohemia, Prague has been fought over and occupied by German, Austrian, French and even Swedish armies. Consequently, it is virtually impossible to write a historical account of the city without frequent reference to the wider events of European history. One of the constant themes that runs throughout Prague's history, however, has been the conflicts between the city's religious factions, and, much later, between the German-speaking community and the Czech nationalists. The history of Prague as the capital of, first Czechoslovakia, and now the Czech Republic, is, in fact, less than a hundred years old, beginning only with the foundation of the country in 1918. Since then, the country's numerous tragedies, mostly focused on Prague, have been exposed to the world at regular intervals – 1938, 1948, 1968 and, most recently (and most happily), 1989.

Legends

The Czechs have a **legend** for every occasion and the founding of Bohemia and Prague are no exception. The mythical mound of Říp, the most prominent of the pimply hills in the Labe (Elbe)

plain, north of Prague, is where **Čech**, the leader of a band of wandering Slavs, is alleged to have founded his new kingdom, Čechy (Bohemia). His brother Lech, meanwhile, headed further north to found Poland. Some time in the seventh or eighth century AD, **Krok** (aka Pace), a descendant of **Čech**, moved his people south from the plains to the rocky knoll that is now Vyšehrad (literally "High Castle").

Krok was succeeded by his youngest daughter, **Libuše**, the country's first and last female ruler, who, handily enough, was endowed with the gift of prophecy. Falling into a trance one day, she pronounced that the tribe should build a city "whose glory will touch the stars", at the point in the forest where they found an old man constructing the threshold of his house. He was duly discovered on the Hradčany hill, overlooking the Vltava, and the city was named *Praha*, meaning threshold. However, it wasn't long before Libuše's subjects began to demand that she take a husband. As Cosmas, the twelfth-century chronicler put it, "resting on her elbow like one who is giving birth, she lay there on a high pile of soft and embroidered pillows, as is the lasciviously wanton habit of women when they do not have a man at home whom they fear". Again she fell into a trance, this time pronouncing that they should follow her horse to a ploughman, with two oxen, whose descendants (the ploughman's, that is) would rule over them. Sure enough, a man called **Přemysl** (which means ploughman) was discovered, and became the mythical founder of the Přemyslid dynasty which ruled Bohemia until the fourteenth century.

Early history

So much for the legend. According to Roman records, the area now covered by Bohemia was inhabited as early as 500 BC by a Celtic tribe, the **Boii**, who gave their name to the region. Very little is known about the Boii except that around 100 BC they were driven from their territory by a Germanic tribe, the **Marcomanni**, who occupied Bohemia. The Marcomanni were a semi-nomadic people and later proved awkward opponents for the Roman Empire, which wisely chose to use the River Danube as its natural eastern border, thus leaving Bohemia outside the empire.

The disintegration of the Roman Empire in the fifth century AD corresponded with a series of raids into central Europe by eastern tribes: first the **Huns** and later the **Avars**, around the sixth century, settling a vast area including the Hungarian plains and parts of what is now Slovakia. Around the same time, the Marcomanni disappear from the picture to be replaced by **Slav tribes** who entered Europe from somewhere east of the Carpathian mountains. To begin with, at least, they appear to have been subjugated by the Avars. The first successful Slav rebellion against the Avars seems to have taken place in the seventh century, under the Frankish leadership of **Samo**, though the kingdom he created, which was centred on Bohemia, died with him around 658 AD.

The Great Moravian Empire

The next written record of the Slavs in the region isn't until the eighth century, when East Frankish (Germanic) chroniclers report a people known as the **Moravians** as having established themselves around the River Morava, a tributary of the Danube. It was an alliance of Moravians and Franks (under Charlemagne) which finally expelled the Avars from central Europe in 796 AD. This cleared the way for the establishment of the **Great Moravian Empire**, which at its peak included Slovakia, Bohemia and parts of Hungary and Poland. Its significance in political terms is that it was the first and last time (until the establishment of Czechoslovakia, for which it served as a useful precedent) that the Czechs and Slovaks were united under one ruler.

The first attested ruler of the empire, **Mojmír**, found himself at the political and religious crossroads of Europe under pressure from two sides: from the west, where the Franks and Bavarians (both Germanic tribes) were jostling for position with the papacy; and from the east, where the Patriarch of Byzantium was keen to extend his influence across eastern Europe. Mojmír's successor, **Rastislav** (850–870), plumped for Byzantium, and invited the missionaries Cyril and Methodius to introduce Christianity, using the Slav liturgy and Eastern rites. Rastislav, however, was ousted by his nephew, **Svätopluk** (871–894), who captured and blinded his uncle, allying himself with the Germans instead. With

the death of Methodius in 885, the Great Moravian Empire fell decisively under the influence of the Roman Catholic Church.

Svätopluk died shortly before the **Magyar invasion** of 896, an event which heralded the end of the Great Moravian Empire and a significant break in Czecho-Slovak history. The Slavs to the west of the River Morava (the Czechs) swore allegiance to the Frankish Emperor, Arnulf; while those to the east (the Slovaks) found themselves under the yoke of the Magyars. This separation, which continued for the next millennium, is one of the major factors behind the distinct social, cultural and political differences between Czechs and Slovaks, which culminated in the separation of the two nations in 1993.

The Přemyslid Dynasty

There is evidence that Bohemian dukes were forced in 806 to pay a yearly tribute of 500 pieces of silver and 120 oxen to the Carolingian empire (a precedent the Nazis were keen to exploit as proof of German hegemony over Bohemia). These early Bohemian dukes "lived like animals, brutal and without knowledge", according to one chronicler. All that was to change when the earliest recorded Přemyslid duke **Bořivoj** (852/53–888/89), appeared on the scene. The first Christian ruler of Prague, Bořivoj was baptized, along with his wife Ludmila, in the ninth century by the Byzantine missionaries Cyril and Methodius (see above). Other than being the first to build a castle on Hradčany, nothing very certain is known about Bořivoj, nor about any of the other early Přemyslid rulers, although there are numerous legends, most famously that of **Prince Václav** (Saint Wenceslas), who was martyred by his pagan brother Boleslav the Cruel in 929 (see p.53).

Cut off from Byzantium by the Hungarian kingdom, Bohemia lived under the shadow of the **Holy Roman Empire** from the start. In 950, Emperor Otto I led an expedition against Bohemia, making the kingdom officially subject to the empire and its king one of the seven electors of the emperor. In 973, under Boleslav the Pious (967–999), a bishopric was founded in Prague, subordinate to the archbishopric of Mainz. Thus, by the end of the first millennium, German influence was already beginning to make itself felt in Bohemian history.

The **thirteenth century** was the high point of Přemyslid rule over Bohemia. With Emperor

Frederick II preoccupied with Mediterranean affairs and dynastic problems, and the Hungarians and Poles busy trying to repulse the Mongol invasions from 1220 onwards, the Přemyslids were able to assert their independence. In 1212, Otakar I (1198–1230) managed to extract a **"Golden Bull"** (formal edict) from the emperor, securing the royal title for himself and his descendants (who thereafter became kings of Bohemia). Prague prospered too, benefiting from its position on the central European trade routes. Czechs, Germans, Jews and merchants from all over Europe settled there, and in 1234 the first of Prague's historic five towns, **Staré Město**, was founded to accommodate them.

As a rule, the Přemyslids welcomed **German colonization**, none more so than King Otakar II (1253–78), the most distinguished of the Přemyslid kings, who systematically encouraged German craftsmen to settle in the kingdom. At the same time, the gradual switch to a monetary economy and the discovery of copper and silver deposits heralded a big shift in population from the countryside to the towns. German immigrants founded whole towns in the interior of the country, where German civic rights were guaranteed them, for example Kutná Hora, Mělník and, in 1257, **Malá Strana** in Prague. Through battles, marriage and diplomacy, Otakar managed to expand his territories so that they stretched (almost) from the Baltic to the Adriatic. In 1278, however, Otakar met his end on the battlefield of Marchfeld, defeated by Rudolf of Habsburg.

The beginning of the fourteenth century saw a series of dynastic disputes – messy even by medieval standards – beginning with the death of Václav II from consumption and excess in 1305. The following year, the murder of his son, the heirless, teenage Václav III, marked the **end of the Přemyslid dynasty** (he had four sisters, but female succession was not recognized in Bohemia). The nobles' first choice of successor, the Habsburg Albert I, was murdered by his own nephew, and when Albert's son, Rudolf I, died of dysentery not long afterwards, Bohemia was once more left without any heirs.

Carolinian Prague

The crisis was finally solved when the Czech nobles offered the throne to **John of Luxembourg** (1310–46), who was married to Václav III's youngest sister. German by birth, but educated in France, King John spent most of his reign participating in foreign wars, with Bohemia footing the bill, and John himself paying for it first with his sight, and finally with his life, on the field at Crécy in 1346.

His son, **Charles IV** (1346–78), was wounded in the same battle, but thankfully for the Czechs lived to tell the tale. It was Charles who ushered in Prague's **golden age** (see p.92). Although born and bred in France, Charles was a Bohemian at heart (his mother was Czech and his real name was Václav). In 1344, he had wrangled an archbishopric for Prague, independent of Mainz, and two years later he became not only king of Bohemia, but also, by election, Holy Roman Emperor. In the thirty years of his reign, Charles transformed Prague into the new capital of the empire. He established institutions and buildings that still survive today and founded an entire new town, **Nové Město**, to accommodate the influx of students and clergy. He promoted Czech as the official language alongside Latin and German and, perhaps most importantly of all, presided over a period of peace in central Europe while western Europe was tearing itself apart in the Hundred Years' War.

Sadly, Charles' son, **Václav IV** (1378–1419), was no match for such an inheritance. Stories that he roasted an incompetent cook alive on his own spit, shot a monk whilst hunting, and tried his own hand at lopping off people's heads with an axe, are almost certainly myths. Nevertheless, he was a legendary drinker, prone to violent outbursts, and so unpopular with the powers that be that he was imprisoned twice – once by his own nobles, and once by his brother, Sigismund. His reign was also characterized by religious divisions within the Czech Lands and in Europe as a whole, beginning with the **Great Schism** (1378–1417), when rival popes held court in Rome and Avignon. This was a severe blow to Rome's centralizing power, which might otherwise have successfully combated the assault on the Church that was already under way in the Czech Lands towards the end of the fourteenth century.

The Bohemian Reformation

Right from the start, Prague was at the centre of the Bohemian reform movement. The increased influence of the Church, and its independence from Mainz established under Charles, led to a sharp increase in debauchery, petty theft and alcoholism among the clergy – a fertile climate for militant reformers like Jan Milič of Kroměříž, whose fiery sermons drew crowds of people to hear him at Prague's Týn church. In Václav's reign, the attack was led by the peasant-born preacher **Jan Hus**, who gave sermons at Prague's Betlémská kaple (see p.106).

Hus's main inspiration was the English reformist theologian John Wycliffe, whose heretical works found their way to Bohemia via Václav's sister, Anne, who married King Richard II. Worse still, as far as Church traditionalists were concerned, Hus began to preach in the language of the masses (ie Czech) against the wealth, corruption and hierarchical tendencies within the Church at the time. A devout, mild-mannered man himself, he became embroiled in a dispute between the conservative clergy led by Archbishop Zbyněk and backed by the pope, and the Wycliffian Czechs at the university. When Archbishop Zbyněk gave the order to burn the books of Wycliffe, Václav backed Hus and his followers, for political and personal reasons (Hus was, among other things, the confessor to his wife, Queen Sophie).

There can be little doubt that King Václav used Hus and the Wycliffites to further his own political cause. He had been deposed as Holy Roman Emperor in 1400, and, as a result, bore a grudge against the current emperor, Ruprecht of the Palatinate, and his chief backer, Pope Gregory XII in Rome. His chosen battleground was Prague's university, which was divided into four "nations" with equal voting rights: the Saxons, Poles and Bavarians, who supported Václav's enemies, and the Bohemians, who were mostly Wycliffites. In 1409 Václav issued the **Kutná Hora Decree**, which rigged the voting within the university giving the Bohemian "nation" three votes, and the rest a total of one. The other "nations", who made up the majority of the students and teachers, left Prague in protest.

Three years later the alliance between the King and the Wycliffites broke down. Widening his attacks on the Church, Hus began to preach against the sale of religious indulgences to fund the inter-papal wars, thus incurring the enmity of Václav, who received a percentage of the sales. In 1412 Hus and his followers were expelled from the university, excommunicated and banished from Prague, and spent the next two years as itinerant preachers spreading their reformist

gospel throughout Bohemia. In 1414 Hus was summoned to the **Council of Constance** to answer charges of heresy. Despite a guarantee of safe conduct from Emperor Sigismund, Hus was condemned to death and, having refused to renounce his beliefs, was burned at the stake on July 6, 1415.

Hus's martyrdom sparked off **widespread riots** in Prague, initially uniting virtually all Bohemians – clergy and laity, peasant and noble (including many of Hus's former opponents) – against the decision of the council, and, by inference, against the established Church and its conservative clergy. The Hussites immediately set about reforming church practices, most famously by administering communion *sub utraque specie* ("in both kinds", ie bread and wine) to the laity, as opposed to the established practice of reserving the wine for the clergy.

The Hussite Wars: 1419–34

In 1419, Václav inadvertently provoked further large-scale rioting by endorsing the readmission of anti-Hussite priests to their parishes. In the ensuing violence, several councillors (including the mayor) were thrown to their death from the windows of Prague's Novoměstská radnice, in Prague's **first defenestration** (see p.141). Václav himself was so enraged (not to say terrified) by the mob that he suffered a stroke and died, "roaring like a lion", according to a contemporary chronicler. The pope, meanwhile, declared an international crusade against the Czech heretics, under the leadership of Emperor Sigismund, Václav's brother and, since Václav had failed to produce an heir, chief claimant to the Bohemian throne.

Already, though, cracks were appearing in the Hussite camp. The more radical reformers, who became known as the **Táborites** after their south Bohemian base, Tábor, broadened their attacks on the Church hierarchy to include all figures of authority and privilege. Their message found a ready audience among the oppressed classes in Prague and the Bohemian countryside, who went around eagerly destroying church property and massacring Catholics. Such actions were deeply disturbing to the Czech nobility and their supporters who backed the more moderate Hussites – known as the **Utraquists** (from the Latin *sub utraque specie*) – who confined their criticisms to religious matters.

For the moment, however, the common Catholic enemy prevented a serious split developing amongst the Hussites, and under the inspirational military leadership of the Táborite **Jan Žižka**, the Hussites' (mostly peasant) army enjoyed some miraculous early victories over the numerically superior "crusaders", most notably at the Battle of Vítkov in Prague in 1420. The Bohemian Diet quickly drew up the **Four Articles of Prague**, a compromise between the two Hussite camps, outlining the basic tenets about which all Hussites could agree, including communion "in both kinds". The Táborites, meanwhile, continued to burn, loot and pillage ecclesiastical institutions from Prague to the far reaches of the kingdom.

At the **Council of Basel** in 1433 Rome reached a compromise with the Utraquists over the Four Articles, in return for ceasing hostilities. The peasant-based Táborites rightly saw the deal as a victory for the Bohemian nobility and the status quo, and vowed to continue the fight. However, the Utraquists, now in cahoots with the Catholic forces, easily defeated the remaining Táborites at the **Battle of Lipany**, outside Kolín, in 1434. The Táborites were forced to withdraw to the fortress town of Tábor. Poor old Sigismund, who had spent the best part of his life fighting the Hussites, died only three years later.

Compromise

Despite the agreement of the Council of Basel, the pope refused to acknowledge the Utraquist church in Bohemia. The Utraquists nevertheless consolidated their position, electing the gifted **George of Poděbrady** first as Regent and then King of Bohemia (1458–71). The first and last Hussite king, George (Jiří to the Czechs) is remembered primarily for his commitment to promoting religious tolerance and for his far-sighted, but ultimately futile, attempts to establish some sort of "Peace Confederation" in Europe.

On George's death, the Bohemian Estates handed the crown over to the **Polish Jagiellonian dynasty**, who ruled *in absentia*, effectively relinquishing the reins of power to the Czech nobility. In 1526, the last of the Jagiellonians, King Louis, was decisively defeated by the Turks at the Battle of Mohács, and died fleeing the battlefield, leaving no heir to the throne. The Roman Catholic Habsburg, Ferdinand I (1526–64), was elected king of Bohemia – and what was left of Hungary – in order to fill the power vacuum, marking the **beginning of Habsburg rule** over what is now

the Czech Republic. Ferdinand adroitly secured automatic hereditary succession over the Bohemian throne for his dynasty, in return for which he accepted the agreement laid down at the Council of Basel back in 1433. With the Turks at the gates of Vienna, he had little choice but to compromise at this stage, but in 1545, the international situation eased somewhat with the establishment of an armistice with the Turks.

The following year, the Utraquist Bohemian nobility provocatively joined the powerful Protestant Schmalkaldic League in their (ultimately successful) war against the Holy Roman Emperor, Charles V. After a brief armed skirmish in Prague, however, victory fell to Ferdinand, who took the opportunity to extend the influence of Catholicism in the Czech Lands, executing several leading Protestant nobles, persecuting the reformist Unity of Czech Brethren, who had figured prominently in the rebellion, and inviting Jesuit missionaries to establish churches and seminaries in the Czech Lands.

Like Václav IV, **Emperor Rudolf II** (1576–1611), Ferdinand's eventual successor, was moody and wayward, and by the end of his reign Bohemia was once more rushing headlong into a major international confrontation. But Rudolf also shared characteristics with Václav's father, Charles, in his genuine love of the arts, and in his passion for Prague, which he re-established as the royal seat of power, in preference to Vienna, which was once more under threat from the Turks. He endowed Prague's galleries with the best Mannerist art in Europe, and, most famously, invited the respected astrologists Tycho Brahe and Johannes Kepler, and the infamous English alchemists John Dee and Edward Kelley, to Prague (see p.61).

Czechs tend to regard Rudolfine Prague as a second golden age, but as far as the Catholic Church was concerned, Rudolf's religious tolerance and indecision were a disaster. In the early 1600s, Rudolf's melancholy began to veer dangerously close to insanity, a condition he had inherited from his Spanish grandmother, Joanna the Mad. And in 1611, the heirless Rudolf was forced to abdicate by his brother **Matthias**, to save the Habsburg house from ruin. Ardently Catholic, but equally heirless, Matthias proposed his cousin **Ferdinand II** as his successor in 1617. This was the last straw for Bohemia's mostly Protestant nobility, and the following year conflict erupted again.

The Thirty Years' War: 1618–48

On May 23, 1618, two Catholic governors appointed by Ferdinand were thrown out of the windows of Prague Castle (along with their secretary) – the country's **second defenestration** (see p.57) – an event that's now taken as the official beginning of the complex religious and dynastic conflicts collectively known as the **Thirty Years' War**. Following the defenestration, the Bohemian Diet expelled the Jesuits and elected the youthful Protestant "Winter King", Frederick of the Palatinate, to the throne. In the first decisive set-to of the war, on November 8, 1620, the Czech Protestants were utterly defeated at the **Battle of Bílá hora** or Battle of the White Mountain (see p.172) by the imperial Catholic forces under Count Tilly. In the aftermath, 27 Protestant nobles were executed on Prague's Staroměstské náměstí, and the heads of ten of them displayed on the Charles Bridge.

It wasn't until the Protestant Saxons occupied Prague in 1632 that the heads were finally taken down and given a proper burial. The Catholics eventually drove the Saxons out, but for the last ten years of the war, Bohemia became the main battleground between the new champions of the Protestant cause – the Swedes – and the imperial Catholic forces. In 1648, the final battle of the war was fought in Prague, when the Swedes seized Malá Strana, but failed to take Staré Město, thanks to the stubborn resistance of Prague's Jewish, and newly Catholicized student populations on the Charles Bridge.

The Counter-Reformation and the Dark Ages

The Thirty Years' War ended with the **Peace of Westphalia**, which, for the Czechs, was as disastrous as the war itself. An estimated five-sixths of the Bohemian nobility went into exile, their properties handed over to loyal Catholic families from Austria, Spain, France and Italy. Bohemia had been devastated, with towns and cities laid waste, and the total population reduced by almost two-thirds; Prague's population halved. On top of all that, Bohemia was now decisively within the Catholic sphere of influence, and the full force of the **Counter-Reformation** was brought to bear on its people. All forms of Protestantism were outlawed, the education system was handed over to the Jesuits and, in 1651

alone, more than two hundred "witches" were burned at the stake in Bohemia.

The next two centuries of Habsburg rule are known to the Czechs as the **Dark Ages**. The focus of the empire shifted back to Vienna, the Habsburgs' absolutist grip over the Czech Lands catapulted the remaining nobility into intensive Germanization, while fresh waves of German immigrants reduced Czech to a despised dialect spoken only by peasants, artisans and servants. The situation was so bad that Prague and most other urban centres became practically German-speaking cities. By the end of the eighteenth century, the Czech language was on the verge of dying out, with government, scholarship and literature carried out exclusively in German. For the newly ensconced Germanized aristocracy, and for the Catholic Church, of course, the good times rolled and Prague was endowed with numerous Baroque palaces, churches, monasteries and monuments, many of which still grace the city today.

The Enlightenment

After a century of iron-fisted Habsburg rule, dispute arose over the accession of Charles VI's daughter, **Maria Theresa** (1740–80), to the Habsburg throne, and Prague, as usual, found itself at the centre of the battlefield. In November 1741, Prague was easily taken by Bavarian, French and Saxon troops, but the French occupation force quickly found itself besieged in turn by a Habsburg army, and in January 1743 was forced to abandon the city. By November 1744, Prague found itself once more besieged, this time by the Prussian army, who bombed the city into submission in a fortnight. After a month of looting, they left the city to escape the advancing Habsburg army. During the Seven Years' War, in 1757, Prague was once more besieged and bombarded by the Prussian army, though this time the city held out, and following their defeat at the Battle of Kolín, the Prussians withdrew.

Maria Theresa's reign also marked the beginning of the **Enlightenment** in the Habsburg Empire. Despite her own personal attachment to the Jesuits, the empress acknowledged the need for reform, and followed the lead of Spain, Portugal and France in expelling the order from the empire in 1773. But it was her son, **Joseph II** (1780–90), who, in the ten short years of his reign, brought about the most radical changes to the social structure of the Habsburg lands. His 1781 Edict of Tolerance allowed a large degree of freedom of worship for the first time in over 150 years, and went a long way towards lifting the restrictions on Jews within the empire. The following year, he ordered the dissolution of the monasteries, and embarked upon the abolition of serfdom. Despite all his reforms, Joseph was not universally popular. Catholics – some ninety percent of the Bohemian population – viewed him with disdain, and even forced him to back down when he decreed that Protestants, Jews, unbaptized children and suicide victims should be buried in consecrated Catholic cemeteries. His centralization and bureaucratization of the empire placed power in the hands of the Austrian civil service, and thus helped entrench the **Germanization** of Bohemia. He also offended the Czechs by breaking with tradition and not bothering to hold an official coronation ceremony in Prague.

The Czech national revival

The Habsburgs' enlightened rule inadvertently provided the basis for the economic prosperity and social changes of the **Industrial Revolution**, which in turn fuelled the Czech national revival of the nineteenth century. The textile, glass, coal and iron industries began to grow, drawing ever more Czechs from the countryside and swamping the hitherto mostly German-speaking towns and cities, including Prague. A Czech working class, and even an embryonic Czech bourgeoisie emerged, and, thanks to Maria Theresa's reforms, new educational and economic opportunities were given to the Czech lower classes.

For the first half of the century, the Czech **national revival** or *národní obrození* was confined to the new Czech intelligentsia, led by philologists like Josef Dobrovský and Josef Jungmann at the Charles University or *Karolinum* in Prague. Language disputes (in schools, universities and public offices) remained at the forefront of Czech nationalism throughout the nineteenth century, only later developing into demands for political autonomy from Vienna. The leading figure of the time was the historian **František Palacký**, a Moravian Protestant who wrote the first history of the Czech nation, rehabilitating Hus and the Czech reformists in the process. He was in many ways typical of the early Czech nationalists – pan-Slavist, virulently anti-German, but not yet entirely anti-Habsburg.

1848 and all that

The fall of the French monarchy in February 1848 prompted a crisis in the German states and in the Habsburg Empire. The new Bohemian bourgeoisie, both Czech and German, began to make political demands: freedom of the press, of assembly, of religious creeds. In March, when news of the revolutionary outbreak in Vienna reached Prague, the city's Czechs and Germans began organizing a joint national guard, while the students formed an Academic Legion, in imitation of the Viennese. Eventually, a National Committee of Czechs and Germans was formed, and Prague itself got its own elected mayor.

However, it wasn't long before cracks began to appear in the Czech-German alliance. Palacký and his followers were against the dissolution of the empire and argued instead for a kind of multinational federation. Since the empire contained a majority of non-Germans, Prague's own Germans were utterly opposed to Palacký's scheme, campaigning for unification with Germany to secure their interests. On April 11, Palacký refused an invitation to attend Pan-German National Assembly in Frankfurt. The Germans immediately withdrew from the National Committee, and Prague's other revolutionary institutions began to divide along linguistic lines. On June 2, Palacký convened a **Pan-Slav Congress** the following month, which met on Prague's Slovanský ostrov, an island in the Vltava. Czechs and Slovaks made up the majority of the delegates, but there were also Poles, Croats, Slovenes and Serbs in attendance.

On June 12, the congress had to adjourn, as fighting had broken out on the streets the previous day between the troops of the local Habsburg commander, Alfred Prince Windischgrätz and Czech protesters. The radicals and students took to the streets of Prague, barricades went up overnight, and martial law was declared. During the night of June 14, Windischgrätz withdrew his troops to the left bank and proceeded to bombard the right bank into submission. On the morning of June 17 the city capitulated – the counter-revolution in Bohemia had begun. The upheavals of 1848 left the absolutist Habsburg Empire shaken but fundamentally unchanged and served to highlight the sharp differences between German and Czech aspirations in Bohemia.

Dualism

The Habsburg recovery was, however, short-lived. In 1859, and again in 1866, the new emperor, Franz-Joseph II, suffered humiliating defeats at the hands of the Italians and Prussians respectively, the latter getting their hands on Prague yet again. In order to buy some more time, the compromise or *Ausgleich* of 1867 was drawn up, establishing the so-called **Dual Monarchy** of Austria-Hungary – two independent states united by one ruler.

For the Czechs, the *Ausgleich* came as a bitter disappointment. While the Magyars became the Austrians' equals, the Czechs remained second-class citizens. The Czechs' failure in bending the emperor's ear was no doubt partly due to the absence of a Czech aristocracy that could bring its social weight to bear at the Viennese court. Nevertheless, the *Ausgleich* did mark an end to the absolutism of the immediate post-1848 period, and, compared to the Hungarians, the Austrians were positively enlightened in the wide range of civil liberties they granted, culminating in universal male suffrage in 1907.

The industrial revolution continued apace in Bohemia, bringing an ever-increasing number of Czechs into the newly founded suburbs of Prague, such as Smíchov and Žižkov. Thanks to the unfair voting system, however, the German-speaking minority managed to hold onto power in the Prague city council until the 1880s. By the turn of the century, German-speakers made up just five percent of the city's population – fewer than the Czechs in Vienna – and of those more than half were Jewish. Nevertheless, German influence in the city remained considerable, far greater than their numbers alone warranted; this was due in part to economic means, and in part to overall rule from Vienna.

Under Dualism, the Czech *národní obrození* flourished. Towards the end of the century, Prague was endowed with a number of symbolically significant Czech monuments, like the Národní divaldo (National Theatre), the Národní muzeum (National Museum) and the Rudolfinum. Inevitably, the movement also began to splinter, with the liberals and conservatives, known as the **Old Czechs**, advocating working within the existing legislature to achieve their aims, and the more radical **Young Czechs** favouring a policy of non-cooperation. The most famous political figure to emerge from the ranks of the Young Czechs was the Prague university professor

Tomáš Garrigue Masaryk, who founded his own Realist Party in 1900 and began to put forward the (then rather quirky) concept of closer cooperation between the Czechs and Slovaks.

The Old Czechs, backed by the new Czech industrialists, achieved a number of minor legislative successes, but by the 1890s, the Young Czechs had gained the upper hand and conflict between the Czech and German communities became a daily ritual in the boulevards of the capital – a favourite spot for confrontations being the promenade of Na příkopě. Language was also a volatile issue, often fought out on the shop and street signs of Prague. In 1897 the **Badeni Decrees**, which put Czech on an equal footing with German in all dealings with the state, drove the country to the point of civil war, before being withdrawn by the cautious Austrians.

World War I

At the outbreak of **World War I**, the Czechs and Slovaks showed little enthusiasm for fighting alongside their old enemies, the Austrians and Hungarians, against their Slav brothers, the Russians and Serbs. As the war progressed, large numbers defected to form the **Czechoslovak Legion**, which fought on the Eastern Front against the Austrians. Masaryk travelled to the USA to curry favour for a new Czechoslovak state, while his two deputies, the Czech Edvard Beneš and the Slovak Milan Štefánik, did the same in Britain and France.

Meanwhile, the Legion, which by now numbered some 100,000 men, became embroiled in the Russian revolutions of 1917, and, when the Bolsheviks made peace with Germany, found itself cut off from the homeland. The uneasy cooperation between the Reds and the Legion broke down when Trotsky demanded that they hand over their weapons before heading off on their legendary **anabasis**, or march back home, via Vladivostok. The soldiers refused and became further involved in the Civil War, for a while controlling large parts of Siberia and, most importantly, the Trans-Siberian Railway, before arriving back to a tumultuous reception in the new republic.

Meanwhile during the course of the summer of 1918, the Slovaks finally threw in their lot with the Czechs, and the Allies recognized Masaryk's provisional Czechoslovak government. On October 28, 1918, as the Habsburg Empire began to collapse, the first **Czechoslovak Republic** was declared in Prague. In response, the German-speaking border regions (later to become known as the Sudetenland) declared themselves autonomous provinces of the new republic of *Deutsch-Österreich* (German-Austria), which it was hoped, would eventually unite with Germany itself. The new Czechoslovak government was having none of it, but it took the intervention of Czechoslovak troops before control of the border regions was rested from the secessionists.

Last to opt in favour of the new republic was **Ruthenia** (officially known as Sub-Carpatho Ruthenia), a rural backwater of the old Hungarian Kingdom which became officially part of Czechoslovakia by the Treaty of St Germain in September 1919. Its incorporation was largely due to the campaigning efforts of Ruthenian emigrés in the USA. For the new republic the province was a strategic bonus, but otherwise a huge drain on resources.

The First Republic

The new nation of Czechoslovakia began postwar life in an enviable economic position – **tenth in the world industrial league table** – having inherited seventy to eighty percent of Austria-Hungary's industry intact. Prague regained its position at the centre of the country's political and cultural life, and in the interwar period was embellished with a rich mantle of Bauhaus-style buildings. Less enviable was the diverse make-up of the country's population – a melange of minorities which would in the end prove its downfall. Along with the six million Czechs and two million Slovaks who initially backed the republic, there were more than three million Germans and 600,000 Hungarians, not to mention sundry other Ruthenians (Rusyns), Jews and Poles.

That Czechoslovakia's democracy survived as long as it did is down to the powerful political presence and skill of **Masaryk**, the country's president from 1918 to 1935, who shared executive power with the cabinet. It was his vision of social democracy that was stamped on the nation's new constitution, one of the most liberal of the time (if a little bureaucratic and centralized), aimed at ameliorating any ethnic and class tensions within the republic by means of universal suffrage, land reform and, more specif-

ically, the Language Law, which ensured bilinguality to any area where the minority exceeded twenty percent.

The elections of 1920 reflected the mood of the time, ushering in the left-liberal alliance of the **Pětka** (The Five), a coalition of five parties led by the Agrarian, Antonín Švehla, whose slogan, "we have agreed that we will agree", became the keystone of the republic's consensus politics between the wars. Gradually all the other parties (except the Fascists and the Communists) – including even Andrej Hlinka's Slovak People's Party and most of the Sudeten German parties – began to participate in (or at least not disrupt) parliamentary proceedings. On the eve of the Wall Street Crash, the republic was enjoying an economic boom, a cultural renaissance and a temporary *modus vivendi* among its minorities.

The Thirties

The 1929 Wall Street Crash plunged the whole country into crisis. Economic hardship was quickly followed by **political instability**. In Slovakia, Hlinka's People's Party fed off the anti-Czech resentment that was fuelled by Prague's manic centralization, consistently polling around thirty percent, with an increasingly nationalist/separatist message. In Ruthenia, the elections of 1935 gave only 37 percent of the vote to parties supporting the republic, the rest going to the Communists, pro-Magyars and other autonomist groups.

But without doubt the most intractable of the minority problems was that of the Sudeten Germans, who occupied the heavily industrialized border regions of Bohemia and Moravia. Nationalist sentiment had always run high in the Sudetenland, whose German-speakers resented having been included in the new republic, but it was only after the Crash that the extremist parties began to make significant electoral gains. Encouraged by the rise of Nazism in Germany, and aided by rocketing Sudeten German unemployment, the proto-Nazi **Sudeten German Party** (SdP), led by a gym teacher called Konrad Henlein, was able to win over sixty percent of the German-speaking vote in the 1935 elections.

Although constantly denying any wish to secede from the republic, the activities of Henlein and the SdP were increasingly funded and directed from Nazi Germany. To make matters worse, the Czechs suffered a severe blow to their morale with the death of Masaryk late in 1937, leaving the country in the less capable hands of his Socialist deputy, Edvard Beneš. With the Nazi annexation of Austria (the *Anschluss*) on March 11, 1938, Hitler was free to focus his attention on the Sudetenland, calling Henlein to Berlin on March 28 and instructing him to call for outright autonomy.

The Munich crisis

On April 24, 1938, the SdP launched its final propaganda offensive in the **Karlsbad Decrees**, demanding (without defining) "complete autonomy". As this would clearly have meant surrendering the entire Czechoslovak border defences, not to mention causing economic havoc, Beneš refused to bow to the SdP's demands. Armed conflict was only narrowly avoided and, by the beginning of September, Beneš was forced to acquiesce to some sort of autonomy. On Hitler's orders, Henlein refused Beneš's offer and called openly for the secession of the Sudetenland to the German Reich.

On September 15, as Henlein fled to Germany, the British prime minister, Neville Chamberlain, flew to Berchtesgaden on his own ill-conceived initiative to "appease" the Führer. A week later, Chamberlain flew again to Germany, this time to Bad Godesburg, vowing to the British public that the country would not go to war (in his famous words) "because of a quarrel in a far-away country between people of whom we know nothing". Nevertheless, the French issued draft papers, the British Navy was mobilized, and the whole of Europe fully expected war. Then, in the early hours of September 30, in one of the most treacherous and self-interested acts of modern European diplomacy, prime ministers Chamberlain (for Britain) and Deladier (for France) signed the **Munich Diktat** with Mussolini and Hitler, agreeing – without consulting the Czechoslovak government – to all of Hitler's demands. The British and French public were genuinely relieved, and Chamberlain flew back to cheering home crowds, waving his famous piece of paper that guaranteed "peace in our time".

The Second Republic

Betrayed by his only Western allies and fearing bloodshed, Beneš capitulated, against the wishes of most Czechs. Had Beneš not given in, however, it's doubtful anything would have come of

Czech armed resistance, surrounded as they were by vastly superior hostile powers. Beneš resigned on October 5 and left the country. On October 15, **German troops occupied Sudetenland**, to the dismay of the forty percent of Sudeten Germans who hadn't voted for Henlein (not to mention the half a million Czechs and Jews who lived there). The Poles took the opportunity to seize a sizeable chunk of North Moravia, while in the short-lived "rump" **Second Republic** (officially known as Czecho-Slovakia), the one-eyed war veteran Jan Sýrový became prime minister and Emil Hácha became president, Slovakia and Ruthenia electing their own autonomous governments.

The Second Republic was not long in existence before it too collapsed. On March 15, 1939, Hitler informed Hácha of the imminent Nazi occupation of what was left of the Czech Lands, and persuaded him to demobilize the army, again against the wishes of many Czechs. The Germans encountered no resistance (nor any response from the Second Republic's supposed guarantors, Britain and France) and swiftly set up the Nazi **Protectorate of Bohemia and Moravia**. The Hungarians effortlessly crushed Ruthenia's brief independence, while the Slovak People's Party, backed by the Nazis, declared **Slovak independence**, under the leadership of the clerical fascist Jozef Tiso.

World War II

In the first few months of the occupation, left-wing activists were arrested, and Jews were placed under the infamous Nuremberg Laws, but Nazi rule in the Protectorate was not as harsh as it would later become – the economy even enjoyed something of a mini-boom. In late October and November 1939, Czech students in Prague began a series of demonstrations against the Nazis, who responded by closing down all institutions of higher education. In 1941 a leading SS officer, **Reinhard Heydrich**, was put in charge of the Protectorate. Arrests and deportations followed, reaching fever pitch after Heydrich himself was assassinated by the Czech resistance in June 1942 (see p.140). The "final solution" was meted out on the country's remaining Jews, who were transported first to the ghetto in Terezín (see p.180), and then on to the extermination camps. The rest of the population were frightened into submission – very few acts of active resistance being undertaken in the Czech Lands until the Prague Uprising of May 1945 (see below).

By the end of 1944, Czechoslovak and Russian troops had begun to liberate the country, starting with Ruthenia, which Stalin decided to take as war booty despite having guaranteed to maintain Czechoslovakia's pre-Munich borders. On April 4, 1945, under Beneš's leadership, the provisional National Front or **Národní fronta** government – a coalition of Social Democrats, Socialists and Communists – was set up in Košice. On April 18, the US Third Army, under General Patton, crossed the border in the west, meeting very little German resistance. The people of Prague finally rose up against the Nazis on May 5, many hoping to prompt an American offensive from Plzeň, which the Third Army were on the point of taking. In the end, the Americans made the politically disastrous (but militarily wise) decision not to cross the demarcation line that had been agreed between the Allies at Yalta. Two crack German armoured divisions, not to mention some extremely fanatical SS troops, remained in position near the capital. Some 1600 barricades were erected, and around 30,000 Praguers held out against the numerically superior German troops, backed up by tanks and artillery, until they finally capitulated on May 8. The Russians entered the city the following day.

The Third Republic

Violent reprisals against suspected collaborators and the German-speaking population in general began as soon as the country was liberated. All Germans were immediately given the same food rations as the Jews had been given during the war. Starvation, summary executions and worse resulted in the deaths of countless thousands of ethnic Germans. With considerable popular backing and the tacit approval of the Red Army, Beneš began to organize the forced **expulsion of the German-speaking population**, referred to euphemistically by the Czechs as the *odsun* (transfer). Only those Germans who could prove their anti-fascist credentials were permitted to stay – the Czech community was not called on to prove the same – and by the summer of 1947, nearly 2.5 million Germans had been expelled or had fled in fear. On this occasion, Sudeten German objections were brushed aside by the Allies, who had given Beneš the go-ahead for the

odsun at the postwar Potsdam Conference. Attempts by Beneš to expel the Hungarian-speaking minority from Slovakia in similar fashion, however, proved unsuccessful.

On October 28, 1945, in accordance with the leftist programme thrashed out at Košice, sixty percent of the country's industry was nationalized. Confiscated Sudeten German property was handed out by the largely Communist-controlled police force, and in a spirit of optimism and/or opportunism, people began to join the Communist Party (KSČ) in droves; membership more than doubled in less than a year. In the **May 1946 elections**, the Party reaped the rewards of their enthusiastic support for the *odsun*, of Stalin's vocal opposition to Munich, and of the recent Soviet liberation, emerging as the strongest single party in the Czech Lands with up to forty percent of the vote (the largest ever for a European Communist Party in a multi-party election). In Slovakia, however, they achieved just thirty percent, thus failing to push the Democrats into second place. President Beneš appointed the KSČ leader, **Klement Gottwald**, prime minister of another *Národní fronta* coalition, with several strategically important cabinet portfolios going to Party members, including the ministries of the Interior, Finance, Labour and Social Affairs, Agriculture and Information.

Gottwald assured everyone of the KSČ's commitment to parliamentary democracy, and initially at least even agreed to participate in the Americans' Marshall Plan (the only Eastern Bloc country to do so). Stalin immediately summoned Gottwald to Moscow, and on his return the KSČ denounced the Plan. By the end of 1947, the Communists were beginning to lose support, as the harvest failed, the economy faltered and malpractices within the Communist-controlled Ministry of the Interior were uncovered. In response, the KSČ began to up the ante, constantly warning the nation of imminent "counter-revolutionary plots", and arguing for greater nationalization and land reform as a safeguard.

Then in February 1948 – officially known as **"Victorious February"** – the latest in a series of scandals hit the Ministry of the Interior, prompting the twelve non-Communist cabinet ministers to resign en masse in the hope of forcing a physically weak President Beneš to dismiss Gottwald. No attempt was made, however, to rally popular support against the Communists. Beneš received more than 5000 resolutions supporting the

Communists and just 150 opposing them. Stalin sent word to Gottwald to take advantage of the crisis and ask for military assistance – Soviet troops began massing on the Hungarian border. It was the one time in his life when Gottwald disobeyed Stalin; instead, by exploiting the divisions within the Social Democrats he was able to maintain his majority in parliament. The KSČ took to the streets (and the airwaves), arming "workers' militia" units to defend the country against counter-revolution, calling a general strike and finally, on February 25, organizing the country's biggest ever demonstration in Prague. The same day Gottwald went to an indecisive (and increasingly ill) Beneš with his new cabinet, all Party members or "fellow travellers". Beneš accepted Gottwald's nominees and the most popular Communist coup in Eastern Europe was complete, without bloodshed and without the direct intervention of the Soviets. In the aftermath of the coup, thousands of Czechs and Slovaks fled abroad.

The People's Republic

Following Victorious February, the Party began to consolidate its position, a relatively easy task given its immense popular support and control of the army, police force, workers' militia and trade unions. A **new constitution** confirming the "leading role" of the Communist Party and the "dictatorship of the proletariat" was passed by parliament on May 9, 1948. President Beneš refused to sign it, resigned in favour of Gottwald, and died (of natural causes) shortly afterwards. Those political parties that were not banned or forcibly merged with the KSČ were prescribed fixed-percentage representation within the so-called "multi-party" *Národní fronta*.

With the Cold War in full swing, the **Stalinization** of Czechoslovak society was quick to follow. In the Party's first Five Year Plan, ninety percent of industry was nationalized, heavy industry (and in particular the country's defence industry) was given a massive boost and compulsory collectivization forced through. Party membership reached an all-time high of 2.5 million, and "class-conscious" Party cadres were given positions of power, while "class enemies" (and their children) were discriminated against. It wasn't long, too, before the Czechoslovak mining "gulags" began to fill up with the regime's political opponents – "kulaks", priests and "bourgeois

oppositionists" – numbering more than 100,000 at their peak.

Having incarcerated most of its non-Party opponents, the KSČ, with a little prompting from Stalin, embarked upon a ruthless period of internal blood-letting. As the economy nose-dived, calls for intensified "class struggle", rumours of impending "counter-revolution" and reports of economic sabotage by fifth columnists filled the press. An atmosphere of fear and confusion was created to justify **large-scale arrests of Party members** with an "international" background: those with a wartime connection with the West, Spanish Civil War veterans, Jews and Slovak nationalists.

In the early 1950s, the Party organized a series of Stalinist **show trials** in Prague, the most spectacular of which was the trial of Rudolf Slánský, who had been second only to Gottwald in the KSČ before his arrest. He and thirteen other leading Party members (eleven of them Jewish, including Slánský) were sentenced to death as "Trotskyist-Titoist-Zionists". Soon afterwards, Vladimír Clementis, the former KSČ foreign minister, was executed along with other leading Slovak comrades (Gustáv Husák, the post-1968 president, was given life imprisonment).

After Stalin

Gottwald died in mysterious circumstances in March 1953, nine days after attending Stalin's funeral in Moscow (some say he drank himself to death). The whole nation heaved a sigh of relief, but the regime seemed as unrepentant as ever. The arrests and show trials continued. Then, on May 30, the new Communist leadership announced a drastic currency devaluation, effectively reducing wages by ten percent, while raising prices. The result was a wave of isolated **workers' demonstrations** and rioting in Plzeň and Prague. Czechoslovak army units called in to suppress the demonstrations proved unreliable, and it was left to the heavily armed workers' militia and police to disperse the crowds and make the predictable arrests and summary executions.

So complete were the Party purges of the early 1950s, so sycophantic (and scared) was the surviving leadership, that Khrushchev's 1956 thaw was virtually ignored by the KSČ. An attempted rebellion in the Writers' Union Congress was rebuffed and an enquiry into the show trials made several minor security officials scapegoats for the "malpractices". The genuine mass base of the KSČ remained blindly loyal to the Party for the most part; Prague basked under the largest statue of Stalin in the world; and in 1957, the dull, unreconstructed neo-Stalinist **Antonín Novotný** – recently alleged to have been a spy for the Gestapo during the war – became First Secretary and President.

Reformism and invasion

The first rumblings of protest against Czechoslovakia's hardline leadership appeared in the official press in 1963. At first, the criticisms were confined to the country's worsening economic stagnation, but soon developed into more generalized protests against the KSČ leadership. Novotný responded by ordering the belated release and rehabilitation of victims of the 1950s purges, permitting a slight cultural thaw and easing travel restrictions to the West. In effect, he was simply buying time. The half-hearted economic reforms announced in the 1965 **New Economic Model** failed to halt the recession, and the minor political reforms instigated by the KSČ only increased the pressure for greater changes within the Party.

In 1967, Novotný attempted a pre-emptive strike against his opponents. Several leading writers were imprisoned, Slovak Party leaders were branded as "bourgeois nationalists" and the economists were called on to produce results or else forego their reform programme. Instead of eliminating the opposition, though, Novotný unwittingly united them. Despite Novotný's plea to the Soviets, Brezhnev refused to back a leader whom he saw as "Khrushchev's man in Prague", and on January 5, 1968, the young Slovak leader **Alexander Dubček** replaced Novotný as First Secretary. On March 22, the war hero Ludvík Svoboda dislodged Novotný from the presidency.

1968: The Prague Spring

By inclination, Dubček was a moderate, cautious reformer – the perfect compromise candidate – but he was continually swept along by the sheer force of the reform movement. The virtual **abolition of censorship** was probably the single most significant step Dubček took. It transformed what had been until then an internal Party debate into a popular mass movement. Civil society, for years muffled by the paranoia and strictures of Stalinism, suddenly sprang into life in the

dynamic optimism of the first few months of 1968, the so-called **"Prague Spring"**. In April, the KSČ published their Action Programme, proposing what became popularly known as "socialism with a human face" – federalization, freedom of assembly and expression, and democratization of parliament.

Throughout the spring and summer, the reform movement gathered momentum. The Social Democrat Party (forcibly merged with the KSČ after 1948) re-formed, anti-Soviet polemics appeared in the press and, most famously of all, the writer and lifelong Party member Ludvík Vaculík published his personal manifesto entitled **"Two Thousand Words"**, calling for radical de-Stalinization within the Party. Dubček and the moderates denounced the manifesto and reaffirmed the country's support for the Warsaw Pact military alliance. Meanwhile, the Soviets and their hardline allies – Gomulka in Poland and Ulbricht in the GDR – viewed the Czechoslovak developments on their doorstep very gravely, and began to call for the suppression of "counter-revolutionary elements" and the reimposition of censorship.

As the summer wore on, it became clear that the Soviets were planning military intervention. Warsaw Pact manoeuvres were held in Czechoslovakia in late June, a Warsaw Pact conference (without Czechoslovak participation) was convened in mid-July and, at the beginning of August, the Soviets and the KSČ leadership met for **emergency bilateral talks** at Čierná nad Tisou on the Czechoslovak–Soviet border. Brezhnev's hardline deputy, Alexei Kosygin, made his less than subtle threat that "your border is our border", but did agree to withdraw Soviet troops (stationed in the country since the June manoeuvres) and gave the go-ahead to the KSČ's special Party Congress scheduled for September 9.

In the early hours of August 21, fearing a defeat for the hardliners at the forthcoming KSČ Congress, and claiming to have been invited to provide "fraternal assistance", the Soviets gave the order for the **invasion of Czechoslovakia** to be carried out by all the Warsaw Pact forces (only Romania refused to take part). Dubček and the KSČ reformists immediately condemned the invasion before being arrested and flown to Moscow for "negotiations". President Svoboda refused to condone the formation of a new government under the hardliner Alois Indra, and the people took to the streets in protest, employing every form of non-violent resistance in the book.

Individual acts of martyrdom, like the self-immolation of **Jan Palach** on Prague's Wenceslas Square, hit the headlines, but casualties were light compared to the Hungarian uprising of 1956 – the cost in terms of the following twenty years was much greater.

Normalization

In April 1969, there were anti-Soviet riots during the celebrations of the country's double ice hockey victory over the Soviets. On this pretext, another Slovak, **Gustáv Husák**, replaced the broken Dubček as First Secretary, and instigated his infamous policy of **"normalization"**. More than 150,000 fled the country before the borders closed, around 500,000 were expelled from the Party, and an estimated one million people lost their jobs or were demoted. Inexorably, the KSČ reasserted its absolute control over the state and society. The only part of the reform package to survive the invasion was **federalization**, which gave the Slovaks greater freedom from Prague (on paper at least), though even this was severely watered down in 1971. Dubček, like countless others, was forced to give up his job, working for the next twenty years as a minor official in the Slovak forestry commission.

An unwritten social contract was struck between rulers and ruled during the 1970s, whereby the country was guaranteed a tolerable standard of living (second only to that of the GDR in Eastern Europe) in return for its passive collaboration. Husák's security apparatus quashed all forms of dissent during the early 1970s, and it wasn't until the middle of the decade that an organized opposition was strong enough to show its face. In 1976, the punk rock band *The Plastic People of the Universe* was arrested and charged with the familiar "crimes against the state" clause of the penal code. The dissidents who rallied to their defence – a motley assortment of people ranging from former KSČ members to right-wing intellectuals – agreed to form **Charter 77** (*Charta 77* in Czech), with the purpose of monitoring human rights abuses in the country. One of the organization's prime movers and initial spokespeople was the absurdist Czech playwright **Václav Havel**. Havel, along with many others, endured relentless persecution (including long prison sentences) over the next decade in pursuit of Charter 77's ideals. The initial gathering of 243 signatories had increased to more than

1000 by 1980, and caused panic in the moral vacuum of the Party apparatus, but consistently failed to stir a fearful and cynical populace into action.

The Eighties

In the late 1970s and early 1980s, the inefficiencies of the economy prevented the government from fulfilling its side of the social contract, as living standards began to fall. Cynicism, alcoholism, absenteeism and outright dissent became widespread, especially among the younger (post-1968) generation. The **Jazz Section** of the Musicians' Union, who disseminated "subversive" western pop music (like pirate copies of "Live Aid"), highlighted the ludicrously harsh nature of the regime when they were arrested and imprisoned in the mid-1980s. Pop concerts, religious pilgrimages and, of course, the anniversary of the Soviet invasion all caused regular confrontations between the security forces and certain sections of the population. Yet still a mass movement like Poland's Solidarity failed to emerge.

With the advent of **Mikhail Gorbachev**, the KSČ was put in an extremely awkward position, as it tried desperately to separate *perestroika* from comparisons with the reforms of the Prague Spring. Husák and his cronies had prided themselves on being second only to Honecker's GDR as the most stable and orthodox of the Soviet satellites – now the font of orthodoxy, the Soviet Union, was turning against them. In 1987, **Miloš Jakeš**, the hardliner who oversaw Husák's normalization purges, took over from Husák as General (First) Secretary and introduced *přestavba* (restructuring), Czechoslovakia's lukewarm version of *perestroika*.

The Velvet Revolution

Everything appeared to be going swimmingly for the KSČ as it entered 1989. Under the surface, however, things were becoming more and more strained. As the country's economic performance worsened, divisions were developing within the KSČ leadership. The protest movement was gathering momentum: even the Catholic Church had begun to voice dissatisfaction, compiling a staggering 500,000 signatures calling for greater freedom of worship. But the 21st anniversary of the Soviet invasion produced a demonstration of only 10,000, which was swiftly and violently dispersed by the regime.

During the summer, however, more serious cracks began to appear in Czechoslovakia's staunch hardline ally, the GDR. The trickle of East Germans fleeing to the West turned into a mass exodus, forcing Honecker to resign and, by the end of October, prompting nightly mass demonstrations on the streets of Leipzig and Dresden. The opening of the Berlin Wall on November 9 left Czechoslovakia, Romania and Albania alone on the Eastern European stage still clinging to the old truths.

All eyes were now turned upon Czechoslovakia. Reformists within the KSČ began plotting an internal coup to overthrow Jakeš, in anticipation of a Soviet denunciation of the 1968 invasion. In the end, events overtook whatever plans they may have had. On Friday, **November 17**, a 50,000-strong peaceful demonstration organized by the official Communist youth organization was viciously attacked by the riot police. More than 100 arrests, 500 injuries and one death were reported (the fatality was later retracted) in what became popularly known as the *masakr* (massacre). Prague's students immediately began an occupation strike, joined soon after by the city's actors, who together called for an end to the Communist Party's "leading role" and a general strike to be held for two hours on November 27.

Civic Forum and the VPN

On Sunday, November 19, on Václav Havel's initiative, the established opposition groups, like Charter 77, met and agreed to form *Občanské fórum* or **Civic Forum**. Their demands were simple: the resignation of the present hardline leadership, including Husák and Jakeš; an enquiry into the police actions of November 17; an amnesty for all political prisoners; and support for the general strike. In Bratislava, a parallel organization, Veřejnosť proti nasiliu or **People Against Violence** (VPN), was set up to coordinate protest in Slovakia.

On the Monday evening, the first of the really big **nationwide demonstrations** took place – the biggest since the 1968 invasion – with more than 200,000 people pouring into Prague's Wenceslas Square. This time the police held back and rumours of troop deployments proved false. Every night for a week people poured into the main squares in towns and cities across the country, repeating the calls for democracy, free-

dom and an end to the Party's monopoly of power. As the week dragged on, the Communist media tentatively began to report events, and the KSČ leadership started to splinter under the strain, with the prime minister, **Ladislav Adamec**, alone in sticking his neck out and holding talks with the opposition.

The end of one-party rule

On Friday evening, Dubček, the ousted 1968 leader, appeared alongside Havel, before a crowd of 300,000 in Wenceslas Square, and in a matter of hours the entire Jakeš leadership had resigned. The weekend brought the largest demonstrations the country had ever seen – more than 750,000 people in Prague alone. At the invitation of Civic Forum, Adamec addressed the crowd, only to be booed off the platform. On Monday, November 27, eighty percent of the country's workforce joined the two-hour **general strike**, including many of the Party's previously stalwart allies, such as the miners and engineers. The following day, the Party agreed to an end to one-party rule and the formation of a new "coalition government".

A temporary halt to the nightly demonstrations was called and the country waited expectantly for the "broad coalition" cabinet promised by Prime Minister Adamec. On December 3, another Communist-dominated line-up was announced by the Party and immediately denounced by Civic Forum and the VPN, who called for a fresh wave of demonstrations and another general strike for December 11. Adamec promptly resigned and was replaced by the Slovak Marián Čalfa. On December 10, one day before the second threatened general strike, Čalfa announced his provisional **"Government of National Understanding"**, with Communists in the minority for the first time since 1948 and multi-party elections planned for June 1990. Having sworn in the new government, President Husák, architect of the post-1968 "normalization", finally threw in the towel.

By the time the new Čalfa government was announced, the students and actors had been on strike continuously for over three weeks. The pace of change surprised everyone involved, but there was still one outstanding issue: the election of a new president. Posters shot up all round the capital urging **"HAVEL NA HRAD"** (Havel to the Castle – the seat of the presidency). The students were determined to see his election through, continuing their occupation strike until Havel was officially elected president by a unanimous vote of the Federal Assembly, and sworn in at the Hrad on December 29.

The 1990 elections

Czechoslovakia started the new decade full of optimism for what the future would bring. On the surface, the country had a lot more going for it than its immediate neighbours (with the possible exception of the GDR). The Communist Party had been swept from power without bloodshed, and, unlike the rest of Eastern Europe, Czechoslovakia had a strong interwar democratic tradition with which to identify – Masaryk's First Republic. Despite Communist economic mismanagement, the country still had a relatively high standard of living, a skilled workforce and a manageable foreign debt.

In reality, however, the situation was somewhat different. Not only was the country economically in a worse state than most people had imagined, it was also environmentally devastated, and its people were suffering from what Havel described as "post-prison psychosis" – an inability to think or act for themselves. The country had to go through the painful transition "from being a big fish in a small pond to being a sickly adolescent trout in a hatchery". As a result, it came increasingly to rely on its new-found saviour, the humble playwright-president, Václav Havel.

In most people's eyes, "Saint Václav" could do no wrong, though he himself was not out to woo his electorate. His call for the rapid withdrawal of Soviet troops was popular enough, but his apology for the postwar expulsion of Sudeten Germans was deeply resented, as was his generous amnesty which eased the country's overcrowded prisons. The amnesty was blamed by many for the huge **rise in crime** in 1990. Every vice in the book – from racism to homicide – raised its ugly head in the first year of freedom.

In addition, there was still a lot of talk about the possibility of "counter-revolution", given the thousands of unemployed StB (secret police) at large. Inevitably, accusations of previous StB involvement rocked each political party in turn in the run-up to the first elections. The controversial *lustrace* (literally "lustration" or cleansing) law, which barred all those on StB files from public office for the following five years, has ended the

career of many a politician and public figure, often on the basis of highly unreliable StB reports.

Despite all the inevitable hiccups and the increasingly vocal Slovak nationalists, Civic Forum/VPN remained high in the opinion polls. The **June 1990 elections** produced a record-breaking 99 percent turnout. With around sixty percent of the vote, Civic Forum/VPN were clear victors (the Communists got just 13 percent) and Havel immediately set about forming a broad "Coalition of National Sacrifice", including everyone from Christian Democrats to former Communists.

The main concern of the new government was how to transform an outdated command-system economy into a **market economy**. The argument over the speed and model of economic reform eventually caused Civic Forum to split into two main camps: the centre-left *Občanské hnutí* or Civic Movement (OH), led by the foreign minister and former dissident Jiří Dienstbier, who favoured a more gradualist approach; and *Občanská demokratická strana*, the right-wing **Civic Democratic Party** (ODS), headed by the finance minister **Václav Klaus**, whose pronouncement that the country should "walk the tightrope to Thatcherism" sent shivers up the spines of those familiar with the UK in the 1980s.

One of the first acts of the new government was to pass a **restitution law**, handing back small businesses and property to those from whom it had been expropriated after the 1948 Communist coup. This proved to be a controversial issue, since it excluded Jewish families driven out in 1938 by the Nazis, and, of course, the millions of Sudeten Germans who were forced to flee the country after the war. A law was later passed to cover the Jewish expropriations, but the Sudeten German issue remains a tricky one, despite the subsequent conclusion of an agreement over the issue.

The Slovak crisis

One of the most intractable issues facing post-Communist Czechoslovakia turned out to be the **Slovak problem**. Having been the victim of Prague-inspired centralization from Masaryk to Gottwald, the Slovaks were in no mood to suffer second-class citizenship any longer. In the aftermath of 1989, feelings were running high in Slovakia, and more than once the spectre of a

"Slovak UDI" was threatened by Slovak politicians, who hoped to boost their popularity by appealing to voters' nationalism. Despite the tireless campaigning and negotiating by both sides, a compromise failed to emerge.

The **June 1992 elections** soon became an unofficial referendum on the future of the federation. Events moved rapidly towards the break-up of the republic after the resounding victory of the Movement for a Democratic Slovakia (HZDS), under the wily, populist politician Vladimír Mečiar, who, in retrospect, was quite clearly seeking Slovak independence, though he never explicitly said so during the campaign. In the Czech Lands, the right-wing ODS emerged as the largest single party, under Václav Klaus, who – ever the economist – was clearly not going to shed tears over losing the economically backward Slovak half of the country.

Talks between the two sides got nowhere, despite the fact of opinion polls in both countries consistently showing majority support for the federation. The HZDS then blocked the re-election of Havel, who had committed himself entirely to the pro-federation cause. Havel promptly resigned, leaving the country president-less and Klaus and Mečiar to talk over the terms of the divorce. On January 1, 1993, after 74 years of troubled existence, Czechoslovakia was officially divided into two new countries: the Czech Republic and Slovakia.

Czech politics since 1993

Generally speaking, life has been much kinder to the Czechs than the Slovaks since the break-up of Czechoslovakia. While the latter have had the misfortune of being led by the increasingly wayward and isolated Mečiar, the Czechs have enjoyed a long period of political stability under Klaus. Under his guidance, the country has jumped to the front of the queue for the EU and NATO, and is often held up as a shining example to all other former Eastern Bloc countries. Naturally enough, given Klaus's political colours, not everyone has enjoyed the fruits of his economic miracle. Prague, though, has attracted more foreign investment than anywhere else in the country – plus thousands of American expats into the bargain – and has been transformed beyond all recognition, its main thoroughfares now lined with brand new hotels, shops and restaurants.

Klaus and his party, the ODS, have certainly proved themselves the most durable of all the new political forces to emerge in the former Eastern Bloc. Nevertheless, in the **May 1996 parliamentary elections**, although the ODS again emerged as the largest single party, they failed to gain an outright majority. They repeated the failure again in November 1996 during the elections for the Czech Senate, the upper house of the Czech parliament. The electorate was distinctly unenthusiastic about the whole idea of another chamber full of overpaid politicians, and a derisory thirty percent turned out to vote in the second round. In the end, however, it was – predictably enough – a series of allegations of corruption over the country's privatization that eventually prompted **Klaus's resignation** as prime minister in November 1997. Those who had grown sick and tired of Klaus's dry, rather arrogant, style of leadership, cheered loudly enough, but few really believe that his main political adversary, Social Democrat leader Miloš Zeman, will actually be able do a better job.

In contrast to Klaus, whose star is clearly waning, **Havel**, Czech President since 1993, looks set to continue for another five-year term, as long as his health holds out. (He had an operation to remove a cancerous tumour from his lung at the end of 1996 and has been in and out of hospital ever since). Havel still commands considerable moral authority in politics, though he is by no means as popular at home as he is abroad. His marriage to the actress Dagmar Veškrnová, seventeen years his junior, in January 1997, less than a year after his first wife, Olga, died of cancer, was frowned upon by many. And his very public fall-out with his sister-in-law, Olga Havlová, over the family inheritance of the multi-million crown Lucerna complex in Prague, didn't do his reputation any favours either.

The Czech Romanies

Nevertheless, the Czechs look like they need Havel's moral guidance more than ever judging by the controversy which catapulted the country into the international media spotlight in late 1997. A misleading documentary shown on the Czech commercial TV channel *Nova* showed life for the handful of Czech Romanies who had emigrated to Canada as a proverbial bed of roses. At last, the documentary seemed to be suggesting,

Princes, kings, emperors and presidents

The Přemyslid dynasty
Princes
Bořivoj I d. 895
Spytihněv I 895–905
Vratislav I 905–921
Václav I 921–929
Boleslav I 929–972
Boleslav II 972–999
Boleslav III 999–1002
Vladivoj 1002–1003
Jaromir 1003–1012
Ulrich 1012–1034
Břetislav I 1034–1055
Spytihněv II 1055–1061
Vratislav II (king from 1086) 1061–1092
Břetislav II 1092–1110
Bořivoj II 1110–1120
Vladislav I 1120–1125
Soběslav I 1125–1140
Vladislav II (as king, I) 1140–1173
Soběslav II 1173–1189
Otho 1189–1191
Václav II 1191–1192
Otakar I (king from 1212) 1192–1230

Kings
Václav I 1230–1253
Otakar II 1253–1278
Václav II 1278–1305
Václav III 1305–1306

Habsburgs
Rudolf I 1306–1307
Henry of Carinthia 1307–1310

The Luxembourg dynasty
John 1310–1346
Charles I (as emperor, IV) 1346–1378
Václav IV 1378–1419
Sigismund 1436–1437

Habsburgs
Albert 1437–1439
Ladislav the Posthumous 1439–1457

Czech Hussite
George of Poděbrady 1458–1471

The Jagiellonian dynasty
Vladislav II 1471–1516
Louis I 1516–1526

The Habsburg dynasty
Ferdinand I 1526–1564
Maximilian 1564–1576
Rudolf II 1576–1612
Matthias 1612–1619
Ferdinand II 1619–1637
Ferdinand III 1637–1657
Leopold I 1657–1705
Joseph I 1705–1711
Charles II (as emperor, VI) 1711–1740
Maria Theresa 1740–1780
Joseph II 1780–1790
Leopold II 1790–1792
Franz 1792–1835
Ferdinand IV (I) 1835–1848
Franz Joseph 1848–1916
Charles III 1916–1918

Presidents
Tomáš Garrigue Masaryk 1918–1935
Edvard Beneš 1935–1938 & 1945–1948
Klement Gottwald 1948–1953
Antonín Zápatocký 1953–1957
Antonín Novotný 1957–1968
Ludvík Svoboda 1968–1975
Gustáv Husák 1975–1989
Václav Havel 1989–1992 & 1993–

they had found a life free from the racism and unemployment that is the reality for most of the Czech Republic's estimated quarter of a million gypsies. The programme prompted a minor exodus of up to one thousand Czech Romanies to Canada. Another *Nova* documentary, this time extolling life for Czech Romanies in Britain, had a similar effect, with several hundred Czech and Slovak Romanies seeking political asylum on arrival at Dover.

Needless to say, in both cases, the Czech Romanies were given a very cold reception. Fascists in both countries demonstrated to have the Czechs repatriated immediately, while the Canadians reimposed visa restrictions on all Czechs, and British Foreign Office officials appeared on Czech and Slovak TV to try and dissuade any further applicants. While racists back in the Czech Republic gleefully plastered up "Gypsies to Canada" graffiti, the positive side effect of all this media attention has been to force Czechs to focus on the institutionalized racism of their society and the casual racism that is acceptable in almost every walk of life. When, some weeks later an African student was stabbed to death in Prague by skinheads, Czech political leaders final-

ly roused themselves into action, and attended a demonstration against the murder. There was, of course, talk of banning the skinhead movement, though a review of the unfair citizenship law, which has branded many Romanies as stateless, would be more useful. Above all, though, there needs to be a concerted campaign of anti-racism and equal opportunities, from above and below, if Czech Romanies are to be persuaded that staying in the country is a viable option.

Czech cinema

Czechs are undoubtedly proud of their film-making. There may be countries with a more vibrant economy, or less corrupt politicans, but everyone knows that the country has produced some of the finest films – and some of the finest film-makers – in the world.

The legacy of the golden age of Czech cinema, the New Wave of the 1960s, is a mixed one. After 1989 a generation of film-makers returned from exile or emerged from obscurity to produce films that were no longer exciting or innovative. For several years they dominated not only the film-making institutions, but also the minds of younger film-makers, whose contemporary works tended to be pale imitations of forgotten classics. Now however, that new generation is winning international recognition for work that appeals to modern audiences. They have had to adapt to commercial pressures, long familiar in the West but relatively new here, and the strength of American distribution chains. The country continues to produce films and personnel of world-class calibre and Czech cinema shows every sign of continuing its long and distinguished tradition.

Interwar cinema: Avant-garde to erotic

From the early days, the Czech contribution to European cinema has not been just great films and outstanding directors. Even in the 1920s,

foreign companies were coming to use the facilities at the Barrandov **studios** in Prague – built by Václav Havel's architect grandfather; and Czech film technicians, like the cameramen Jan Roth and Otto Heller, were much in demand abroad.

With around thirty films produced annually, the Czech **avant-garde** were excited by the possibilities of cinema. The leading theoretician of the Devětsil group, Karel Teige, saw not only the possibility of an art for the masses, but what he called "pure cinematography", an opportunity to escape from (bourgeois) objective realism. The Czech public was perhaps less discerning. The most famous prewar film, *Extase* (1933), was notorious not for the Devětsil motifs of circles, trains and picture-poem montages from the director **Gustav Machatý**, but for the (briefly naked) appearance of a young Slovak actress, later to become known the world over as **Hedy Lamarr**. Machatý never recovered from his initial success and his career was dogged by proposals to make a pornographic sequel.

There were initially strong ties with early **German cinema**. Paul Wegener's expressionist classic *The Golem* (1920) was based on the Prague legend. Karl Junghans made *Such is Life* (1929) with a Czech cast, and Přemsyl Pražský's silent classic *Battalion* (1927) showed the extent of German influence. However, the coming of sound and the rise of fascism propelled Czech film-makers in different directions.

Czech theatre had an important influence on film, with **E.F. Burian** switching from directing for the stage to the screen and Voskovec and Werich bringing their successful blend of comedy and politics from the Liberated Theatre in Prague (now the ABC Theatre, just off Wenceslas Square) to films like *Your Money or Your Life* (1932) and *The World is Ours* (1937). Their domestic popularity was enormous, comparable to that of Chaplin in the West, and Werich in particular remained a powerful figure in Czech culture long after the war. He continued writing and making films and records well into the 1970s, ceasing only when the authorities threatened to prevent him receiving vital throat surgery.

Nazi occupation and nationalization

The **Nazi takeover** did not spell the end of Czech film production. Although many people in the film industry took their talents into exile – notably the director Karel Lamač, and actors Hugo Haas and Jiří Voskovec – others managed to continue working during the occupation.

One reason they were able to do so was that the Germans envisaged a major role for the film industry in Czechoslovakia. Goebbels personally supervised the expansion of Barrandov studios, partly as an excuse to pursue his relationship with the Czech actress, Lida Baarova. Over one hundred features were produced for the Reich as well as many documentaries, including the notorious propaganda film (supposedly called *Hitler Gives the Jews a Town*) depicting Theresinstadt as a Jewish spa resort.

In 1945, Czechoslovakia found itself with the largest undamaged film complex in Europe but the surviving community of film-makers had already decided how best to manage it. As President Beneš put it, "If there is anything in our country ripe for nationalization, it is film!"

Public support for the arts was not unknown in Czechoslovakia (theatre had been subsidized since the 1880s) but after the war cinema acquired a new prominence. In October 1945 the **Prague film academy (FAMU)** was founded and film students started to gather in the *Café Slavia*. A surge of movie-making began, under the direction of Vítězslav Nezval, once *Devětsil* poet, then Minister of Information. With other studios badly damaged, Barrandov again became an international production centre, whilst Vávra, Frič and Weiss (fresh back from his spell at the British Crown Film Unit) demonstrated the strength of domestic talent.

Meanwhile, freed from commercial pressures and advertising fashions by nationalization, Czech **animation** began to bloom. **Jiří Trnka**, a master of puppet animation, produced *The Czech Year* in 1947, while Hermína Týrlová and Karel Zeman experimented with combining filters, live action and cut-out cartoons at the Baťa studios at Zlín.

Under the Communists

When the Communists took power, they inherited a centralized film industry and quickly began implementing the new orthodoxy of **social realism**. Vávra, Frič, Trnka – even Burian – were all curbed by the new bureaucracy, and bright talents, such as student directors Vojtěch Jásny and Karel Kachyňa, were prevented from making feature films.

The authorities were not consistent, however. While for most of the 1950s Czech cinema produced an unappetizing diet of girls in love with tractors, war epics and uninspiring biographies, some unusual gems emerged. **Alfred Radok** (founder of the *Laterna magika* theatre company) made *The Longest Journey* (1950), a striking portrait of the Terezín ghetto, and **Martin Frič** made a two-part intellectual comedy about the limits of absolute power, based on the golem myth and starring Jan Werich: *The Emperor's Baker* and *The Baker's Emperor* (1951). Zeman managed his surreal *The Invention of Destruction* in 1957 and Trnka produced *The Cybernetic Grandma* in 1962 – demonstrating that animation is perhaps harder to control politically than normal film.

After the ideological savaging of the Stalinist era, when feature film production dropped as low as eight films a year, a slightly more relaxed attitude prompted a series of questioning and often elegant films from directors like Ladislav Helge (*The Great Solitude*, 1959 – on the difficulty of being a rural party official), and Zdeněk Brnych (whose *Local Romance*, 1957, produced the term "dingy realism").

The Czech new wave

Although still subject to political interventions and the occasional clampdown, production reached 35 films a year in the early 1960s. One of the most powerful films of Czech cinema was the historical epic *Markéta Lazarová* (1960), a tale of barbarity in thirteenth-century Bohemia directed by Frantisek Vlacil. Only recently have western audiences had a chance to see its arresting images and ravishing camerawork by Bendrich Batka. The great partnerships of Czech cinema between directors **Jan Kadar** and **Elmar Klos**, and between scriptwriter **Jan Procházka** and director **Karel Kachyňa** got under way. Vojtěch Jásny and Štefan Uher both found their way past the censor and inspired a new and bolder generation.

Assisting these film-makers were various young students from FAMU. They were not only directors, but cameramen like Jan Kučera and Miroslav Ondříček, and editors such as Miroslav Hájek. As economic sluggishness produced turmoil within the Communist Party, these students were to find a new contemporary voice and lead the Czech **New Wave**.

Their teachers showed the way. Jásny's *Cassandra Cat* (1963) starred Werich in a fairy tale about a cat who saw people in their true colours; Kadar and Klos's *The Shop on Main Street* (1964) described the fascist puppet state of wartime Slovakia; and Kachyňa's *Long Live the Republic* looked at the liberation from the Nazis with a new objectivity (1964).

The student directors took the contemporary feel and the flexibility modern cameras allowed to produce stunning low-budget films. **Věra Chytilová** completed her *Something Different* (a woman's point of view) in 1963. **Miloš Forman** was filming his first feature, *Black Peter*, out on the streets in the same year. **Jan Němec** took Arnošt Lustig's autobiographical story of boys fleeing from the Nazis and turned it into a terrifying vision of youth in a hostile world with *Diamonds of the Night* (1964). **Pavel Juráček** brought Kafka back to Prague with *Josef Kilian* (1964), a nightmare tale of a man trying to find the shop from which he had borrowed a cat. A number of young directors were brought together to produce a series of short films, *Pearls at the Bottom* (1965), each based on a short story by the surrealist writer Bohumil Hrabal.

The New Wave was characterized by energetic and innovative camera work, a brazen questioning of assumptions and a darkly humorous accuracy in observing contemporary mores. As the political uncertainty in the Party deepened, the films became more daring: in *Daisies* (1966) Chytilová showed two girls having a food fight at an official banquet; in *The Fireman's Ball* (1967) Forman hilariously satirized bureaucratic incompetence; and in *The Report on the Party and the Guests* (1966), Němec depicted a chilling party where the guests couldn't leave. Trnka contributed the blatantly allegorical *The Hand* (1966), and in the same year **Jiří Menzl** won an Oscar for his delightfully irreverent look at wartime resistance – *Closely Observed Trains*, again based on a Hrabal story.

By the time the tanks rolled in, even stronger films were in production. Jaromír Jireš' version of Milan Kundera's mournful novel about the 1950s, *The Joke*, came out – briefly – in 1969, as did Evald Schorm's bitterly funny *End of the Priest* (with a script by Josef Škvorecký). Menzl's *Larks on the String* (1969) had the same lead (Vlastimil Brodský) in a Hrabal tale of love and politics amongst the labour gangs at a Kladno steel works. Most terrifying, in *The Ear* (1970), Kachyňa

and Procházka produced an image of an entire society under surveillance.

All these films were **banned**, along with Vojtěch Jásny's lyrical portrait of a disintegrating rural community in *All My Good Countrymen* (1969), arguably the finest film of the period, and the short, blatantly allegorical *Uninvited Guest*, which starred a youthful Pavel Landovsky as a mysterious visitor who arrives one night in a Prague apartment and refuses to leave.

Post-1968: normalization and exile

The era of normalization blighted the burgeoning Czech film industry. While Chytilová and Menzl produced some interesting work in the 1970s, and Miroslav Ondriček became one of the world's most valued cameramen, little of note emerged from Czechoslovakia in the drab decades after 1969. Dozens of film-makers fled, including Kadar and Němec, while many of those who stayed found themselves excluded from regular film-making and isolated from international film trends.

The most successful **director in exile** has undoubtedly been **Miloš Forman**. His most famous films, *Amadeus* (which was filmed in Prague) and *One Flew Over The Cuckoo's Nest*, had a particular relevance to Czechoslovakia, where artists still suffered the vagaries of official patronage, and mental hospitals were just one of numerous institutions used to curb individual will. These films only secured public release in the country after the revolution of 1989.

Several major **foreign films** were made in Czechoslovakia throughout the seventies and early eighties, including *A Bridge Too Far* (which turns out to be the railway bridge over the Vltava near Dobříš), *Slaughterhouse 5* and *Yentl* (a picture of Barbra Streisand still hangs proudly in Prague's main kosher restaurant). However, domestic production plummeted.

One outstanding Czech film-maker who just about continued to function was **Jan Švankmajer**, although he had to move to Bratislava for a while to evade official restrictions. He was not associated with the New Wave, partly because he had not been at FAMU, and partly because he saw himself as primarily a surrealist rather than solely a film-maker. He used an enforced break from film-making to conduct "touch experiments", exploring the nature of objects. When he returned to animation, he produced a series of stunning films including *Dimensions of a Dialogue, Down to the Cellar* and the feature-length *Alice*. In recent years he has been acknowledged in the West as one of the giants of contemporary animation. He continues to work with his dedicated team combining live action, puppets, animation and opera to produce a devastating version of *Faust* (1994) and exposing the everday world of bizarre perversions in *Conspirators of Pleasure* (1996) (which featured a Czech TV newsreader having her toes sucked by live carp as she describes the day's events). Currently he is developing a CD Rom about the world of alchemists, Arcimboldo and Rudolph II's Prague.

The Velvet Revolution and after

The revolution, in which FAMU students played a prominent part, raised enormous expectations of Czech cinema. These were further encouraged when Czech audiences for the first time had an opportunity to view some of the finest films that had been buried in the archives. Film-makers too emerged from obscurity; Dagmar Víhanová had disappeared after a provocative documentary about morale in the Czech army. In 1996 she re-emerged with a deeply disturbing masterpiece *Fortress*. However, the **immediate post-revolutionary era** was largely disappointing. New wave giants like Němec, Menzl and Chytilova produced films that were frankly embarrassing; certainly no competition for the flood of western imports as audiences were treated to a twenty-year backlog of mainstream films. Like all art forms, cinema suffered a loss of direction when both Communist and opposition orthodoxies vanished.

Tank Division (Wit Olmer, 1990) was the first privately financed Czech film since the 1940s. It recouped its budget, but its script (based on a Škvorecky story) is typical of the films from the immediate post-revolution era; a mildly amusing tale of boys growing up, full of cheap anti-Communist gibes, awash with nostalgia and laced with tedious sexism. It was clear that the years of isolation and restriction had taken their toll, less in terms of a depletion of technology and skills, but more in their impact on creative thinking. During the revolution, Švankmajer had painted a banner calling for "More Imagination Please", but there was little sign of film-makers heeding his call.

Meanwhile, foreign crews began flocking to use cheap Czech **facilities** and **locations**. Recent productions include Emír Kustarica's award-winning *Underground* and the big-budget *Mission Impossible*. A host of production companies have sprung up to serve the international advertising industry and some young Czechs are among the leading commercial directors world wide. But the foreign films generated insufficient revenue to finance local productions. The privatization of the huge Barrandov film studios, mass lay-offs and threats of turning the place into a theme park or a vast supermarket complex provoked enormous controversy. Reluctantly, the government was forced to concede that Czech cinema is a vital national asset and has set up grants to fund it.

A new generation of film-makers is now benefiting from this system, most famously Jan Svěrak. He won a student Oscar for *Oil Gobblers*, a witty satire about disasterous ecological policies under the Communists. In 1992 his *Elementary School* was nominated for an Oscar for the best foreign-language film and in 1997 he won the award with *Kolja*, a sentimental account of the humanizing influence of a Russian boy on a cynical Czech. Jan Hřejbeik directed the first Czech musical for decades with *Big Beat* (1993) about the arrival of rock'n'roll in Dejvice, and Jiří Brabec used grotesque tales and illustrations from the 1930s to make *The Bloody Novel* (1993), a very Czech horror film and a technical masterpiece, including a whirlwind history of cinematography. Petr Zelenka produced his debut *Knoflikáři* in 1997, shaking off the sentimentality of much Czech cinema with a black comedy about responsibilty.

Although the country has a loyal and remarkably sophisticated film audience, it is simply too small (especially now Czechoslovakia has split in two) to support a major domestic film industry. Inevitably, cinemas are now filled with the latest offerings from Hollywood (or with uniformly dire local imitations). There are, nevertheless, real prospects for a revival of Czech cinema. Television has discovered it is cheaper to fund local production, with characters and stories people recognize, than merely to buy foreign blockbusters. Government grants, however small and haphazardly administered, coupled with investment from private production companies and co-production deals with other Europeans mean there is now a serious attempt to foster domestic production. The pressures for international standardization are familiar throughout Europe, but the Czechs have a better chance than most.

David Charap

Books

The recent upsurge of interest in all things eastern European has had a number of positive repercussions in the publishing world. There's certainly a much wider choice of Czech fiction than ever before, and art and architecture don't lag too far behind. There's now a whole load of books published only in Prague, which cater for the city's large English-speaking ex-pat community, and which are well-nigh impossible to obtain anywhere else (a list of English-language bookstores in Prague can be found on p.24). Where two publishers are given in the selection below, the first is the UK publisher, the second the US. O/p means the publication is out of print.

History, politics and society

Peter Demetz *Prague in Black and Gold; Scenes from the Life of a European City* (Penguin/Hill & Wang). Demetz certainly knows his subject, both academically and at first hand, having been brought up here before World War II (where his account ends). His style can be a little dry, but he is determinedly un-partisan, and refreshingly anti-nationalist in his reading of history.

R. J. W. Evans *Rudolf II and his world* (Thames & Hudson, UK). First published in 1973, and still the best account there is of the alchemy-mad emperor, but not as salacious as one might hope.

Jan Kaplan and Krystyna Nosarzewska *Prague: The Turbulent Century* (Könemann, Prague). This is the first real attempt to cover the twentieth-century history of Prague with all its warts. The text isn't as good as it should be, but the book is worth it just for the incredible range of photographs and images from the century.

Karel Kaplan *The Short March: The Communist Takeover in Czechoslovakia, 1945–48* (C. Hurst Co, UK); *Report on the Murder of the General Secretary* (I. B. Tauris/Ohio State University Press, o/p). *The Short March* is an excellent account of the electoral rise and rise of the Communists in Czechoslovakia after the war, which culminated in the bloodless coup of February 1948. *Report on the Murder of the General Secretary* is a detailed study of the most famous of the anti-Semitic Stalinist show trials, that of Rudolf Slánský, number two in the Party until his arrest.

Callum MacDonald *The Killing of SS Obergruppenführer Reinhard Heydrich* (Papermac, UK). Gripping account of the build-up to the most successful and controversial act of wartime resistance, which took place in May 1942, and prompted horrific reprisals by the Nazis on the Czechs.

Callum MacDonald and Jan Kaplan *Prague in the Shadow of the Swastika* (Quartet, UK). Excellent account of the city under Nazi occupation, with an incisive, readable text illustrated by copious black-and-white photos.

R. W. Seton-Watson *The History of the Czechs and Slovaks* (Shoe String Press US, o/p). Seton-Watson's informed and balanced account, written during World War II, is hard to beat. The Seton-Watsons were lifelong Slavophiles but maintained a scholarly distance in their writing, rare amongst émigré historians.

Elizabeth Wiskemann *Czechs and Germans* (Macmillan, o/p/AMS Press, o/p). Researched and written in the build-up towards Munich, this is the most fascinating and fair treatment of the Sudeten problem. Meticulous in her detail, vast in her scope, Wiskemann manages to suffuse the weighty text with enough anecdotes to keep you gripped. Unique.

Essays, memoirs and biographies

Margarete Buber-Neumann *Milena* (Panther/Arcade). A moving biography of Milena Jesenská, one of interwar Prague's most beguiling characters, who befriended the author while they were both interned in Ravensbrück concentration camp.

Karel Čapek *Talks with T. G. Masaryk* (Catbird Press, UK). Čapek was a personal (and political) friend of Masaryk, and his diaries, journals, reminiscences and letters give great insights into the man who personified the First Republic.

Jana Cerná *Kafka's Milena* (Souvenir Press/Northwestern University Press). Another biography of Milena Jesenská, this time written by her daughter, a surrealist poet, whose own works were banned under the Communists.

Timothy Garton Ash *We The People: The Revolutions of 89* (Penguin/Vintage). A personal, anecdotal, eye-witness account of the Velvet Revolution (and the events in Poland, Berlin and Budapest) – by far the most compelling of all the post-1989 books. Published as *The Magic Lantern* in the US.

Patrick Leigh Fermor *A Time of Gifts* (Penguin). The first volume of Leigh Fermor's trilogy based on his epic walk along the Rhine and Danube rivers in 1933–34. In the last quarter of the book he reaches Czechoslovakia, indulging in a quick jaunt to Prague before crossing the border into Hungary. Written forty years later in dense, luscious and highly crafted prose, it's an evocative and poignant insight into the culture of *Mitteleuropa* between the wars.

Václav Havel *Living in Truth* (Faber); *Letters to Olga* (Faber/Holt); *Open Letters: Selected Prose*; *Disturbing the Peace*; *Summer Meditations* (all Faber/Vintage); *The Art of the Impossible* (Knopf, US). The first essay in *Living in Truth* is "Power of the Powerless", Havel's lucid, damning indictment of the inactivity of the Czechoslovak masses in the face of "normalization". *Letters to Olga* is a collection of Havel's letters written under great duress (and heavy censorship) from prison in the early 1980s to his wife, Olga – by turns philosophizing, nagging, effusing, whingeing. *Disturbing the Peace* is probably Havel's most accessible work yet: a series of autobiographical questions and answers in which he talks interestingly about his childhood, the events of 1968 when he was in Liberec, and the path to Charter 77 and beyond (though not including his reactions to being thrust into the role of president). *Summer Meditations* are post-1989 essays by the playwright-president, while *The Art of the*

Impossible: Politics as Morality in Practice, is a collection of speeches given since he became the country's president in 1990.

Václav Havel et al *Power of the Powerless* (M. E. Sharpe, US). A collection of essays by leading Chartists, kicking off with Havel's seminal title-piece. Other contributors range from the dissident Marxist Petr Uhl to devout Catholics like Václav Benda.

Miroslav Holub *The Dimension of the Present Moment* (Faber & Faber, UK); *Shedding Life: Disease, Politics and Other Human Conditions* (Milkweed, US). Two books of short philosophical musings/essays on life and the unverse by this unusual and clever scientist-poet.

Antonín Klimek and Zbyněk Zeman *The Life of Edvard Bene Beneš: Czechoslovakia in Peace & War* (Clarendon Press). Beneš is a fascinating figure in Czech history, revered as number two to Masaryk while the latter was alive, only to find himself held responsible firstly for the Munich debacle, and secondly for allowing the Communists into power in 1948.

Heda Margolius Kovaly *Prague Farewell* (Indigo/Holmes & Meier). An autobiography that starts in the concentration camps of World War II, ending with the author's flight from Czechoslovakia in 1968. Married to one of the Party officials executed in the 1952 Slánský trial, she tells her story simply, and without bitterness. The best account there is on the fear and paranoia whipped up during the Stalinist terror. Published as *Under a Cruel Star* in the US.

Angelo Maria Ripellino *Magic Prague* (Picador/University of California Press). A wide-ranging look at the bizarre array of historical and literary characters who have lived in Prague, from the mad antics of the court of Rudolf II to the escapades of Jaroslav Hašek. Scholarly, rambling, richly and densely written – unique and recommended.

William Shawcross *Remember Dubček: Dubček and Czechoslovakia 1918–1990* (Hogarth Press, o/p/Simon & Schuster, o/p). Biography of the most famous figure of the 1968 Prague Spring, updated to include Dubček's role in the 1989 Velvet Revolution.

Michael Simmons *The Reluctant President* (Methuen, o/p). The definitive (and so far the only) biography of Václav Havel, by the long-time *Guardian* reporter.

Josef Škvorecký *Talkin' Moscow Blues* (Faber/Ecco Press). Without doubt the most user-friendly of Škvorecký's works, containing a collection of essays on his wartime childhood, Czech jazz, literature and contemporary politics, all told in his inimitable, irreverent and infuriating way. Published as *Head for the Blues* in the US.

■ **Ludvík Vaculík** *A Cup of Coffee with My Interrogator* (Readers International). A Party member until 1968, and signatory of Charter 77, Vaculík revived the *feuilleton* – a short political critique once much loved in central Europe. This collection dates from 1968 onwards.

Zbyněk Zeman *The Masaryks – The Making of Czechoslovakia* (I. B. Tauris, UK). Written in the 1970s while Zeman was in exile, this is a very readable, none-too-sentimental biography of the country's founder Tomáš Garrigue Masaryk, and his son Jan Masaryk, the postwar Foreign Minister who died in mysterious circumstances shortly after the 1948 Communist coup.

Czech fiction

Josef Čapek *Stories about Doggie and Cat* (Albatros, Prague). Josef Čapek (Karel's older brother) was a Cubist artist of some renown, and also a children's writer. These simple stories about a dog and a cat are wonderfully illustrated, and seriously postmodern.

Karel Čapek *Towards a Radical Centre* (Catbird Press, US); *The War with the Newts* (Hydra Books/Catbird Press); *Nine Fairy Tales* (Northwestern University Press in US). Karel Čapek was the literary and journalistic spokesperson for Masaryk's First Republic, but he's better known in the West for his plays, some of which feature in the anthology, *Towards a Radical Centre*.

Ladislav Fuks *The Cremator* (Marion Boyars, UK); *Mr Theodore Mundstock* (Four Walls Eight Windows, US). Two readable novels – the first about a man who works in a crematorium in occupied Prague, and is about to throw in his lot with the Nazis when he discovers that his wife is half-Jewish. The second is set in 1942 Prague, as the city's Jews wait to be transported to Terezín.

Jaroslav Hašek *The Good Soldier Švejk* (Penguin). The former, by Bohemia's most bohemian writer, is a rambling, picaresque tale of Czechoslovakia's famous fictional fifth columnist, Švejk, who wreaks havoc in the Austro-Hungarian army during World War I.

Václav Havel *The Memorandum* (Eyre-Methuen, o/p/Grove-Atlantic, o/p); *Three Vaněk Plays* (Faber, o/p); *Selected Plays 1984–87* (Faber, UK). Havel's plays are not renowned for being easy to read (or watch). *The Memorandum* is one of his earliest works, a classic absurdist drama that, in many ways, sets the tone for much of his later work, of which the *Three Vaněk Plays*, featuring Ferdinand Vaněk, Havel's alter ego, are perhaps the most successful. The 1980s collection includes *Largo Desolato*, *Temptation* and *Redevelopment*; freedom of thought, Faustian opportunism and town planning as metaphors of life under the Communists.

Bohumil Hrabal *Closely Observed Trains* (Abacus/Northwestern University Press); *I Served the King of England* (Picador/Vintage); *Too Loud a Solitude* (Deutsch/Harcourt Brace); *The Little Town Where Time Stood Still* (Abacus/Pantheon, o/p); *Dancing Lessons* (Panther/Harcourt Brace). A thoroughly mischievous writer, Hrabal's slim but superb *Closely Observed Trains* is a postwar classic, set in the last days of the war and relentlessly unheroic; it was made into an equally brilliant film by Jiří Menzl. *I Served the King of England* follows the antihero Dítě, who works at the *Hotel Paříž*, through the decade after 1938. *Too Loud a Solitude*, about a waste-paper disposer under the Communists, has also been made into a film, again by Menzl. *The Little Town Where Time Stood Still* was the last work Hrabal completed before his death in 1997. *Dancing Lessons* is a short tale from 1964, composed of a single sentence, a rambling monologue by a 70-year-old shoemaker to six sunbathing women.

Alois Jirásek *Old Czech Legends* (Forest Books/Dufour). A major figure in the nineteenth-century Czech *národní obrození*, Jirásek popularized Bohemia's legendary past. This collection includes all the classic texts, including the story of the founding of the city by the prophetess Libuše.

Franz Kafka *The Collected Novels of Franz Kafka*; *Letters to Felice*; *Diaries* (all Penguin/Schocken). A German-Jewish Praguer, Kafka has drawn the darker side of central Europe – its claustrophobia, paranoia and unfathomable bureaucracy – better than anyone else, both in a rural setting, as in *The Castle*, and in an urban one, in one of the great novels of the twentieth century, *The Trial*.

Ivan Klíma *A Summer Affair* (Penguin, UK); *My Merry Mornings* (Readers International); *My First Loves* (Penguin/Norton); *Love and Garbage* (Penguin/Vintage); *Judge on Trial* (Vintage); *My*

Golden Trades (Penguin/Macmillan); Waiting for the Dark, Waiting for the Light (Penguin/Grove-Atlantic); The Spirit of Prague (Granta, UK); Ultimate Intimacy (Granta/Grove-Atlantic). A survivor of Terezín, Klíma is another writer in the Kundera mould as far as sexual politics goes, but his stories are a lot lighter. Judge on Trial, written in the 1970s, is one of his best, concerning the moral dilemmas of a Communist judge. Waiting for the Dark, Waiting for the Light is a pessimistic novel set before, during and after the Velvet Revolution of 1989. The Spirit of Prague is a very readable collection of biographical and more general articles and essays on subjects ranging from Klíma's childhood experiences in Terezín to the current situation in Prague. Ultimate Intimacy is his latest novel, set in the cynical post-revolutionary Czech Republic.

Milan Kundera Laughable Loves; The Farewell Party; The Joke; The Book of Laughter and Forgetting; The Unbearable Lightness of Being; The Art of the Novel; Immortality; Slowness; Testaments Betrayed (all Faber/HarperCollins); Life is Elsewhere (Faber/Penguin). Milan Kundera is the country's most popular writer – at least with non-Czechs. His books are very obviously "political", particularly The Book of Laughter and Forgetting, which led the Communists to revoke Kundera's citizenship. The Joke, written while he was still living in Czechoslovakia and in many ways his best work, is set in the very unfunny era of the Stalinist purges. Its clear, humorous style is far removed from the carefully poised posturing of his most famous work, The Unbearable Lightness of Being, set in and after 1968, and successfully turned into a film some twenty years later. Slowness is his latest novel, a slim volume set in France, and his first work written in French. Testaments Betrayed is a fascinating series of essays about a range of subjects from the formation of historical reputation to the problems of translations.

Arnošt Lustig Diamonds of the Night; Night and Hope (both Quartet/Northwestern University Press); Darkness Casts No Shadow (Quartet/Avon, o/p); A Prayer for Kateřina Horovitová (Overlook Press in US); Indecent Dreams (Northwestern University Press in US). A Prague Jew exiled since 1968, Lustig spent World War II in Terezín, Buchenwald and Auschwitz, and his novels and short stories are consistently set in the Terezín camp.

Gustav Meyrink The Golem (Dedalus/Dover); The Angel of the West Window (Dedalus/Ariadne). Meyrink was another of Prague's weird and wonderful characters who started out as a bank manager, but soon became involved in cabalism, alchemy and drug experimentation. His Golem, based on Rabbi Löw's monster, is one of the classic versions of the tale, set in the Jewish quarter. The Angel at the West Window is a historical novel about John Dee, an English alchemist invited to Prague in the late sixteenth century by Rudolf II.

Jan Neruda Prague Tales (OUP). Not to be confused with the Chilean Pablo Neruda (who took his name from the Czech writer), these are short, bittersweet snapshots of life in Malá Strana at the close of the last century.

Leo Perutz By Night Under the Stone Bridge (Harvill Press/Arcade, o/p). A Jewish-German Praguer who emigrated to Israel and wrote a series of historical novels. This one is set in Rudolfine Prague, and, among other things, tells the story of the emperor's love affair with the wife of Mordecai Maisl.

Karel Poláček What Ownership's All About (Catbird Press/Independent Publishers Group). A darkly comic novel set in a Prague tenement block, dealing with the issue of fascism and appeasement, by a Jewish-Czech Praguer who died in the camps in 1944.

Rainer Maria Rilke Two Stories of Prague (University Press of New England, US). Both tales deal with the artificiality of Prague's now defunct German community, whose claustrophobic parochialism drove the author into self-imposed exile in 1899 (for more on Rilke see Poetry, p.276).

Peter Sís The Three Golden Keys (Pavilion/Doubleday). Short, hauntingly illustrated children's book set in Prague, by Czech-born American Sís.

Josef Škvorecký The Cowards; The Miracle Game (both Faber/Norton); The Swell Season; The Bass Saxophone (both Vintage/Ecco Press); Miss Silver's Past; Dvořák in Love (both Vintage/Norton); The Engineer of Human Souls (Vintage/Pocket Books); The Republic of Whores (Faber/Ecco Press). A relentless anti-Communist, Škvorecký is typically Bohemian in his bawdy sense of humour and irreverence for all high moralizing. The Cowards (which briefly saw the light of day in 1958) is the tale of a group of irresponsible young men in the last days of the war, an antidote to the lofty prose from official authors at the time, but hampered by its dated Americanized translation.

Josef Škvorecký The Mournful Demeanor of Lieutenant Boruvka; Sins for Father Knox; The Return of Lieutenant Boruvka; The End of Lieutenant Boruvka (all Faber & Faber/Norton). Less well known (and understandably so) are Škvorecký's detective stories featuring a podgy, depressive Czech cop, which he wrote in the 1960s at a time when his more serious work was banned. The later book, The Return of Lieutenant Boruvka, is set in Škvorecký's new home, Canada.

Zdena Tomin Stalin's Shoe; The Coast of Bohemia (both Dent, UK, o/p). Although Czechborn, Tomin writes in English (the language of her exile since 1980); she has a style and fluency all her own. Stalin's Shoe is the compelling and complex story of a girl coming to terms with her Stalinist childhood, while The Coast of Bohemia is based on Tomin's experiences of the late 1970s dissident movement, when she was an active member of Charter 77.

Ludvík Vaculík The Guinea Pigs (Northwestern University Press, US). Vaculík was expelled from the Party in the midst of the 1968 Prague Spring; this novel, set in Prague, catalogues the slow dehumanization of Czech society in the aftermath of the Soviet invasion.

Jiří Weil Life With a Star; Mendelssohn is on the Roof (Collins, o/p/Farra, Straus & Giroux). Two novels written just after the war and based on Weil's experiences as a Czech Jew in hiding under Nazi-occupied Prague.

Poetry

Jaroslav Čejka, Michal Černík and Karel Sýs The New Czech Poetry (Bloodaxe/Dufour). Slim, but interesting volume by three Czech poets; all in their late forties, all very different. Čejka is of the Holub school, and comes across simply and strongly; Černík is similarly direct; Sýs the least convincing.

Sylva Fischerová The Tremor of Racehorses: Selected Poems (Bloodaxe/Dufour). Poet and novelist, Fischerová is one of the new generation of Czech writers, though in many ways she is continuing in the Holub tradition. Her poems are

by turns powerful, obtuse and personal, as was necessary to escape censorship during the late 1980s.

Josef Hanzlík Selected Poems (Bloodaxe/Dufour). Refreshingly accessible collection of poems written over the last 35 years by a poet of Havel's generation.

Miroslav Holub Supposed to Fly; The Jingle Bell Principle; Poems Before and After (all Bloodaxe/Dufour); Vanishing Lung Syndrome (Faber/Field Translations Series). Holub is a scientist and scholar, and his poetry reflects this unique fusion of master poet and chief immunologist. Regularly banned in his own country, he is the Czech poet par excellence – classically trained, erudite, liberal and westward-leaning. Vanishing Lung Syndrome is his latest volume; the other two are collections.

Rainer Maria Rilke Selected Poetry (Picador, UK). Rilke's upbringing was unexceptional, except that his mother brought him up as a girl until the age of six. In his adult life, he became one of Prague's leading Jewish-German authors of the interwar period.

Jaroslav Seifert The Poetry of Jaroslav Seifert (Catbird Press, US). Czechoslovakia's only author to win the Nobel prize for literature, Seifert was a founder-member of the Communist Party and the avant-garde arts movement Devětsil, later falling from grace and signing the Charter in his old age. His longevity means that his work covers some of the most turbulent times in Czechoslovak history, but his irrepressible lasciviousness has been known to irritate.

Literature by foreign writers

Bruce Chatwin Utz (Pan, UK). Chatwin is one of the "exotic" school of travel writers, hence this slim, intriguing and mostly true-to-life account of an avid crockery collector from Prague's Jewish quarter.

Lionel Davidson The Night of Wenceslas (Reed Consumer Books/St Martin's Press). A Cold War thriller set in pre-1968 Czechsloavkia that launched Davidson's career as a spy-writer.

Martha Gellhorn A Stricken Field (Virago, o/p /Penguin, o/p). The story of an American journalist who arrives in Prague just as the Nazis march into Sudetenland. Based on the author's own experiences, this is a fascinating, if sentimental, insight into the panic and confusion in "rump"

Czecho-Slovakia after the Munich Diktat. First published in 1940.

Philip Roth *Prague Orgy* (Arrow, UK). A novella about a world-famous Jewish novelist (ie Roth) who goes to Communist Prague to recover some unpublished Jewish stories. Prague "is the city I imagined the Jews would buy when they had accumulated enough money for a homeland", according to Roth. A coda to Roth's Zuckerman trilogy.

Art, photography and film

The Castle of Prague and its Treasures (Flint River Press/Vedome). Heavy, coffee-table book with excellent colour photos of all the main sights, plus exclusive coverage of the castle interiors – many by Plečnik – which remain closed to the public.

Czech Modernism 1900–1945 (Little Brown/Museum of Fine Arts, Houston). Wideranging and superbly illustrated, this American publication records the journey of the Czech modern movement through Cubism and Surrealism to Modernism and the avant-garde. The accompanying essays by leading art and film critics cover fine art, architecture, film, photography and theatre.

Devětsil – Czech Avant-Garde Art, Architecture and Design of the 1920s and 30s (Museum of Modern Art, Oxford, UK). Published to accompany the 1990 Devětsil exhibition at Oxford, this is the definitive account of interwar Czechoslovakia's most famous left-wing art movement, which attracted artists from every discipline.

Disorientations – Eastern Europe in Transition (Thames & Hudson, UK). A self-explanatory book of photos accompanied by Pavel Kohout's text.

Ivan Margolius *Prague – A guide to Twentieth-century Architecture* (Artemi/Knickerbocker). Dinky little pocket guide to all the major modern landmarks of Prague (including a black-and-white photo of each building), from the Art Nouveau Obecní dům, through functionalism and Cubism, to the Fred & Ginger building, currently in construction.

Language

The official language of the Czech Republic is Czech (český), a highly complex western Slav tongue. Any attempt to speak Czech will be heartily appreciated, though don't be discouraged if people seem not to understand, as most will be unaccustomed to hearing foreigners stumble through their language. If you don't know any Czech, brush up on your German, since, among the older generation at least, this is still the most widely spoken second language. Russian, once the compulsory second language, has been practically wiped off the school curriculum, and the number of English-speakers has been steadily increasing especially among the younger generation.

Pronunciation

English-speakers often find Czech impossibly difficult to pronounce. In fact, it's not half as daunting as it might first appear from the "traffic jams of

consonants", as Patrick Leigh-Fermour put it, which crop up on the page. An illustration of this is the Czech tongue-twister, *strč prst skrz krk* (stick your finger down your neck). Apart from a few special letters, each letter and syllable is pronounced as it's written – the trick is always to **stress the first syllable** of a word, no matter what its length; otherwise you'll render it unintelligible.

A Czech language guide

There are very few **teach-yourself Czech** courses available and each has drawbacks. *Colloquial Czech* by James Naughton is good, but a bit fast and furious for most people; *Teach Yourself Czech* is a bit dry for some. The best portable **dictionary for Czech** is the *kapesní slovník*, most easily purchased in Prague. The *Rough Guides* also produces a useful Czech phrasebook.

The Alphabet

In the Czech alphabet, letters which feature a **háček** (as in the č of the word itself) are considered separate letters and appear in Czech indexes immediately after their more familiar cousins. More confusingly, the consonant combination *ch* is also considered as a separate letter and appears in Czech indexes after the letter *h*. In the index in this book, we use the English system, so words beginning with *c*, *č* and *ch* all appear under *c*.

Short and long vowels

Czech has both short and long vowels (the latter being denoted by a variety of accents). The trick here is to lengthen the vowel without affecting the principal stress of the word, which is invariably on the first syllable.

a like the u in c**u**p
á as in f**a**ther
e as in p**e**t
é as in f**ai**r
ě like the ye in **ye**s
i or y as in p**i**t
í or ý as in s**ea**t
o as in n**o**t
ó as in d**oo**r
u like the oo in b**oo**k
ů or ú like the oo in f**oo**l

Vowel combinations and diphthongs

There are very few diphthongs in Czech, so any combinations of vowels other than those below should be pronounced as two separate syllables.

au like the ou in f**ou**l
ou like the oe in f**oe**

BASIC WORDS AND PHRASES

Yes	*ano*
No	*ne*
Excuse me/don't mention it	*prosím/není zač*
Sorry	*pardon*
Thank you	*děkuju*
Bon appétit	*dobrou chuť*
Bon voyage	*šťastnou cestu*
Hello/goodbye (informal)	*ahoj*
Goodbye (formal)	*na shledanou*
Good day	*dobrý den*
Good morning	*dobré ráno*
Good evening	*dobrý večer*
Good night (when leaving)	*dobrou noc*
How are you?	*jak se máte?*
Today	*dnes*
Yesterday	*včera*
Tomorrow	*zítra*
The day after tomorrow	*pozítří*
Now	*hnet*
Later	*později*
Leave me alone	*dej mi pokoj*
Go away	*jdi pryč*
Help!	*pomoc!*
This one	*tento*
A little	*trochu*
Large/small	*velký/malý*
More/less	*více/méně*
Good/bad	*dobrý/špatný*
Hot/cold	*horký/studený*
With/without	*s/bez*

GETTING AROUND

Over here	*tady*
Over there	*tam*
Left	*nalevo*
Right	*napravo*
Straight on	*rovně*
Where is . . .?	*kde je . . .?*
How do I get to Prague?	*jak se dostanu do Prahy ?*
How do I get to the university?	*jak se dostanu k univerzitě?*
By bus	*autobusem*
By train	*vlakem*
By car	*autem*
On foot	*pěšky*
By taxi	*taxíkem*
Ticket	*jízdenka/lístek*
Return ticket	*zpateční*
Railway station	*nádraží*

Bus station	*autobusové nádraží*
Bus stop	*autobusová zastávka*
When's the next train to Prague?	*kdy jede další vlak do Prahy?*
Is it going to Prague?	*jede to do Prahy?*
Do I have to change?	*musím přestupovat?*
Do I need a reservation?	*musím mít místenku?*

QUESTIONS AND ANSWERS

Do you speak English?	*mluvíte anglicky?*
I don't speak German	*nemluvím německy*
I don't understand	*nerozumím*
I understand	*rozumím*
Speak slowly	*mluvíte pomalu*
How do you say that in Czech?	*jak se tohle řekne česky?*
Could you write it down for me?	*mužete mí to napsat?*
What	*co*
Where	*kde*
When	*kdy*
Why	*proč*
How much is it?	*kolík to stojí?*
Are there any rooms available?	*máte volné pokoje?*
I would like a double room	*chtěl bych dvou lůžkovy pokoj*
For one night	*na jednu noc*
With shower	*se sprchou*
Is this seat free?	*je tu volna?*
May we (sit down)?	*můžeme (se sednout)?*
The bill please	*zaplatím prosím*
Do you have . . .?	*máte . . .?*
We don't have	*nemáme*
We do have	*máme*

SOME SIGNS

Entrance	*vchod*
Exit	*východ*
Toilets	*záchody/toalety*
Men	*muži*
Women	*ženy*
Ladies	*dámy*
Gentlemen	*pánové*
Open	*otevřeno*
Closed	*zavřeno*
Danger!	*pozor!*
Hospital	*nemocnice*

continued overleaf

No smoking	*kouření zakázáno*
No bathing	*koupání zakázáno*
No entry	*vstup zakázán*
Arrival	*příjezd*
Departure	*odjezd*
Police	*policie*

DAYS OF THE WEEK

Monday	*pondělí*
Tuesday	*uterý*
Wednesday	*středa*
Thursday	*čtvrtek*
Friday	*pátek*
Saturday	*sobota*
Sunday	*neděle*
Day	*den*
Week	*týden*
Month	*měsíc*
Year	*rok*

MONTHS OF THE YEAR

Many Slav languages have their own highly individual systems in which the words for the names of the month are descriptive nouns – sometimes beautifully apt for the month in question.

January	*leden* – ice
February	*únor* – hibernation
March	*březen* – birch
April	*duben* – oak
May	*květen* – blossom
June	*červen* – red
July	*červenec* – redder
August	*srpen* – sickle
September	*zaří* – blazing
October	*říjen* – rutting
November	*listopad* – leaves falling
December	*prosinec* – slaughter of pigs

NUMBERS

1	*jeden*	14	*čtrnáct*	90	*devadesát*
2	*dva*	15	*patnáct*	100	*sto*
3	*tří*	16	*šestnáct*	101	*sto jedna*
4	*čtyři*	17	*sedmnáct*	155	*sto padesát pět*
5	*pět*	18	*osmnáct*	200	*dvě stě*
6	*šest*	19	*devatenáct*	300	*tři sta*
7	*sedm*	20	*dvacet*	400	*čtyři sta*
8	*osm*	21	*dvacetjedna*	500	*pět set*
9	*devět*	30	*třicet*	600	*šest set*
10	*deset*	40	*čtyřicet*	700	*sedm set*
11	*jedenáct*	50	*padesát*	800	*osm set*
12	*dvanáct*	60	*šedesát*	900	*devět set*
13	*třináct*	70	*sedmdesát*	1000	*tisíc*
		80	*osmdesát*		

Consonants and accents

There are no silent consonants, but it's worth remembering that r and l can form a syllable if standing between two other consonants or at the end of a word, as in Brno (Br-no) or Vltava (Vl-ta-va). The consonants listed below are those which differ substantially from the English. Accents look daunting – particularly the háček, which appears above c, d, l, n, r, s, t and z – but the only one which causes a lot of problems is ř, probably the most difficult letter to say in the entire language – even Czech toddlers have to be taught how to say it.

c like the **ts** in boats
č like the **ch** in chicken

ch like the **ch** in the Scottish loch
ď like the **d** in duped
g always as in goat, never as in general
h always as in have, but more energetic
j like the **y** in yoke
kd pronounced as **gd**
l like the **lli** in colliery
mě pronounced as mnye
ň like the **n** in nuance
p softer than the English **p**
r as in rip, but often rolled
ř like the sound of **r** and **ž** combined
š like the **sh** in shop
ť like the **t** in tutor
ž like the **s** in pleasure; at the end of a word like the **sh** in shop

Prague's leading personalities – past and present

Beneš, Edvard (1884–1948). Hero to some, traitor to others, Beneš was president from 1935 until 1938 – when he resigned, having refused to lead the country into bloodshed over the Munich Crisis – and again from 1945 until 1948, when he aquiesced to the Communist coup.

Čapek Josef (1887–1945). Cubist artist and writer and illustrator of children's books, Josef was older brother to the more famous Karel (see below); he died in Belsen concentration camp.

Čapek, Karel (1890–1938). Czech writer, journalist and unofficial spokesperson for the First Republic. His most famous works are *The Insect Play* and *R.U.R.*, which introduced the word *robot* into the English language.

Dobrovský, Josef (1753–1829). Jesuit-taught pioneer in Czech philology. Wrote the seminal text *The History of Czech Language and Literature.*

Dubček, Alexander (1921–92). Slovak Communist who became First Secretary in January 1968, at the beginning of the Prague Spring. Expelled from the Party in 1969, but returned to become speaker in the federal parliament after 1989, before being killed in a car crash in 1992.

Dvořák, Antonín (1841–1904). Perhaps the most famous of all Czech composers. His best-known work is the *New World Symphony,* inspired by an extensive sojourn in the USA.

Fučik, Julius (1903–43). Communist journalist murdered by the Nazis, whose prison writings, *Notes from the Gallows,* were obligatory reading in the 1950s. Hundreds of streets were named after him, but doubts about the authenticity of the work, and general hostility towards the man have made him *persona non grata.*

Gottwald, Klement (1896–1953). One of the founders of the KSČ, General Secretary from 1927, Prime Minister from 1946 to 1948, and President from 1948 to 1953, Gottwald is universally abhorred for his role in the show trials of the 1950s.

Hašek, Jaroslav (1883–1923). Anarchist, dog-breeder, lab assistant, bigamist, cabaret artist and People's Commissar in the Red Army, Hašek was one of prewar Prague's most colourful characters, who wrote the famous *Good Soldier Švejk* and died from alcohol abuse in 1923.

Havel, Václav (1936–). Absurdist playwright of the 1960s, who became a leading spokesperson of Charter 77 and, following the Velvet Revolution, the country's first post-Communist president.

Havlíček-Borovský, Karel (1821–56). Satirical poet, journalist and nationalist, exiled to the Tyrol by the Austrian authorities after 1848.

Hrabal, Bohumil (1936–97). Writer and bohemian, whose novels were banned under the Communists, but revered world wide.

Hus, Jan (1370–1415). Rector of Prague University and reformist preacher who was burnt at the stake as a heretic by the Council of Constance.

Husák, Gustáv (died 1991). Slovak Communist who was sentenced to life imprisonment in the show trials of the 1950s, released in 1960, and eventually became General Secretary and President following the Soviet invasion. Resigned in favour of Havel in December 1989.

Jirásek, Alois (1851–1930). Writer who popularized Czech legends for both children and adults and became a key figure in the Czech national revival.

Jungmann, Josef (1773–1847). Prolific Czech translator and author of the seminal *History of Czech Literature* and the first Czech dictionary.

Kafka, Franz (1883–1924). German-Jewish Praguer who worked as an insurance clerk in Prague for most of his life, and also wrote some of the most influential novels of the twentieth century, most notably *The Trial.*

Kelley, Edward. English occultist who was summoned to Prague by Rudolf II, but eventually incurred the wrath of the emperor and was imprisoned in Kokořín castle.

Kepler, Johannes (1571–1630). German Protestant forced to leave Linz for Denmark because of the Counter-Reformation. Succeeded Tycho de Brahe as Rudolf II's chief astronomer. His observations of the planets became the basis of the laws of planetary motion.

Kisch, Egon Erwin (1885–1948). German-Jewish Praguer who became one of the city's most famous investigative journalists.

Klaus, Václav. Known somewhat bitterly as "Santa Klaus". Prime Minister since (1992–97), confirmed Thatcherite, and driving force behind the country's present economic reforms.

Komenský, Jan Amos (1592–1670). Leader of the Protestant Czech Brethren. Forced to flee the country and settle in England during the Counter-Reformation. Better known to English-speakers as Comenius.

Mácha, Karel Hynek (1810–36). Romantic nationalist poet, great admirer of Byron and Keats and, like them, died young. His most famous poem is *Máj*, published just months before his death.

Masaryk, Jan Garrigue (1886–1958). Son of the founder of the republic (see below), Foreign Minister in the postwar government and the only non-Communist in Gottwald's cabinet when the Communists took over in February 1948. Died ten days after the coup in suspicious circumstances.

Masaryk, Tomáš Garrigue (1850–1937). Professor of Philosophy at Prague University, President of the Republic from 1918 to 1935. His name is synonymous with the First Republic and was removed from all street signs after the 1948 coup. Now back with a vengeance.

Mucha, Alfons (1860–1939). Moravian graphic artist and designer whose Art Nouveau posters and artwork for Sarah Bernhardt brought him international fame. After the founding of Czechoslovakia, he returned to the country to design stamps, bank notes, and complete a cycle of giant canvases on Czech nationalist themes.

Němcová, Božena (1820–62). Highly popular writer who became involved with the nationalist movement and shocked many with her unorthodox behaviour. Her most famous book is *Grandmother*.

Neruda, Jan (1834–91). Poet and journalist for the *Národní listy*. Wrote some famous short stories describing Prague's Malá Strana.

Palacký, František (1798–1876). Nationalist historian, Czech MP in Vienna and leading figure in the events of 1848.

Purkyně, Jan Evangelista (1787–1869). Czech doctor, natural scientist and pioneer in experimental physiology who became professor of physiology at Prague and then at Wroctaw University.

Rieger, Ladislav (1818–1903). Nineteenth-century Czech politician and one of the leading figures in the events of 1848 and the aftermath.

Rilke, Rainer Maria (1876–1926). Despite having been brought up as a girl for the first six years of his life, Rilke ended up as an officer in the Austrian army, and wrote some of the city's finest German *fin-de-siècle* poetry.

Smetana, Bedřich (1824–84). Popular Czech composer and fervent nationalist whose *Má vlast* (My Homeland) traditionally opens the Prague Spring Music Festival.

Svoboda, Ludvík (1895–1979). Victorious Czech General from World War II, who acquiesced to the 1948 Communist coup and was Communist President from 1968 to 1975.

Tycho Brahe (1546–1601). Ground-breaking Danish astronomer, who was summoned to Prague by Rudolf II in 1597, only to die from over-drinking in 1601.

Tyl, Josef Kajetán (1808–56). Czech playwright and composer of the Czech half of the national anthem, *Where is my Home?*

Werfel, Franz (1890–1945). One of the German-Jewish literary circle, which included Kafka, Kisch and Brod.

Žižka, Jan (died 1424). Brilliant, blind military leader of the Táborites, the radical faction of the Hussites.

A glossary of Czech words and terms

brána gate.

český Bohemian.

chata chalet-type bungalow, country cottage or mountain hut.

chrám large church.

divadlo theatre.

dóm cathedral.

dům house.

dům kultury generic term for local arts and social centre; literally "House of Culture".

hrad castle.

hřbitov cemetery.

hora mountain.

hospoda pub.

hostinec pub.

kaple chapel.

katedrála cathedral.

kavárna coffee house.

klášter monastery/convent.

kostel church.

koupaliště swimming pool.

Labe River Elbe.

lanovka funicular or cable car.

les forest.

město town.

most bridge.

muzeum museum.

nábřeží embankment.

nádraží train station.

náměstí square.

ostrov island.

palác palace.

památník memorial or monument.

pasáž indoor shopping mall.

pivnice pub.

radnice town hall.

restaurace restaurant.

sad park.

sál room or hall (in a chateau or castle).

schody steps.

svatý saint; often abbreviated to sv.

třída avenue.

ulice street.

věž tower.

vinárna wine bar or cellar.

Vltava River Moldau.

vrchy hills.

výstava exhibition.

zahrada garden.

zámek chateau.

An Architectural Glossary

Ambulatory Passage round the back of the altar, in continuation of the aisles.

Art Nouveau French term for the sinuous and stylized form of architecture dating from 1900 to 1910; known as the Secession in the Czech Republic and as *Jugendstil* in Germany.

Baroque Expansive, exuberant architectural style of the seventeenth and mid-eighteenth centuries, characterized by ornate decoration, complex spatial arrangement and grand vistas.

Chancel The part of the church where the altar is placed, usually at the east end.

Empire Highly decorative Neoclassical style of architecture and decorative arts, practised in the early 1800s.

Fresco Mural painting applied to wet plaster, so that the colours immediately soak into the wall.

Functionalism Plain, boxy, modernist architectural style, prevalent in the late 1920s and 1930s in Czechoslovakia, often using plate-glass curtain walls and open-plan interiors.

Gothic Architectural style prevalent from the fourteenth to the sixteenth century, characterized by pointed arches and ribbed vaulting.

Loggia Covered area on the side of a building, often arcaded.

Nave Main body of a church, usually the western end.

Neoclassical Late eighteenth- and early nineteenth-century style of architecture and design returning to classical Greek and Roman models as a reaction against Baroque and Rococo excesses.

Oriel A bay window, usually projecting from an upper floor.

Rococo Highly florid, fiddly though (occasionally) graceful style of architecture and interior design, forming the last phase of Baroque.

Romanesque Solid architectural style of the late tenth to thirteenth century, characterized by round-headed arches and geometrical precision.

Secession Linear and stylized form of architecture and decorative arts imported from Vienna as a reaction against the academic establishment.

Sgraffito Monochrome plaster decoration effected by means of scraping back the first white layer to reveal the black underneath.

Stucco Plaster used for decorative effects.

Trompe l'oeil Painting designed to fool the onlooker into believing that it is actually three-dimensional.

Index

direct orders from

		UK£8.99	US$14.95	CAN$19.99
Amsterdam	1-85828-218-7	UK£8.99	US$14.95	CAN$19.99
Andalucia	1-85828-219-5	9.99	16.95	22.99
Australia	1-85828-220-9	13.99	21.95	29.99
Bali	1-85828-134-2	8.99	14.95	19.99
Barcelona	1-85828-221-7	8.99	14.95	19.99
Berlin	1-85828-129-6	8.99	14.95	19.99
Belgium & Luxembourg	1-85828-222-5	10.99	17.95	23.99
Brazil	1-85828-223-3	13.99	21.95	29.99
Britain	1-85828-208-X	12.99	19.95	25.99
Brittany & Normandy	1-85828-224-1	9.99	16.95	22.99
Bulgaria	1-85828-183-0	9.99	16.95	22.99
California	1-85828-181-4	10.99	16.95	22.99
Canada	1-85828-311-6	12.99	19.95	25.99
China	1-85828-225-X	15.99	24.95	32.99
Corfu	1-85828-226-8	8.99	14.95	19.99
Corsica	1-85828-227-6	9.99	16.95	22.99
Costa Rica	1-85828-136-9	9.99	15.95	21.99
Crete	1-85828-316-7	9.99	16.95	22.99
Cyprus	1-85828-182-2	9.99	16.95	22.99
Czech & Slovak Republics	1-85828-121-0	9.99	16.95	22.99
Dublin Mini Guide	1-85828-294-2	5.99	9.95	12.99
Edinburgh Mini Guide	1-85828-295-0	5.99	9.95	12.99
Egypt	1-85828-188-1	10.99	17.95	23.99
Europe	1-85828-289-6	14.99	19.95	25.99
England	1-85828-301-9	12.99	19.95	25.99
First Time Europe	1-85828-270-5	7.99	9.95	12.99
Florida	1-85828-184-4	10.99	16.95	22.99
France	1-85828-228-4	12.99	19.95	25.99
Germany	1-85828-309-4	14.99	23.95	31.99
Goa	1-85828-275-6	8.99	14.95	19.99
Greece	1-85828-300-0	12.99	19.95	25.99
Greek Islands	1-85828-310-8	10.99	17.95	23.99
Guatemala	1-85828-189-X	10.99	16.95	22.99
Hawaii: Big Island	1-85828-158-X	8.99	12.95	16.99
Hawaii	1-85828-206-3	10.99	16.95	22.99
Holland	1-85828-229-2	10.99	17.95	23.99
Hong Kong	1-85828-187-3	8.99	14.95	19.99
Hotels & Restos	1-85828-306-X	12.99	19.95	25.99
Hungary	1-85828-123-7	8.99	14.95	19.99
India	1-85828-200-4	14.99	23.95	31.99
Ireland	1-85828-179-2	10.99	17.95	23.99
Italy	1-85828-167-9	12.99	19.95	25.99
Jamaica	1-85828-230-6	9.99	16.95	22.99
Kenya	1-85828-192-X	11.99	18.95	24.99
Lisbon Mini Guide	1-85828-297-7	5.99	9.95	12.99
London	1-85828-231-4	9.99	15.95	21.99
Madrid Mini Guide	1-85828-353-1	5.99	9.95	12.99
Mallorca & Menorca	1-85828-165-2	8.99	14.95	19.99
Malaysia, Singapore & Brunei	1-85828-232-2	11.99	18.95	24.99
Mexico	1-85828-044-3	10.99	16.95	22.99
Morocco	1-85828-040-0	9.99	16.95	21.99
Moscow	1-85828-118-0	8.99	14.95	19.99
Nepal	1-85828-190-3	10.99	17.95	23.99
New York	1-85828-296-9	9.99	15.95	21.99
New Zealand	1-85828-233-0	12.99	19.95	25.99
Norway	1-85828-234-9	10.99	17.95	23.99
Pacific Northwest	1-85828-092-3	9.99	14.95	19.99

In the UK, Rough Guides are available from all good bookstores, but can be obtained from Penguin by contacting: Penguin Direct, Penguin Books Ltd, Bath Road, Harmondsworth, West Drayton, Middlesex UB7 0DA; or telephone the credit line on 0181-899 4036 (9am–5pm) and ask for Penguin Direct. Visa and Access accepted. Delivery will normally be within 14 working days. Penguin Direct ordering facilities are only available in the UK and the USA. The availability and published prices quoted are correct at the time of going to press but are subject to alteration without prior notice.

around the world

Paris	1-85828-235-7	8.99	14.95	19.99
Poland	1-85828-168-7	10.99	17.95	23.99
Portugal	1-85828-313-2	10.99	17.95	23.99
Prague	1-85828-318-3	8.99	14.95	19.99
Provence	1-85828-127-X	9.99	16.95	22.99
Pyrenees	1-85828-308-6	10.99	17.95	23.99
Rhodes & the Dodecanese	1-85828-120-2	8.99	14.95	19.99
Romania	1-85828-305-1	10.99	17.95	23.99
San Francisco	1-85828-299-3	8.99	14.95	19.99
Scandinavia	1-85828-236-5	12.99	20.95	27.99
Scotland	1-85828-302-7	9.99	16.95	22.99
Sicily	1-85828-178-4	9.99	16.95	22.99
Singapore	1-85828-237-3	8.99	14.95	19.99
South Africa	1-85828-238-1	12.99	19.95	25.99
Soutwest USA	1-85828-239-X	10.99	16.95	22.99
Spain	1-85828-240-3	11.99	18.95	24.99
St Petersburg	1-85828-298-5	9.99	16.95	22.99
Sweden	1-85828-241-1	10.99	17.95	23.99
Thailand	1-85828-140-7	10.99	17.95	24.99
Tunisia	1-85828-139-3	10.99	17.95	24.99
Turkey	1-85828-242-X	12.99	19.95	25.99
Tuscany & Umbria	1-85828-243-8	10.99	17.95	23.99
USA	1-85828-307-8	14.99	19.95	25.99
Venice	1-85828-170-9	8.99	14.95	19.99
Vietnam	1-85828-191-1	9.99	15.95	21.99
Wales	1-85828-245-4	10.99	17.95	23.99
Washington DC	1-85828-246-2	8.99	14.95	19.99
West Africa	1-85828-101-6	15.99	24.95	34.99
More Women Travel	1-85828-098-2	10.99	16.95	22.99
Zimbabwe & Botswana	1-85828-186-5	11.99	18.95	24.99
Phrasebooks				
Czech	1-85828-148-2	3.50	5.00	7.00
Egyptian Arabic	1-85828-319-1	4.00	6.00	8.00
French	1-85828-144-X	3.50	5.00	7.00
German	1-85828-146-6	3.50	5.00	7.00
Greek	1-85828-145-8	3.50	5.00	7.00
Hungarian	1-85828-304-3	4.00	6.00	8.00
Italian	1-85828-143-1	3.50	5.00	7.00
Japanese	1-85828-303-5	4.00	6.00	8.00
Mexican	1-85828-176-8	3.50	5.00	7.00
Portuguese	1-85828-175-X	3.50	5.00	7.00
Polish	1-85828-174-1	3.50	5.00	7.00
Spanish	1-85828-147-4	3.50	5.00	7.00
Swahili	1-85828-320-5	4.00	6.00	8.00
Thai	1-85828-177-6	3.50	5.00	7.00
Turkish	1-85828-173-3	3.50	5.00	7.00
Vietnamese	1-85828-172-5	3.50	5.00	7.00
Reference				
Classical Music	1-85828-113-X	12.99	19.95	25.99
European Football	1-85828-256-X	14.99	23.95	31.99
Internet	1-85828-288-8	5.00	8.00	10.00
Jazz	1-85828-137-7	16.99	24.95	34.99
Millennium	1-85828-314-0	5.00	8.95	11.99
Opera	1-85828-138-5	16.99	24.95	34.99
Reggae	1-85828-247-0	12.99	19.95	25.99
Rock	1-85828-201-2	17.99	26.95	35.00
World Music	1-85828-017-6	16.99	22.95	29.99

Stay in touch with us!

ROUGH*NEWS* is Rough Guides' free newsletter. In three issues a year we give you news, travel issues, music reviews, readers' letters and the latest dispatches from authors on the road.

I would like to receive ROUGH*NEWS*: please put me on your free mailing list.

NAME . . . .

ADDRESS . . . .

Please clip or photocopy and send to: Rough Guides, 1 Mercer Street, London WC2H 9QJ, England or Rough Guides, 375 Hudson Street, New York, NY 10014, USA.

MAP 1

N

HRADČANY

MALÁ STRANA

Čertovka

River Vltava

Loreta

Černínský palác

Strahovský klášter

Loreta

Martinický palác

Sternberský palác

Vojenské muzeum

St Vitus Cathedral

Lobkovický palác (German Embassy)

Schönbornský palác (US Embassy)

Vrtbovská zahrada

Schönbornska zahrada

Panna Maria Vítězná

sv Mikuláš

Panna Maria pod řetezem

Pražský hrad (Prague Castle)

Jízdárna

Jelení příkop

Královská zahrada

Míčovna

Belvedér

Píseckà brána

Bílkova vila

Chotkovy sady

Hanavský pavilón

Senát

British Embassy

Sněmovna

sv Tomáš

Valdštejnský palác

Valdštejnská jízdárna

M

Karlův most (Charles Bridge)

Vojanovy sady

Na Kampě

0   200   Metres

MAP 4

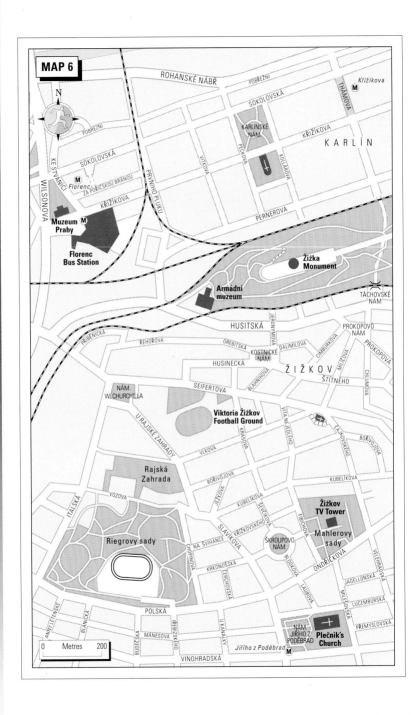